Praise for Alex L

A PARALLEL UNIVERSE

A great read, yet a masterful portrayal of the big picture—the web of laws denying registered people basic human rights. Landon's lucid account makes you think you knew this all along, and Halleck's fictional Fernandez characters, with their sometimes zany adventures, illustrate the suffering and survival of convicted people. Thank you for your wisdom!

—*Janice Bellucci, J.D., executive director Alliance for Constitutional Sex Offense Laws*

The book will be challenging to people deceived by leaders into believing that "designer laws" and "hate laws" (Megan's Law, Jessica's Law, International Megan's Law, etc.) actually protect children.

— *Thomas L. Gayton, civil rights lawyer, author "Long Journey Home"*

Most child molestations and "kidnappings" are committed by family members, yet the public feels there are sex predators infesting every park. How did we come to this? Landon and Halleck suggest that America has become a prison-industrial complex. And the sex registry? Though it contains people who did nothing more than urinate in public, or as a teen have sex with a girlfriend, Americans picture these lists as protecting them against criminals. Like canaries in a coal mine, the authors warn that the air of freedom is getting so rare that we may soon choke on our own feeble breath.

— *Michael Hogan, Ph. D., author of 18 books including "The Irish Soldiers of Mexico" (basis of MGM movie)*

This book doesn't fit neatly into one category. It's a novel, textbook, editorial, a narrative taken from the headlines, a primer on the U.S. legal system and how it can be overwhelmed by the very fears we seek to quiet. Halleck and Landon inform the reader by citing case histories and legal doctrine, never talking over our heads.

— *Sandra K. Waterkotte, North Carolina*

Interweaving law with storytelling in alternate chapters, Landon (a lawyer) and Halleck (a novelist), reveal the "parallel universe" created by sex-crime legislation. What makes this universe parallel to, instead of part of, reality is its utter irrationality. As a former federal prosecutor, I thought I knew something about sex-crime laws, but this book opened my eyes to what happens in real life.

— *Art Campbell, professor of law, author "Law of Sentencing"*

Author Biographies

ALEX LANDON is an attorney specializing in criminal law for over 50 years. He has taught Corrections and Sentencing for 38 years at the University of San Diego School of Law.

As a student in the 1960s, he was motivated by decisions of the Supreme Court in its "civil rights era," and as an attorney handled civil rights cases such as the "Camp Pendleton 14" (black Marines reacting to KKK activity on base). Continuing to focus on protecting his clients' civil rights, he also litigated over dreadful conditions at San Diego jails and Juvenile Hall.

Making the Sixth Amendment right to a lawyer a reality likewise became part of Landon's civil rights focus. "San Diego didn't have a public defender until 1968, my first year of law school," he said, adding that in some parts of the country, people had been executed for crimes such as robbery, while others got away with grisly crimes, such as the murder of black teenager Emmet Till.

Landon's concern about people convicted of sex offenses grew out of this core interest in civil rights. "They don't have the same civil rights as other people—that's counter to the Constitution. Laws are prejudiced against them. They should be able to travel and live where they need to." His involvement in Alliance for Constitutional Sex Offense Laws was sparked by ACSOL's focus on constitutional rights.

He was chair of the Board of the Institute for Criminal Defense Advocacy at Cal Western (where the California Innocence Project was created), president of California Attorneys for Criminal Justice and executive director of the Defenders Program of San Diego, Inc. and Community Defenders, Inc., while maintaining a law practice including capital cases. He is a frequent speaker at seminars and public programs.

ELAINE HALLECK is a writer, graphic designer and illustrator who came of age during the Vietnam War and the mistrust of government it spawned. She worked under Detroit's first black mayor, Coleman Young, and for the Detroit Metro Times, a newspaper emphasizing racial justice.

While a copy editor at a Southern California newspaper in the early 2000s, she was struck by the lynching atmosphere in the media and legal arenas, which was sparked by a frightful series of abduction-murders of white girls. After contacting California Attorneys for Criminal Justice and Alex Landon, she embarked during the following years on collaborating with Landon in educating the public on sex offending, while swimming upstream against reaction to the Catholic-priest-molestation and #MeToo scandals and other countercurrents such as proliferating bad laws and new technologies supporting them.

She lived in Guadalajara, Mexico, for 18 years, reporting for The Guadalajara Reporter until 2022.

A PARALLEL UNIVERSE

Not Science Fiction
But You May Wish it Were

by

Alex Landon and Elaine Halleck

PM Library

Copyright@2023 by Alex landon and Elaine Halleck

ISBN 978-1-63649-693-1

All rights reserved. No part of this book may be used or reproduced in any manner whatsoever without written permission, except in the case of quotes for personal use and brief quotations embodied in critical articles or reviews.

PM Library

An Imprint of Poetic Matrix Press
www.poeticmatrix.com

Printed in the United States of America

Table of Contents

Introduction

"What brought you to this topic?" people sometimes ask us, especially to this revised and greatly extended second edition that is emerging over 10 years after the first one, and into a world that generally seems just as hostile towards registered people as 2011 was.

For one of us, Alex Landon, with decades of specialized experience in criminal law and a feel for injustice, the answer is easy: insight derived from knowledge of the burdens borne by clients convicted of "sex crimes"— which we sometimes put in quotation marks because they can include streaking and skinny-dipping.

For others who advocate reform, such as Elaine Halleck, the answer lies in having a convicted relative or friend. (In her fictional chapters, many details were invented or altered, except for macro-level events, such as the political.) Knowing a convicted person was also the inspiration for Janice Bellucci (Chapter 25), a former aerospace and government-contract lawyer who founded the Alliance for Constitutional Sex Offense Laws, spurred by harsh experiences she learned about from a book her plumber wrote, based on his conviction over three decades earlier. Just so, the list is long of activists and board members in ACSOL who have dear ones convicted and registered for sex crimes.

Literature and history give examples of reformers spurred by special, and often secondhand, experience of the justice system—experience usually opaque to lawmakers and the average Jane or Joe. In Mark Twain's novel "The Prince and the Pauper," Prince Edward, after accidentally exchanging places with a young pauper and landing in prison during his vagabond travels, throws out absurd laws after he is restored to his royal position—Twain's fanciful explanation for King Edward VI's reputation as merciful. Closer to the present, former U.S. President Trump permitted his son-in-law Jared Kushner, spurred by Kushner's father's prison time, to champion a prison-reform law, the First Step Act of 2018.

Similarly, the friends and relatives of people convicted of sex crimes, with their up-close experience of the justice system, are much better poised than the average person to know about the "parallel universe" that consigns people on public sex-offender registries to a perpetual purgatory that is hidden from everyday view. It has probably been mostly these friends and relatives who have been responsible for the positive and encouraging developments that prompted this new edition, over 10 years after the first one and over 20 years after some key events mentioned.

Among the pluses are the emergence of super-credible people speaking out against registration, such as former Los Angeles County District Attorney Jacquelyn Lacey, as well as Patty Wetterling, the mother of murdered boy after whom a bad law was named, and once a prominent

3

promoter of such laws. There are more positives in the successes of groups, such as ACSOL, that have been recently organized.

The first edition focused on the decade between the portentous year 2000 and 2010, when terror over 9/11 and various cases of child kidnapping led Americans, even though crime was dropping, to enact laws that overprotect children and overburden everyone else. Alex Landon dubbed those laws—at least the ones mostly named after photogenic white girls with articulate parents—"designer laws," and we also focused on such laws' racist aspects. In the 21 years since our first edition's earliest dated chapter, this focus on racism has been borne out and taken up by prestigious journalists.

Some negative developments spurring our second edition are newer laws, particularly the abysmal International Megan's Law of 2016. This law, along with dogged refusal by the people who push bad laws to recognize their torrent of dreadful results—for everyone, not only convicted people—led us to another nickname: hate laws.

We recognize that not every person who supports bad laws—or thinks they do—is motivated by hate. We also realize that not every person convicted of a sex crime was a streaker, skinny-dipper, or Romeo-and- Juliet couple. There are a few who, for example, brutally raped 7-year- olds—and a person needs a lot of emotional intelligence to distinguish between such horrific criminals and people who commit the vast majority of sex crimes, which, as Alex Landon discovered in his practice, could be perpetrated by almost anyone.

So we recognize that it takes exceptional insight to begin to read this book, with its counterintuitive perspective. We thank you for starting and hope to inspire you to help create a better world with no more victims and no more senseless cruelty.

Alex Landon and Elaine Halleck

August 2022

1. Golden State or police state?

2001 to Summer 2002

ALEX LANDON

This is a story about tragedies. But not the type you may be thinking of, the type that politicians and the media often want you to think about. In fact, the victims of the tragedies you will read about here are the same people that politicians generally depict as villains—the accused and convicted people I have spent my life defending.

The other victims in my story are ordinary people such as yourselves, who have been frightened and misled into spending a staggering amount of money on a false quest for security that has bankrupted us—financially and perhaps morally.

And although it may seem incredible, ordinary citizens and convicted people are often one and the same. This trend was revealed by the U.S. Justice Department's Bureau of Justice Statistics in 2001. It reported that an alarming 5.6 million Americans—about one in every 37 adults—had "prison experience," which means they were either imprisoned at the end of 2001 or had been at one time. (1) Of course, women go to prison, but the majority of the 5.6 million people are men, and it breaks down to 5 percent of all white men, 7.7 percent of all Hispanic men and 17 percent of all black men.

To add some perspective, 5.6 million people is over a million more than the entire population of Ireland. It is more than the population of many European countries. And keep in mind that the shocking figure from this government study does not even include people arrested and held in jails for a short time. Neither does it include people convicted but not sent to prison—the ones who get probation or alternative sentences. And to put things in perspective over time, the number of Americans sent to prison in 2001 was triple the number 25 years earlier, in 1974. The reason is that the whole justice system—laws, arrests, sentences—has been getting tougher. Later I will try to explain why.

Think about it—one in every 37 adults. There are probably more than 37 adults in your apartment building or on your block. We could infer from this study that at least one of the people on your block probably has spent time in prison, if it were not for a sad quirk in the system: many convicted people's lives are so ruined by prison that later, they are not able to live in a decent neighborhood. They can't get jobs, and they have emotional and family problems. So, too often, they end up living a twilight-zone existence in neighborhoods that most of you have been fortunate enough to avoid.

I began by saying that this is a story about tragedies. A story has a setting—a time and place. The time of our story begins just after the turn of the millennium and continues beyond its two decades. Several chapters focus on the summer of 2002, during which public officials and the media seized on three shocking crimes and whipped up a witch-hunt atmosphere —a sort of perfect storm—that had devastating effects. I have dubbed it the Summer of the Abducted White Girl. We will also look at developments in later years—especially 2010, which often seemed like a replay of 2002—but to start, that summer just after the millennium and 9/11 offers a clear view of a sad, but I hope instructive, slice of life.

The setting of our story, of course, is the United States—frequently, California, where a lot of this tragedy takes place. California is the state where I was born and have worked all my life. I went to law school in San Diego and I now practice law and teach there. I was president of California Attorneys for Criminal Justice, chair of the Board of the Institute for Criminal Defense Advocacy at Cal Western (where the California Innocence Project was conceived) and active in a state-funded organization, Volunteers in Parole.

California is the most populous state in the country, the richest state. It is the crown jewel of the United States, the sunny Golden State where a lot of people's dreams have focused—whether dreams of striking gold in the mountains, of making it in Hollywood, or of finding a place that is prosperous yet "laid back," to use that 1970s buzzword.

Some beach areas in San Diego have a peculiar yellow highway caution sign with a silhouette of a surfer carrying his board. But there's another yellow caution sign you sometimes see that is truly bizarre. It shows silhouettes of a man, woman and child holding hands and running. It's the Watch Out for Illegal Aliens sign.

And of course, surfers don't elicit the reaction that illegal immigrants do. You might see this reaction, as I have, when you are whizzing along a downtown freeway and suddenly a helicopter appears above, weaving and swooping in obvious pursuit. You crane your neck to watch, trying not to end up in a crash, and you see an officer has joined the chase, pursuing what might be an incarnation of that fleeing person in the yellow sign.

The average person, looking up at the cop running along a narrow ledge on a steep embankment through the tangled mat of ice plants, might wonder, "Who would do that for a living?" The answer is, a lot of people, although not always in such arduous circumstances.

I say that to point up how the sad statistics I mentioned have played out in California. During the same few decades I spoke about earlier, while the number of imprisoned people has been shooting up, not surprisingly, the Golden State has undergone a prison-building boom. If you drive around California expecting to see sunny beaches, stunning parks and rolling agricultural fields, instead, you may be surprised at how many prisons you see.

Somebody has to work at these prisons and in the vast machine that sends people to live in them. These workers may be cooks, judges, secretaries, doctors, counselors, teachers, nurses, lawyers, probation officers, social workers, psychologists and, of course, guards. Some are members of the California Correctional Peace Officers Association—the state prison guards' union. In 2002, according to Joe Domanick, the "liberal" Gov. Gray Davis signed a contract giving guards a whopping 37 percent raise when other groups received none. (2) In 2006, still with Davis' help, prison guards were set to earn $73,000 a year. (Compare that to what a California teacher made around that time: an average of about $54,000, according to the American Federation of Teachers.)

California's prison boom is what led a drug addict from Illinois who was locked up in a San Diego county jail to recite the jailhouse buzz about the Golden State: "Come on vacation, leave on probation."

The prison boom is what led an education manager who worked at the same institution, a man who had studied to be a Jesuit priest and who hobnobbed with cops, to sum up the situation: "California is a police state."

Was it the prison boom that led a Spanish linguistics professor who was teaching in Los Angeles to make the same dim pronouncement about California? Having been born and raised in a certifiable police state—Spain under Nazi-sympathizer Franco—the professor was in a good position to know. He said he had been particularly taken aback by the profusion of police helicopters patrolling the skies, something that those of us who have lived here a long time may have stopped noticing.

"Summer of the Abducted White Girl"

Some pieces in the puzzle that make up the picture of a police state fell into place when I noticed how many prison guards come out of military service to work in California prisons, and when I read an article in the Los Angeles Times not long after 9/11 saying that the Pasadena police "homeland security" efforts had been bolstered by using military-surplus helicopters. Another piece in the puzzle became clear when I took a look at a state map, pockmarked with 33 state prisons and countless county and local jails and noticed its similarity—a superficial but nevertheless striking similarity—to a map showing California's 24 military bases.

In the 1950s, former General and President Eisenhower warned us about the "military-industrial complex" and recently others have started to identify a "prison-industrial complex." But I am getting a glimmering of something that combines it all—a "military-prison-industrial complex which brings our nation's unfortunate and intrusive foreign adventures to the home front.

The foreign military incursions of the United States are sometimes traced to fears—of Communism, Islamic extremism, whatever. It is said that these fears were based on reality—or a smidgen of reality—but then veered off the deep end. That is what happens with "complexes"—when entrenched interests take on a life of their own and go out of control. Something like this happened on the domestic front during the Summer of the Abducted White Girl. Three girls in the U.S. Southwest disappeared and two were later found dead. It hit a nerve, probably the same nerve that was raw from the attacks of 9/11. Then the reaction, pumped up by politics and money, lurched into absurdity.

Sociologist Barry Glassner tried to inject some rationality into this reaction, when, during that summer, he was quoted in the Los Angeles Times saying, "It's hard to imagine any serious danger to children that is less likely than kidnapping by a stranger."

But a perfect storm is not built on rationality. And so, in the midst of the panic, at a booth at the Orange County Fair, officers appeared decked out in uniforms with SWAT-style lettering that screamed, incongruously, PROBATION. The officers were inviting grim-faced fairgoers clustered around a computer to look at Megan's list. In another era, probation was a relatively benign affair in which officers were seen as helpers to their charges. In that era, in other fairs, it was the Reptilian Man or the Hermaphrodite who supplied the chills, but during the summer of 2002, Megan's list filled the bill. Ladies and gentlemen, step right up and see the Amazing Sexual Predator.

2. The cross and the cloud

December 31, 1999

ELAINE HALLECK

Danny Fernandez wasn't a complainer. In fact, he was cheerful. His mother always said he had a bounce in his step.

Anyway, what did he have to complain about? He may have lived in a country where a lot of people had trouble pronouncing his last name, but why should that bother him? His mostly Mexican American world was tucked into a little middle class pocket—albeit lower middle class—between Los Angeles and Orange County. His world didn't normally bring him into contact with many people who weren't Hispanic. There were his bosses at Colpro, the occasional neighbor, Danny's not-exactly-ex-wife Patty—just enough to spice things up.

Life had been good to Danny so far. At 37, he was short but decent looking, healthy, and not fat, even if he did eat a few too many giant take-out burritos from Andre's with cream and fried eggs and everything else. Things were easier for him than they had been for his mom. She had been raised by Mexican parents on the move, and in her youth during the 1940s the border had been a completely different place. But now, in 1999, it was a waste, a no-man's land, with cops patrolling on motorcycles, trucks and helicopters. Later would come motion sensors, dirigibles, and more.

In fact, Danny's Uncle Roberto, who lived in Tijuana, said that besides all the anti-immigration action, the desert area just north of the border had three big lockups—a state penitentiary, two county jails and one detention center for teenagers. All of it was heavily patrolled by cops, and you didn't dare set foot there unless you were one.

But Tio Roberto said when he was young, he had walked back and forth across the dry hills every day from his home in Tijuana to go to work at his job in a flower growing operation in a suburb of San Diego. Back then, the border had been a porous, natural thing, perhaps in recognition of the fact that California had belonged to Mexico until it was lost—sold, according to the official version—around the time of the American Civil War. Danny had learned about the American Civil War in high school in Delaney, another California town with a huge state prison, but he didn't learn much about how California and several other states had become part of the United States, nor why Mexicans still felt bad about this.

But Danny Fernandez didn't care about all that. He had a toehold on the American dream and he was moving up. Most people would say he was happy. For 17 years, he had held the same good job running the silk-screening department at a big sporting goods manufacturer. He had a son, Trevor, and a daughter, Kari, two "beautiful kids" whom he praised whenever possible, just as he did his mother—"a good woman." He carried photos of the kids dressed in baseball uniforms in his wallet and showed them to everyone he met, whether they asked or not. He usually pointed out Trevor's green eyes—like Patty's—although not too loudly if Kari was around, because it might make her feel bad. Kari took after Danny and all his blood relatives, with eyes so brown they were almost black, light brown skin and black hair.

Danny may have been happy, but he did have some gnawing fears—about what, he couldn't precisely say. Maybe it was because of the way things had gone with Patty. She had left him and the kids when Kari was still in diapers and gone off to West Virginia or North Carolina or somewhere. Maybe she left because Danny had been giving her a hard time about too much partying—after all, they had two kids to think about. These days, Patty showed up from time to time and the kids were so happy to see her that Danny would let her stay on the couch as long as she was in town. But secretly, he always wished she would leave—sooner rather than later.

Now, on the eve of the biggest New Year's that Danny, his mother and his kids would ever know, the one where 1999 rolled into 2000, Danny's tiny fears were magnified by the general mood of apprehension, the talk about a "millennium bug" that would wipe out all the computers after the clock struck 12. Somewhere in the back of his mind, there was also what he'd heard about the year 2012—that it was the last year recorded on the Mayan calendar, or was it the Aztec? Somehow, 2000 sounded a whole lot closer to 2012 than 1999 had.

Whatever the reason, Danny had a strange feeling on that afternoon of New Year's Eve, 1999. Surely the feeling was magnified by the sound —at times incredibly loud, but so familiar that it formed a part of his subconscious world—of a helicopter circling the area. The feeling made him take out the gold-edged Bible given to him by his mother and put it on a table near the TV. Maybe it was because he knew Pope John Paul was going to be on TV with a message about the big New Year, along with the Dalai Lama and somebody else.

After Danny took a shower and before he put on his uniform, he dug out from his underwear drawer the gold cross, another gift from his mother, and put it around his neck. Kari and Trevor weren't home—they were already over at his mom's apartment—and Danny wouldn't be with them to celebrate the big night. He had to work the late shift. It wasn't so bad, though—he would make double time. But they said that whatever you were doing at midnight on New Year's Eve, you'd be doing for the rest of the year. Probably that prediction would be stronger this year, the turn of the millennium.

———

Great, he thought. I'm going to be working the whole year? With no woman? He usually told himself that life was OK without a woman. He had his kids and his mom and, even if he didn't have anybody to sleep with, he could beat off, which wasn't so bad, especially considering what a disaster his marriage to Patty had turned into. They should never have gotten married. But they'd been in Reno, and they already had Trevor, and they were pretty messed up from all the partying, and Patty's mother, who was there too, said she'd pay for the wedding.

Perhaps it was from thinking about Reno, or maybe because, after all, it was New Year's Eve—something made Danny get a beer from the fridge. He'd have a quick one before work. He almost never did that. He only drank on weekends, maybe when Jorge came over to watch a game.

Through the kitchen window, he noticed Jake Dykowski and his strange little daughter Ashley in front of their house next door. Jake was smoking, but Danny knew he didn't smoke—cigarettes, at least. Danny guessed they were doing a little early partying, but he was a little shocked that Jake was smoking in front of Ashley. It took some guts to do that, because the police helicopter was still circling. It had already been a half hour, Danny realized, glancing at his watch. But maybe Jake thought there was no problem, since he used to be a Marine.

In the darkening late afternoon light, the Dykowski's house was all lit up, like they were going to have a party. Danny grabbed his truck keys, his baseball cap and his beer, locked the front door to the tiny, three-room house, and headed Jake's way. Ashley was wearing short shorts and sitting on the cement step leaning on her father's shins, her blonde hair cascading across her bare thighs in a mass of glistening ringlets.

"Happy New Year, dude," Jake said when Danny approached. Ashley didn't say anything, just looked at him. But when Danny put one of his legs on the step, she scooted close and rubbed up against his leg like an affectionate cat. Danny felt a little reaction. Ashley was only 11, but she was already a developed girl, who looked like she was going to take after her mother in the boobie department. But as soon as he could, without Ashley falling over, he moved his leg away. She's something, that girl. She's probably the way she is because of her mother.

Danny had known the family since he had moved into the neighborhood, when Patty was still living there and Kari and Ashley were babies. Having gringos as his next-door neighbors was part of what had made Danny like the neighborhood. And, for some inexplicable reason, the whole Dykowski family always seemed to like the whole Fernandez family. Sometimes it seemed like the Dykowskis, even Jake, had a thing for Hispanics. Ashley had always been crazy about Trevor, who was the rare blond, green-eyed Hispanic. And Ashley was Kari's best friend. The mother, Janine Dykowski, although she seemed to Danny to have a seriou mean streak toward her children, was super nice and even flirtatious toward Danny. But Danny had seen right away where that could go. When Jake made a couple of nasty comments, Danny realized he didn't want to be on his neighbors' bad side—especially neighbors who were both Marines stationed at Camp Pendleton. Besides, Janine may have been sexy, but Danny didn't like the way she treated kids.

Danny could hear Janine screeching inside the house—probably at Ashley's little brother—and he finished up his chatter with Jake and took a last swig of beer. He turned down a toke when Jake offered him one "for the road." He still couldn't believe Jake was smoking in front of Ashley, and what Jake said next surprised him more.

"This stuff is pretty good. If you want, I can sell you a bag, so you can bring in the New Year right." Danny thanked him but declined, glancing down at Ashley, who seemed to be in her own world and not paying any attention, thank goodness. Danny didn't do much smoking anymore, or anything else. Beer was his poison, and never before work, or hardly ever. As if to underline Danny's shock, the roar of the police helicopter got louder again as it came near. Now they were blaring out something over the loudspeaker. At first, it was too loud and indistinct to make it out, but when they could actually see the great beast, the words became clear enough to make out: "Hispanic male, five-foot-seven." Danny looked at Jake and they both burst out laughing. It was a description that fit Danny. It was a description that fit a lot of guys in the area.

"Dude, you better run for it. I'll hold them off," Jake joked.

It was already nearly dark when Danny got in his Ford truck and drove 30-minutes, mostly on the freeway, to Colpro. On Vista Drive, about a half mile before the Colpro plant, he veered off on a side street just in time to avoid a traffic stop the cops had already set up to nab New Year partyers. Waiting in the long line would have made him late for work and, besides, he didn't know if that one beer would have been a problem.

Danny had no love for cops, especially considering what had happened when he was 18. He and his cousin Moises had been stealing tires, and a white guy had fired a gun at them while they were running away, killing Moi. Danny had run back to help Moi and ended up getting arrested. Nothing happened to the guy who killed Moises, and it had left Danny with a bitterness toward cops, tempered by a firm resolution he made at the time not to get in trouble again. Now that he was the sole source of support for Trevor and Kari, there was no question of it. The kids counted on him. In his heart of hearts, he knew they were his reason for living.

It was a short crew that night at work, but there was an urgent order of golf bags that needed logos silk-screened on them. Danny clambered up the metal stairs to the big press and started the setup. While he was waiting for one of the guys downstairs to find him some ink and solvent, he sat down near the production whiteboard. He wished he had another beer, or at least a Coke.

He picked up a marker and, way up near the top of the whiteboard, drew a 3-D cross. It didn't have Jesus on it, but just to make sure it looked like Jesus' cross, he drew it sitting on top of a mountain. Just under the mountaintop, he drew the number 2000, also 3-D. Then, for no reason he was aware of, he drew a cloud above all of it, and put some dark shading on the underside of the cloud. He was going to draw a little helicopter among the clouds, but then Gary came upstairs with the supplies. "Happy New Year, dude," Gary said, looking at the drawing. "That's kinda depressing, ain't it?"

3. The baby kissers

Fourth century B.C. to 2005

ALEX LANDON

Since 1947, California has had a system for registering people convicted of sex crimes. This may surprise you if you only knew about the newer measures—the Megan's laws, Jessica's laws, and so on—laws that I call "designer laws" because they have been sold to the public based on the "human interest" of their titles and their supposed ability to have prevented notorious crimes.

Often the parents of children murdered in these notorious crimes have a role in initiating designer laws. Such parents, of course, are assailed by complex emotions, such as grief, shock and guilt. And they are taken advantage of by much larger forces. One of these larger forces is undoubtedly the mass media, which finds it easy to publicize laws that are cleverly packaged to grab the attention—and usually to frighten—the public.

Another of these larger forces might be the California Correctional Peace Officers Association—the prison guards union. This union took up with the father of a murdered girl, Polly Klaas, to promote California's infamous "three strikes" law. (It is understandable why prison guards would promote this law, because it resulted in an increase in the prison population and, thus, better job prospects for guards.)

Another larger force might be politicians. Often one who is up for reelection is eager to hitch his or her wagon to a tragic tale that can capture the public imagination and boost a politician's publicity to levels beyond their wildest hopes. Campaigning politicians who lay claim to a child's murder are doing the modern equivalent of old-fashioned baby-kissing. But we would all be better off if they stuck to kissing babies, because designer laws tend to be bad laws that hurt everyone.

Even politicians such as California's former Attorney General Bill Lockyer get into the act. This is a shame because an attorney general is a trusted figure, one from whom people expect a sober approach. Yet, instead of fulfilling the public trust, one of Lockyer's Megan's law reports gave new life to discredited urban myths, claiming without any basis that "convicted sex offenders are among the most likely criminals to reoffend and create new victims." (1) Didn't Lockyer notice that at the same time, a U.S. Justice Department Web site was calling it "a myth" that sex offenders commit new sex crimes at a higher rate than other, general criminals reoffend? The Justice Department cited three large studies showing recidivism for sex offenders was only 10.9 to 13.4 percent, (2, 3) compared to about 50 percent for people convicted of crimes of a more general nature.

Besides being engulfed by emotional storms and conniving politicians, another thing that designer-law parents have in common is that most are white. Apparently, only white parents and white children have what it takes— a mix of political savvy, appeal and perhaps the ability to evoke a particular type of fear—to get rolled up with sex crimes into a designer-law snowball.

The disadvantage of being a black or brown child who suffers a crime and is apparently forgotten may create a sense of sad poignancy among their relatives. Combine the disadvantages of being a black or brown victim with the disadvantages of being a black or brown convicted person —heavily over-represented in prison—and it is easy to see why people of color get upset with the criminal justice system. We've all heard the stories from the Old South, about the rampant fears in that era that white women were going to be raped by recently freed slaves and the lynchings and injustice against African Americans that resulted. If, after you read about events during the summer of 2002, it seems like this ugly snapshot of lynchings was somehow beamed up to the 21st century in slightly transmuted form, then it will be clear that our criminal justice system has not advanced as much as some of us like to think.

Crimes of "incontinence"

With this background about sex crimes, designer laws and racial bias, you may wonder if, in the distant past, extremely strong reactions to sex crimes were as normal as they seem now. Have sex crimes always been the crimes that grab all the fear and loathing?

If we check out Renaissance Italy and ancient Greece, what we see looks pretty different from today. In his 14th century Italian epic classic, The Inferno, Dante put sexual sinners in the higher echelons of Hell. He reasoned that hot-blooded sexual sins, which he called sins of "incontinence," were less bad than sins of cold malice, such as usury and other monetary crimes. Dante inherited the concept from Aristotle. But in modern American society, incontinence is something that happens to old people in nursing homes, and on the evil meter, sex crimes take the prize.

By the colonial era in New England, a most severe reaction toward people accused of sex crimes was already evident, judging from two works of literature that give us a clue that in early America, things had changed a lot since the days of Dante and Aristotle. The Frenchman Alexis de Tocqueville, who in the 1800s wrote his observations about traveling in the United States, noticed that Americans showed a peculiar ire toward sex crimes. He attributed this to the Puritans, whose stamp on the national character was indelible, and to a desire to safeguard freewheeling American women who traveled about unprotected by men.

Nathaniel Hawthorne's classic novel The Scarlet Letter also shows a young nation with Puritan roots that was prone to castigate sexual transgressions. As most Americans know from their high school literature class, Hawthorne depicted the rage that a town vented against Hester Prynne and a minister who fell in love with her. Few works of early American literature mention slavery—and the fear of angry, marauding slaves—as a factor in creating this harshness toward sex crimes. But it is worthwhile to remember that slavery existed in most of New England in early colonial times and that the slave trade and the settling of America went hand in hand. So it may be plausible, as suggested above, that overly harsh treatment of sex crimes is related to racism and racial fears.

"High tech vs. Sexual Predator"

Returning now to the 20th century, specifically 1947, we find that California gained a distinction of sorts as the first state to require police registration for people convicted of sex crimes. California enjoys a reputation as the state that pioneers "progressive" laws and it is expected that eventually other states will follow suit. But many other states didn't get around to requiring registration until the 1990s.

The idea of having to register with police, especially lifetime registration, should be inherently abhorrent to people in a nation "conceived in liberty." So even this low-tech, 1947-style registration is contrary to important American principles, except in cases where someone is demonstrably dangerous.

A few years later, with the advent of computers, the Internet and high technology, things got even worse. Since high tech seems to take on supernatural proportions in the public mind, our mental images of internet-related sex crimes and high tech "solutions" to sex crimes have become badly warped. Viewing online child pornography and people over 18 chatting online with people under 18 using social media have begun to seem extremely threatening. To many people, the nascent internet appeared a perilous place swarming with "predators," a dehumanizing term that in itself is a bit strange and was not used much until recently. (Before 1995, the term was "Mentally Disordered Sex Offenders," which then mutated to the far more frightening "Sexually Violent Predators.") And judging from police publicity, the great and well-funded police machine—which by the way includes a lot of our entertainment media—has played a role in convincing people that the danger from the internet is grave. Once

16

again, this publicity effort protected police officers' job security and ensured that tax dollars kept rolling in.

If the dangers of high technology were depicted in hysterical terms, high tech solutions to sex crimes began to be billed as the savior. This started in the 1990s, with technology that purported to control sex crime. If there had been a movie, it could have been called High Tech vs. Sexual Predator. As computers boomed, the high-tech superheroes started appearing.

The first saviors on the scene were two national laws, Megan's law and the Jacob Wetterling Act, unless you count the primarily federally funded National Center for Missing and Exploited Children, which was connected to the TV show "FBI's Most Wanted" and began before the 90s. (Remember the connection between police forces and entertainment that was mentioned above? This is only the most flagrant example.) All these efforts were inspired by child victims. The two laws provided for "community notification" about people convicted of sex crimes, and had boatloads of federal money attached to them.

As high-tech measures made their way through the waning years of the 20th century, they evolved—metastasized may be a better word—from databases and 900 numbers into CD-ROMs and on into other technologies. They generated progeny too—the Amber Alert, Jessica's law, and so on—forming a web of laws. In fact, it began to seem as if relatives of crime victims felt they were shirking a duty if they didn't start a campaign for a new law, although they were often urged and made to feel obligated by police and politicians.

Now we once again arrive at the slice of life we are looking at, just after the turn of the millennium, when the unfortunate events of that terrible summer of 2002 began to unfold.

At around this time, the annual registration of sex offenders in California, abetted by the birth of Megan's list a few years earlier, had lurched forward to encompass staggering numbers of men—93,000 Californians, (4) or about one out of every 135 California men. Arriving at this figure is not rocket science. You take population figures from the 2000 Census, subtract people under 18, and divide half of the remainder by the total of listed people at that time. And if you had done the calculation for other states, you would have found figures even more shocking, for example, the rate in Alaska, where one out of every 63 men was listed. (This process admittedly assumes that very few women were on the list.) The above words, "staggering" and "shocking" do not mean that the world is in reality overflowing with dangerous sexual deviants. Quite the contrary. In fact, the list wouldn't be objectionable if it contained only truly dangerous people. But only a tiny fraction of the 93,000 people listed in California at that time—about 1,700 people listed as "high risk"—were truly dangerous. (4) The other 91,300—who were misleadingly called "serious"—were nothing like the paroled man who killed young Megan Kanka in New Jersey. Yet his specter continued to drive public opinion.

Experience has shown me that most child molestation is situational—it occurs in situations in which the two people already know each other and the man does not show a pattern of such behavior. An adult may turn to a young person due to stress, alcohol or convenience. There is none of the stalking, lurking or violence you see in many TV dramas. In fact, my child-molest clients generally have jobs and more stable lives than drug and property offenders. And contrary to the urban myth that convicted child molesters are "incurable pedophiles," in reality, we usually find that they are neither.

Above, it is mentioned that, rather than being "incurable," sex offenders have a relatively low re-offense rate. As for the pedophile myth, only a tiny group of these men fit the American Psychiatric Association's definition of a pedophile—a person who shows a sustained attraction for prepubescent children. Most people convicted of "child molestation" actually commit their offense against developed teenagers. And sometimes "molesters" are teenagers, or almost teenagers, themselves.

Some people convicted of child molestation are not criminals at all. Frequently, they are men falsely accused in bitter divorces. It is not uncommon for attorneys to see cases in which charges are made by mothers grasping for ways to disable the father during bitter custody disputes. This can halt visitation in a heartbeat and leave the accused men paralyzed with fear.

People convicted of sex offenses can also be men convicted on questionable date rape charges or young men who get caught having consensual sex with an underage girl. Registered sex offenders can even include people convicted for "indecent exposure"—for example, urinating in public. This certainly doesn't merit lifetime registration with police.

The scarlet letter

All this information should make us very cautious in spotlighting people convicted of sex crimes. But nevertheless, all 93,000 people on Megan's list in 2002 were turned into lepers by the list—with counterproductive results for them and the rest of us. Listed people lived in terror of public exposure from the CD-ROM. Their wives are sometimes harassed, and their children taunted at school. Vigilante actions such as murder threats, fire bombings, shootings and beatings as a result of Megan's list have been documented.

18

As an example, consider what was on Alaska's Megan's list in 2002. Alaska's list—the list that, as already mentioned, spotlights one out of every 63 Alaskan men—was already on the Web then. One person immediately noticeable under the A's, was a slight young man, five-feet-five inches, apparently of Native background, who wore a melancholy expression and a headset pulled down around his neck like any other twenty-something. The Web site said he had committed an offense at the age of 18. What would a lifetime of derision do to his chances of overcoming his past? Since loneliness and depression can cause sex offenses, making it difficult for people to find friends or jobs, Megan's list is one way to push them into reoffending. Thus, a perverse result of Megan's list could be increased recidivism. The feeling many thinking people will carry away from this Web site is shame—overwhelming shame at being a voyeur in a system that subjects people to this wearing of the scarlet letter.

In California, at the beginning of the summer of 2002 Megan's list was available by dialing a 900 number or by going to the local sheriff station, signing a form saying you agreed not to improperly use the list or to harass registered people, and then viewing the list from a CD-ROM as a sheriff looked on. Very tame stuff compared to what was coming.

But even under this "old fashioned" system, which included a warning that harassing or discriminating against a listed person was illegal, a public defender in Vista, California, said he got at least 40 calls a year from people, some of whom had been convicted decades ago, who were getting hate mail or not getting jobs because of Megan's list. Lawyers are likely to be the only ones who hear the stories of these terrified people. Because where else could they turn? To police? Reporters? Ex-offenders are too afraid of further public exposure to complain, and they believe police will not be sympathetic.

A public electrified

That year, it was still winter in southern California when the doubly tragic chain of events began. First, a girl named Danielle Van Dam went missing. Weeks later, after a tremendous police effort and the prompt arrest of a neighbor, her body was found. The case electrified San Diego for months going on years. In another example of the link between police and entertainment, several TV stations preempted regular daytime shows for live coverage of the neighbor's trial when it began in June. Newspapers too, capitalizing on the possibility of increased readership during the panic, were scrambling for headlines with any imaginable angle on the story, including some about Megan's list—"Database spotlights sex offenders in area," one of the many newspaper stories announced.

One reason for this overwhelming media interest was that the girl's family lived in a middle-class subdivision. As the Los Angeles Times noted, quoting a Poynter Journalism Institute spokesman, "We tend to, in the media ... place more weight with children who are white, children who come from economic circumstances that are middle or upper level." Another reason for the interest was surely that Danielle Van Dam was very cute. In a heavily publicized photo, her charming smile and blonde hair in pigtails plucked at the public's heartstrings.

There had still been only one killing when one little newspaper complained about the "inconvenience" of having to go to a sheriff's station to see the Megan's list CD-ROM. This was the start of many contradictions. Although the Danielle Van Dam case was clearly the reason for the media's sudden interest in Megan's list, the neighbor arrested in Danielle's killing had no police record except drunken driving. He would never have been on Megan's list, so it couldn't have prevented the crime. But that didn't stop the growing clamor to beef up the list. Many people in San Diego pointed enviously at Alaska's Web map. But its legality was due to be decided by the U.S. Supreme Court, so a full-scale Web map for California was on hold.

Then two more disappearances occurred in the U.S. southwest. They were girls who were just as appealing as Danielle Van Dam. News photos showed Samantha Runnion, who lived in Orange County near Los Angeles, to be a cherubic, curly haired child. And Elizabeth Smart, who lived in Salt Lake City, was an appealing teen with blonde hair in French braids.

Elizabeth Smart was not found for many months and, thankfully, she was alive. But Samantha Runnion's body was found quickly, and a man was arrested almost as quickly. This was the result of overwhelming publicity in the media and another massive effort on the part of police, including Orange County Sheriff Michael Carona, who made a splashy TV appearance saying the killer was going to strike again soon, which won him acclaim from no less than President George W. Bush, and the nickname "America's sheriff."

However, once again, the arrested man had never been convicted of a sex crime. And even if he had been listed, the abduction site of Samantha was about 50 miles from his home, making it further impossible that people in the girl's neighborhood could have pinpointed him as suspicious. In fact, the absence of both of the summer's suspects from Megan's list points up a major problem with the list—that it promotes an unwarranted sense of security. Nevertheless, a loud outcry to make Megan's list more easily accessible erupted. Do something ... anything, the public seemed to say, even if it is outrageously expensive, even if it makes the situation worse, even if it tramples on cherished American liberties, even if it is illogical, even if it is a useless panacea.

One of many "improvements" to Megan's list implemented during the Summer of the Abducted White Girl was a scaled down Web map in San Diego County with colored circles showing approximate locations of registered people's homes. Former County Supervisor Dianne Jacob promoted it with incredible statistics, claiming on KFMB radio that "An average sex offender, in their lifetime, commits 360 sex offenses." (5) This was outrageous nonsense. But it was effective publicity, because most people simply take such statements at face value without doing any further research. Life is far too busy to double check "reliable sources," such as an elected county official who apparently has no reason to lie. The Web map was up and running within months.

Nobody seemed to take notice that at least two technicians who worked on the map, according to the North County Times, expressed doubts about the map, calling it "a massive effort" and "a huge undertaking and a very labor-intensive project." In the panic that was building, no expense was considered too outlandish—a harbinger of even more outlandish expenditures to come.

The panic developed as quickly as mushrooms in a spring rain. The three girls took on mythical proportions. Many people could rattle off the names "Danielle, Samantha and Elizabeth" without a second thought.

"Terrorism against babies"

Newspapers sometimes are more accurate and in-depth than electronic media. One paper ran a story citing FBI statistics showing that the rate of child abductions by non-family members was actually decreasing a bit and had held steady for about a decade. And some reporters noticed the similarity of the child abduction scare to the previous summer's shark attack scare, concluding that the media had a tendency to trumpet and magnify whatever frightening events would increase their ratings. But these stories were deep inside the paper, while front page stories—as well as almost all coverage on TV and radio—gave the impression that a rash of child abductions was in progress. And the "rash" seemed to justify the need for an all-out war mentality.

Illustrating the panic, it was not uncommon then to read opinions drawing parallels between the fight against child abductions and the fight, also very much in the news since the 9/11 attacks, against terrorism. In the North County Times, a social worker claimed child sexual abuse was rampant, compared people who did it to "terrorists" and described the involved children and teens as "babies."

With terrorist attacks an all too recent memory, what could be more alarming than a vision of a great number of apparently ordinary people engaging in terrorism against babies? But what did it cost our society to believe in this vision? We didn't need a crystal ball for the answer—a look at the recent past told the tale.

In the 1980s, there had been a series of questionable allegations that created a similar panic reaction. A wave of accusations—based on questioning of children by social workers—swept not just California, but the nation, in which people were imprisoned for alleged sexual abuse of children. There was the Akiki case in San Diego, the McMartin case in Los Angeles, the Stoll case in Bakersfield and several in other states. Although these accusations were made in locations that were very distant from one another, hard-to-believe allegations of Satanism and torture were made in many of them. (6)

In many cases, the charges were dismissed, or the defendants were acquitted, or the convictions overturned—sometimes after accused people were imprisoned for years. In at least one instance, when one of the questioned children reached adulthood, he wrote about being interviewed when he was 9 years old at L.A. County's Children's Institute International. In 2005 Kyle Zirpolo recalled his long-ago questioning at the Institute. It seemed to go on for weeks, he wrote. Kyle said that when he told social workers that nothing happened, they didn't believe him. "I remember thinking to myself, 'I'm not going to get out of here unless I tell them what they want to hear." (7)

The finale to the extremely expensive prosecution of teachers from the McMartin Pre-School may have been ignominious, but the bureaucracy devoted to the alleged abuse had already mushroomed, including an increased number of people employed by Child Protective Services. In California, the number of people working in prisons and in Child Protective Services shot up. Prison construction and guards' salaries shot up.

The racial slant

In its intensity, this 1980s panic, including the McMartin case, foreshadowed the one that was developing during the summer of 2002. Of course, in 2002, real crimes had taken place, while many people thought the 1980s panic was a matter of snowballing accusations conjured up by overzealous officials. Another big difference was that the 2002 panic was diverted into an increasing public clamor for high tech "solutions."

And in the 2002 panic, some people noticed a racial slant—a slant like the one mentioned earlier that operates in the social recipe that produces designer laws. Los Angeles Times reporters noted that two African American children, Alexis Patterson and Jahi Turner, disappeared under similar circumstances around the same time as "Danielle, Samantha and

Elizabeth," but their cases remained obscure. The Times also pointed out unsolved crimes that had occurred in the previous decade but had not drawn much attention. Three of these five child killings that went unheralded and unsolved had happened to children with Hispanic names.

The article explained the discrepancy in attention given by the media and police by pointing to the certain advantages—"The [Elizabeth] Smart case had lots of compelling video and pictures"—and by noting that police had been hampered by a shortage of Spanish speaking officers to investigate the abductions of Hispanic kids.

It wasn't fair, logical or wise, but "Danielle, Samantha and Elizabeth" would continue to drive far-reaching developments during and beyond that 2002 Summer of the Abducted White Girl.

4. Trial

March 2001, to February 2002

ELAINE HALLECK

Sometimes Esperanza Fernandez tried to think when it had all begun. She was thinking about it today, a cold morning in February 2002, as she drove to work. The sun was barely up, but already the freeway was thick with fast moving traffic—people apparently going to work as early as she was.

Pera had known something was wrong over a year ago—or was it getting close to two years now?—when Danny started dragging around with a long face, when he stopped eating, when his weight began dropping. When, with quivering lips and welling eyes, he finally told her he was in trouble, she wasn't surprised.

But Pera was an optimistic person. After all, her name, Esperanza, means hope. Maybe Danny had gotten his optimism from her, although Pera knew where hers came from. It came from God, from the Virgin. Her faith wasn't the most learned variety, considering her early, itinerant life, but she knew St. Paul said to always keep praying, always keep giving thanks, no matter what.

Pera went to church regularly. Danny didn't, although he considered himself Catholic. He started going every Sunday, though, after that detective came to his house, beat on the door with something heavy and metallic, and came storming in to accuse Danny. Or maybe it was after that neighbor of Danny's called—later they found out the police had been taping the call—accused him of molesting her daughter, and said her husband was coming over with a gun.

Something's wrong with that woman, Pera thought. Always screaming at her children, always wearing short shorts. She started Ashley, or Tiffany or whatever her name was—Pera could never remember—in modeling when she was only a baby. Why would she let her daughter come over for sleepovers with Kari, with no woman in the house?

Pera remembered one day at the courthouse. The mother was dressed all in black, down to her stiletto heels. She had hair down to her waist, like her daughter's, although her daughter's was blonde. "Child molester! You're going down!" she had screamed at Danny in the hallway. Pera just looked at her.

Inside the court, she was just as raucous. But she quieted down when her daughter came in with a blond prosecutor, who had on a grey pantsuit that couldn't hide the fact that she looked to be anorexic.

In contrast, Ashley was chubby. And not all that cute. To Pera, it seemed like a career as a model was a long shot for her. And that day she was wearing a weird outfit: short shorts in a bib overall style that Esperanza figured was to make her look younger than 12, or to hide her breasts, which were already bigger than Pera's.

Danny had frozen when Ashley and the prosecutor came in. The prosecutor stood between Danny and Ashley and gave the girl a demonstration of how to raise her hand and swear to tell the truth.

Danny later told Pera he was surprised that a Bible hadn't been included in the swearing-in. But there was a Bible in the courtroom that day—the one Danny had brought. He had it on the table where he sat with his lawyer. In his left hand, he held the cross Pera had given him years ago, with its chain tightly wound around his fingers.

For Pera, the worry had started in force the day her son cried and said he was in trouble. Yet it wasn't as bad that day as it got later. At first, it was just another problem, like all the others. She knew problems would come out right if she had faith in God and worked hard. This is America, Pera thought, where nothing can hold you down forever. Here, there were always opportunities, another chance to do better. Even when Chucho, a heroin addict, left her, he went up to San Francisco and got in a Salvation Army program, and now he was better, and was back in L.A., although they didn't live together anymore.

The problem really didn't seem so bad then—not on the day when Danny said he was in trouble, not during the four days after they came to arrest him and Pera was frantically helping him cash in his retirement plan so he could get out of jail, not even on that day in the courtroom when it seemed like the whole world was on the side of a 12-year-old girl and nobody except Pera and the lawyer were on her son's side.

No, it was later. Maybe it was the day Danny made his plea bargain, when he told her with an incredulous and choking voice that he had to register with police as a sex offender "every year on my birthday, for the rest of my life."

This news really sunk in a month or so later, when Pera changed apartments so she would have room for Trevor and Kari. Between the signing of the rental agreement and explanations about the complicated security procedures, the manager of her new complex had gone to great lengths to point out to Pera the existence of a 900 number that she could call, "with some difficulty," the manager said, bristling with irritation, to access "Megan's list"—a national database for obtaining information on convicted sex offenders living in the area. At that, Pera had gone a little numb, wondering how it would impact Danny after he got out of the

25

detention facility and came to live with them. The manager even had a picture of a sex offender posted in the window of the office. Her boyfriend was a police officer, she explained.

Now Pera was getting off the freeway. It was chilly for Los Angeles, as chilly as her heart got after she glanced up through the polluted haze at a white cross on a distant mountaintop and then looked back down and saw hawkers in the middle of the intersection selling newspapers with an unusual urgency. Pera could see the headline was in screaming capital letters, as if there had been another 9/11 attack. But she couldn't make it out. When she got close to one of the hawkers, she noticed his breath was making a white cloud in the cold air. He turned then, so she could read the headline. GRISLY DISCOVERY. She knew what it was about—they had found the girl's body—and she knew it would affect Danny, although right then she didn't know exactly how.

5. Whimpers

1972 to 2005

ALEX LANDON

During the months before the summer of 2002—before the chain of events that began that Summer of the Abducted White Girl—anyone observing the scene in Southern California might have taken a certain Lutheran minister's arrest as emblematic of some important features of life in the United States.

It was a defining moment for several reasons. Pastor Michael Skoor was accused of child sexual abuse. A furious reaction followed. The sexual nature of the case and the response presaged both the disappearances of three white girls and the broader sex scandal involving Catholic priests, which took hold of the popular mind and the media just a short time later, triggered by a series of articles in the Boston Globe.

Pastor Skoor's case attracted hardly any attention compared to the two soon-to-break stories of the abducted girls and the Catholic priests, but it did create a spectacular whirlwind of outrage among people close to the situation. A local newspaper reported that, after being threatened with 100 years or life in prison, the 54-year-old minister got 29 years. "Hopefully, he'll die in prison," the prosecutor then said, at which members of the pastor's flock broke into cheers, apparently seconding her death wish.

Prosecutors have uttered worse than this, but the scene was unusually ugly, possibly because one expects religious people not to cast stones so enthusiastically. However, what really drew my attention to Rev. Skoor's case was how it had come to the attention of police. The pastor had been experiencing suicidal urges and sought counseling. His psychiatrist reported him to authorities after he apparently talked about his behavior with the boys.

So we see that, in essence, it was his psychiatrist's report to authorities that put Rev. Skoor in prison. In fact, the psychiatrist was required to report him. This may shock some readers, unless they have been paying attention to developments in the helping professions during the last few decades. Many people are still under the impression that what someone says to a psychiatrist, and other medical doctors, is confidential. The principle of confidentiality, which is also called "privilege," is an ancient principle that originated with Hippocrates and is with us today in the Hippocratic oath doctors take.

Principles vs. sex

The Hippocratic oath with its pledge not to harm the patient is an ancient principle that forms one of the foundations of modern society. Earlier in this book, another ancient idea that has become outmoded was mentioned—Aristotle's and Dante's perception that sex crimes are less severe than some other crimes. Now we see that, in more than one instance, pillars are crumbling under the weight of changing attitudes toward sex crimes. This confirms what a wise minister once noted—that principles are most likely to be overlooked when sex is involved.

But let's get back to "privilege" or confidentiality, which mean that people who have certain relationships to you cannot—or should not—be forced to report you to police or testify against you.

A Catholic priest in a confessional operates under a "seal of confession," which is related to the separation of church and state. He will not divulge what you say in confession, no matter what you confess. It is similar with your lawyer, doctor and your husband or wife. What you say to them is protected by the ancient principle of confidentiality, which nowadays, as we will see, sometimes has little more legal weight than a custom—in other words, very little.

One prominent instance in which confidentiality between parent and child was attacked came to light on Mother's Day 2003, several years after the sex scandal involving former President Bill Clinton. Monica Lewinsky wrote an editorial in the Los Angeles Times criticizing investigating prosecutors who had threatened to force her parents to testify against her. (Incidentally, a person cannot be forced to testify against himself or herself either, although the principle here is not confidentiality, but the Fifth Amendment to the U.S. Constitution. The Fifth Amendment is also under fire in regard to sex crimes, as we shall see in another chapter.)

A big blow to confidentiality in the field of psychology came in a landmark 1972 decision by the California Supreme Court in the Tarasoff case, which was not about a sex crime, although it did involve a man who murdered a woman. The decision punished a psychologist for not warning the woman about the client's threat of murder, which the client later carried out. As D.F. Tweedie, the former president of the California Correctional Psychologists Association, pointed out, the Tarasoff decision was by no means unanimous (it was 4-3) but it is "now taught as if it were gospel."

So, almost 40 years after the Tarasoff decision, and with only a few whimpers of protest from the helping professions, this great breach of confidentiality has grown to include other professions and situations, although this growth is not widely recognized.

"It's just in this one case," one psychologist said when discussing Rev. Skoor's case and his psychiatrist's "mandatory reporting" of child sexual abuse. But child sexual abuse is not the only case. There are now mandatory reporting laws for other crimes: domestic violence, elder abuse, child abuse and, as is evident from the Tarasoff case itself, threats of violence. And now, even a client's long-past and nonviolent behavior must sometimes be reported. And not only clients are in danger of being reported by their therapists. If a client mentions a third party who may have done something illegal, therapists must sometimes report it. In fact, a web of reporting obligations exists and it is not easy for therapists to keep abreast of them, as you can see from the comment of the psychologist just mentioned. And not just psychologists, psychiatrists and other psychotherapists face this requirement for mandatory reporting—doctors and teachers do too. Each California teaching credential threatens teachers with six months in jail for failing to report "reasonably suspected" child abuse.

Psychotherapists are involved with the courts due to mandatory reporting, as expert witnesses or, as will be detailed further ahead, doing court-ordered treatment. Consider one San Diego woman we will call Giselle who decided to get a doctorate in psychology when she was in her forties. She received her education at a respected institution in San Diego, but then, after one of her last classes—Ethics—she became discouraged and abandoned the field.

What a loss of a good future psychologist, not to mention the loss of money and of a dream. Giselle had seen herself working in the humanistic mode, helping people overcome their emotional problems. She didn't know she was practically going to be deputized. But after her Ethics class and her early, clinical experience, she suddenly realized how involved psychologists were with the courts. She was shocked to learn that the state licensure exams, which she was about to take, required knowledge of so many state laws, such as mandatory reporting. And she was also shocked to learn what the consequences were for making a mistake.

"You could lose your license and never be able to practice again, or spend lots of money defending yourself."

A professor who taught the Ethics class at the institution Giselle attended, when asked to comment, seemed discouraged, both about Giselle's situation and the state of ethics in the field. The professor acknowledged that in 2002, even the state licensing exam was moving away from testing clinical abilities—and clinical abilities were, of course, what Giselle was interested in. The exam, as the professor reported, would soon focus primarily on "legal and ethical" issues, such as when a therapist has to turn in a client.

And that brought the professor to the topic of confidentiality and child sexual abuse. "Confidentiality is your important ethical principle.

I support protecting kids, but it [mandatory reporting] interferes with the therapeutic relationship." In fact, many psychotherapists speak of the therapist-client bond as a primary key to success, although, as will be shown in the pages ahead, there is a significant group of practitioners who do not think highly of this bond, mostly because it is not in their financial interest to do so.

Most therapists try to deal with the new requirements for mandatory reporting by having their patients read and sign a warning when they begin therapy. It is sort of a Miranda warning, similar to the famous line we all know from television shows—"Anything you say may be held against you in a court of law."

But these pro forma warnings are not enough. The therapist-client bond is so important that many therapists work very hard at cultivating ways to put the client at ease. Perhaps if a therapist were to warn patients every session, or every hour—although that would surely interfere with the therapist-client bond—it might be enough to remind clients not to be lulled into forgetting that what happened to Pastor Skoor could happen to them.

But even this "remedy," when you think about it, reflects a sorry state of affairs. Imagine a young mother with postpartum depression who is having fantasies about killing her baby—a scenario that is not uncommon. Do you think this mother will take her problem to a counselor if she has any inkling of the trouble she could cause herself and her family? Medical doctors now have "reporting" requirements too—laws requiring them to turn patients in to police. So think about a parent whose child is injured in a fall. Perhaps they will hesitate to take the child to a doctor or hospital, thinking they may get a doctor who is "obsessed with child abuse," as attorney Tracy Emblem described the San Diego doctor who treated a child in the case of Ken Marsh. Marsh was convicted of child murder based on this doctor's testimony, yet the murder conviction was overturned 21 years later, and Marsh was finally released from prison. Do you think any parent who knows about this case or about similar false accusations would be eager to take an injured child for treatment?

Do you think psychotherapists would be willing to stay in a client's face—every session or more often—about their role as police deputies? If not, then you can probably see, as Giselle did, that psychotherapists' involvement with courts destroys their very reason for existence. It creates a brave, new type of psychotherapist that might make anyone who just finished George Orwell's "1984" feel queasy. It creates a psychotherapist who not only doesn't complain about the government's demands—he or she welcomes them. It creates "police therapists."

Of course, not all helping professionals have always given in to the unreasonable demands of the state. In 2005, there were legal maneuvers in California involving the suspicion that lethal injections cause people to suffer severe pain during executions and several anesthesiologists backed out when the state asked them to participate in an execution. Although technicians had been performing lethal injections for years, when a court decided that a doctor must oversee the process, the anesthesiologists' refusal left California unable to carry out the execution of Michael Morales. These doctors stood by their Hippocratic oath.

The actions of these doctors was inspiring. But certainly not all medical doctors have acted in such an exemplary manner. In fact, an Oklahoma physician, not a mere technician, was the one who had come up with the very same three-drug protocol that the principled California doctors later rejected, a protocol which, although it looks a lot like a medical procedure, is aimed at extinguishing a life. Sadly, this doctor-developed process became standard in the 35 states that kill convicted people via lethal injection.

6. The Amazing Sexual Predator

December 1999 to spring 2002

ELAINE HALLECK

Kate Michel sometimes woke up in the middle of the night, anxiously looked around the bedroom in her small apartment in Orange County and wondered where she was. It had started happening more after Danny's crisis started, even though she wasn't even that well acquainted with her dancing partner. Now she lay in bed, wishing that the pleasant sleep she had just been enjoying would come back and wash away the nagging memories that had begun marching around in her head.

Kate—blonde, slim, serious and pleasant looking, although not gorgeous—sometimes wondered why she had moved to California. Boredom, probably. With Corey grown and only her beloved cat Oscar depending on her, there wasn't any reason to stay in her job as a TV news writer—a job that paid very well, but that she had long since grown disenchanted with. Cats were portable, and Kate's friend Sandra had urged her to come to Los Angeles. So, Kate made a short visit to celebrate New Year's Eve 2000—the big one—with Sandra and her husband.

Then, on February 14, 2000, in her white Toyota, Kate left Detroit permanently. Glancing at the back seat where Oscar crouched in his cage, which was sandwiched between heaps of her other possessions, she wondered if the fact she was leaving on Valentine's Day had some cosmic significance. Hopefully it did, and hopefully it was positive, because Kate's love life couldn't have been much worse than what it had been in Detroit. And then she started calling L.A. home—along with all those others who considered Orange County to be L.A.

Sandra wasn't one of them. She lived with her husband in Eagle Rock, a part of Los Angeles that, if not really upscale, had character. Sandra joked that Kate was "behind the Orange Curtain," referring to how conservative Orange County was. Sandra was right. Kate couldn't detect a bit of the crazy leftist radicalism California was so famous for. She realized it was mostly a big myth, created by a couple pockets of liberalism—San Francisco and central Los Angeles—and by infamous religious cults, Hollywood stars, the Black Panthers and even maniacs like Charles Manson.

In Detroit, Kate had considered herself liberal, if she ever stopped to think about it, but not radical. But here she was practically the most far-left person she knew, even at the Unitarian congregation she attended. Although the congregation had some Jews and atheists, Kate thought if it had been suddenly transported to Detroit, it could have been taken for an ordinary Protestant church.

Perhaps the biggest factor in her decision to come West was the job she got as an art history lecturer at a community college. She almost had a doctorate in the subject—something else done out of boredom, although she had never finished her dissertation and in fact was still working on it. Her near-Ph.D., along with the cachet from her impressive sounding television job, plus help from her friend Candace, who taught mathematics at the same college, had landed her the job, which actually wasn't as great as she had hoped.

But what the heck—at least now she was in the Golden State and out of the grey Detroit winters that alternated between bone-chilling cold and muddy slush, neither of which were so bad unless you had to drive in it, which of course you did. Kate remembered one winter when there hadn't been a sunny day for two months. When the sun finally made an appearance, you felt like running naked down the slushy street, which could have had something to do with the seasonal depression you were suffering from.

But Kate was proud of being from Michigan. For one thing, Michigan had probably saved her from getting a boob job. "I see a lot of silicone here," said her friend Mona on one of the many days they ventured out to walk on the beach together. Mona was a married, unemployed, Jewish doctor Kate had met at the Unitarian church. Neither of them was cast in the mold of a typical beachgoer that warm day. Mona was short, dark-haired and chubby and didn't do a thing in the way of make-up or clothes. Kate was prettier, but she too was low key.

They usually came to the beach to walk and to talk. One thing they often discussed was the death penalty. Not an everyday topic, but Mona was actively against it, and her interest appealed to Kate's serious side as well as to the news writer that was still alive inside her.

On any number of these beach walks, Mona might have thrown out a rhetorical question, such as, "Did you know that the use of the death penalty in the good old United States is on par, or worse, than in countries we consider very totalitarian—like China, Russia and South Africa when it still had apartheid?"

Kate more or less knew, although she lacked Mona's ability to produce facts and figures with such gusto and at a moment's notice. But, indeed, Michigan's lack of the death penalty was another reason Kate was proud of her home state. It was one of only 12 states that didn't execute people. From 1976, when the death penalty had been re-legalized in many states, until then, at the turn of the millennium, 25 years later, the number of people on death row in the United States had steadily increased. California, along with other Western states, especially Texas, had added plenty to the U.S. total, although because of a lot of complexities, California hardly ever got around to executing the people warehoused on Death Row.

Still wishing she could get back to sleep, Kate turned over in bed, trying to get more comfortable. Maybe she should count sheep, she thought, instead of letting the death penalty disturb her.

But she couldn't seem to forget the death penalty, probably because, with Mona's exhortations often in the back of her mind, this depressing topic and the legal system were two of the things Kate had been researching, along with Giotto's "Lamentation," a 13th century Italian fresco she was writing her dissertation on. Her zeal for research had been among the talents that had made her a natural as a news writer. Once she got her teeth in a topic, she never let go. She discovered this propensity, along with a talent for writing, almost accidentally, in an Indian philosophy class in her undergraduate days. After reading one of Kate's papers, the professor called Kate to his office, for no reason she could figure out until he asked for the definition of a couple of words in her paper, and Kate realized that he didn't believe she had written it herself. He thought she had plagiarized it.

With Mona and their beach talks constantly kindling Kate's interest in the death penalty, Danny's problems had catalyzed yet more interest in the criminal justice system. As Oscar snoozed on her lap, she often sat at the computer looking up data until Oscar's weight put her legs to sleep and she had to kick him off and stand up. She read about the death penalty, the conviction rate of prosecutors, sentencing, the age of consent, and Megan's law, which Danny's mother had told her was an obsession of their apartment manager, although Kate hadn't even heard of it before she knew Danny. She decided she must've been out sick on the days it was in the news in Michigan.

This research—and maybe the worrying about Danny, which often disturbed her sleep—were about the only ways Kate felt much contact with her old dancing partner during the long period when he was weighed down—"devastated," in his words—by his impending arrest and trial. Despite the hopeful Valentine's Day omen, after over a year in California, Kate still didn't have a boyfriend, and although Danny seemed like a pretty bad candidate, her interest in him had taken on some intensity. He was such a cheerful person—or at least had been—and being an attentive, single father of two cute kids was certainly a point in his favor.

Even though Danny and his problems might have been what was disturbing her sleep, it no longer seemed strange to Kate that she was researching sex crimes, in particular sexual abuse of children. But it

34

certainly seemed bizarre to her friends, even Mona, once she realized that Kate's research interests had strayed beyond the death penalty.

"I'm wondering what brings a topic like this into someone's life," Mona said one day, many walks after their first one. Kate hadn't answered, and now she turned over in bed again, wondering what Mona had meant by that. Was she trying to suggest that Kate was attracting the topic? Perhaps even that Kate had been a victim of child sexual abuse herself? She remembered reading in some authoritative source like Cosmopolitan magazine that 60 percent of women had been sexually abused, but that a lot of them didn't remember it! At the time she had not questioned the figure, but now she felt a lot more critical. Pretty hard to prove, she thought, knowing how easily a writer could come up with facile facts that nobody questioned.

Kate had no doubt about what had brought the subject into her life. It was Danny's problem—the accusation of child molestation or "lewd conduct" as he said the police termed it—and the fact that he told her he didn't do it, once he was willing to tell her anything at all about it. When he disappeared from their Latino dance class, after a few months of acting and then starting to look like a cancer victim, Kate panicked. Just before he disappeared, she had finally gotten him to tell her what was wrong. He said that the girl, although she was only 12, was very developed and a little Lolita as well. To illustrate his point, he told Kate that once, when this girl was sleeping over with Danny's daughter and Danny was watching football with a friend, they asked her why she had so many boyfriends. "They like these," she'd laughed, cupping one breast in each hand—Danny aped her actions as a demonstration for Kate. Then the girl had rushed out of the room giggling.

Kate had seen Danny's kids once or twice when they waited for him at dance class at the college. Trevor was quite a hunk for only 13, and the girl Kari was cute too. What a shock and coincidence it had been to see them turn up one day, walking along the driveway in her apartment complex. They had moved there with Danny's mother when he'd been sent to a prison—or whatever it was—for a couple of months.

What else had brought the topic into her life? It's the injustice, plain and simple, she thought, getting up from her rumpled bed to get a glass of water. She had always been one to instantly defend the underdog. Maybe that was why she'd learned Spanish, starting in St. Mary's High School in Hamtramck, where most everybody else was taking Latin or French. Why take Latin when Spanish was the closest thing to it, and Latin was only used in church anyway? Yes, Spanish was definitely the most useful foreign language for an American and best of all, it belonged to underdogs.

Ironically, soon after she got to know Danny, she realized her Spanish was better than his. He was second-generation Mexican American and even his mother said her own Spanish was rusty.

Danny had started taking the dance class to get back to his roots, he said. He picked up the salsa and cumbia steps very well, but the teacher complimented Kate most lavishly, saying she had a natural ability. Why a Polish girl—her last name Michel had been changed from an unpronounceable one—should be a natural at Latin dance was a perplexing question, but there it was. She'd danced with Danny twice a week for months. He had been very reliable. But he never came back to class after he disappeared that time—she later found out that he had spent four days in jail after being arrested.

When he unexpectedly didn't show up for that class, it had thrown Kate into a panic. She knew Danny had been afraid of getting arrested. But she didn't have his phone number. So, like a good researcher, she called his job, where she managed to talk to his friend, who told her he'd call Danny's house and tell him Kate was trying to contact him. The next day, Danny's mother, Pera, phoned her.

What else had brought the subject into Kate's life? There was the way her blood boiled—and the way it was starting to boil again as she lay in bed sleeplessly—when she thought about a girl for whom sexual touching was an exciting new toy being bundled off to a hospital for questioning by protective social workers. There was the pounding in her temples when she heard later about the humiliation Danny was enduring in court- ordered "therapy," and about him hemorrhaging money for this "therapy," on top of bail, lawyers, and everything else. Where was he supposed to find the money to raise his kids? she wondered. It seemed to Kate that California had reaped a bonanza when it accused Danny. Guys like him must be keeping the state economy afloat.

Kate doubted that the girl had suffered any harm from the childish touching and undressing. In fact, she thought it more likely that Danny was the one who'd been harmed—though she came to this conclusion little by little. And this was despite another conclusion that also came to her little by little—one that she had told herself all along was a possibility —that Danny "did it."

For Kate's friends, serious consideration of whether or not he "did it" did not tarry months in coming—rather, the question sprang from their lips the moment Kate told them about her dancing buddy's problem. The other constant was a similar theme in her friends' reactions—all but Sandra, dear Sandra, the petite and beautiful daughter of a family of Lebanese American doctors.

Running through that group of surprisingly similar reactions, Kate could discern threads of the collective unconscious—more specifically, the white, American, female, collective unconscious. And these surprisingly constant views alarmed her. In fact, Kate wondered if Sandra's reaction was unusual because she was unusual ethnically. And extremely smart— Sandra herself wasn't a doctor but a linguist. So Kate rewarded Sandra's good sense by making an admission—and she surprised even herself with her late-in-dawning realization: "He says he didn't do it, but I think he might have. I might never know the truth," she told her friend one day when they were walking in a lagoony park not far from the ocean. (Kate walked with both Mona and Sandra, and sometimes thought the strength of these friendships was in direct relation to the length and frequency of their walks.)

*

Now Kate, still sleepless in her Orange County apartment, wondered when she had first glimpsed that disturbing strand of the white, American, female consciousness.

Probably, it was in Abigail, a television production professor at the community college. Although Abigail at 20-something was a lot younger than Kate, the two were friendly because of their common background in TV. Kate liked Abigail because she wasn't a stunning beauty, but she had a down-to-earth prettiness and she didn't play up—or fudge—every asset to the nth degree, as did many women Kate saw in California. Also, like Kate herself, Abigail had just moved West, which probably went a long way in accounting for her unpretentious looks.

It was the spring of 2002, Kate remembered, and she had been organizing a lecture on Art Deco in the college's slide library, with a commercial art book open on an unrelated page. Abigail walked by, stopped, and did a double take at a photo from the 80s showing a young, scantily clad Brooke Shields in a Lolita-type pose.

With sleep still eluding her, Kate even remembered how Abigail had bent over the table, and how her long brown hair had fallen forward over her shoulders. Abigail may have been unpretentious, but her shiny hair was like something from a shampoo commercial. Kate's hair had once been like that—even that color—but Miss Clairol, abetted by the advent of grey hair, had turned her into the blonde she had been for years. And now, even on this sleepless night, she remembered the wistfulness Abigail's untreated hair had aroused on her, the longing for the lost treasures of youth, even though they had been unappreciated pleasures at the time. "Isn't that kind of thing illegal?" Abigail had asked. Kate's ruminations on hair aside, Abigail was zeroing in on the Brooke Shields photo.

"Is it?" Kate answered. "It's from the 70s or 80s. I think it was less illegal then. The age of consent has been going up. Maybe I'm showing my age, but it looks pretty tame to me." The photos reminded Kate of what Danny had told her about the girl, Ashley. Perhaps that was why at that moment, she couldn't resist raising the topic of Megan's law with Abigail. She also blurted out something about men getting in trouble with young girls when a lot of girls—especially in star struck California—were doing their best to look as enticing as possible.

Abigail didn't waste a second in replying. "I know about Megan's law! I did a project on it for my real estate class." Abigail explained that she and her husband wanted to buy a house, and she was studying to become a real estate agent in her spare time.

"I printed out the Attorney General's reports," Abigail continued, sounding a little out of breath. "And I went to a sheriff's station and looked up the sex offenders in my zip code." But she suddenly stopped short. "What's the age of consent?"

"It's when someone is considered legally capable of consenting to sexual relations," Kate said, lowering her voice so a guy at a nearby table wouldn't hear. "Hey, you know," she added, "I read that the age of consent in Mexico and other Latin countries is 12."

Abigail, now seeming as conspiratorial as Kate, began whispering too. "Well, 12 is pretty young, don't you think?"

"Girls start puberty now at 9 or 10," Kate retorted. She remembered how she had almost given up hope before her period finally started at 17. "It's because of the hormones they feed cows to fatten them up. They're in the milk and meat."

Abigail slightly lifted one eyebrow. "I grew up on a farm and ... I never heard about that."

"Did you have cows?" Abigail admitted she hadn't.

"Well," Kate continued, "I knew a guy from farm country in Iowa. He said that the guys who mixed the cow feed were growing breasts!"

Abigail still looked skeptical. "Anyway, I showed it all to my real estate teacher. He said 'Yuk.'"

It took Kate a second to realize that Abigail had switched back to the topic of the Megan's law reports. Abigail looked a little crestfallen, as if she had expected a different reaction from her real estate teacher. Then she offered to lend Kate the reports, maybe hoping that Kate would show more enthusiasm. Abigail showed up the next day with the reports, organized in three very big binders.

*

When Kate finished reading the notebooks about a week later, she had to agree with Abigail's real estate teacher—yuk.

She had read most of them in a park one day—they were too depressing to read indoors. In the middle of reading, she found herself fantasizing about tossing the reports—three-ring binders and all—off a bridge. She confessed this to Sandra over lunch at a restaurant later that day.

"What bridge?" Kate's intelligent, artistic friend deadpanned. "There aren't many around here. A freeway overpass or the pier would be better." But in spite of her jokes, Sandra began studying the pages, her eyes now almost hidden by her curly, black hair.

Kate scanned the menu. "I think I'll have an omelet," she said distractedly. "They're horrible," she reiterated.

"They are?" queried Sandra. Looking worried, she turned her large brown eyes, framed by incredibly long lashes, directly at Kate.

Kate smiled, understanding the confusion. "No, I mean the reports. I don't even know if I can say exactly why—the mentality. Everything has been sort of twisted.

"Can I take them for a few days?" Sandra asked. "I can do a discourse analysis on them."

"Oh yes, please, I beg of you," Kate agreed. "Get them out of my sight." By the time Sandra returned the notebooks, she seemed to have gone through them thoroughly. "The sections that are the weirdest are the ones they call 'Success Stories,'" she told Kate. "It was creepy to notice who was checking up on who. A lot of it was between family members —they had a daughter-in-law checking up on her father-in-law, a sister checking on her brother, even a wife on her husband. The police get right in there between family members and dig out the dirt. I would say that family values take a real beating with that law."

After they ordered lunch, Sandra continued. "Another thing I noticed had to do with what they call 'hits'—that's when someone identifies a person by using Megan's list. They had 52 anecdotes about 'hits'—I counted them. But 36 of them were on men who weren't even doing anything illegal! At the time of the 'hit' at least, the men were basically just existing. A lot of them weren't even prohibited from contact with kids as a condition of their parole, or at least it wasn't mentioned. But the consequences of the 'hits' were really severe." Sandra once again had her earnest brown eyes turned full on Kate, almost as if she were pleading. "Some of them lost a position, or a job opportunity, or sometimes a relationship because they got fingered. I'm kind of surprised the attorney general would admit to it. It seems like discrimination."

"Somewhere in there it says it's illegal to use Megan's list to discriminate or harass people on the list," Kate put in. "That's just baloney." She was starting to get steamed again—even as she lay in bed, no closer to sleep than she had been a half hour ago.

"Well," Sandra had continued, "I noticed they never actually said someone lost a paying job because of Megan's list. The ones they mention were volunteer jobs. They did report that somebody didn't get a job he applied for because someone identified him on Megan's list. They were really kind of crafty the way they worded it. I can't believe that nobody has lost a job—or worse—because they were listed."

"Danny says he'll have to work at the place where he works now all his life. He thinks he'll never be able to get another job."

"I hope he never gets laid off," Sandra said. "And speaking of discrimination, I counted the Hispanic names on the list your friend printed." She pulled the list out of a pocket in one of the notebooks and waved it at Kate. "There were a lot."

*

Not long after this, Kate spotted Abigail in the library, and took the notebooks out to her.

Abigail was using one of the school computers, and seemed very intent on it. "Hi," Kate said, gently setting the stack of binders by Abigail's keyboard. From the screen, a page entitled "Age of Consent" jumped out at Kate. Kate almost jumped herself. Abigail noticed.

"It does say it's 12 in Mexico," Abigail admitted, a little pained. After a second, she added, "Well, you can't apply the standards of other societies here."

Kate wobbled her head equivocally. "Why not? Some Hispanic men might be on Megan's list for breaking a law they didn't even know about. It's not like it's on billboards. Even if it were, maybe they don't read, maybe they don't read English."

"Is that what happened with your friend?" Abigail asked, looking at Kate out of the side of her eye.

"Oh. I told you about him?" Abigail nodded yes. "Well, kind of. Well … no. I mean, he speaks English, but … I think he was charged with 'Lewd behavior toward a child under 14' or something. But, well, he does come from the Mexican cultural background and … I noticed a lot of Hispanic names on your list were charged with the same offense and, anyway, if a girl is developed, it seems weird to me that she has to wait eight or nine years, until she's 18, before it's OK to do anything without getting somebody in trouble. Eight or nine years is a lifetime to kids. In 'Romeo and Juliet,' Juliet was 13. In the United States, the age of consent has been going up. Now it's 18 here in California, but it's 16 in some states, or even 14. Did you notice that on the Web page? But overall, the trend is up. When you think about it—the age of puberty going down while the age of consent goes up—it's really a perfect recipe for sending a lot of guys to prison! Is that what women's liberation has come to? I thought it was about letting girls and women make their own decisions."

Kate was a little surprised at the abundance of verbiage that had just come out of her. She was also surprised, now that she thought about it, that Abigail was looking up the age of consent—what they'd talked about just last week. Kate hadn't thought she'd had that much impact on Abigail.

She searched for a compliment that wouldn't sound condescending. "Are you a researcher at heart, like me?" she asked.

"I guess I'm just curious," answered Abigail. "But I'm not too happy about doing it here in the library. What if someone sees me? In fact, I thought this page might be blocked. But at home our Internet died."

Kate's gaze went to the malevolent binders. She patted the stack and threw diplomacy to the winds. "You know, if they said 'person' instead of 'predator,' it would give you a completely different impression. A predator is an animal. It's dehumanizing when they misuse language like that. Your word choices can make a huge difference. You know how, when you're writing for TV, if you say 'sweetheart' instead of 'lover,' it makes a huge difference."

Abigail shrugged. "I wasn't a writer. And I mostly worked on ads." They were both silent for a moment as Abigail apparently processed Kate's remark about the word predator. "Well, what about that predator who killed Danielle Van Dam?" she said, almost triumphantly.

Aha, Kate thought. That explains her interest in collecting this information! But Kate had been following the Van Dam news story too, particularly in view of Danny's problem, so she replied, "Well, that guy wasn't convicted of a sex crime before—so he wasn't even on Megan's list. So why is everybody talking about Megan's list all of a sudden, like it could have prevented that crime? And besides, the guy hasn't been convicted yet for the murder. Maybe he's innocent."

"Well, somebody did it!" Kate didn't reply to this statement of the obvious and after a second, it seemed as if something more had suddenly occurred to Abigail. "If he gets convicted, then can I call him a predator?" As if to underscore her point, she clicked the Age of Consent window abruptly closed.

Kate might have reacted to Abigail's dig, but she still felt encouraged —so what she said did have some effect on Abigail! And now she was further astounded that the page that appeared where "Age of Consent" disappeared was called "Big Agro—The Truth About Meat."

"Well, we don't have language police, do we?" Kate answered slowly, staring at the Truth About Meat page. "But the point is that when they call people names like that, especially when the names are sanctioned by the authorities, it's demeaning. And dangerous! The guy is still a human being. Look what happened after the Nazis started calling Jews vermin. Then it got easier for ordinary Germans to look the other way when the Nazis started exterminating the vermin. And look at the n-word, you know, for black people." Kate didn't even want to say it out loud. "That's only a word too, but I don't think there's any word that's more offensive."

Abigail shrugged a little and looked away, pressing her unlipsticked lips together. Kate did appreciate Abigail's fresh, uncomplicated appearance.

But why was someone like her, raised on a farm in Vermont, she'd said, fixated on something so creepy, so Big Brother, as Megan's law? It must be fear. That Van Dam crime was pretty awful—the killer apparently snatched the girl out of her bed in a comfortable suburban home in the middle of the night. And the press was really playing it up.

But now, Kate began to get drawn into the "Truth About Meat" page. It had a large, leering cartoon of a lascivious looking cow with hot pink lipstick on her cow lips and her udder in a Victoria's-Secret-type brassiere. Kate leaned forward to look closely at the page.

"That's it!" she said, pointing at the text. "Di ... ethyl ... stil ... bes ... trol. That's what they feed cows! It's the morning-after pill. It used to be used for miscarriages but it caused cancer. I read it caused some 7-year- old girls in Puerto Rico to start menstruating—they'd eaten some meat that was shipped there after it was rejected by the USDA because it had too much diethylstilbestrol. Imagine what it does to boys. I heard it's illegal in Europe." She pointed at the screen and repeated a headline. "'Cows on Drugs.' That's good."

But this avalanche of information didn't seem to agree with Abigail —she clicked that window closed too. "I gotta go," she said, and began packing up her Megan's law binders. "I'm starting to feel like my real estate teacher—yuk."

"I guess we all agree about that," Kate told her.

"So you got interested in Megan's law because of your friend?" she asked Kate.

The remark brought Kate up short as she realized, she's just as suspicious about my interest in Megan's law as I am about hers. Kate was a little entertained by the idea. "Do you think we're both obsessed?" she asked, smiling. But, getting no answer from Abigail, she shrugged. "Well, I'm a research freak. But, yes, it's mostly because of my friend. I don't think he deserves it." Kate watched Abigail, still very serious, stuff the binders in a big tote bag. Suddenly Kate felt sorry for Abigail, sure that, husband or no husband, she felt uprooted and scared in Los Angeles. She probably wanted to be sure to move into a neighborhood where there weren't any bogeymen. After all, the man accused of kidnapping Danielle Van Dam was the Van Dam's neighbor. Abigail's worries about sex offenders were probably even related to property values. Once again, Megan's list made Kate think about discrimination—this time, about housing discrimination against blacks, which had been a big issue when she was growing up in Detroit.

*

Not long after that, another uprooted and overwhelmed friend with a taste for Megan's list materialized in Kate's life. Marlene, a friend from

Detroit, called and, almost overnight, showed up on Kate's doorstep with her 6-year-old daughter Eve. Beautiful Marlene, a long-legged blonde who turned lots of heads, was fleeing her second husband.

As Marlene sat on Kate's sofa one afternoon with Eve, pushing strands of disheveled, now dirty blonde hair out of her eyes as she looked through a telephone book for a women's shelter and to make an appointment to get food stamps, she offered Kate her explanation as to why she had to run away from her second husband.

"I caught him looking at child porn on the Internet." Marlene said flatly. The soul-shaking discovery had prompted her to grab Eve and dash across the country in her beat up Honda Civic. Kate was afraid to ask for details, so she remained silent. "That kind of thing is incurable, you know," Marlene added.

Kate wanted to protest. She wanted to explain about Danny, about what happened to him, and why she didn't think he was any different from most guys, and that he was going to suffer needlessly. Then, as with Abigail, when Kate began to explain what was happening to him and how it pained her, Marlene exhibited a surprising familiarity and fascination with Megan's list.

"I'm a young mother," Marlene stated, glancing at little Eve, arrayed across the sofa in an indefinably odd position, intent on her Game Boy. "I'm glad to know where the pervs are."

"Pervs"? Kate mumbled. This was novel. Kate knew Marlene as a person who would never dream of using derogatory language against any racial group. Yet here she was, calling people on Megan's list—and by extension, Danny—"pervs."

Kate suspected that if she scratched a bit deeper, Marlene would exhibit something more than fascination. And sure enough, a couple of weeks later, just before Marlene had to return east because of legal threats from Eve's father, when Marlene and Kate weren't focusing on Danny, Marlene came out with, "Basically, I don't give a damn if their lives are somehow less full because they chose to have sexual experiences with young girls. As I'm always telling Eve, we need to learn to live with the consequences of our choices." Kate glanced at the little girl, again lost in her Game Boy, and now showing signs of a nervous tic—an occasional, sideways jerking of her head.

Kate remembered the harping on "choices" that had filled her daughter Corey's school days—and how it had irritated her even then. She thought again about Danny, and started to get angry at Marlene's lack of sympathy for him.

"That's how you would describe it?" Kate asked. "'Their lives are made less full?' It's more like their lives are ruined. I don't think you would say it like that if you knew someone who was on Megan's list.

People like Danny are not space aliens. It could be your brother or someone you know."

But it turned out that was just the problem.

"When I was a girl, my cousin bothered me. I hope he's on Megan's list. I hope he rots in hell," retorted Marlene, her pretty face turned sour by the memory. Kate lost the energy to argue and decided not to probe further, not to ask what "bother" meant or if it was an action so grave as to warrant the "consequences" that rained down from Megan's list. Marlene apparently didn't want to dwell on it either. She changed the subject to something almost equally surprising—Alaska's Megan's list.

As it turned out, Marlene was not only keeping tabs on the "pervs" in California, but also on those in Alaska—via Alaska's Megan's list Web site. But she's thousands of miles away and doesn't have any plans to travel even remotely in that direction! Kate realized that, just as with Abigail, Marlene's interest in Megan's list and "pervs" must reflect the upheaval in her life. After all, Marlene had just dragged herself and her daughter across the country, had no idea where she was going to live or work, and was surviving on public charity.

But was the upheaval in her life the only cause of her fascination with Megan's list? Or was she also indulging a taste for thrills, like going to a slasher movie? With Megan's list you could have it all — you could be a wholesome young mother defending your children and meanwhile, you got a few chills and thrills from deeply pondering pervs and their pictures. When Marlene charged out of L.A., Kate thought her chances of a happy life in the near future were dim. Bitter divorces are everywhere you look, Kate reflected. Maybe that's why Megan's list is so popular.

*

Kate couldn't seem to stop the train of errant friends from visiting her bedroom that night. Next Mona's spirit turned up, speaking eloquently, just as the real Mona did, of her full-blown mindset about Megan's list.

On a day when Kate and Mona had been taking another of their walks, out Mona's opinions had come, like a gust of salty ocean air. All of this was starting to make Kate wonder how she, a former news writer, could until recently have been completely ignorant of Megan's list, while all her friends practically had love affairs with it.

But Mona's opinion had a novel focus. While Abigail and Marlene had zeroed in on fear, loathing and even titillation, for Mona the whole thing boiled down to power. As a wintry ocean wind made them pull sweatshirts and jackets tighter, Mona had assured Kate that sex crimes derived "not really from a sexual motive, but from a desire for power."

Although Mona was the first to voice this idea, Kate would soon discover that, like all the surprisingly similar ideas her girlfriends were expressing about Megan's list and sex crimes, the power theme was not uncommon either. You'd think power wouldn't be such a negative idea for women, considering how often it's mentioned by them, Kate reflected. There's that classic feminist book and catch phrase, "Sisterhood is Powerful," plus any number of similar slogans: "empowerment for women," "strong and beautiful," even the embarrassing feminist anthem of the 70s with its line, "I am strong; I am invincible; I am woman." But when it comes to men—or at least women thinking about them—power is clearly a bad thing.

Kate had long been accustomed to thinking about the power some women enjoyed in the play between the sexes. Perhaps this was because, as a girl and woman who was attractive only in a rather subdued way, she had always noticed—and envied—the tremendous power enjoyed by the prettiest girls to make guys behave rather strangely, almost like street dogs. She remembered how, in sixth grade, a group of boys, responding to some unseen force, had inexplicably shown up to sit on the doorstep of one of her prettiest friends while Kate was visiting. Kate had been puzzled and envious.

Maybe Mona was right, at least in part, Kate thought that night in her darkened bedroom. Maybe men recognize how powerless they can be in the face of their hormones and desires. Maybe some of them resent women for it. But for women to talk unilaterally about men wanting power as a bad thing seems like a refusal to recognize that women like power too—that's certainly clear from all the feminist slogans.

*

The power theme—and more—came up again soon after her old friend Marlene's visit and her new friend Mona's pronouncements. The next time was when Polly, a college roommate Kate hadn't seen in ages, visited Los Angeles with her family. Kate remembered Polly as an enthusiastic Baptist and enthusiastic feminist who had majored in social work. After graduation, Polly had often been desperate for work, finding mostly low-paid state or local bureaucratic positions. Now, to Kate's amazement, Polly reported she had found a niche as a counselor for child victims of sex abuse. At that, Kate just had to bring up Danny and his problems and, as if by magic, Polly produced not only the familiar theme, but some new twists.

It was during dinner in a Chinese restaurant not far from where Polly's husband and teenage son were touring Universal Studios. "The perps are after power and control more than sex," Polly pronounced confidently. Kate, remembering Marlene's surprising "pervs" from the not-too-distant past, now contemplated "perps."

Kate had been thinking about what Mona said about power, so she might at least have tried some brilliant argument on Polly, such as, "And what brings you to that conclusion?" But her mouth was full of Cantonese Seafood Medley, and she was stuck on "perps" as if it were a fishbone in her throat.

"And sometimes, if a guy perps his girlfriend's child," Polly continued, "it's a way to get even with her, if the relationship has gone bad." Polly was apparently undaunted by any inkling that Kate was half choking on Cantonese Seafood Medley as she tried to think how to respond. How could she resist this wall of female power paranoia? And there was something else in the back of her mind: "predator" ... "pervs" ... now "the perps" ... even a verb "to perp." All beginning with p.

Kate had learned as a news writer that it is often better to ask questions than make pronouncements. Sometimes, just repetition was good—that way, the person might see how bad something sounded. Finally swallowing her food, Kate squeaked, "perp?" like a mouse with hiccups.

"Perpetrator," Polly said, a little condescendingly.

"But you said a guy perps his girlfriend's child."

"That means he perpetrates his girlfriend's ... he sexually abuses a child."

"I've never heard of perps or perping."

"Well, that's what we say. I work with ... mental health professionals. We see it all the time."

"Perping?"

"Sexual abuse." Polly shifted in her seat. "I'll tell you one story. I was working with a woman who walked into their apartment when the boyfriend was sexually abusing her 16-year-old daughter. There was a gun in the apartment. She picked it up and shot him dead. She went to prison and was out in two years. That story has certainly stayed with me, although I'm not supporting all perps being shot."

"Do you support some perps being shot?"

Polly sighed heavily, shifted in her seat again and even gave a barely discernible roll of her eyes. "A woman I work with says they should all be killed. It's incurable, you know."

Kate almost jumped. Where have I heard that before? Feeling a little bit evil, she said, "Perping?"

"No ... well yes. Pedophilia. Being attracted to children. It's the peds who are the real danger."

Kate gave a little half gasp, half snort. Peds—another p word!

"But you said the girl was 16. That's not a child. Isn't 16 old enough to get married? I think my grandmother got married when she was 14." Kate thought about Nana, her grandmother on her father's side, the American born child of parents from Bohemia. Now, all of Kate's former life in Michigan seemed something on the other side of the sun, and Kate would have given anything to spend an afternoon with Nana.

46

"It's underage," Polly said, undeterred. "Some professionals say they should be castrated."

"Well, you said the perps, or the peds, are after power and control more than sex. If they just want power, why should not having sex organs stop them?"

"Well, it's their professional opinion."

"What kind of professionals are they?" Kate asked.

"Psychologists. Psychiatrists."

"Psychologists are castrating people?"

"No, of course not. But they consult. They recommend it. I think it's voluntary. The perp agrees to it to get out of prison. The state does the surgery, I suppose. The prison authorities."

"That sounds creepy. It sounds a little like shock therapy. If the person is doing it to get out of prison, that's not really a free choice, is it?" At that moment, opportune or inopportune, the waiter appeared to collect the dishes and ask about dessert. Talk of castration had dimmed Kate's appetite, but Polly ordered banana cream pie.

Kate didn't feel much like laughing, but she did so, dryly. "Isn't that kind of Freudian, Polly?" To Polly's uncomprehending stare, she added, "We're talking about castration, and you order banana cream pie."

Polly smiled and looked down shyly. "Well, nobody believes in Freud nowadays."

"No?" It was news to Kate, but she didn't have the heart to pursue it. She was tired and wanted this meal to be over, to get away from Polly. "So do you think your friend did it?" Polly asked.

Kate's answer to the perennial question surprised even herself. "I don't care much if he did. He's a decent person. He doesn't deserve what's happening to him."

*

Somewhere in the midst of what was happening to Danny came September 11, 2001. He told Kate he didn't care much because he'd had his own September 11. Kate understood. And she found that her own reaction was similar to his. But how could it be that something happening to a person she didn't even know very well was coloring her perceptions?

Or was it only Danny's problems that were making Kate's feelings so different from everybody else's? I'm about as far away as you can get in the continental United States from New York and 9/11, Kate realized. Yet she was astonished — both at her lack of surprise at 9/11 and the intensity of most people's reactions. Her lack of surprise was due to the fact that, for a long time, she'd been hearing terrorism experts say that something like 9/11 was only a matter of time. And, after all, the World Trade Center had already been attacked once. Who would work there after that? But a lot of people did. And a lot of people watched the attacks endlessly on TV, something that Kate didn't do because she'd stopped watching television when she stopped working at WXYZ-TV.

But now, analyzing her friends' bizarre opinions about sex crimes and Megan's list was as inexplicably fascinating to Kate as repeatedly watching the Twin Towers crash was to most other people.

The next opinion to fall into line belonged to Candace, the mathematics professor who had helped Kate get the job at the college. Kate had met Candace during graduate school at Wayne State. Stout and no-nonsense and given to wearing dark business suits, Candace had been a bit of a rebel and an active member of the professor's union. Although she was white, in true Detroit super-liberal style, Candace had distinguished herself by campaigning for the university to hire more blacks in teaching positions. Over lunch in the Orange County college cafeteria, infamous for its bad food, Kate had been recounting some of Danny's saga to Candace. Candace really wanted to talk about the professors' union at the community college, or the lack of one, but she allowed herself to be distracted by this semi-interesting talk of a guy accused of a sex crime.

"Did he do it?" Candace asked as she swirled large curlicues of mustard on her French fries. By now, the question didn't faze Kate. She took a deep breath and watched as Candace turned her attention to her diet coke— Kate even fantasized that Candace was about to put mustard in it too. Candace not only lacked the frills one might expect from her name, but showed such bad sense in food that Kate could not understand how her obvious intelligence could hold up under the constant stream of sludge entering her mouth. Still, one of her more endearing qualities, besides her general sociability and enthusiasm, was that she was totally impervious to California chic.

"I don't think so. I'll probably never know for sure. But the thing I'm upset about is Megan's law and ... Danny has to register with police as a sex offender every year for the rest of his life and be subject to who-knows-what—maybe his picture on telephone poles."

"We should put up signs about a professors' union on telephone poles," Candace said drily. "We are getting screwed here! This place is medieval." She pushed three or four French fries in her mouth and chewed them firmly as Kate steeled herself to talk about the union. But suddenly Candace lit up. "Megan's law!" she said with even more excitement than she had shown about the union. "It's like Oprah's law!" It went without saying that Candace was a big Oprah fan.

Kate stayed silent, holding her breath, bracing herself. She wanted to avert her eyes from the glaring yellow French fries and, next to them, a puffy yellow muffin, both on foam plates. Candace deftly ripped the greasy, pleated paper from the muffin and plunged ahead. "You know, Oprah was molested when she was young. So she had a law passed. It created a national database to look up child abusers."

Kate absently wondered if Candace liked Oprah because they both had weight problems. She realized that somewhere in the dim reaches of her memory, she had known about Oprah's law. "I didn't realize laws like that were so big. I still think it's a shame though. Laws like that cover a lot of people who don't deserve it. Like my friend."

"But aren't you defending white males?" asked Candace, sinking her teeth into the muffin as a few yellow crumbs dropped on the table.

Kate stared. She must not have mentioned to Candace that Danny was Hispanic. Kate's mouth opened a little, then closed. She wanted to say, What's wrong with defending white males? But she suspected that white males were Candace's candidate for the Great Satan—perhaps it was so for every self-respecting feminist.

Every self-respecting, brain dead feminist, Kate thought. And I've been brain dead too, thinking that anything that rights—or seems to right—the incredible injustices against black people must be okay.

Candace chewed the muffin calmly and took a sip of diet Coke, seemingly unaware of the little storm raging inside Kate.

"Danny's not a white male," Kate finally replied. "He's brown." Now is it OK to defend him? she wanted to add.

7. Blue is green

1950 to 2002

ALEX LANDON

In the case of the pastor convicted of child molesting, we saw that when a psychotherapist's patient doesn't realize he or she is in the presence of a deputy, psychotherapy can lead to criminal conviction, turning a doctor into an active player in a police state. And when this happens, the sacred principles of doctor-patient confidentiality and "do no harm" get a big kick in the pants.

But the chicken-and-egg relationship can be reversed too. Not only can psychotherapy lead to conviction, frequently conviction leads to psychotherapy—court-ordered psychotherapy. And often, when this happens, more than just those two principles are damaged.

Consider "Ed," a San Diego man convicted of drunken driving, describing an "ignition interlock device" that analyzes people's breath and prevents them from starting their cars after drinking. "You get one of those after you take the classes," he explained.

Why not before?

"Then the therapists wouldn't get their money."

He continued, "The therapist says blue is green. If you don't go along, he makes a note. If you don't say anything, they write 'Not participating.' They put the notes in your file and if you get in trouble again, they unseal it·

With this, Ed identified the corrupting effect of money and self-interest on court-ordered therapy, the tendency of this type of therapy to degenerate into brainwashing, and the broken principle of confidentiality as well.

D.F. Tweedie, of the California Correctional Psychologists Association, added his insight on the money issue. In 2002, this psychologist who came from a family line of psychologists, observed that the profession had changed, becoming so ill-paid that he would discourage his children from entering it. (1) He said it was nearly impossible to work in the classic mode in which the client receives thoughtful—and expensive—attention from a private therapist. Instead, the "California Department of Corrections is one of the largest, if not the largest, employers of psychologists in the world," he wrote in the Los Angeles Times.

Rocking and rolling with prisons

So private psychologists have to mope at the side of the dance floor while prison psychologists rock and roll—on taxpayer money.

In our society, chock full of prisons, there exists a wide world of "therapists" of one stripe or another who are dancing with the prison system and for whom confidentiality is a quaint anachronism: prison psychologists and counselors, parole and probation officers, child protection workers, and school psychologists whose chats with misbehaving youngsters sometimes put kids in juvenile institutions behind high fences with razor wire.

In times past, it was a different world. Parole and probation officers, for example, used to think of themselves as helping professionals, not as police officers. In fact, one of the founders of the social work movement, Charlotte Towle, warned early social workers not to associate with the courts. But this pioneer's ideas have been drowned in a tsunami of social workers who not only are associated with the courts—they are employed by them and function almost like police. "Almost" means that such social workers are not subject to the constitutional restraints that police are. So with this association have come benefits that the ambitious Dr. Faustus, who sold his soul to the devil, would recognize. As one lawyer put it, "P.O.s are God."

Our brave new world also includes therapists who run court-mandated "classes" on domestic violence, sex offenses, drug abuse, shoplifting and drunken driving. In fact, a great many common crimes now result in a "sentence" of "therapy." Some of these programs are effective, but some are awash in abuses. And can you imagine which area has the worst abuses? You guessed it—therapy for people convicted of sex offenses.

Sometimes court-ordered therapy is good, or at least a big improvement over prison. Several years ago, there was a change that sent many California drug offenders into treatment programs instead of to prison (although the programs have been bedeviled by problems). Programs for sex offenders can be good too, although Eric Lotke, a specialist in sex offender treatment, writes that "the public trial, shame and humiliation of getting caught appears to deter most sex offenders from further misconduct." (2) But Lotke's common sense is not often recognized, and courts are stricken with a panic mentality that sees a sex maniac lurking inside every Tom, Dick and Harry and looks for therapists with the same mentality.

Therapy factories

So when court-ordered therapy is bad, it can be really bad. And the sad fact is that there are more than a few bad-egg therapists. Often these are poorly educated individuals who are far from being doctors—M.D.s or Ph.Ds. They do en masse, one-size-fits-all "therapy" which they unblushingly refer to as "aggressive," apparently overlooking the inherent contradiction between the terms "therapy" and "aggressive." These under-qualified therapists are frequently the ones to whom the courts direct a steady stream of paying, convicted clients. These bad eggs may be the lowest bidders, or the best at scaring the courts or telling them what they want to hear, whether it is true or not.

The San Diego psychology professor mentioned in an earlier chapter sounded like an example of a good therapist — or at least a therapist who was trying to be ethical considering that current standards make it next to impossible. He said that when a probation officer wanted to know what was going on in his sessions with a convicted client, he told the P.O. to "back off." Respecting confidentiality, this therapist would only say if the client was attending.

Other practitioners, especially less educated ones who run the therapy factories that offer cheaper, group therapy and are the only ones that many convicted people can afford, tend to be just the opposite of the professor. One of the courts' favored therapists in a large metropolitan area in California was a social worker who enthusiastically touted his "public safety" role. (But he balked at describing his work as police work though, although "public safety" is how police describe themselves. The reason was probably that, after all, "policeman" still doesn't have such a nice ring as "therapist.") In fact, this man said he would never want to run his "therapy" groups without having a "strong relationship" with parole officers and regular reporting to them. If the convicted men didn't pay their therapy bills or do their "homework," if they forgot an appointment or committed some similarly loathsome act, the practitioner would make a bad report to P.O.s and off they would go to prison.

One psychologist of the same stripe, a man who ran a prison program and even called himself an expert in ethics, related a shocking account about a convicted man who admitted during treatment to committing a murder unrelated to the reason he was in prison in the first place. And as a result, the psychologist said, seemingly unperturbed, the man was sentenced to life in prison.

But was this ethical? Wasn't this an instance of self-incrimination where there are rights under the Fifth Amendment to the U.S. Constitution?

No problem, the psychologist said. He had told the convicted man up front that he was going to pursue "acceptance of responsibility" and "if you tell us about crimes that have not been adjudicated, we may have to report you, if you tell us names."

"It's ethical if you proceed with fully informed consent," he added.

In actuality, the operant phrases are "voluntary consent" and "free power of choice," stronger expressions which were established after World

War II at the Nuremberg Medical Trial. Perhaps now that memories of Nazi medical atrocities against prisoners have faded, this "ethicist" overlooked how much weaker his "fully informed consent" was. He also overlooked the fact that prisoners are not considered capable of freely choosing because, ever since "voluntary" medical experiments on prisoners were halted in the United States in the middle of the 20th century (many of them had been done on African Americans), prison has been recognized as an inherently coercive setting where "voluntary consent" simply doesn't happen.

And what about doctor-patient privilege, the principle based on the Hippocratic oath? This psychologist didn't hesitate in his reply. "Medical practitioners don't have privilege. That's only given to defense attorneys," he said, betraying another gaping hole in his knowledge of ethics. More should be expected from a PhD psychologist and one can only conclude that simply saying you are an ethics specialist does not mean that you are—or that you are practicing good ethics.

In fact, court-ordered psychotherapy and counseling can become so twisted and can put convicted people in such terrible binds that in the worst cases we can no longer dignify them with the names psychotherapy and counseling. "Police-affiliated therapy" or "treatment" seem more apt. And instead of the words psychotherapist, therapist and counselor, with their benign implications, simply "practitioner" is more fitting. In the pages ahead, you might think that even "practitioner" is too good a word, and that the words "interrogator" and "inquisitor" are more fitting.

8. Dios mio

Spring 2001 to Summer 2002

ELAINE HALLECK

Kari Fernandez didn't like the yukky new apartment, but at least the rain had stopped. Why did they have to move in the first place? With the buckets of rain that came down the day they packed up Dad's truck, it seemed like God didn't think it was a good idea either. Now their stuff was in piles in the new living room because the place was smaller than their other house. Dad said it was the best he could do on short notice.

Perched on top of the piles, like crowns for clowns, were those silly old Mexican sombreros that they got from Tio Roberto in Tijuana.

Kari, Trevor and Dad hadn't moved that far, but it was in a different district. Instead of MacManus, Trevor and Kari were going to Wheeler where they didn't know anybody. Kari was in fourth grade and Trevor sixth.

Right now, Trevor was snoring. He was 13 and just started this. But Kari couldn't get to sleep. Rikki the chihuahua was curled up by her feet—he liked to sleep with her best—and he was out cold, which was something, because when he was awake, he never calmed down. Kari guessed most chihuahuas were like that. They're Mexican dogs, she thought, our kind of dogs.

She wished she could go out in the living room and sleep on the couch with Dad, like she use to when she cried because she didn't know when Mom was coming back. To help her get back to sleep, Dad would sit her down next to the hamsters' aquarium or the parakeet cage while he told her little known facts about animals. "Do you know how you can tell a female parakeet from a male? By the bump on the beak." Dad liked animals. It was one of the things he and Kari had in common. Also trucks. She helped him pick out his Ford—the color at least—a really cool eggshell blue.

But anyway, if she went in the living room now and laid down on the sofa, Dad would say, "Princess, you got to sleep in your own room with Trevor and Rikki. Rikki will miss you." Dad said he got Rikki, who they'd only had about a week, to get his mind off his problems. Maybe it worked because Rikki was a worry, always running in and out the door and up the hill, sniffing around in the tall grass. There were coyotes up there.

What Dad said was strange. What problems was he trying not to think about? Tata said Kari shouldn't worry, just say a prayer every night for their family and before you knew it, things would be better.

Moving out of a nice house to this dinky apartment didn't make any sense. Well, their old house had been pretty dinky too, but they lived there ever since Kari remembered and it was cool. They knew a lot of people and she could walk to baseball and she had her best friend next door, at least she thought she was her best friend till not so long ago.

Kari guessed Ashley—or the blonde bombshell as Trevor called her, though not to her face—wasn't a true friend. Maybe Ashley considered Kari the booby prize—oops, she shouldn't use that word, but she didn't mean it the bad way. Maybe Ashley was only nice to her because of Trevor, who was a blondie and kind of hot. Kari was a year younger than Ashley, and chubby, and dark, and very Mexican looking, so Ashley probably considered Kari not so cool. Well, Ashley was chubby too but not the same way as Kari—Ashley was an older kind of chubby.

It was fun because her and Ashley slept over at each other's houses a lot, mostly Ashley at Kari's. Ashley's house wasn't so fun. Her mother screamed a lot, at Ashley, her little brother, her father. She never screamed at Kari, in fact she never talked to her, but with all that screaming, Kari figured it was just a matter of time.

Ashley's room was full of her awards and pictures, starting from when she was a baby, wearing super cool dresses and even make-up. Once in a while, they would hole up in there, with her mom's screams in the distance. The thing was, they could never mess up Ashley's room. If her mother stuck her head in and saw a couple plates or whatever, she would have a cow right in their ears. Or if Ashley got her hair messed up—which was down to her waist and she used gel to get the curls right—that'd be another reason for her mom to wig out.

One day over at their old house, Kari answered when Mrs. Dykowski called. She asked for Dad and sounded like she was getting ready to scream. Dad took the phone. At first he looked mad, then something else, and then he waved at Kari to go in the other room. They stayed talking for a long time. Poor Dad, Kari thought. She would not want to talk to Ashley's mom for a long time.

Sometimes Ashley told her things that were shocking, but kind of interesting. She told Kari what boobies means, which when she said it in front of Dad he told her not to, it wasn't nice. She asked what word should she use, and he said he didn't know, ask Tata. Tata thought it was funny. "I say boobs sometimes," Tata laughed. "But I guess you could say breasts or bust."

Ashley probably told Kari about boobies because she definitely had them. She must have been wearing a bra since about the age she started being in those contests—two days old. Way different from Kari who still didn't need a bra and only wore one because she begged Tata after her friends started getting them and the big thing with guys was to run up behind you and snap your bra—if you had one!

That reminded Kari of what Ashley did one night when she slept over, and Dad and Jorge were having beer and burritos from Andre's and watching a game. Ash was as wired up as Rikki that night (although they didn't have Rikki then) and kept asking where was Trevor, who for all Kari knew had ridden his bike over to Suzanne O'Brien's again. Kari guessed Ashley wanted Trevor as one of her admirers. She had a lot of boyfriends—or at least she talked a lot about them.

That night, Ashley and Kari were in the bedroom watching a video and having burritos too. They started jumping between Kari's bed and Trevor's and pretty soon they were sweaty and Ashley's hair was a big mess and she took off her sweater and showed her tank top with glitter on it. Ashley always wore stuff like that—even to school—and so did her mom. "She shouldn't even come out of the house like that," Tata said once when she saw Ashley's mom.

So Dad and Jorge were in the other room and there was a lot of football noises and Ashley runs out there in her Bebe top and Kari heard Jorge ask about her boyfriends and everybody laughed. Kari stuck her head out of her room just in time to see Ashley put one hand on each bosom and say, "They like these!" and then come tearing back into her room.

Being a single father and all, Dad didn't have much of a social life. But Dad said him and Mom weren't ever getting back together. Now, laying in bed and trying to get to sleep, Kari heard the TV in the other room with the sound low. She thought about Dad's Bible on the table out there. Why was he so interested in it all of a sudden? He usually kept it in a box under the table along with an album with pictures, mostly of her and Trevor.

That made her think of another strange thing. One day at the old house, Kari was home with a fever and Dad was home because he was working nights. Someone banged on the front door really hard and woke her up in the bedroom and she heard Dad asking who it was and he must have let him in, because they talked for a long time. Later, she asked Dad who was that guy and he said he was a policeman warning everybody about something. The photo album was on the table then, open to a page where there use to be a baby picture of Trevor with no clothes on. Now there was just a empty space. She asked, where's Trevor's picture? Dad didn't say anything, just closed the book. It was so weird that sometimes Kari thought maybe she dreamed it because of her fever.

Pretty soon, Dad gave her his gold cross and told her to wear it for him. What did that mean—"for him"? Why couldn't he wear it for himself? But she wore it. She only took it off in the shower and then she put it right back on again.

When she got well and went back to MacManus, things seemed different. She didn't walk home with Ashley anymore. Ashley's parents picked her up every day and she didn't ask if Kari wanted a ride. When she told Tata about it, Tata just rolled her eyes and said, "Oh, that family." And then, before she knew it, they moved. That would be the end of Kari and Ashley. And Kari had known her all her life. She asked Dad if she would ever see Ashley again and he shook his head, but he didn't tell her any answer. He acted like he didn't like Ashley anymore. But before, he took Ashley places with them and he tickled her when he tickled Kari and when they all fell asleep watching TV, he carried Ashley in the bedroom just like her and Trevor.

*

The previous Sunday, Kari heard Tata talking in Spanish with some ladies after church. So later, Kari asked Tata where she was born. "I'm not sure," Tata said, and laughed a little.

Kari thought, how can you not be sure? Kari knew where she was born—at the Mission-Verde hospital. Dad reminded her every time they drove by. "And I was there for the whole thing, from the time your mom started having her pains until my little princess was all wrapped up in her pink blanket."

That was the same hospital where the lady almost took them that horrible day. Tata must have talked her out of it and so they had to talk to her in a little room by the principal's office, one by one—her, Trevor and then Tata. Kari was crying most of the time, because by then she knew Dad was in jail.

"The reason he's in jail, Kari," said the lady, "was because Ashley Dykowski said he did things to her that he shouldn't have done, like touching her on her private parts. Do you know what that means?" Kari said yes.

"So, Ashley—I mean, Kari—we want to know if anything like that ever happened to you."

Who was "we?" Kari wondered. She didn't say anything and then the lady said, "Kari, sometimes older people, even fathers, do things to kids that make them feel yukky. After the kids tell us about it, they feel better. And, Kari, don't worry that you'll get in trouble if you say yes. You won't get in trouble."

Right, Kari thought, but other people will. She didn't like how the lady kept saying her name either.

"No," Kari said.

The lady had a tape recorder going. "OK, Kari. Do you mean, No, nobody ever touched you on your private parts?"

"Yeah," she said.

"So nobody ever touched you on your private parts. Is that right?" "Yeah."

"How about during tickling or horseplay? Did anybody ever do it then?" Kari wasn't sure what horseplay was. Did she mean like when Sam Swantek snapped her bra? She remembered once Trevor got in trouble for snapping a girl's bra and Mrs. Weiner said it was inappropriate. She hadn't known what inappropriate meant and Tata said it just means bad, but they don't like to say bad, she didn't know why. Kari decided she wasn't going to tell the lady about Sam Swantek.

"Sometimes we tickle and ... horseplay," Kari said.

"Did anybody ever touch you on your private parts when they were tickling or wrestling with you?"

"No."

Things went on like this. Finally, the lady let Kari leave and then Kari sat in a chair near the office reception while Trevor and then Tata went in the room. Somebody had called Tata—Kari didn't know how long she'd been there.

While Kari was sitting in the office, one of the kids in her grade came in and saw her. Now everyone would know she was in trouble! Probably her eyes showed she was crying. She touched Dad's cross she had around her neck. But then she started thinking about where he was right now, and it got her crying again. Her stomach felt bad, like she might throw up. Tata had bought her coke from the machine. Kari didn't want it but Tata told her to drink it slow and she bought her some cheetos too. Tata asked the lady at the desk, is there anything to read in here, like some comic books? There wasn't. When Tata had to go in the room with the lady, she gave Kari a fat book she was reading called One Red Rose.

Kari looked at the cover and believe it or not the main person in the book was a lady named Ashley. She hated that name, she hated Ashley, the big liar. Pretty soon Trevor came over and sat down by Kari and she showed him the book. On the front was a picture of a pretty lady and she had long, red hair and a big bust. Look, Kari said to Trevor, her name's Ashley and she's just like our friend Ashley.

"Our friend? She's not our friend. She's a big fat butt," Trevor said. Kari looked at him. It was true that Ashley was kind of fat, but they weren't supposed to call people butts. Trevor took the book and, on the cover, right on the lady Ashley's red dress, he took his pen and wrote, in tiny little capital letters, ASS. Kari took the book back. They definitely weren't supposed to say ass or write it. Now what was she going to do when Tata came back and saw the book?

"Assly, that's her name," Trevor whispered. It made Kari laugh, she couldn't help it. They both started laughing, and the lady behind the desk looked at them and Kari tried to stop but it was really hard. For the longest time, Trevor and Kari didn't look at each other, but every once in awhile his shoulders started shaking. Kari got tears from laughing that mixed with the ones from crying.

After Dad got out of jail those four days, they started going to Mass at Holy Trinity. That meant that after Mass, Dad had to try talking Spanish to some guys there. Dad would hold Kari's hand and when they talked to him in Spanish, he laughed and squeezed her hand and it hurt. He couldn't talk Spanish very good but he understood some. Kari and Trevor didn't talk or understand it either.

"I do so speak Spanish!" Trevor sometimes said. "Taco! Burrito! Carne asada!"

Dad said that in jail, they didn't have any carne asada, but he hung with the Hispanic guys and went to prayer meetings with them. Kari was saying prayers then too, laying in bed at Tata's house holding tight on Dad's cross around her neck. She didn't think she ever felt that bad, except when Mom went away.

Tata didn't cry when Dad was in jail, but she made a million phone calls and got the rosary out of Dad's truck. Once, Kari told Tata she didn't know what to say when she prayed. Tata taught her to say a prayer in Spanish. Ave Maria madre de Dios ruega por nosotros los pecadores a la hora de nuestra muerte, Amen.

Kari didn't know what it meant, except that it was to Mary, and pecadores meant sinners. But she memorized it, and said it a lot, and it made her feel better. But she thought hamsters and parakeets and chihuahuas made her feel better than prayers.

Finally, after about a million years—really it was only four days— Tata went to get Dad. When he got out of the car, Kari was the first one he went for. He hugged her and cried for a long time, even though Chucho was there. Kari cried too and later she gave Dad back his gold cross. She was afraid to ask if everything was going to be OK, even later when he took them to Ponderosa to celebrate. "I don't care if it's expensive," Dad said.

At night, Jorge came over with his woman and brought Dad a dress shirt in a package and a tie. Dad made Jorge do up the tie like when you wear it, because Dad didn't know how. Then he put it on a hanger, all ready to pop it over his head when it was time, when he had to go to court. Kari guessed Ponderosa was the last time they went anywhere in the truck. Pretty soon after that, Dad had to give it back to the bank and he got a motorcycle. Trevor got all excited about the motorcycle, but Dad told him, "You're not driving it." To Kari, it wasn't as cool as the truck.

Things were OK for a while, but pretty soon Rikki got killed. He was always going out the door and one time he didn't come back. Dad said in the night he heard some yelping from the hill. The next day Trevor brought Rikki home in a Kentucky Fried Chicken box he found. A coyote got him. Trevor was crying. He said he was sure it was Rikki even if there wasn't much left. Kari wouldn't look. Dad cried again and said, "Rikki was a good boy."

Pretty soon, they blew up the World Trade Center in New York. At school they sat around all day and watched TV and went out on the field for flag assembly instead of having it on TV. They saw the blowup a million times and people running and crying and everything. Trevor said it was awesome. Dad said he didn't care much because he already had his own 9/11. At Dad's work they printed up a lot of American flags and Trevor and Kari put one in their window. It was like July Fourth but you weren't supposed to be happy like on July Fourth; you were supposed to hate the terrorists, Trevor said. Kari hated them some, but she hated Ashley worse.

The only good thing about their new place was baseball. The team she used to be on wasn't good. But the new team by Wheeler was good. Even Ashley was on the old team and everybody knows beauty queens can't play sports for anything, especially fat beauty queens. Kari knew she shouldn't think of Ashley as fat, because she was too—or chubby.

Kari had always been good at baseball. Tata said Dad used to be good at soccer. It was from being Mexican. Especially now that Kari was on a good team, Dad loved to come and take pictures and watch her play, except when he had to work. Even if they lost, which they hardly ever did, and even if they didn't buy hot dogs, because they had to watch their money, they always had an awesome time.

*

Trevor saw Ashley at a dance at Pio Pico. He said it was bound to happen. She came right up to him and asked, "Are you mad at me?" He told her no.

"No?" Kari asked him later.

"I'm not mad at her. I hate her," he said. After that, he said bad stuff to his friends about her. "I told them she's a witch."

A witch? Kari though she knew what he really said. "I'm gonna get her," he told Kari.

"Ay, Trevor, you better leave her alone."

"Why? She should leave us alone. She's a big liar."

"Yeah, but Trevor, she could cause more trouble ... for Dad, I mean."

"How?" he said. Later in his notebook Kari saw a picture he drew. It was a big naked pink butt and some poop too. He wrote on it: ASSLY, and all around it, LIAR, LIAR, LIAR, a million times. Kari tore it in little pieces and put them in an empty milk carton in the garbage.

Trevor wanted a new dog, but Dad said not now, wait and see if Tata's gonna move in with us. Kari hoped she did! She wanted a dog too, though.

She asked Dad what was going to happen about Ashley and he said he didn't know yet, but don't worry. She asked him if he was gonna go to jail, because Trevor said Ashley said to Norberto Nogales, who told Sam Swantek, that Dad is going down. And Sam told Trevor. Dad said it was possible.

Kari said, "Dad, why did she say you did things to her?" And he said that he didn't know—that maybe her parents didn't like Mexicans. Kari told him, "No, they like Mexicans. They liked us. And remember what we saw at the beach?"

Tata had driven all of them to the beach the weekend before and when they were going in the parking lot, there was Ashley and her father. The Dykowskis didn't see the Fernandezes, and the Fernandezes sure didn't wave. Ashley had on a bathing suit that showed a lot. Anyway, there was a guy with the Dykowskis, a Hispanic guy, pretty dark and a lot older than Kari, maybe 18. Ashley was all over him, right there with her father watching.

"Dios mio," Tata said, and they drove to another part of the lot and Tata checked to make sure the Dykowskis were gone before they got out. Kari never heard Tata say Dios mio before, but she knew it means, "Oh my God."

Anyway, after Dad said he was maybe going to jail, Kari cried in her room. That night she couldn't get to sleep, and when she did, she dreamt that Dad was dead and wasn't gonna make them any more carne asada. When she woke up, she was really crying. Trevor, who usually didn't wake up for anything, came over and gave her a piece of toilet paper and patted her head. After a while, he said, Don't worry, Chucho makes pretty good carne asada.

Kari didn't think Dad was sleeping too good either. All of a sudden, he had a bunch of medicine in the bathroom—stuff for sleeping, Oxycontin for when he hurt his hand in the press, Prozac, and something for when his back hurt.

Pretty soon after that, Dad told her that for sure he was going away for a few months. "To jail?" Kari said, and she started to cry. But no, he was gonna keep his job, but he had to sleep at a place far away and they couldn't visit him. Dad hugged her and said, it's not for very long and I'll call you every day. But he was crying a little too.

One night late, he tiptoed through Kari and Trevor's room to go to the bathroom. He almost closed the door and turned on the light.

Dios mio, she heard him say. That was the first time she ever heard him say that too. Kari got up and whispered through the crack in the door, "What's wrong?" He showed her the red marks all over his neck and chest. He said it was hives.

Kari asked, "Like for bees?" But Dad said it was another kind, she forgot what. Next morning he went right away to the doctor and got more medicine. Kari wondered could he take all that medicine to the facility. He had started packing his stuff in a corner of the living room. He put some books there. That was strange because he never had books before—only the Bible. She looked at them. There was a writing notebook, and also a book Your Erroneous Zones, but it didn't look good. One Red Rose was a lot better.

Kari looked inside the notebook. She knew she shouldn't have. There were some loose pages that said Tower of Hope, Sex Offender Program Goals and Tasks, Bartek M. Michalewicz, MSW, LCSW.

Kari froze. Sex offender. So that was what all this was. Feeling a little scared, she flipped through the pages. She understood some of it—she thought she could already read a little better than Dad—and she understood some of the list of goals: "To accept responsibility," "To build self-esteem," "To understand that choices have consequences." In school the teachers were always talking about stuff like that. There was also a big list of tasks.

In the notebook, she found some pages Dad wrote. On the top in red there was a check mark and a signature, like for her homework. Down below, Dad had written the same thing, over and over, line after line. I take full responsibility for bringing pain in my children's lives by my deviant acts. I take full responsibility for the pain I caused my mother by my deviant acts. I take full responsibility for the pain I caused my father by my deviant acts. I take full responsibility for the pain I caused Esther by my deviant acts. I take full responsibility for the pain I caused Ashlee by my deviant acts.

On and on. When he ran out of people that he accepted responsibility for causing pain to by his deviant acts, he just put the same ones over again until he had two pages. Kari thought he should've put Rikki. She didn't even know who Esther was, maybe a cousin. She didn't know what deviant was either. And she wondered why he spelled Ashley's name wrong. Kari thought about it a lot. Later, she asked Dad, "What are those books for? What's your ... erroneous zones?"

"I don't know. I didn't read it yet. It's for a class."

"What's the name of the class?"

"I don't know." He acted like he didn't want to talk about it anymore. He finally said, "It's at a place called Tower of Hope."

"That's a weird name for a school."

"It's a weird place, period."

"Dad, do you think Ashley is a weird name?"

He turned his head quick and stared at her. After a second he said, "No ... why?"

"Trevor calls her Assly but it's a joke. How do you spell Ashley anyway?"

Dad looked disappointed. "Kari," he began sternly, then seemed to think better of it, and said, "I don't know how you spell it."

Kari still wanted to know what was deviant. She waited till later when she was watching TV in her room and pretended she heard something on TV and came out and asked, "Dad, what's deviant?"

Well, she didn't fool him. He asked, "Kari, have you been looking where you shouldn't be looking?"

"No."

"I can't hear you."

"Maybe. It was in the book." They heard Trevor ride up on his bike outside, talking to some other kids.

"It means bad, I guess, or weird," Dad said quickly.

"What about inappropriate?" Kari asked. "Why don't they say inappropriate? That means bad too."

Dad gave Kari a funny look and said he didn't know. Anyway, Kari thought, if the class is to build his self-esteem, why do they have him say over and over that he's bad? Kari didn't even think Dad probably knew what deviant was before. But he sure knew it now—applied to himself. Kari decided that his class sounded like what was bad—not Dad.

Then Dad surprised Kari. "I spelled Ashley wrong because ... I thought maybe they could use it against me, like a confession." She hadn't fooled him about that part either.

"Did you confess in your class?"

"I had to. If I didn't, they would of said I committed perjury."

That bothered Kari because she knew he didn't do it. How long was he going to have to go on in this class, lying and being an actor?

"When is the class done?" she asked.

"Maybe when I finish the tasks. Somebody else asked, but they gave a long answer, and I didn't understand."

Then Trevor came in and threw his helmet in the corner near the hamster aquarium and the helmet hit it and Kari felt sorry for Eenie and Meenie.

Dad got mad. "Trevor, be careful of the hamsters! Where you been anyway? You're not supposed to be out after dark."

Trevor said, "I tried to get back but I was far away."

"It's been dark a long time. Where were you?"

"By Sam's house."

"You know better than that. That's way over by our old house. What were you doing over there?"

"Nothing. Riding around."

"You went all that way to do nothing?"

Trevor didn't say anything. He opened the refrigerator. "It's not so far. Isn't there any coke?"

"I'm waiting for an answer. There isn't any coke because we're cutting down. It's expensive and it's not good for you."

"Oh Christ," Trevor said. "Am I supposed to drink water?"

"What was that?"

Kari tensed because she knew they were not supposed to say "Christ!" or even "Kripes," which Tata said sounded too much like "Christ."

"Kripes. Should I drink water?"

"Say Dios mio," Kari whispered to Trevor.

"Listen to me, Trevor. I don't want any more riding around late when I'm at the facility. If Tata tells me you're doing it, I'm gonna be mad. And watch your mouth. I'm depending on you to set a good example. You're gonna be the man of the house for a while."

Trevor got some water and he and Kari went in their room. "Guess what?" he told Kari. "We rode over to Dykowski's. We put some dog caca in a paper bag and put it on their porch and set it on fire."

Kari sucked in her breath. "What happened?"

"I don't know. Sam rang the bell and we took off. It was Sam's idea— they stomp on it to put out the fire and get the caca all over them."

"Oh my God!" Kari whispered. She almost said Dios mio.

*

Did things like this happen to other people? That's what Kari couldn't figure out. If she could have told anybody else about it, maybe she could have known if her family was normal or not.

Like one day at baseball, Norberto Nogales's brother Ivan came up to Trevor and said, "I heard your father did something sick to Ashley Dykowski."

"It's a lie," Trevor said. He was so mad Kari thought he was going to hit Ivan. When Dad came to pick them up, Trevor told him. Dad didn't say anything. Later he had to go to the facility, and when he came back he couldn't come to baseball anymore. One of his rules of probation was he couldn't be around kids, except for Kari and Trevor. He wouldn't even drop them off at baseball now. Now that they were all living together in a new apartment, Tata drove them to baseball and Dad stayed home. He slept or watched TV. He wasn't even allowed to come to school, so no parent-teacher conferences. He said before Kari and Trevor were born, he used to surf and Chucho called him Negrito cuz his skin got so dark. Well, he wasn't Negrito anymore—he was real white because he never went anywhere.

It wasn't from Ivan or Norberto Nogales that word about their curse started getting around. It was from another, older guy at school, who brought in a list of names and addresses of sex offenders. He was the kid of the manager of where Kari and her family lived now—Green Manor. The manager, Mary Ann, went to the same church as Ashley, called Cavalry Nondominational. Mrs. Dykowski taught Sunday school there and she got her picture in the paper at the sheriff station looking at the list of sex offenders. It said she was getting the list to protect the little children in her Bible class. Kari thought Mrs. Dykowski gave the list to the manager, the manager gave it to her kid and the kid gave it to the school principal. Dad was on the list.

After that, somebody wrote "Predater Puke" in marker on Trevor's locker. You can't get marker off, so Trevor had to write over it and just then, the principal walked by. So Trevor got a detention. He told Tata and Kari about it that night, and Tata said something in Spanish that wasn't Dios mio, and when Kari asked her what it meant, she wouldn't say. Tata just said that they had to be tight with their family now and say the rosary. That was her advice for a lot of things—say the rosary.

While Dad was in the facility, Trevor and Sam Swantek started a band and they practiced at home. Trevor was trying to stay home more, like Dad said, and band practice was probably Trevor's way of trying to stay home more. But Kari didn't think Tata was too happy about the noise. Anyway, Sam brought his guitar over to their house and left it there. Kari had a nerdy keyboard Dad got her when she was about one year old and Trevor played it. Kari played it a little too but she mostly sang. First they named the band Rikki Dog, after you know who, but then later, after Dad got home, Trevor said he wanted to call it Predater Puke.

"No way," Sam said.

"How about The Sex Offenders then?" Trevor said. Kari liked that name OK, but she wasn't exactly a major player in the band, because of being a little sister. She sang pretty good, though. Sometimes when she sang, she saw Sam and Trevor staring at her. Kari liked Sam and she thought he kind of liked her, even though she was chubby. She lost some weight when Dad was in the facility because she didn't feel like eating. She wished she'd lose more. Once Kari showed Sam and Trevor the picture Ashley took of Kari lying like a cat on a rug in front of Ashley's Playboy poster. Kari was wearing Ashley's black push-up bra that could make anybody look good, probably even a guy, and her lower half was draped in a faux-fur blanket.

"Cool," Sam said. Kari was elated.

Well, Sam said he didn't like The Sex Offenders any better than Predator Puke. Pretty soon after that, Dad said Sam better not come over anymore. It was the same reason as for baseball. So Sam took his guitar back home and that was the end of the band.

One day, after Trevor had gotten in trouble for the marker, he was standing by a bus with Ivan and Norberto Nogales in it. When the bus took off, Trevor picked up one of those brown, spikey things that hang on trees and threw it at the bus. He threw good and the nut made a big noise and the bus stopped like a bomb hit it and the driver came out and yelled at him. So he got in trouble again. Now he even has to go to juvenile court. Tata says everybody is too nervous after 9/11, and they have zero tolerance, especially for Hispanics, and after all, it was only a nut.

But Dad was about as mad at Trevor as the bus driver was. Trevor didn't defend himself, because he didn't want to tell Dad the things everybody was saying about him. So finally Kari explained it all to Dad. He didn't say much, but he calmed down.

Dad said now that he was home, they needed to get a bigger apartment because Tata was going to keep on living with them and Trevor and Kari weren't little kids anymore. He said they needed a girls room and a boys room, and the same for the bathrooms.

So Tata and Kari went to the office to ask if there were any bigger apartments. Mary Ann wasn't very nice and she said there weren't any apartments either.

"I don't believe her. This complex is huge," Dad said later. "People are always moving in and out. There's a lot of Marines from Camp Pendleton here. They're being shipped out to Afghanistan. When we first moved in, the manager was real friendly and there were like 10 apartments to pick from."

But that was before Dad's name was on that police list.

When they were in the manager's office, they thought the manager was gonna say something about the list, because she said to Tata that her name wasn't on the rental contract. Tata said it was because she came later, and naturally she didn't say it was because Dad had to go to the facility.

Mary Ann had a radio going and a man was talking and Kari noticed Tata start tapping her fingers up and down the way she does when she's getting mad.

Suddenly Tata asked the manager, "Do you like Jon Johnson?" You could tell by the way Tata said it that she didn't. Kari didn't know who Jon Johnson was, but she realized he must've been the guy from the radio show that was on right now.

The manager stopped writing and looked up at Tata. "It's not a matter of liking Jon Johnson or not. Jon Johnson puts out some very important information." Tata just looked back. Mary Ann went back to writing.

All of a sudden, Tata said, "Are you talking about Jon Johnson's Sex Offender of the Week show?"

The manager flipped a page and put her hand on the table kind of hard. "Well, maybe if Jon Johnson had been doing that show earlier, little Danielle or that little angel Samantha wouldn't have been abducted and their bodies found in the desert. There's a lot of it going on—there's Elizabeth

Smart, too." When she said it, she looked at Kari all of a sudden, like she was thinking maybe she should watch her mouth in front of kids.

"It wouldn't have made any difference," Tata shot back. "The men they arrested for Danielle and Samantha had never been convicted of any sex crimes before. They weren't on Megan's list. That's where Jon Johnson gets his information—from CDs at the sheriff's office. In the paper, it said that in California for the last 10 years, only about 10 kids were kidnapped and killed by strangers, like Samantha. There's no crime wave. It only seems like one, because of people like Jon Johnson. Jon Johnson does it for ratings."

Kari was thinking he did it so he could have his name repeated a million times a day, like now.

"Well, what are we supposed to do? Nothing?" Mary Ann said.

Kari started wondering if Megan's list was like the list of sex offenders that the manager's son took to school. It must've been. She never heard of it before, but Tata knew all about it. Just then, Kari looked down at the end table by her chair. On the table was sitting a newspaper called Orange County Shopper, and she almost jumped when she saw the front-page headline, "Megan's List: A Useful Tool for Parents."

She picked it up quietly and showed it to Tata, who looked at it, and then said to the manager, "Yes. Doing nothing would be better than doing something useless. Megan's list is useless. It's worse than useless. It hurts a lot of innocent people."

Now Kari knew Tata was talking about Dad and she knew the manager knew it too, but nobody said anything like that. Tata's brave remark just sat there on the manager's desk for a minute.

Then all heads turned toward the radio because Jon Johnson was announcing a guest. Some Orange County official was going to talk about "a new Internet map that's going to make Megan's list even more useful." Well, it looked to Kari like there was no getting away from Megan's list and how useful it was, except maybe in the shower. And since Tata and the manager were arguing about it, they just had to listen to Jon Johnson. The manager turned up the radio and even put down her pen. The guest said she was getting money to make a map for the Internet and put on it stars for all the houses of people who were on Megan's list. Kari didn't dare look at Tata, but she knew she was thinking, Dios mio—that means us! The guest said it was going to cost a lot, but nothing was too much to help keep our most precious oddities safe.

Kari didn't have time to ask Tata what our most precious oddities were, because the guest was giving out important information a mile a minute. "These people have lost their privacy rights. They're criminals, repeat offenders. Study after study has shown that people convicted of child molestation are incapable of being cured. They have a 100 percent recidivism rate. They should be locked up for life with the first conviction."

Tata let out kind of a snort. "How can she say that?"

"Why would she lie?" the manager replied. But she didn't seem too happy about the news either, because right after it was over, she looked mad and said, "Well, we're going to have a lot of red and yellow stars right here at Green Manor. At least for now."

Kari didn't like how she said "At least for now," but she didn't have time to worry about it because the guest started talking about the red and yellow stars, which were for the two types of sex offenders—the really-bad, who were called high-risk, and the not-so-bad, who were called serious. She thought of the reading groups in first grade. But then, stars meant you were good, not bad.

She wanted to ask Tata if they were going to be red or yellow. She leaned over and said, very quietly, "Are the reds and the yellows like ... deviants?" But Tata just shook her head no.

Well, later Kari found out Dad was a yellow. So was everybody else in the area. In fact, it was hard to find any reds but just the same she felt sorry for them — they must've really been catching it.

When the Internet map for the sex offenders came online, Tata had just bought Kari a computer. The first time she tried to look for Dad's star, the Web page was so busy she couldn't even get on it.

"It's all the deviants checking to see if their star is there," Trevor said while he sat on his bed and watched. Now Trevor was saying "deviant" too.

It was after baseball, so pretty soon Kari decided to take a bath and Trevor said to leave the computer on, he wanted to use it. "Dad says it's only for me," Kari said. "He thinks you'll go looking for pictures of girls."

"You think I'm a deviant?" Trevor asked. Kari didn't say anything. She figured that he probably knew it was true that he'd go looking for girls' pictures. But she didn't like that word deviant.

She turned off her computer and went to take a bath. Meanwhile, she heard Trevor start to play the keyboard.

"Hey!" he yelled in to Kari, who was already in the tub. "Sing some of that song Sam wrote about Rinky Dinky Rikki Dog. Remember?"

He turned on some automatic drumbeat on her keyboard and started playing. He'd been practicing a lot and it sounded good. So Kari sang. The parts she didn't remember she made up, and her voice sounded pretty good with all the reverberation in the bathroom.

By the end, although Kari was sitting in the bathtub with the shower curtain closed, she could tell Trevor was standing just on the other side of the bathroom door. "Wow," he said. "You sounded good."

"There's a lot of reverb in here."

"Maybe I should come in there with you and we could record it."

"In the tub?"

"Yeah, I guess we'd get electrocuted though."

"You're crazy," she said.

He came in the bathroom and sat on the toilet cover and played for a while. Then Kari decided it wasn't a good idea. The shower curtain was totally closed, but Tata and Dad weren't home, and she was afraid they could get in some kind of trouble.

"Go heat us up some pizza in the microwave," she told him. So he did. Then she got out of the tub and got dressed.

Her ideas about the kind of trouble Dad could get in and the kind of trouble she and Trevor could get in, turned out to be not so far wrong.

9. Inquisition

The 1940s to 2006

ALEX LANDON

"He had the plethysmograph," said a convicted man, Gene, suppressing a shudder. He was talking about a practitioner in a "therapy factory" in a large, metropolitan area. The convicted man, who was in his 60s and had a distinguished military record in Vietnam, was not in that particular practitioner's group, but he said everyone in his group shuddered about this practitioner and was afraid of being sent to him, because he had the penile plethysmograph.

There is a paper on it entitled, "Assessments of Sex Offenders by Measures of Erectile Response." And you too may have to suppress a shudder while reading it.

The paper explains how a man's penis is hooked up, after which he is "seated comfortably" in a recliner chair in an isolated room and shown explicit movies or played explicit tapes. According to one source, a typical tape might go something like this: "You're in a room alone with a young girl. A young girl of the age you prefer. She's very pretty, the age you really like. She smiles at you." The tape becomes more detailed and explicit. Meanwhile, the man's "penile tumescence" is measured either by "the air displaced by changes in penile volume in a glass cylinder enclosing the penis" or by "the mercury-in-rubber strain gauge and the Barlow metal band strain gauge." If it is a movie, a video camera might be focused on the man or he might have to do a "signal detection task" while watching the movie, to make sure he is paying attention.

"Some of these guys should have been at Auschwitz," commented Gene.

The history of this rather creepy device, the penile plethysmograph, can be traced to Czechoslovakia in the 1940s, and it was supposedly geared for detecting unusual types of sexual arousal—although based on the above scenario, it seems as if almost anybody might be aroused by that enticing description of being alone with a pretty, young girl.

Later the inventor of the penile plethysmograph migrated to Canada. In North America, the device seems to have fallen on fertile ground and, according to the Association for the Treatment of Sexual Abusers (ATSA), it was enthusiastically discussed, developed and experimented with. (And in case women were feeling left out, a female version was developed too, the ATSA website points out.)

However, despite the device's warm reception in some quarters, psychiatrists didn't think much of it. The fourth edition of the American

Psychiatric Association's Diagnostic and Statistical Manual of Mental Disorders pointed out that the "reliability and validity of this procedure in clinical assessment have not been well established."

But, as with other thought-probing techniques, such negative scientific assessments have not had much effect on the use of the devices on one group of particularly vulnerable and voiceless individuals—convicted people, especially those in prison or on parole. In fact, despite the thumbs down by the American Psychiatric Association, the use of the penile plethysmograph for sex offenders, as recently as 2004, has been recommended by the ATSA—a group whose members, incidentally, are not required to have nearly as high a level of training as psychiatrists.

Junk science rules

But the convicted man mentioned above is apparently not the only one to have found the penile plethysmograph sinister. So, in the 1990s, another technique, the Abel Assessment for Sexual Interest, hit the market. It was promoted as superior to the plethysmograph because men didn't even have to remove their clothes to take it.

Another reason the Abel test has been touted as the enlightened alternative is most likely because it employs computers instead of clunky glass cylinders and metal gauges. People simply sit at a computer, which records their "reaction time" as they look at pictures of various types of people in various states of dress and undress and report whether they feel aroused or disgusted.

A more familiar device that is used to interrogate people accused of all types of crimes, not only sex crimes, is of course the lie detector or polygraph, which measures breathing, heart rate, blood pressure and perspiration. The polygraph has been used by counterespionage agents for 50 years, but in civilian life, there have been many legal challenges. Now, most private businesses are banned from using polygraphs for employment screening, and test results are inadmissible as evidence in most state courts.

Nevertheless, in 2002, probably in response to the post-9/11 surge in security measures and the use of the lie detector in one high-profile but unfounded espionage case, the National Academy of Sciences produced a 333-page report calling polygraph testing "junk science, with results so inaccurate that they tend to be counterproductive." In plain English, these scientists said that the lie detector lies.

But in the parallel universe of sex-crime "therapy," where principles that are respected in other settings are frequently ignored, lie detectors, penile plethysmographs and the Abel test have been frequently used. If a paroled person does not want to cooperate, he will be found in violation of his conditions of parole and off to prison he goes. Apparently, where sex crimes are concerned, junk science rules.

"The polygraph is a wonderful prop for the interrogation" of naive suspects, said David Faigman of the University of California San Francisco Hastings College of Law in the Los Angeles Times, noting how police or police-affiliated therapists use the polygraph to make people nervous and even confess.

Criminology professor Bill Thompson, Ph.D., J.D., of the University of California, Irvine, was even more vociferous in criticizing the polygraph, the Abel test and the plethysmograph. Using them to pressure people into confessions reminded him of "the Spanish Inquisition," he said. "Most academic psychologists are skeptical. A group of clinicians that are employed by law enforcement uses them, but there's not much published validation." They are "practitioner-driven technique(s) without an academic foundation. The only people doing it (validity studies) are the people who use it. University people don't use the penile plethysmograph. The users are not very objective. It's a continuing problem in the forensic sciences."

Despite these gaping problems, in settings such as police-affiliated therapy, in which accused or convicted people have "voluntarily" agreed to participate and waive important rights, there is no telling how any of these techniques—penile plethysmograph, Abel test or polygraph—will be used. Experience indicates that many times they are used as punishment, to frighten people and to generally keep them on a short leash. (The punishment can be financial too, as a lie detector test can cost $200 or more and the subject often has to pay for it himself.)

Judith Becker of the University of Arizona Tucson is considered an expert on the penile plethysmograph. She says it should be used "as an assessment tool," "when the person is an admitter," and that it "can't be used to say if a person did an offense" because it gives "lots of false negatives" and "some false positives."

However, she added that there are no standards in use for administering the plethysmograph. Every lab that administers the test gives different directions to the client, she said, and the stimulus varies and the way it is scored varies. In other words, her recommendations about how to use it are often not followed.

What about the Abel test? Is it more reliable or used more carefully? According to one attorney, the Abel is "expensive" for licensed users, such as therapists, and they are forbidden to divulge its methodology. A costly, secretive test would not seem to lend itself to rigorous validation by independent studies, which the criminologist Thompson said are necessary to get beyond junk science. And, just as you might suspect, by 2004, most research on the Abel test had been published by Gene Abel himself, according to the expert Becker.

In fact, Thompson called forensic science, which includes the three techniques we are discussing, "a service industry for law enforcement." Such technologies as the Abel, he said, were mostly developed outside mainstream science with little controlled research that would eliminate the bias of those who market the tests. Faigman compares them to bloodletting.

But clearly, now that these Frankensteins have been let out of the lab, they have run amok, especially in the obscurity of prisons and police-affiliated therapy, where the people caught in the grip of such monsters are too ashamed and afraid to talk about what is going on. In addition, many defense attorneys feel obligated to ask accused clients to take the Abel, knowing that some courts put stock in it, and hoping that the results will seem to show a client does not have dangerous "sexual interests." (Notice that "sexual preferences" is not used in the Abel, which would invite unwelcome comparisons with homosexuality—and, indeed, the penile plethysmograph, according to author David M. Friedman, was used by the Czechoslovakian government early on to detect and change the sexual preferences of homosexuals.)

A bedrock protection

Rarely does an ordinary person get a chance to witness one of these Frankensteins running amok. But in a U.S. Supreme Court decision in 2002, made during the Summer of the Abducted White Girl, anyone who wants to read the decision can get a glimpse of how sex offender "therapy" works in prison, using one of these "scientific" devices, the lie detector.

This decision in McKune v. Lile put another bullet in the already badly maimed body of convicted people's rights—rights that are precious because they were bought with the blood and tears of American founders who fled European countries that did not respect these rights and because they also protect people who aren't criminals. (1)

The issue in McKune v. Lile revolved around the Fifth Amendment's protection against forcing people to incriminate themselves. The question was whether a prison warden could send Mr. Lile, a man convicted of a sex crime, to a worse, more dangerous prison because he refused to participate in "therapy." In the "therapy" offered in the first prison, a polygraph would be used to extract confessions from Mr. Lile, which could then be the basis for prosecuting him for earlier crimes (other than the one he was in prison for), such as child sex abuse.

It was a hotly contested decision (the vote was 5 to 4) and those on the losing side evidenced some blood and tears of their own. They called it a "watershed" decision attacking one of the "bedrock" protections in our system. Some used "rack and screw" to describe the polygraph—words that may seem like exaggerated terms describing ancient Inquisition devices used in dungeons until you realize that the pressure exerted on Mr. Lile indeed put him in danger of his life, since people convicted of sex crimes are sometimes killed in prison.

Although in some "therapy" programs, immunity from further prosecution is offered, many convicted people feel bewildered and under fire during such therapy. So, if the convicted person isn't a lawyer and if the therapist doesn't explain things clearly—and many of them don't, preferring to keep convicted people in the dark—confusion and fear rule the day.

And, although we saw earlier that lie detectors, penile plethysmographs and Abel tests are widely considered junk, police and police-affiliated therapists enthusiastically embrace them. Although expert Becker said that the Abel gives false negatives and false positives, on a website, Gene Abel himself promoted it is as "a tool in the detection of child molesters who deny the behavior." And the director of a large "therapy factory" in California publicly reported that he often combines the Abel test with weekly lie-detector tests to "break through" denial. So it is clear that police-affiliated therapists, undeterred by the widespread criticism of these devices, freely use them, as well as other unsavory forms of pressure.

One of these tests—perhaps the weirdest one, the penile plethysmograph—received a legal blow, although not a knockout, in 2006. A federal court saved Matthew Weber, convicted of possessing child pornography on his computer, from having his mind probed and his penis wired up to determine if his thoughts and desires had been cleansed after three years in prison. (2)

It was a small victory in the legal ping pong that hopefully will someday land the penile plethysmograph in the same junk heap as the rack and screw. But those who employ the penile plethysmograph seemed undaunted. One can only wonder if it was bravado or disregard for the court that led Thom Mrozek, of the U.S. attorney's office in Los Angeles, to comment in the Los Angeles Times that the court ruling "will have no effect on our aggressive enforcement program."

10. The sex police

September 2001, to September 2002

ELAINE HALLECK

Pera Fernandez remembered watching Danny on his second-to-last day at court. It had already been nine months of waiting on pins and needles. And what a draining nine months it had been as she watched her boy spend everything he had, including several thousand borrowed from Chucho, and then declare bankruptcy.

Danny had lost weight along with money. Now his pants hung so loose they would have fallen off if he hadn't done up the belt so tight. Pera had started bringing him carry-out sweet-and-sour shrimp, burritos—anything to tempt him to eat.

Much of the time she had been with Danny at the courthouse, that great gleaming place that could be seen for miles around, with its endless parking lots and security checks, she read novels and sometimes said the rosary. That helped her feel calm, and since Danny was so nervous, he needed her to be calm.

The lawyer helped too. Pera liked him. Whenever he saw Danny, he gave him a friendly slap on the shoulder, and it seemed to cheer Danny up, as if the lawyer were injecting energy through Danny's shoulder in that brief moment. The lawyer did other little things too—like thanking Pera for coming to court and walking Danny to the car after Danny told him the girl's parents had threatened to kill him and had even driven by his new place.

But that day, even Pera was on pins and needles, despite the lawyer's good cheer. It was just after 9/11, something that Danny and Pera had barely noticed in the background of their own trauma. The lawyer was trying to put together a plea bargain in which Danny would plead guilty to two counts. The lawyer said going to trial would be too risky. Anyway, after that long year, Danny and Chucho were both pretty much out of money. It was great how Chucho came through, considering he wasn't even Danny's real father. But it would've taken more money than either of them could scare up to pay the thousands more to go to trial.

The lawyer said the prosecutor insisted on two counts because each one was considered a "strike." That way if Danny ever got in trouble again, it would be a third strike and he'd go to prison for life. It made Pera shudder. To her, that seemed pretty severe for somebody who'd never been in trouble, except for that time he was a teenager and had tried to steal tires. Now Pera's mood was tainted by a bad dream she'd had the night before.

In the dream, she was trying to bury herself in the basement of a huge, dark building while two large, blind robots were mechanically searching and searching. It wasn't clear what they were trying to find or why, but Pera thought it was only a matter of time till they got her.

From a bench in a hallway outside the courtroom, she watched Danny and the lawyer huddle along the opposite wall. Danny looked good, if wan, in his blue shirt and tie, the same one he wore to every court date. But his face was so serious. Sitting bent over with his elbows on his knees, he looked smaller than usual, and Pera felt a big surge of affection for her boy. She thought about the time when he was little, and he accidentally pushed his hand through a window and cut his wrist and they had to rush him to a hospital. The Hispanic mother-son connection was beating strong, even though they were so far removed from Mexico. And Danny really had the father-daughter bond with Kari just like what Pera remembered having with her father.

What were they talking about now? Pera knew Danny wanted her out of earshot, and that was fine. He hadn't even really wanted her to come to court, but she'd insisted. When the girl, Tiffany or Brandy or whatever her name was, had come in the courtroom, once with the prosecutor and once with another lady, the prosecutor had requested that Pera leave. Afterward, Danny said he was glad. He felt so ashamed he wanted to curl up and die. Once, he recognized the mother of a friend of Kari's, who was a court secretary, and he scrunched down in his seat. Later, walking through the hallway, he spotted a TV reporter. He put his head down and seemed to hold his breath and clutch his Bible tighter until they were well past.

Later, Danny told her that he and the lawyer had been talking about the final deal, the plea bargain. Part of it was that he would have to get counseling.

"It's pretty rough," the lawyer said. "You have to follow the sword." What did that mean—"Follow the sword"? It sounded manly. Pera thought it had something to do with the fact that initially Danny said he was innocent, but finally pleaded guilty.

Despite these early glimmers of a problem, Esperanza, true to her name, was optimistic. Who wouldn't want some free counseling? Danny drank too much, and counseling would help with that, wouldn't it? All things considered it must be a good thing.

As for what he had supposedly done with that girl, Pera didn't see that Danny had any problem there. He said he didn't do anything, but she thought anybody would say that. And if he had done it, as far as she was concerned, the girl had asked for it. He shouldn't have done it, but she asked for it, Pera thought.

But even though Pera started out in favor of the counseling, little things soon began to raise doubts in her mind. The first was the discovery that counseling wasn't free after all—Danny would have to pay for it. It seemed strange that they were saying it was "pretty rough," and yet he'd have to pay for it.

No, Danny's counseling wasn't free, and it wasn't "free will" either. They were forcing him to do it. Danny's lawyer said that, technically, Danny was choosing counseling as part of his plea bargain, instead of taking a "crap shoot," as the lawyer put it, on a jury trial. With a jury, the charges would have been more serious and the sentence would probably have included prison. So if Danny hadn't said yes to the deal that included counseling and a very attractive work furlough program, he would've stood a big chance of going behind bars. Basically they were forcing him to get the counseling. It didn't sound right to Pera.

There were other disturbing glitches too—little evil trolls that popped up leering just when Pera hoped things might finally be getting better. For example, counseling was only one of the things Danny would have to pay for. Now that he was bankrupt from paying the lawyer and the bail bond company, he was going to have to pay to live in the work furlough facility for a few months — and the rent wasn't cheap. He also had to pay for each appointment with his probation officer all during his three-year probation. Since when did prisoners have to pay for being in jail and talking to cops?

And at his first appointment, this probation officer told Danny he had to pay still more: for therapy for the girl and reparation to the parents for time they took off work for court.

Going to jail of course was a bad thing, and Pera told herself she should be glad Danny didn't have to do that, especially considering what she heard happened in prison to people convicted of child molesting. But this bleeding him dry for years was something she never expected. When would it stop?

That test Danny had to take was another thing. Early on, his lawyer had asked him to go to somebody's office and take a test on a computer. He had to look at pictures—of people without many clothes on, Danny said—and push a button to say if he felt aroused or not. Danny called it the Abel test.

When Pera asked him, Danny said he guessed the test was used in his favor. After all, his lawyer had asked him to take it. One day at the court building, she got up the nerve to ask about it. The lawyer replied that the results had been "very favorable."

Well good, Pera thought, but what if it had been unfavorable? Would everybody have just ignored it? That was strange, but what came next was stranger.

Before Danny's final sentencing, he had to be evaluated by the probation officer. Well, the P.O. asked Danny about his sexual experiences and Danny told him he had sex when he was 17 with a 26-year-old girl. When the judge read this in the P.O.'s report, the whole sentencing came screeching to a halt. Apparently, the judge thought this experience made Danny a worse danger than ever, so he had to go and have another evaluation from the same guy he had taken the Abel test from. And of course, he had to pay for it himself. And based on that evaluation, they increased Danny's probation from three years to five!

And guess where he ended up being sent for counseling? To the same guy who had given him the Abel test and the evaluation! The lawyer called him "the sex crimes guru for the whole county." Now, how objective could that guy be? If he said in his report that Danny was dangerous, Danny would become a paying customer—and the worse he made Danny sound, the longer Danny would be a customer.

Pera didn't like the sound of it. So she asked the lawyer if Danny had to go for counseling to this guy. According to the lawyer, he didn't—he could go somewhere else. When Pera suggested this to Danny, it bothered him. He didn't seem to want to rock the boat by asking to change therapists. Besides, he didn't know what the other therapists would be like. "I just want to get through this," he said.

But getting through it turned out to be harder than he thought. Even before counseling started, Danny was so terribly nervous anticipating it that he started breaking out in hives and had to start on steroids. Then, after the first session of "following the sword," Pera asked him what happened.

"I survived," he said. "When somebody new comes, everybody in the group has to take a turn standing up and saying what they did. I was so nervous I didn't even hear what the other guys said. When it was my turn, I cried. I said I did it. My lawyer told me I had to, or they would get me for perjury. Then a black guy in the group said he didn't like what I said, so I had to do it over."

There always seemed to be bad feelings between blacks and Hispanics, Pera thought, especially around Los Angeles. But why did Danny have to be at the mercy of it?

Danny went on. "I thought, 'What do you want, man? I said I did it. I cried. Isn't that enough?' But that's how it is. We're supposed to pick on each other."

Then he changed the topic. "They gave me a bunch of papers with the tasks on them. One of them is I have to tape myself beating off and play it for the group."

After a moment to digest this, Pera reached out to the table in front of her and, to steady her nerves, rested her hand there. It was shaking. She didn't say anything, but she was stunned, first by these incomprehensible bits of news and then by the wave of fury that washed over her. This wasn't therapy, she thought. It was humiliation.

78

Finally she managed, "When you finish all the tasks, do you get out?" But Danny didn't know and didn't want to ask. He was bending over backward to do everything his P.O. and therapist wanted, to be cooperative. He was so scared they'd take Trevor and Kari away.

In fact, one day Danny told Pera that his therapist, a guy by the name of Michalewicz, said he "couldn't believe" that hadn't happened already. Pera knew this really upset Danny. All along, from the time the child protection people came to school, losing Trevor and Kari had been Danny's nightmare. And now his therapist was hinting about it. Was he going to make it happen? That was probably the reason Danny didn't want to ask when therapy would be finished, or about switching to another therapist.

"What kind of a name is Michalewicz?" Pera asked. She could barely remember it, and had no idea how it was spelled.

"I don't know—gringo," Danny said. It was a joke, but he wasn't laughing very hard.

Getting laid off from work was Danny's next nightmare. He knew he'd never be able to get another job now that he was convicted and on Megan's list. And losing his job would mean he couldn't pay his therapy bills and reparations anymore. Then his therapist or P.O. would send him to prison. It's a vicious circle, Pera realized—like they are trying hard to make him fail. A P.O. and a therapist were supposed to be your friends, she thought. But instead, they're getting him coming and going.

Danny told her about a guy in his group named Robert, whose crime was going in a lady's house and playing with her underwear.

"And he went to jail for that?" Pera said, incredulous. "Did he break in the house? Maybe he was a friend or relative!" Danny said that he didn't think Robert broke in. He thought Robert worked for the lady. But he said Robert went to prison for two months.

"I didn't know it was a crime to play with underwear," Pera said, and Danny looked at her like he was surprised. She said she always thought things like that were considered strange, but basically harmless.

Danny replied that the other day Robert confessed he had gone looking for underwear in garbage bins.

"There's no cure for you. The next step is prison," the therapist told him. Then the therapist made Robert go for new lie detector tests and for another test in which the therapist puts the guy's penis in a machine to see what his true desires are.

Again, Pera was aghast. But these were the new and strange commonplaces in Danny's world.

"It sounds like your therapist is ..." She groped for a word and finally found one. "... sick." Danny got quiet. Pera knew she shouldn't have said it.

Then Danny said, "Yeah, he's the king of the deviants," and gave a little laugh.

Once, early on, when Danny was in the facility but going to therapy once a week and coming to visit her and the kids in a few stolen moments when he was on his way to work, Pera asked if he was making friends with any of the other men in therapy. He looked at her a moment, as if it was dawning on him that she didn't understand something important. Then she remembered the guy who had picked on Danny at his first session, the time he cried.

"We're not allowed to contact each other outside. They're afraid we'll get together and do something bad."

Danny said the only friendly thing that happened at therapy was during break. Then some of the guys smoked in the parking lot, looked at the therapist's black Lamborghini and joked that they'd paid for it. Danny didn't smoke, but sometimes he went out with them anyway.

"Does the therapist ever say anything about drinking?" Pera asked. "Not so far," Danny said.

Strange, she thought, when alcohol was probably responsible for the whole thing. Instead, the therapist kept saying the guys had a "condition" like cancer. "Like cancer? What's the name of your condition?"

"I don't know. We broke the law, so he says we're deviant. It's his favorite word."

"Breaking the law isn't a disease, is it?"

"He's always talking about deviant fantasies. We have to report our fantasies. We're not allowed to have fantasies about anyone under 18. When we go to the P.O., he gives us lie detector tests and asks us if we had any sexual activity or fantasies we didn't tell our therapist about."

Pera wondered, how do you know someone's age in a fantasy? Do you ask them to show their fantasy ID? She had heard that in Mexico it was legal for girls a lot younger than 18 to have sex. So if Danny visited Mexico, was he allowed to have fantasies about girls younger than 18 while he was there? But she knew he wasn't allowed to even leave the state while he was on probation, so she didn't bring any of this up. Besides, he didn't look too happy at the moment.

"What if you fail the lie detector test?"

"I think then he would send us to prison."

"Has that happened to anyone?"

"I don't know. Guys disappear from the group sometimes and we don't know what happened to them."

"Does anybody ask?" "No."

"Do the counselors ask you if anybody is thinking about suicide?"

"Not so far."

Pera felt herself getting upset again. What if the person died? What if he committed suicide? Danny said the therapist hated them. Pera didn't like the way Danny was starting to look and act—not gaining back the weight he'd lost, taking a lot of different medicines, sleeping all the time. He even walked different, kind of dragging. She knew he would never consider suicide, because of the kids. But if they were gone, then she would really be afraid for him. Once, after the cops came to his house but before they arrested him, he said he'd thought about suicide, and about running to Mexico. But he couldn't do either, because of the kids.

"And you," he added, looking Pera in the eyes. "Besides, I don't hardly speak Spanish."

But he liked everything Mexican. One Saturday much later, after Danny got home from the facility and they were all living in the same apartment, they went to the swap meet. Walking from the parking area to the main area, Trevor and Kari were ahead, and Pera noticed Danny do a double take at a girl in tight jeans and a bright halter top. After a minute, she said, "Hijo, how are you ever going to have a girlfriend with us all cramped into that little apartment?"

She had never talked to him before about girlfriends and she thought she saw him squirm, whether from irritation or embarrassment, she didn't know. Or maybe it was the fact that he wasn't divorced from Patty, and didn't seem to be moving in that direction. Pera liked Patty but knew she wasn't a good mother and that Danny didn't want to go back with her. Besides, Pera was aware that she herself hadn't set a good example—neither matrimony nor divorce had ever figured in her life.

Danny didn't say anything.

"We need a bigger apartment, so you can have company," Pera added.

"If I have a girlfriend, I don't have to bring her home. Besides, that's not the only problem. I don't have money and I don't have a car. And I'm convicted. Who's going to want to go out with me?"

She hadn't thought of any of that, except maybe the convicted part. Not many girls would want to go out on a motorcycle. She had thought that maybe he was interested in that girl who lived in their complex, the one from his dance class, way back when. She looked like maybe she wouldn't mind a motorcycle. But Danny didn't see much of her, maybe because he had no money.

"And I don't have time," he added.

"Where there's a will, there's a way," Pera said. Then she was sure she had irritated him.

"Besides, I really can't have a girlfriend. I can have a fantasy girlfriend; that's about it. We have to report everything, and they believe in celibacy. I guess if you're married, it's OK."

Pera knew that "they" were the counselors. "If you don't go along, what happens?"

"We don't like to ask. They say we have to have celibacy to stop being deviants."

"Deviants?" she repeated. The word wasn't familiar.

"Put it on the radio!" Danny said with a little smile as he nodded toward some people walking within earshot. He lowered his voice. "It's Michalewicz's favorite word. He gets mad if we don't say it. Another word he loves is 'taking responsibility.' Like if we say we made a mistake or something, then he says we're not taking responsibility."

"Que cabron! I thought he was supposed to be helping you."

One day Danny's P.O. called up and made him go and get a lie detector test. It was because of the girl who had just been kidnapped, Samantha. Before he went, he called his lawyer and asked if he had to.

The lawyer said that even if Danny wasn't on probation, he'd probably tell him to go. Not because the police had the right to make Danny do it, but if he didn't, they'd find some way to make him sorry. But since he's on parole, the answer was definitely yes. If he didn't, his P.O. would say he was breaking his rules of probation, which are whatever the P.O. wants them to be that day. And Danny would go to jail. So Danny went for the lie detector test. And he had to pay for it too.

As for Danny's attitude about therapy, soon his tone changed. One day he even said he liked it. "The guys look up to me. I work hard on my tasks." After everything she'd heard before, Pera found it hard to believe he really liked it.

After a few seconds, as if reading her mind, Danny said, "You can't help but be brainwashed." Shaking his head, he added an explanation. "There's one guy in the group who's there for having sex with his own daughter."

"So who's the king of the deviants now?" Pera asked, feeling a little daring. Again, Danny looked at her, puzzled.

Pera recalled how at first Danny had mentioned guys who were in therapy for silly things. There was the underwear fondler and another guy who got convicted for skinny dipping in his own pool when two 12-year-old girls saw him.

But now he mentioned the serious cases. He'd said men in the group were supposed to pick on each other—wasn't that what Danny was doing now? Of course, Pera didn't dare say this. But was that why Danny's focus was on the other end of the spectrum now? Maybe since he hadn't had relations with Ashley and she wasn't related to him, it put him in one of the least pecked positions in the group's pecking order. And at the top was the chief pecker, Michalewicz, whose psychological health was beyond question—except in the mind of one lonely deviant's mother.

Pera had seen Danny take his Bible to therapy, and later he told her the therapist suggested certain Bible readings. And as time went on, Danny got more religious—being a leper would do that to you, wouldn't it? Pera might have been happy about this, except that his new interest in religion had a focus she didn't like.

"I hope I don't go to Hell," he said, tight-lipped. Pera looked at him steadily, and he broke eye contact and added, "I'm already there."

So much for liking therapy, she thought.

Her own reaction to what Danny was going through surprised her. She used to be proud to be a Mexican American, proud to be an American—although she'd never put it that way. She only realized her feelings had changed one day when she read a newspaper story saying somebody had taken pot shots with a rifle at that huge court building that had taken her boy in its jaws and spat him out. Only a few windows had been broken. But Pera found herself mentally cheering the shooters—Go! Go!

Later the change became more extreme. As the first anniversary of 9/11 approached, she was driving on the freeway near the court. Between clumps of trees, she glimpsed the court's soaring bluish windows whizzing by and she found herself imagining an airplane flying into the side of that glassy monster. When she became aware of the image, she stopped herself, shocked, and made the sign of the cross. She saw her hand shaking. But later the fantasy returned, and it was harder to push away.

11. Spy vs. Spy

2001 to 2009

ALEX LANDON

"Did you ever have a nightmare, and you were so glad when you woke up?" Gene, a man convicted for touching his teenage stepdaughter asks, after spending several years in both military and civilian courts, in a detention facility, on probation, and in "therapy."

The gist of Gene's plaintive musing is that after all those years, he was still struggling to wake up from his long "nightmare." His statement could have come from one of the other residents in the parallel universe— people long imprisoned without charges by the U.S. military in Guantanamo, Cuba, during the warlike atmosphere after 9/11, or the vast crowds of immigrants invisible in U.S. detention centers during that same time period after the passage of the Homeland Security Act in 2002.

"I'd rather go on a hundred combat missions than stand in a courtroom again, with my family looking on, waiting to be sentenced by a judge," Gene added, referring to his honorable service in Vietnam.

Gene's story illustrates more than one point. First, it puts a chink in the notion that sex offenders are a special breed of incorrigible maniacs who are incapable of learning from their mistakes.

And it shows the uncertainty as to whether Gene's nightmare could ever end. So it is for many people convicted of sex crimes, who suffer lifetime repercussions, including authoritarian restrictions and "therapy," all in mistaken service to this myth of incorrigibility and incurability, which, as we will see, has been promoted by some of the people who are supposed to be helping them.

Another reason for mentioning Gene's story is simply because of its military dimension. In my chapter about the War on Crime, parallels between the military and civilian worlds in their approaches to crime are discussed. But for now, let's look at the civilian world of court-ordered therapy and see how its foundations in adversarial thinking lie in the military world.

These foundations are sometimes exposed when an aggressive mentality shows itself in court-ordered therapy, the same mentality that a bellicose general might have when he sees a sinister enemy lurking on every foreign shore, in every strange face. (And, just as in military misadventures, an important factor at work is economic self-interest, which further distorts a "therapist's" thinking.)

Bells ringing, dogs salivating

Up to now, you may have been thinking that the "therapy" programs criticized in this book don't sound anything like any psychotherapy you ever imagined. If so, you were right. A lot of court-ordered therapy, especially the kind practiced in one-size-fits-all "therapy factories," got its start in places that will not strike you as very "therapeutic": in laboratories where experiments were done on salivating dogs responding to bells, and in Cold War military and spy chambers where interrogation, psychological pressure, "truth drugs" and brainwashing were the order of the day.

In the wide world of psychology, two important—and basically contrasting—currents of thinking are humanism and behaviorism. Sigmund Freud and later people, such as Carl Rogers, are described as founders of humanism. (And incidentally, humanistic thinking is not necessarily the same as non-religious thinking. Humanism is often traced back to the European Renaissance, when the classical thought of ancient Greece and Rome was rediscovered after the Dark Ages. It is probably fair to say that the Roman Catholic Church, for one, considers itself a humanistic institution, as evidenced in its opposition to capital punishment and abortion.)

On the other side of the fence is behaviorism, which got its start in those un-therapeutic sounding settings—for example, in the Russian Ivan Pavlov's study of dogs who salivated in response to ringing bells, once they had been conditioned to connect the sound with dinner. A lot of court-ordered therapy for sex offenders (and shoplifters, substance abusers, etc.) doesn't utilize classical, humanistic models of psychology. Instead, such "therapy" is based on behaviorism, with its world view that tends to peg people as brimming over with dangerous impulses that need to be controlled. Psychologists of a behavioral stripe have developed CBT— cognitive-behavioral theory or cognitive-behavioral therapy—which was summed up by one self-described "aggressive" CBT practitioner like this: "My clients are telling me, 'Help me, I can't control my behavior.'" Just as you might expect from a therapy that started with getting dogs to salivate by ringing bells, CBT is a repertoire of techniques that are often criticized as mechanical. (And doesn't the word "mechanical" conjure up "therapy factories"?) One of CBT's signature techniques is aversive conditioning in which a person is repeatedly exposed to repulsive stimuli—a drunken driver forced to watch videos of bodies mangled in car accidents, for example.

The "aggressive" practitioner claiming his clients are telling him "Help me" went on to scoff at humanist Carl Rogers' idea that the client's relationship with the therapist is sufficient to cause change. He also derided humanistic therapy as "sissy, touchy-feely stuff," that simply "doesn't work." However, D.F. Tweedie, of the California Correctional

Psychologists Association, cautioned against an overly optimistic estimation of CBT. He said that CBT is indeed easier to quantify and lends itself to controlled trials, such as studies that ascertain whether a target behavior goes away after treatment and, if so, for how long. (Weight loss was an example he used of a condition that was readily quantifiable.) However, that does not necessarily mean that CBT is the most effective, he said. Humanistic or psychoanalytic practices could be just as effective, but they are more difficult to verify. (1) (And they are certainly more expensive, because they require more thoughtful analysis.)

After Pavlov and during the Cold War (the 1950s and 60s), behavioral and cognitive-behavioral therapy, as mentioned above, started getting a lot of use by Americans, when CIA and spy-agency interrogators tried it on hostile subjects. During that era, which is often called paranoid and conformist, the U.S. military, steeped in a spy-versus-spy mentality, was "by far the country's major institutional sponsor of psychological research," according to writer Ellen Herman. (2)

In a Central Intelligence Agency (CIA) interrogation handbook from 1963 entitled "KUBARK Counterintelligence Interrogation," deceptive behavioral techniques are laid out, starting with attempts to foster bonding with the interrogator that are a mainstay of brainwashing techniques: "Provide adequate evidence of sympathetic interest," "establish rapport," adopt a manner that is "friendly and patient," "use the subject's first name," say the handbooks from the past. But all this friendliness is a sham. The idea is to get the subject to "take the final step of accepting the interrogator's values" and overcoming the "inward conviction that no man in his right mind would incriminate himself by providing the kind of information that is sought." Behaviorism, we see, has been mixed up with self-incrimination since early in its short history.

Some other unsavory tricks mentioned in the handbook and also implicated in brainwashing are: good-cop/bad-cop techniques (a "kind" interrogator is a foil for another "harsh" one); manipulation and control of the environment (very long questioning sessions); simple threats of legal ramifications; and group techniques such as encouraging the subject's peers to pick on him or telling the subject that his partner in the next room already confessed.

Excuses, not reasons

Anyone who has been reading along up to this point will have noticed that some of these interrogation tricks sound quite familiar. That is because they have made their way into "therapy" done on people who, like captured spies, are not free to leave, are subjected to pressure to make them incriminate themselves, and, if they do, are not protected by confidentiality—in short, the kind of "therapy" described in this book.

Consider one prison psychologist, highly respected in the field of sex offenses, writing about a typical session in which he got subjects to "accept responsibility." Spy vs. spy group pressure techniques can be seen in the prison psychologist's description of how convicted men made "disclosures" followed by rounds of "challenges" from the therapist and group members. And the spy manual's "manipulation and control of the environment" can be seen in the prison psychologist's description of an individual session focusing on one person—it had "a typical duration of six hours." (Compare these six hours with session times in the shrinking world of non-police therapy, where individual sessions run 50 minutes, and group sessions 1 1/2 hours.)

Besides his "challenges" and long sessions, the prison psychologist reveals his roots in spy interrogations when he catalogs the many ways his patients—better called "subjects"—engage in "denial." This denial, he wrote, may take the form of "excuses," "distortions," or "minimization"— never "reasons," which would yield an entirely different picture.

In his words: Sex offenders deny they committed the offense. They say they were framed. They say the victim did not resist, that the victim tricked them into believing she was older. They say the victim did not suffer long-term harm, had many previous sex partners, an unsavory reputation or was sexually provocative. If sex offenders pointed to outside factors influencing their behavior, these too were shot down as "excuses." Stress, the offender's own past victimization, their childhoods, being drunk, even Satan—all were simply one more "excuse" on the damning checklist for the "therapist" to tick off.

The content of the prison psychologist's list of "excuses" has a remarkable similar feel to a list in the CIA manual that ticks off personality types. In the CIA list there is a parade of scurrilous types: the orderly-obstinate character, the greedy demanding character, the optimistic impulsive undependable character, etc. Truly, this list and the prison psychologist's are brethren in their adversarial spirit. Just as the spymeister's scheme does not admit of any sanguine character types, the prison psychologist's list likewise reeks of a suspicious spirit, and lacks any trace of fellow feeling, advocacy, or therapeutic bond. The spy/"patient" is simply a mass of bad traits, suitable for being pummeled into submission by the interrogator/"therapist." As a boss in a "therapy factory" summed up his mindset about men convicted of child molestation, "These guys are very deceptive. They'll get you believing they are just misunderstood, and they actually really like children."

The prison psychologist didn't stop with his choice of "excuses" instead of "reasons," He continued to frame the situation in accord with his dismal expectations by using more linguistic devices. For example, he overwhelmingly chose "sex offenders" in his long document to describe those whom another type of therapist might have called "clients," "patients," "prisoners," "people" or "men." In fact, he used "men" twice, but both times in instances where if "offender" had been used, it would have been redundant—for example, "offenses made by offenders."

But plug in "men" instead of "offenders" in his paper (or in the summary three paragraphs above), and the effect is markedly different. The prison psychologist's vocabulary choice has the subtle but strong effect of dehumanizing convicted people.

There are several more problems with the prison psychologist's reasoning. Saying that convicted people have "excuses" instead of "reasons" is not only unfair, it is illogical and flies in the face of reality.

If there is no reason for something, then why did it happen? Out of pure caprice? The prison "therapist" even ruled out Satan, listing the Prince of Evil as yet another "excuse." I would have thought that after all the other "excuses" were rejected, the devil was the only remaining possibility.

Uncle Joe

But in reality, convicted people usually do have reasons for what they do. In fact, some of their reasons are the very ones the prison psychologist tossed in the garbage. If someone makes a mistake while they are drunk or depressed, his or her state of mind may not excuse the mistake, but it certainly goes a long way toward explaining it. Especially in these increasingly intolerant times, it is important to keep in mind that many sex crimes, especially child molestation, are done by ordinary people, not by a special breed of dangerous, deceptive maniacs who do them for no reason. Some experts, even among the ranks of police, say that they agree with the idea that ordinary people commit sex offenses. During the panicky summer that is the focus of this book, FBI agent Mark Hilts was quoted in the New York Times saying that some child abductors are not primarily interested in children at all — their "preferred partner might be an adult female," he said, but because of poor social skills they don't feel comfortable with them. In the North County Times, Capt. Lori Bird of the Family Protection Division of the San Diego Sheriff's Department said, "Your chance of your kids being molested by a registered sex offender are tiny compared to the danger of them being molested by Uncle Joe, by their coaches and neighbors." Perhaps police-affiliated therapists don't want to see the ordinariness of many people convicted of sex crimes, because it would take away from their presumed expertise and it would impact their pocketbook, undercutting their claim that convicted people need years of "therapy"—from them.

This ordinariness also conflicts with the therapists' fear of convicted people. Yes, fear. For behind the aggressive facade, some of the unprincipled therapists betray an underlying terror and an awareness of being over their head. One, a woman in the San Diego area, said that psychologists doing sex-offender treatment are not bothered by the lack of therapist-client confidentiality because they "don't want all the pressure on themselves of deciding if a person is dangerous." Another female therapist who worked with people convicted of sex crimes told horror stories about them, such as one about a 6-month-old girl whose father molested her so badly that she needed reconstructive surgery. The story may well have been true, but it was certainly an exceptional situation. Experience shows that very few molest clients use violence, have full-fledged intercourse with young people, or molest infants..

"Aggressive"

What do these scare stories gain for some therapists? For one thing, a feeling that they are exempt from having to treat their clients decently. A social worker with a master's degree who works in a "therapy factory" said plainly that many people were amazed to think he might treat his clients "like human beings." (The therapist's use of "human" here is enlightening, coming from someone who turns his back on humanistic theory.) He too said he "would never want to be involved in sex-offender groups without having a strong relationship and regular reporting to parole officers." Why? Because his clients were people who "rape infants and push stuffed animals in their orifices. Why should I worry about violating their rights?" If this social worker's claim is correct, if indeed his clients included rapists of infants, the question must be asked: why was someone with a master's degree treating them? So one of the things that such practitioners may fear, or should fear, is their own lack of expertise—being over their heads. Such "therapists" likewise manifest a problem with their low level of education when they say that their clients have a "disease" or "condition"— "like cancer," as they frequently claim.

It is a mystery what "disease" these "therapists" are referring to, at least in the cases of the vast majority of people convicted of sex crimes. If they mean pedophilia, this is hardly ever the case. The American Psychiatric Association's bible for mental health, the Diagnostic and Statistical Manual, defines pedophilia as recurrent and longstanding fantasies involving prepubescent children. Most people convicted of "child molesting" do so with teenagers or young teens—not prepubescent children. And all too often, the "child molesters" themselves are teenagers or very young adults and they "molest" a younger, consenting teen.

As for other types of sex crimes—possession of child pornography, rape, indecent exposure, goosing somebody on a bus, etc.—we are on even shakier ground if we say they are caused by diseases. We cannot say with confidence that a murderer, drug lord, or bank robber has a disease. Why should anyone assert that sex offenders are different?

Calling a sex crime a "disease like cancer," has other benefits for the unethical therapist besides exempting them, as they claim, from practicing ethically.

For if you have a serious disease, then, just as with cancer, this would seem to justify "aggressive" treatment—and such "therapists" frequently call their programs "aggressive." So, once again, one has to wonder: if a client really has a terrible disease, why should someone who is so far from being a doctor treat them?

Indeed, it sometimes seems as if the most unethical "therapists" have the least education. The "stuffed animals in their orifices" therapist mentioned above was a social worker with only a master's degree, as are many individuals who run "therapy factories" for people convicted of sex crimes. In fact, according to their 2002 websites, two professional organizations for professionals doing court-ordered therapy, the Association for the Treatment of Sexual Abusers and the California Coalition on Sexual Offending, required at most a master's degree for membership. And they required no specified educational level for other members working in the criminal justice system, such as parole agents and polygraph givers, who may only need a high school diploma.

Perhaps that explains why many such police-affiliated therapists are not troubled by the lack of voluntary consent or doctor-client confidentiality in their "therapy" programs. The foundation of the principle of confidentiality is the Hippocratic oath, which medical doctors (including psychiatrists) take, and for which some psychologists, by virtue of their PhD (in Latin, philosophiæ doctor), feel at least a pang of yearning. And the principle of voluntary consent was likewise articulated for medical doctors in the Nuremberg Medical trials after World War II and focused on the medical atrocities committed by Nazi doctors.

A social worker with a master's degree normally has far less expertise than a doctor, but it seems that many police-affiliated therapists with little education want to have it both ways. They don a white coat and claim they are treating "diseases" when it impresses the court and seems likely to increase their business and professional status. But then they toss off the white coat and ignore medical principles such as confidentiality and voluntary consent when observing them would displease the court and harm their business.

In fact, one wonders if the drop in the employment outlook of Ph.D. psychologists, as mentioned by the prison psychologist Tweedie, is connected to the fact that more and more police-affiliated treatment is done by under-educated and unprincipled "therapists" who charge less for their services and, untroubled by any principles that may apply to doctors, happily cooperate with parole officers and the like. (By no means do all full-fledged psychologists observe classical principles, but some make an effort, as mentioned in an earlier chapter.)

On the ATSA's 2002 Standards and Guidelines Web page, this group of police-affiliated therapists made no bones about forcing people into therapy (lack of consent) and working hand in glove with police (lack of confidentiality). "Criminal investigation, prosecution and a court-order ... are important components of effective intervention and management," they stated. They also promoted "external motivation"—a more palatable term than "forcing"—explaining that voluntary consent or "internal motivation ... may not be sufficient for treatment engagement and compliance."

Contrast that with what a San Diego marriage and family therapist said about confidentiality. "When the court wants to find out if therapy is working, it's not a real therapy situation. The patient is thinking what information is getting back to the court and this causes a real conflict. Therapists hate to work in that kind of situation. I wouldn't do it." Besides, she added, the pay for that kind of work is generally low, confirming what the prison psychologist reported earlier.

But there are plenty of practitioners who will do it, such as those in ATSA, who, disposing of confidentiality and voluntary consent with a few high-sounding phrases, spread a rich icing on their cake, claiming that, although "sexual abusers are treatable ... there is no known 'cure'" and "management of sexually-abusive behavior is a life-long task for some." With such self-serving statements, they once again ratchet up the fear factor to justify their lack of principles and, at the same time, conveniently lock in lifelong, paying clients for themselves.

If committing sex crimes is an incurable disease, as these practitioners claimed, then the exit door out of therapy is effectively blocked. And besides guarding the exit like Rottweilers, some police-affiliated therapists are as busy as elves at the "therapy" entrance door too, drawing in paying clients for all sorts of reasons.

Some do evaluations for courts of the same people they will end up having for years as captive "clients." They apparently are not bothered by the problem mentioned by Mindy Mechanic, a psychology professor at California State, Fullerton: "A clinician doing both evaluation and treatment is in a conflict of interest." (3) And some clinicians have other conflicts of interest. The practitioner who told the "6-month-old-needing-reconstructive-surgery" horror story as well as the "stuffed-animals-in-their-orifices" practitioner both mentioned doing victim counseling. This most likely explains their problematic lack of sympathy for their convicted clients. Perhaps these "therapists," have been blinded by their need for income or have never been educated about the dangers of a therapist's own emotional conflicts.

In the article "On Mitigating Professional Arrogance in the Treatment of Sex Offenders," psychiatric social worker Jerome Miller recognized how the pocketbook impacts principles when he mentioned the dwindling educational requirements for therapists of all stripes and the pressure to "hang out a shingle" and start making an income.

He explained the growing acceptance of questionable therapies such as CBT by the dumbing-down mechanisms of the insurance industry and its constant pressure to reduce costs and find something that seems to work—and work quickly. CBT does not allow much thoughtful analysis, he wrote, and earlier humanistic models would require a deeper—and costlier—approach.

"More aware of human life"

Miller and therapists who have stayed on the humanistic side of the fence, and even one who may be on the fence, have some enlightening things to say to their CBT-loving colleagues who cannot cope with a client who doesn't seem truthful.

Professor Mechanic, who said she didn't treat perpetrators, simply explained that a therapist is normally in an advocate position toward the patient and that it usually doesn't even matter if he is telling the truth or not. She allowed that in treating perpetrators, skepticism is important but noted that for years she treated a crime victim and "it turned out that she was lying."

She implied that a perpetrator's motivation for lying might be very strong and that a way to avoid that problem was granting him immunity. Court ordered treatment is "an arm of the police" and "inquisitorial," she stressed. "The only time a child molester gets treatment is if he's in trouble with the law" and he doesn't "want to be there," she said. "In early research on sex offenders, they were given immunity." (3)

Jerome Bruner, himself one of the founders of the cognitive psychology movement—the C in CBT—expressed serious doubts about therapists who are preoccupied with a client's truthfulness. He suggested in "Acts of Meaning" that whatever a client says (including rationalizations, lies and fantasies) can be understood on its own merits. Rather than worry about a client's lies or denial, Bruner focused on the need to understand accused people's stories: "It does not matter whether the account conforms to what others might say who were witnesses, nor are we in pursuit of such obscure issues as whether the account is 'self deceptive' or 'true.' Our interest rather is only in what the person thought he did ... what kind of plights he thought he was in."

Miller again blames marketplace pressures for some therapists' inability to deal with a patient's deceptions. In his view, "The story is as important as the 'factual' history. Indeed, it may be more important. It's why I've never been particularly distressed by a client who could not from the beginning tell the whole 'truth.' That usually comes later in the relationship. But reaching that point is impossible if one rejects the story out of hand, thereby demeaning the person even though he or she [may] be self-manufactured from whole cloth."

CBT therapists, in contrast, are singularly focused on the client's deception and denial. And yet they seem to be engaged in a number of their own deceits, including some self-deceit. Some exaggerations already mentioned: the client's dangerousness, his "disease," the CBT practitioners' own expertise, their own objectivity, the practitioners' minimization of their own economic interests—all can distort their professional judgment. Other deceptions include: the practitioner's linguistic distortions, their slippery dismissal of important principles such as voluntary consent and confidentiality, and the failure to honestly inform clients about parameters of "therapy," such as rules, length of treatment, and so on.

This long list of deceptions leads one to think that perhaps CBT itself —its quick-fix, superficial nature—causes the deficiencies in therapists. The deceits of cognitive-behavioral therapy (that the therapist is well and patient is sick)—indeed, the denial—ensure these deficiencies. A therapist with a different orientation who was treating sex offenders, if one existed, might be in analysis himself or herself, and might then be struck by unsettling similarities between himself and "deviants," or might even notice the sadism underlying some practices in court-mandated therapy.

Think back to the CBT therapist who decried his patients' deceptiveness and scoffed at the humanistic idea that the relationship with the therapist is sufficient to effect change. Two points seem important: first, maybe that particular therapist was easy to deceive. Humanistic therapists, by contrast, seem to expect deception and work with it. Second, maybe the client's relationship with that particular therapist was not sufficient to effect change, because that therapist didn't have what it takes—educationally, emotionally or intellectually. And perhaps the missing ingredient was the therapist's view of the client not as a robotic mass of stimulus and response, but as a human being, albeit an errant human being, who deserves to have their basic human rights respected.

One convicted person beautifully summed up the difference between CBT and humanism. Richard, a perceptive person who had been a lawyer before conviction, spent a short time as a client in a "therapy factory" before he realized the "therapist" was abusive. Taking advantage of his savvy, a savvy that many less educated clients cannot muster, Richard was able to arrange with his probation officer to switch therapists.

He soon realized the new therapist had a completely different approach. Now Richard was glad to be in therapy, he said. Consciously or unconsciously, he hit the nail on the head when he explained that the new therapist was "much more aware of human life."

12. War on Sex

1970s to fall, 2002

ELAINE HALLECK

By late fall of 2001, Kate Michel had long since come to the realization that, in her defense of Danny, a cause that seemed to have dropped on her from the sky, she was swimming upstream against a flood of friends and acquaintances who were amateur psychologists, amateur cops and haters of predators, pervs, perps, peds, power—haters even of Freud and white men.

Kate had long considered herself a true-blue feminist, but now, after she had listened with displeasure while Candace ripped white men, and other friends invoked the "sex crimes are about power" theme, it was obvious to her that there was a problem.

That problem revolved around feminism.

At this point in her life, post-post-divorce and in a totally new environment, most of Kate's friends were women, except for Danny and a cousin she barely knew but who apparently lived in the area—and whom she was trying to look up with the help of her uncle from Hamtramck.

She thought back to how her feminist sympathies had grown up in the ashes of the Vietnam war and the civil rights movement of the 1960s and 70s. In fact, after the war faded and she felt that civil rights for blacks had, at least in theory, been addressed, her twin causes seemed to boil down to the environment and feminism. It was so easy to transform that insult college students once hurled at cops putting down antiwar and civil rights demonstrations—"Fascist pigs!"—into "Male chauvinist pigs!" referring of course to men, especially white men, who resisted the advance of feminism.

Anyway, calling police "Fascist pigs" lost favor once women started joining the police force in droves and old bogeymen cops who swept rape under the rug gave way to Lacey and What's-her-name. (Kate never actually saw the show but you couldn't work in TV without knowing something about it.) Besides that, there were victims rights, rape crisis centers and even a new, mind-bending crime Kate had read about somewhere called "post-consent rape."

If Kate had had any hesitation about forgiving cops for being "Fascist pigs," it diminished when, on the heels of the seriously misbehaving police of the 60s and 70s, there arrived a wave of police public relations. To win back women, cops and their promoters took to the airwaves and press. "Police are your friends," they said—of course, not in so many words. These savvy cops started up neighborhood watch programs and "community policing" and the like. You forgot all about their fire-hosing black demonstrators or tear gassing antiwar demonstrators.

And Kate recalled that these new PR-hip cops also began to ply women with horrifying stories about horrifying crimes that scared them silly. She remembered being scared enough to lose a night's sleep by one of them who was a guest on a program at the TV station where she worked. She supposed his theme was ostensibly self-protection, but the effect of his detailed descriptions of chilling crimes was a huge feeling of horror and panic, rather than any sense of power.

Yes, besides offering employment to women, cops in the 70s and 80s painted themselves as heroes who protected damsels in distress. So "fascist pig" cops faded quickly, but "male chauvinist pigs" did not. After all, women could become cops, but women generally couldn't become men.

In her enthusiasm for feminism, Kate had once shared the sentiments of her college friend, that idealistic counselor of abused children, Polly — she of the perps and peds—and many other friends. But somewhere along the line, feminism seemed to have taken on sacred proportions in Polly's world—although not in Kate's. On Polly's wedding day, Kate remembered being underwhelmed by Polly's glowing summary of her new husband. "The best thing about him is that I know he would never do anything sexist," Polly had gushed.

Now Kate's feeling of "sisterhood" toward Polly, although she never verbalized it that way, had vanished and she found herself wondering how she could ever have considered herself like Polly. The whole comic "p" business hadn't done much to put things in a comic light.

Later, even the universe, in the form of a parakeet, seemed to want Kate to lighten up. One day just before Danny entered the "facility," he had unexpectedly called and then shown up at her doorstep with a sheet-covered cage containing a parakeet that needed pet sitting. And the little yellow peeper's name was Polly. Oscar was as delighted as Kate, although Kate knew it was for different reasons.

But when Kate and Oscar watched Polly the parakeet carry on a near constant monologue while performing acrobatics, instead of lightening up, Kate reflected—not very benevolently—about Polly the college friend, who seemed to be parroting views—castration! incurable!—that had mutated from innocent and inspiring ideas into something sinister.

In college, Kate had loved Ashley Montague's The Natural Superiority of Women, a book she and Polly read for a class on women's issues. Both of them had delighted in Montague's idea that all the great civilizing advances were made by women, while men had been straying from the hearth and generally causing trouble.

96

And in the 1970s, as Kate, Polly and most of her other friends were reading Germaine Greer's and Susan Brownmiller's horrifying classics about rape, they were coming to agree with the seemingly inescapable conclusion that something was very wrong with men. "Misogyny," a male condition that was presented as practically a mental illness, became part of their vocabulary. And later, Kate laughed along with the rest at jokes about "testosterone poisoning," and laughed even harder at a Phyllis cartoon about a world without men: "No crime and lots of fat women."

Kate, with her interest in political analysis, had gone a little farther. Put women in charge and the U.S. government would not be causing pollution, death and destruction wherever it went.

But now, Kate sensed she was changing, inexorably heading away from the sunny circle of her friends and their shared feminist passions and out into the cold and unknown. And all because of Danny? One lonely underdog? A guy I barely know?

Indeed, feminism, or some lowest common denominator of it, seemed implicated in a lot of the bad things that were happening to Danny.

Starting way back when he had still been coming to dance class, Kate remembered that he had told her that the prosecutor assigned to his case was female. Since then, every one of the sex crime prosecutors Kate ran across in her search for information related to Danny's plight seemed to be female. She also read reports about women law students volunteering in droves at rape counseling centers. There had to be some women lawyers who weren't sex crime prosecutors—maybe a lot—and even women on the defense side of the ring.

But from all appearances, feminism had inspired women lawyers to gravitate to prosecution—sex-crime prosecution in particular—probably because they were crimes on women's turf, Kate thought. These prosecutors and prosecutors-to-be wanted to right wrongs against women, such as cold and skeptical treatment of rape victims, just like women doctors specializing in pediatrics or gynecology wanted to right the wrongs said to be perpetrated by legions of male doctors wielding cold minds, cold hands and cold instruments.

One spring morning after Danny got out of the "facility," he walked over to Kate's apartment to pick up Polly the parakeet. He sat on the sofa while Oscar sat near his feet and staring longingly at Polly's cage, once again covered with a sheet in preparation for the parakeet's trip back to Danny's. Oblivious to Oscar's obvious emotion, Danny was describing his therapy, which he called a "class." And it became apparent to Kate that in the "class" that Danny was enduring, feminism had a role.

"Our therapist hates us," Danny said. "We call him 'the man.' Or sometimes Asshole."

"To his face?" Kate was wide eyed.

"No, during break. But now we don't have him anymore. What a relief. We got a new one—a girl. She's a lot nicer. I asked her why therapy makes us feel so bad. She said that was the humiliation phase—it's part of Mickey's plan."

The humiliation phase? Mickey? This reminded Kate of something she couldn't put her finger on. She hadn't actually watched TV shows like Columbo, except in passing, but she knew the airwaves were full of cop shows and it must have been from one of them that she had heard about the "good cop-bad cop" routine. This new woman therapist certainly sounded more congenial than "Mickey," and her chummy reference to the first therapist made it sound as if her role might be as foil to Mickey the evil therapist.

Another strange thing was that Danny said he took his Bible to therapy, among his "workbooks," and now the new therapist was suggesting Bible readings. But hadn't the therapy had been ordered by the court—what about separation of church and state? Still, that worry seemed academic compared to others Kate couldn't articulate yet. One of them was related to the fear Danny evidently felt during therapy, a process Kate thought should be benevolent. Things fell into place when Danny offered more information about his new "girl therapist."

"She says we're supposed to ..." He stopped in mid-sentence. "When are you supposed to say 'woman,' anyway?" he asked, frowning.

"Maybe when they're over 16," Kate mumbled. But no, 16 sounded too young for "woman." "You should probably call your therapist a woman," she added, starting to feel silly for participating in this.

What irritated her when she thought about it later was that Danny's therapist apparently thought sexism—including linguistic fads like "woman" versus "girl" that changed every few years—was relevant to sex crime. Did they seriously believe that if you used "girl" incorrectly that it had something to do with committing a sex crime? So she started to wonder what the real point of the "class" was. Was it actually just to keep tabs on Danny during probation? All this other stuff—the feminist indoctrination, the humiliation—was to punish, and fill the time while satisfying some therapist's ideological whims. It all sounded vaguely un-American, like something out of Red China in the 1950s.

But Danny's conversion from sex criminal and presumed sexist pig to feminist not only included his vocabulary, but his thoughts too. The next time Kate saw him—at the garbage bin where they sat on a nearby flower berm talking for twenty minutes—he told her he had to report all his fantasies. Not only that, he had to detail all his sexual activity, including masturbation. And of course, anything with underage girls. Who would report that, Kate thought, unless they wanted to get in big trouble? But not only were underage girls verboten, everyone else was too—he was expected to be celibate. That was a cold shower on any lascivious thoughts Kate might have been entertaining.

Danny must have been reading her mind, because what he said next floored her. If she became his "significant other," she would be invited to attend therapy with him.

"They keep us on a pretty short leash," he explained to Kate's horrified stare.

She may have spent a second or two considering going to therapy with him. But she quickly nixed it, still agog at the idea of involving police in a possible romance. "I'll go to dance class with you," she said. "But not your sex offender class."

"I'm never going back to dance class," Danny lamented. "I read in the paper that now the colleges and universities are making us register with campus police—besides our regular registration."

Kate had read that too. It was part of the reaction to the girls' abductions in the summer. She had considered complaining to the regents but had put it out of her mind. They'd just think she was a pervert-lover. But what a stupid rule it was. Keeping Danny off campus wouldn't protect anybody. He was no danger. It would just push him more and more outside of regular society. And that, if anything, might make Danny more dangerous than he would ever have been otherwise.

Over the next few days, Kate thought about Danny, as well as about Polly, whose constant burbling chatter and clambering she and Oscar both missed. She decided to make some cookies and take them to Danny's apartment. He wouldn't have to report that, would he?

On the day she delivered the cookies, Danny offered her a beer. They drank it with potato chips on his balcony in the late afternoon sun. "This is relaxing," he said. "This is the best I've felt in a long time, even though I'm taking Prozac."

"Oh!" Kate said, indicating her glass. "Is it OK to drink then?"

Danny didn't know. But he did know that one of Prozac's side effects was that "it reduces your sex drive." The therapists encouraged the Prozac, he said—it helped him be celibate—and they backed it up, like they did everything, with lie detector tests.

Kate suddenly found her beer was warm and flat and the sun was glaring. Her stomach started to hurt. So these police therapists—that's what she had found herself calling them—they were using drugs too? She had read in her research about them using libido quelling drugs, usually on institutionalized people. Sometimes the castration Polly had mentioned was done chemically. But why were Danny's therapists trying to reduce his sex drive? He wasn't violent. He wasn't a pedophile. Again the idea occurred to her that his therapists were "making a mountain out of a molehill," as her mother used to say. They were treating him like a psycho.

And if they treated him like a psycho, couldn't that make him act more like a psycho? Couldn't it actually screw him up rather than straighten him out? Danny may have had his problems—in fact, Kate was more convinced than ever that he had a drinking problem and had indeed touched the girl as he was accused of doing—but in his attitudes towards women, sex and sexism, he wasn't any different than about 50 percent of the guys she knew. That meant that half of her male friends might do the same thing under the same circumstances—specifically, when drunk and hanging around a Lolita. So there were a lot of guys out there who were going to be candidates for thought cleansing and indoctrination.

But again, what for? Danny didn't have any mental "condition," as he told her his therapists put it. Or was his "condition" simply being a man? Suffering from the "testosterone poisoning" of that old joke? Were the therapists, in fact, trying to root out Danny's very sex drive, because they saw it as inherently diseased? If so, how different was that from the bad old hysterectomy-happy gynecologists that women complained about—the ones who saw women's bodies as inherently diseased?

Kate suddenly retrieved from her memory banks the word "misanthropist"—or was it "misandrist"? Man hater. Phooey to "misogynist," she grumbled—Danny's therapists were misanthropists!

And yet Danny didn't show any irritation, maybe because of the Prozac, or maybe because he was more or less being brainwashed. Although he had no idea how long this therapy would last, he seemed to want nothing more than to be cooperative, and "get through" the murky program that stretched interminably into his future—and, Kate was realizing, into his pants. Yes, Danny was a "Stepford husband"—like those ultra-submissive automatons in the old movie "The Stepford Wives."

"Thank you for being my friend," Danny said to Kate that sunny afternoon as she got up to leave. "You make me feel like a man."

Kate felt like crying. She knew he'd had two or three beers and she knew that, in bringing cookies and trying to help out, she was doing what a million self-help books would deplore as "rescuing." In fact, she'd seen a pile of self help books in a corner of Danny's apartment—courtesy of his therapist, he'd said. Would any of what she was doing pass muster with these authors who sneered at women who "love too much," or had relationships with men who were not their "equals"?

She'd stopped at Danny's on her way home from work, so instead of parking in her garage, she'd driven clear to the other end of the gated complex and parked around the corner from his apartment. Now, as an all-too coincidental reminder of the slogans she'd just been contemplating, she found on her windshield a warning notice from Green Manor Management. "Illegal Parking Has Consequences."

Stupid flyer. Somebody here is in cahoots with all the world's school-marm platitudes, Kate thought, crumpling up the notice and throwing it toward the brush that loomed just beyond Danny's apartment—a hilly expanse that led to who knew where. Now she was a litterer too. She felt like doing something with consequences.

Little did she know she would soon have her chance. Driving the short distance through the apartment complex, she came upon a knot of four women near the mailboxes. Kate stopped and got her mail, noticing a letter with a return address: Mickey Michalewicz from Hamtramck— Uncle Mickey, who had retained the original version of the family name. Kate supposed he was too old to use e-mail. Probably he was writing to give Kate her cousin Bart's phone number.

But Kate barely thought about this as she focused on the four women. She was practically brushing elbows with them. She hardly ever saw anyone in the complex, except in the laundry room, so she was mystified as to why these ladies were standing around in the hot sun, with handbags and sunglasses. One carried a large, covered coffee mug and a notebook. The notebook sounded a little buzzer in Kate's brain. She didn't recognize any of the women, but that didn't mean anything. She hardly knew anyone in her complex except Danny, his mother and kids.

One of the women seemed to be staring at Kate, but since the woman had on big, black, wraparound sunglasses, Kate couldn't be sure.

"Do you know where ..." the woman looked at a paper in her hand and had to remove her sunglasses to read, "... apartment 15J is?"

Now Kate could see that the woman's eyes were red and damp, like her nose. She was either crying or had bad allergies. Kate stared at her, but the lady wouldn't meet her eyes.

"J ...," Kate murmured. She knew her own apartment was in the B building and Danny's was in T, but that was all. "I'm not sure. There's a map over there ..." She pointed, but then saw that the others were already headed in that direction. "Or you could ask at the manager's office," she suggested.

"No," the answer came quickly, "she's ..."

Before the wet-faced woman could finish, one of the others called out almost exultantly, "This is him!" She was pointing at a glass-covered notice board next to the map. From her distance, Kate could see a black and white photocopied picture of a man's face. Oh no. She looked again at the woman near her car door and now realized she was definitely crying. In fact, the mere sight of the photocopied face, from 50 feet away, had produced a fresh gush of tears.

"What is it?" Kate asked, not sure what "it" meant.

"A serious sex offender," the woman said, her voice now warbling and wheezing. "They did community notification on him at Wheeler. We all have kids there. We came over to ... meet him," she blurted out, barely able to get out the last phrase.

"Oh gosh," Kate said. She was trying to remember something, about "serious." She leaned into her open car window, grabbed the box of tissues off the front seat and held it out to the crying woman.

"I've got one, thanks." She fished a limp, crushed one out of her pocket and dabbed her nose. With that, her plastic coffee cup slid through the crook of her elbow and thumped on the driveway, leaking coffee. The woman whirled around as if she were being attacked on all sides by leaping toads.

"Well ..." Kate began, as the others, now returning from the map, drew closer. "Don't panic. 'Serious' isn't so bad." Her mind was scrambling to recall something she had learned in her research.

"Serious? I thought it said 'serial,'" said another woman, also in sunglasses.

Finally, Kate's brain clicked. "No, it's 'serious.' And 91,000 men in California are listed as serious sex offenders. You can be 'serious' for only one offense. The other category—'high risk'—those are the dangerous people. There's only one or two thousand of them. The 'serious' ones aren't the ones to worry about."

"Well, why are they called serious if it's not serious?" said another woman. She was wearing a hot pink jogging suit and matching fanny pack and used a tone of voice like she was talking to a silly child or a hopelessly benighted person. "Why are the sheriffs doing community notification on him if he's not dangerous?"

"Well they shouldn't," Kate said. "It scares people for no reason. And the 'serious' ... well, the state is probably afraid to call them 'not serious.' Then people would say they're minimizing things."

"Oh, come on."

Although Kate was normally bad at arguing, she remained undaunted. "And besides, people have cars nowadays. Why does it matter where somebody lives, or if it's near a school? They can always just drive somewhere if they're determined to do something. Who walks anymore, anyway—especially around here?"

"Let's go talk to him," said the woman in pink to the others. "I have to go shopping after."

"What did he do, anyway?" Kate asked.

"The police told us he picked up a teenage boy in a video game place," said Pink Fanny Pack. "He just got out of prison."

"So he paid for it," Kate said, assuming the guy had done something worse than walk off into the sunset with a teenage boy. "I'm sure he just wants to be left alone."

"Yes, I'm sure he does. But we're not going to forgive and forget. We've got little children to worry about. Do you have children?" asked Pink Fanny Pack, looking at Kate suspiciously.

Kate didn't answer this. Instead, she shot back, "Leave the poor guy alone. What are you going to do—string him up?" She was surprised at herself.

Pink Fanny Pack gave Kate a long disgusted stare, then turned away and started to move off, including the crying one, who still wouldn't look at Kate. Kate didn't know what to do. Get in her car, back up, and follow them? That would just cause a worse scene. But after they were out of sight, she went to look at the map herself, then drove slowly to the J building. She wasn't going to confront them, but she wanted them at least to know somebody was watching.

As Kate passed the manager's office, she saw her looking out the window. And who, Kate wondered, let those lovely ladies through the gate? They don't live here, and the complex is secured like it holds the Queen's jewels.

Kate parked where she could watch the confrontation, which took about five minutes. She saw a woman come to the door first, to be replaced by a man. The man came outdoors on the landing and closed the door behind him. He was looking at the ground. While they were talking, the man's neighbors pulled into the garage below the apartment in a Hummer. A couple wearing combat uniforms got out, walked up the stairs and slowly passed the group on the landing, hesitating and exchanging a few words with them.

Kate sat in her car with the motor off and windows down. Once the weeping lady looked Kate's way. Then Pink Fanny Pack also turned to look.

They're all white, Kate reflected. Maybe just a coincidence. She knew they'd be offended at being compared to the Ku Klux Klan and, indeed, they were not going to lynch anybody. But just because their vigilante actions were toned down versions of the past, didn't seem to take away from the viciousness. Kate knew from reading Abigail's Megan's law notebooks that it was illegal to harass listed people. But who could this guy complain to? The cops? They'd be the last people he'd want to contact and they wouldn't help him anyway. And in Abigail's notebook, the attorney general had poo-pooed the whole idea of harassment, saying none had been reported, Kate thought, steaming.

And what about Danny? Will something like this happen to him? Why hadn't it already? How many others like him live in the complex? Kate knew the manager was in on this. She had posted the sign. She's probably trying to get rid of this man. And she'll probably be trying to get rid of Danny. Kate felt sick with worry. Yes, Danny's suffering and her friends' reactions to it were shooting holes in Kate's treasured feminist worldview. And soon new chinks started appearing. One developed out of the big military footprint she noticed in Southern California, so different from anything around Detroit. Apparently, all the U.S. military services found sunny California just as attractive as everybody else. Kate had already grown used to hearing thunderous booms from munitions practice, seeing big groups of helicopters flying in formation, lumbering transport helicopters, fighter jets practicing maneuvers and, off the coast, beyond the bathers and surfers enjoying the waves, huge, grey ships moving about in the glittering sea. And it wasn't just vehicles. Enlisted people were evident all around Orange County and Los Angeles, a lot of them from the huge Camp Pendleton Marine base just to the south.

And more than a few were women. At the community college where Kate taught, it wasn't unusual to hear these twenty-something girl soldiers extolling their SUVs as emblems of liberation. In addition, Kate overheard one girl remark to a friend that her stretch as a U.S. soldier in Dubai was cool because they had KFC and you could get servants cheap. Her comment followed the much publicized mistreatment of Iraqi POWs at a prison better described as a dungeon, in which female soldiers had participated. All of that had sunk Kate's hopes that if women were just allowed into male roles, as she in her feminist phase had long dreamed, it would cure the world of pollution, exploitation, cruelty and war.

It was certainly true that Kate had now fallen off the feminist bandwagon. And she had bruised herself in the process. She didn't expect much sympathy from her women friends. They all seemed to be as staunchly feminist as she had once been. She didn't expect much sympathy from Mona either, considering she had, it seemed to Kate, once mindlessly parroted the feminist party line and claimed that sex crimes were "about" power.

But amazingly, judging by the tales that Mona soon began telling, maybe, just maybe, she was crossing the line into Kate's camp.

Surely Mona's change was due to her new job. She had been out of work ever since she had a bad car accident a few years earlier. But recently, she had finally found a job. True to her interest in the downtrodden and her opposition to the death penalty—probably the main reasons she and Kate were becoming friends—Mona had taken a job as a doctor treating men in a San Diego County minimum security prison near the border with Tijuana. It was a hugely long trip from Orange County to the prison, something Kate thought Mona would hate, considering her accident. But she only had to do it once a week because she took a train to and from San Diego and stayed a couple nights with her sister there.

Although Mona had only been working at the jail a few weeks, she was already filling Kate's ears with stories. "Do you know one of the first things I saw there?" In the huge parking lot outside the West Mesa Detention Facility, which it shares with an institution for incarcerating juveniles and a longer term prison, where Mona also worked sometimes, Mona said she had seen "a Brinks-type armored truck" parked at the entrance.

"What was it doing?" Kate puzzled.

"What do you think? Carting away the money!"

"Money from who?"

"Who else could it be from? The guards? No, the inmates."

Kate was mulling that over when Mona dropped yet another story on her. "When I leave the jail, it's about a five-mile drive on a two-lane road to the highway. One night when I was leaving I saw a tiny little woman and a little kid walking away from the prisons in the gully alongside the road."

Kate suspected that Mona, being a tiny little person herself, had a lot of sympathy for other tiny little people. "What'd you do?"

"Well, I pulled over. I think they were as afraid of me as I was of them. But I gave them a ride to the highway. The woman didn't even speak Spanish—I think she was from an indigenous tribe in Mexico—but she spoke some English. She told me her husband had been in jail at the prison where I work and when he was released, he didn't take his money. You know, inmates earn a great big 50 cents a day working in the laundry or kitchen. She said he was afraid to go back to get his money because there's a sign in the parking lot that says any former prisoner can get arrested for being on the property. So she went instead. But she couldn't get it. I suppose the armored truck will eventually cart it away."

Mona had still worse stories from the dark side.

"Do you know what the three main crimes that men are locked up for there are?" she asked Kate on a sunny spring day when the two of them were walking barefoot on the San Onofre beach, distinguished by its location near the Camp Pendleton Marines base and a nuclear power plant, both of which were almost constantly on their minds because of the booms from artillery practice and the reactors looming behind the sandy knolls.

"The three main crimes? Let's see—overdue library books, making tainted cheese, and ... I don't know, yelling at their kids in a shopping mall."

Mona stared at Kate and slowly said, "No," then sharply, "Ow!" She stopped and lifted one of her feet to examine it, pointing out clumps of little clear blobs scattered in the surf-soaked sand. "Something got me." As they moved to dry sand and put on their shoes, Kate backtracked. "Those are some crimes I was just reading about—jail for overdue library books was in a city in Michigan. But right here in California, since the 1980s, it's been a felony to make contaminated cheese, even by accident.

"The other one was ... well, my mechanic's mother stopped in a mall parking lot because her granddaughter was in the back trying to get out of her car seat. She got out and yelled at her. She shook a finger in her face. A surveillance camera in the lot got it, and the next day a Child Protection person shows up at her house and undresses the kid to look for bruises."

Eventually, Kate let Mona explain about the three main crimes that men were in her minimum-security facility for. They were drugs, drunk driving and domestic violence.

"The three D's!" Kate said. She'd never told Mona about perps, pervs and peds. But now her mind started turning the three D's over and over like a new toy. Kate had already been thinking a lot about feminism, so it wasn't a stretch to characterize drugs, drunk driving and domestic violence as offenses on women's turf. Most obvious was domestic violence. Demands to prosecute domestic violence had been a staple of feminists in the 1970s and 80s.

The evidence for drinking and drugs was more circumstantial, but still strong. Mothers Against Drunk Driving had been founded by a woman whose daughter was killed by a drunk driver. And the old link between women's suffrage and Prohibition of alcohol was no secret. What about drugs? Well, the war against drugs had also been vigorously embraced by at least one woman, as in Nancy Reagan's Just Say No campaign.

But when Kate expressed her theory, Mona wrinkled her nose. "Domestic violence, OK, I can see that. But the others ..." she trailed off, saying it wasn't just men who were going to prison. More women were in jail now too, as Mona saw when she sometimes worked at a women's prison about 20 miles from the Mexican border.

Kate would have argued that the fact that there were more women in prison didn't dilute her feminism-bashing theory, but was an unintended and probably unavoidable consequence of feminists getting on the law and order bandwagon. But she didn't make that argument. She didn't have to. Because it wasn't long before Mona seemed ready to do an about-face on the whole matter. That was one reason, besides her sympathy for underdogs, that Kate liked her — she wasn't afraid to change her mind.

What had set off Mona's slide into Kate's camp was something else that happened, this time at the big state prison where Mona substituted once in a while, about a mile away from the minimum security place that was her usual gig. She had treated a boy there—Jason Fisher—who was doing life for raping and killing a 12-year-old girl early in 2001, well before the three girls and the recent scare.

Technically the "boy" was a man, but Jason had been only 19 at the time of the murder and still seemed a boy to Mona—maybe because she was treating him for cystic acne. Later, the prison counselor gave her a magazine article he had kept about him—the cover story in a newspaper Sunday magazine. As Kate and Mona sat in a restaurant after their walk, pushed off the beach by the tiny jellyfish that had stung Mona's feet and a blustery wind, Mona produced the magazine and slid it across the table toward Kate. "Murder. Just Because," screamed white letters from an all- black cover.

The waiter took away her plate and Kate pulled the magazine closer, spreading it out on the table. Her journalistic sixth sense pricked up at the scent of something familiar—yellow journalism, the insertion of sensationalistic ideas, usually done in catchy headlines, which were always at a premium and very powerful because they were often the only part of the story people read.

She tried to distill the essence from the words staring at her. "Murder. Just Because." What was it? That it happened for no reason? "Just Because"? Yes, that was it. And in case a reader didn't get it, the idea was echoed in sub-headings inside. "This Summer's Child Kidnappings and Murders Have People Wondering Why." The editors answered this question, declaring that when the 19-year-old spotted the girl, "He Was Thinking Something Far Worse: 'Why Not?'"

She began leafing through the pages. "Mona, did you notice? They're implying Jason didn't have a reason for the murder, like he did it out of boredom or pure evil—something that may have been true in the case of Charles Manson, I suppose. But is it true of this kid? In the story, do they mention any reasons?"

"I think so." Mona chewed on a piece of parsley and then seemed to remember. "Yes. He and his father tried to commit suicide together the night before the killing. The police had come to their house and found child pornography on Jason's computer. The next day when he thought about doing the kidnapping, he remembered the child porn charges. He said to himself, 'Well, if I'm going to jail, I may as well go for a crime that's worth going to jail for.'"

"Ooh," Kate exhaled. "Tough law enforcement causing more crime. Some people criticize Megan's list for the same reason. It makes people desperate and angry ... lonely ... depressed ... so it increases the re-offense rate. They don't have anything to lose so they're liable to do anything."

Mona was quiet, toying with a spoon. Suddenly, she spoke. "The article also said the kid's mother was on her deathbed at the time of the murder. And he drank too much and smoked pot. And he was unpopular. He said he panicked when he realized the girl might identify him after the rape."

"That's an awful lot of reasons," Kate said. "That's what bothers me. Sometimes the media twist things to make a better story, to make it creepier. In the headline, they say he didn't have any reason for what he did, but in the story, they mention a million reasons."

Mona still had not dropped the thread of this talk a week or so later. This time, she and Kate were on a walk around a tidal inlet and marsh. "Maybe you're on to something about feminism filling the prisons," she announced.

Kate was nearly floored. "You agree with me?"

"I was thinking about that kid, Jason, and that the magazine said he didn't have any reason, or any excuse, for what he did. Just pure evil, or something like that. I was talking to the counselor again. I like him, but … well, he's on a board that recommends people for early release. He said he recommended an abused woman who committed a crime against the man who abused her."

"Did she kill him?" Kate asked, remembering Polly's story—her not supporting all perps being shot.

"I don't think so. But the counselor asked me a question—'Who could be more deserving of early release than that?' he said. I didn't say anything, but later I thought about Jason getting life for something he did when he was 19. I suppose the counselor would've called all Jason's reasons 'excuses,' just like the magazine did. I suppose that when the counselor picked that woman for early release, he passed over somebody else, maybe a man. Men who are in jail for domestic violence tell me they never get early release—the board thinks they're going to go right back out and do it again. I guess the counselor would've said the woman had good reasons for the crime she committed. And that anything a man says in defense of himself is nothing but excuses."

Kate could sense the conclusion coming. It was like a curtain lifting. She raised her finger to shush Mona and lifted her eyes up, waiting for clarity. "So that's it," Kate interrupted. "Women have reasons, but men have excuses." She shook her head, half in disgust, half in disbelief.

13. A parallel universe

1896 to March 2003

ALEX LANDON

"It's a little like being black or gay," said Richard, a former lawyer who lived in San Diego. It was autumn of 2002, and he was talking about being registered on Megan's list for an offense involving touching his teenage daughter seven years earlier.

Richard had successfully completed several years of probation and court-ordered treatment, had married a second time and had two young children. But when his homeowner's association found him on Megan's list, they let it be known he was not welcome at meetings. As the premise of Megan's law is ostensibly to warn communities about dangerous people, perhaps it is not surprising that Richard's board took the list at face value and didn't question if he was truly dangerous. They trusted the California legislators who had tailored the basic federal version of Megan's law for the nation's most populous state. Probably neither the legislators nor the condominium board knew that the U.S. Department of Justice, in its publication "Myths and Facts about Sex Offenders," called California's Megan's list "extreme." (1)

Richard's perception about the housing repercussions he suffered might have been echoed by a San Diego teenager we will call Nick, whose conviction years earlier while he was still a boy was impinging on his freedom of housing in 2002. In 2003, several years after Nick's offense with a younger teenager had been addressed by the juvenile court, the 18-year-old found he could not live with his parents in their condominium. After board members learned about his past, they told the parents that Nick's presence would bring property values down. Would you agree that forcing this teenager to live alone rather than with his parents put the community in greater danger than otherwise?

Aside from his housing problems, another ill result of the lawyer Richard's conviction was that he had been forced to stop practicing law. At the age of 40, he changed to accounting, because he knew an accountant could have an independent business—a necessity considering that anyone convicted of a sex offense becomes even more professionally untouchable than the average convicted person, due to the ease of pinpointing them on Megan's list.

As if restrictions on his housing and profession weren't enough, Richard didn't travel out of state on business. He couldn't because he didn't want to chance running afoul of the labyrinth of regulations requiring people convicted of sex offenses to register with police within a short time of entering a state. To use a mundane example as a comparison, would you want to drive through another state if you had heard that you might have to apply for a new driver's license within 24 hours of entering it? With Megan's list the stakes are much higher, because the scary fact is that, for any convicted sex offender, failure to register can be considered a second offense, with very grim consequences, which in California could include triggering the three strikes law and a life sentence.

"We know where you live"

Richard's worries about professional restrictions caused by police registration might have been seconded by somebody who wasn't even an offender herself — the wife of the Alaskan plaintiff who, early in the 21st century, was at the center of an unfolding challenge to Megan's law before the U.S. Supreme Court. This couple was begging for relief from Alaska's online Megan's list because the woman had found it impossible to carry on her profession considering that their home was listed as the residence of a dangerous sex offender.

Richard's worries might also have been similar to those of another man, "Leonard," whose story of threats and beatings was related by an attorney in a state Public Defender's office. As a result of exposure by Megan's list, Leonard had been attacked by a vigilante group with a broom handle and bottles. And the group had jeered, "We know where you live!"

Public defenders and other lawyers who are familiar with Megan's list can often relate many such stories about physical violence. Yet in its 2001 Megan's law report, California's Attorney General claimed that "to date there has been no reported misuse" (harassment or vigilantism) resulting from the public sex-offender notification service. (2) Who knows? — maybe it was technically true. And if so, the underlying story was probably that no harassment had been reported. But remarkably, a headline in a county sheriffs' magazine around that time used the same words the mob had used to taunt Leonard—"We know where you live"—to crow about Megan's law and the resolution of the Danielle Van Dam case. (Megan's law played no role in the resolution, but logic was apparently not the magazine's forte.) With such jeers coming from public authorities themselves, it is easy to see why listed people threatened by vigilante action and discrimination don't turn for help to sheriffs.

Richard's story, along with these others, shows how Megan's law in effect torpedoes a person's profession and home, and gives license to small-mindedness, paranoia and vigilantism. For many of us, if we were threatened both on the home and work front, we would be sweating bullets on a regular basis. However, although Richard was indeed afraid, he regarded all these impediments without rancor or a sense of entitlement, possibly because he was a stoic and fervent Catholic, "People do not seem to understand the principle of transformation. It is at the heart of our heritage. People are redeemable. They can change. They can grow into a more beautiful state of being."

Richard's faith and stoicism served him well, and, by early 2003, anticipating the upcoming U.S. Supreme Court decision about Megan's list, he found himself daring to hope. "The Supreme Court will move the whole argument into the area of due process for the offender, and away from the extremities which have been driving this issue for much too long."

That was his optimistic take, but in the background lurked a dose of grey reality. "If it is unfavorable, California may then move toward names, addresses and pictures on the Internet. That would be scary, but if it is what comes, I will just deal with it and pray for guidance. What I was in the past I am not anymore."

Bad days, bad decades

In March 2003, the Court announced its long-awaited decision. (3) In a 6-to-3 decision, the court upheld Megan's list as practiced in Alaska which, at the time, had one of the harshest versions. This new decision relating to sex crimes echoed the kind of thinking the Court had just shown when it permitted a Kansas prison warden to continue denying people convicted of sex crimes their constitutional protection against self-incrimination. In fact, two such harsh decisions on sex crimes so soon after the Summer of the Abducted White Girl make one think that the justices in faraway Washington, D.C., were aware of the panic that was still simmering in the Southwest. And, as we shall see in a later chapter, still more reactions that occurred in the nation's capital a bit farther down the line make this conclusion inescapable.

A run of dismal decisions coming from the U.S. Supreme Court may surprise many people who have a sanguine view of the Court. Many positive opinions of the court are based on landmark civil rights decisions made during the 20th century, such as one in 1954 (Brown v. Board of Education) aimed against racial segregation in schools. (Not all Americans saw this decision as positive, as was seen in the resurgence of white supremacy groups around six decades later.) Other decisions that were similar to Brown chipped away at widespread discriminatory practices such as "anti-miscegnation" laws, separate train cars, literacy tests, poll taxes and the like.

But despite these decisions that many of us saw very optimistically, the Court has also had its bad days, or its bad decades. Sometimes the public memory and history books can be very selective, glossing over the

Court's less-shining moments. Keep in mind that the sad 1896 Supreme Court decision Plessy v. Ferguson, upholding "separate but equal" facilities, led to 58 more years of discrimination against African Americans. And in 1927, another sorry practice the Court let stand was a 35-year-long "eugenics" policy, which, in California and other states, resulted in the forced sterilization of over 20,000 "degenerates" and "morally delinquent" people, such as prostitutes and men and women who had children out of wedlock.

Only a few critics saw the 2003 decision on Megan's law as another of these less-than-shining moments that stigmatized "degenerates" for life. For Richard, who had hoped and prayed for a decision that would move the nation away from extremism—from vigilantism and housing, business and travel restrictions—it was a sad moment. Now, following the Court's lead, states that had been hesitating would begin adopting the draconian version of Megan's law that Alaska embraced—and soon, worse. In addition, coming on the heels of the summer of 2002, the decision would encourage a wave of new repressive measures—Sons of Megan's law, if you will. And the Supreme Court's imprimatur would allow a lot of old absurdities to stay in force.

Examples of such absurdities abound, but one mentioned by Paul Gerowitz of California Attorneys for Criminal Justice was a man who earned lifetime status as an untouchable for driving by a group of high-school girls and calling them whores, breaking a statute called Annoying or Molesting a Person Under the Age of 18. Another more absurd example was a man arrested taking a leak by a building in a deserted area in San Diego County near the border at Tijuana. The statute here was California Penal Code Section 314, indecent exposure, an offense for which you must register as a sex offender. The man only avoided lifetime registration under Megan's law because his case was dismissed by a rational judge. Another all-too-common and absurd example is the 19-year-old who has sex with a younger teenage girlfriend whose parents get angry, and who is then branded for life as a sexual offender.

Of course, none of the offenses mentioned here are admirable behavior, but they should be classified as annoyances rather than assaults, especially when you consider the gargantuan cost of policing tens of thousands of such low-level former offenders or—in the case of a man arrested for taking a leak near the border—non-offenders.

"Unusual" crimes, unusual punishment

Yes, there was bitter disappointment about the decision, especially on the part of convicted people suffering severe consequences from Megan's list. But for attorneys, a very small silver lining behind the gloomy cloud was the opportunity to see, spelled out in black and white courtesy of Justice Anthony Kennedy writing for the majority, the myths and distortions that propel the juggernaut against people convicted of sex crimes.

The crux of the Court's reasoning ostensibly resided in Justice Kennedy's statement that Megan's list didn't punish because it was not intended to punish. No, he said, Megan's law isn't punishment at all—it is merely a regulatory device, like a measure that forbids a 15-year-old to drive. The utility of this dubious proclamation was that it allowed the justices to snatch the matter out of reach of what the Constitution says about punishment—its prohibitions against ex post facto (retroactively increased) punishment and against cruel and unusual punishment, as spelled out in the Eighth Amendment.

But in Justice Kennedy's written decision, the majority judges appeared worried that perhaps their statement that Megan's list wasn't punishment rang hollow. For they went on to dance a clumsy tango of contorted statistics and questionable information, as if to say that, just in case you didn't buy their centerpiece argument, they might as well try to prove that these sex offenders were unusually incorrigible, that sex crimes were unusually frequent, and that the victims suffered unusual trauma. It was as if, in trying to skate around the matter of cruel and unusual punishment—emphasis on unusual—they were arguing that everything about sex crimes and sex criminals was unusual, and so maybe such unusual crimes really did require unusual punishment.

Let's look at their claims, saving the worst for last, and begin with unusually frequent and unusually traumatic.

When Justice Kennedy described "sex offenders and their dangerousness as a class," he was reflecting a claim from the state side of this argument, namely from U.S. Solicitor General Theodore Olson in 2001, that sex offenses were rising dramatically. "The average number of individuals imprisoned for sex offenses increased at a faster rate than that for any other category of violent crime," Olson had written, even mentioning a claim that "For every known perpetration, another 150 were not reported" (4).

Authoritative-sounding claims about an "explosion" of sex offenses have been ricocheting around the American collective unconscious for decades—and not just during panics such as in the summer of 2002. Earlier, we read about the exaggerated claims made by the secret police for sex crimes—people who work in the tax-supported service industry that has grown up to ferret out lechery, Child Protective Services.

These are claims that come out of nowhere—and are impossible to prove. You might hear, "An average sex offender, in their lifetime, commits 360 sex offenses" or "20 percent of U.S. children will be sexually exploited." Wild claims, such as the one Olson made about 150 unreported sex crimes for every known one, are just the tip of the iceberg. An entire movement has grown up in some quarters, based on what are called "victim studies," which cite astronomical rates of sex offenses based on simply asking people if they have ever been sexually abused.

But studies like this are like trying to grab hold of a big, slippery bar of soap because, first of all, if crimes are not reported, there is no way of knowing with any certainty how many of them there are. Secondly, as we saw in the infamous McMartin case, wishful thinking can be involved in claims of sexual abuse, both by children who want to please authorities and by adults who, in this age of 12-step groups and lionized victims, may yearn to join a symbolic brotherhood or sisterhood of suffering. Third, even with reported crimes, experience tells us that some people make false claims of sexual abuse, especially in deteriorating marriages where one spouse is eager to make the other one look bad. As a psychologist specializing in sex offenders, Howard Barbaree, pointed out, that is why arguing about a sex crime explosion based on victim studies can be like medieval arguments over how many angels could dance on the head of a pin.

However, not only these facts contradict Solicitor General Olson's picture of a sex-crime explosion. Also throwing Olson's claims in doubt is information from another arm of the very same Department of Justice, for which Olson supervised litigation before the Supreme Court. In fact, it was a bit ironic that in March, 2003—the same month and year as the Megan's law decision—a U.S. Justice Department Bureau of Justice Statistics study was publicized showing that the number of actual crimes had in reality been dropping, while the percentage of those crimes that got reported to the police was going up. (5) For example, the report said that 49 percent of crimes were reported to police in 2000, versus only 43 percent from 1992 to 1999.

Other sources had noted this trend for some time. "Much of the apparent rise in sex offending is related to increased reporting rather than increased offending," wrote Eric Lotke, a specialist in sex offenses, adding that "enforcement is more aggressive and definitions of sex offenses are more expansive than ever before." (6)

So we see that the first prong in the justices' assertion—that sex crimes deserve unusual measures because they are unusually frequent—is on very shaky ground.

Now consider what Justice Kennedy said about the unusual trauma suffered by victims.

"Sexual offenders inflict a terrible toll each year on this Nation and its citizens," he stated in the decision, no doubt drawing inspiration from what Olson had written about trauma in a brief in 2001. "Children who are sexually assaulted are more likely than other children to develop severe psychosocial problems" and "more likely than other youths to become sex offenders as adults." (7)

The Justice Department apparently has many rooms, for once again, Olson was contradicted by another part of the very same department he worked for. On the Justice Department's "Myths" Web site at that time, we could read, "Most sex offenders were not sexually assaulted as children and most children who are sexually assaulted do not sexually assault others." (8) (The careful reader will note that Olson's statement and those on the "Myths" Web site are apples and oranges, and that they might both be true while creating entirely contradictory impressions in the mind of a casual reader.)

We can only wonder what the justices would have thought if they had checked one "opinion of the week" against the other. But, probably giving credence to Olson in his trusted role, the justices just accepted the statistics presented in his brief. And, regrettably, the other side did not present any information on victim trauma, perhaps because in the pro-victim atmosphere that has persisted for decades in the United States, it is untenable to express skepticism about what victims suffer without releasing a storm of rancor.

If the other side had presented such information, it might have been on the order of what the feminist writer Camille Paglia said a few years before then—releasing a storm of rancor—about the tendency of rape-crisis-center counselors to create in victims more trauma than necessary by "sympathetically" telling victims to expect a lifetime of psychological problems. "Coercive compassion," was her term for insulting clients by implying they are special, frail little creatures. (9)

Others have called the phenomenon "socially constructed trauma," a topic discussed in another chapter. In summary, "socially constructed trauma" is trauma that is suffered after a crime, but that results from the disdainful reaction of society to the victim, not directly from the crime itself. For sex crimes, these disdainful reactions include distaste toward the victims, finger-pointing over their participation in sexual encounters and, yes, the presumption they will go on to become molesters themselves.

And now for unusually incorrigible, the third myth on which the Court based some of its decision about Megan's list. The notion of astronomical sex offender recidivism—their "incurability," if you will—is probably the most widespread and powerfully misleading idea about sex offenders and is at the heart of the matter.

What did Kennedy say about recidivism in the Court's decision about Megan's list? "Frightening and high," he wrote, spotlighting "grave concerns over the high rate of recidivism among sex offenders." (10)

It is a good bet that Kennedy and the rest of the majority weren't frightened about the man who urinated near a deserted area, the man who yelled "Whores!" or the man who goosed a teenager in a subway. And they apparently hadn't been reading the U.S. Justice Department's

"Myths and Facts about Sex Offenders" which stated, "Recidivism rates for sex offenders are lower than for the general criminal population." (11) Instead, they probably had once again relied upon the problem-ridden information supplied by Solicitor General Olson.

Cut and pasted

In fact, much "information" about sex offenders seems to exist in its own self-contained universe, where it is cut and pasted—with telling permutations—between one source and another, often between one legal brief and another. In this parallel universe, falsehoods abound that, when repeated often enough, start to sound like the truth.

Victims-rights organization, which generally have an axe to grind, are perhaps one of the most notorious disseminators of faulty information. They often seem to simply pull information out of their hats, without citations, but because they present it with a gloss of authority, many people buy it. Most of us are far too busy to spend time checking facts from supposedly sober organizations, and normally we feel automatic sympathy for the parent of a child victim and even feel a little guilty thinking that they might be fabricating information. In the winter of 2003, a newsletter published by Marc Klaas, the father of a murdered girl, boldly claimed, "There is not one documented case of a pedophile ever having been cured" and, "It is a ... fact that whenever a sexual deviant is anonymously released into the community, the probability is virtually guaranteed that the offender will revert to deviant behavior." (12)

A state attorney general should be several notches above such victim organizations, but unfortunately, in at least one case, he was not. In his 2000 report on Megan's Law, former California Attorney General Bill Lockyer claimed, "Convicted sex offenders are among the most likely criminals to re-offend and create new victims." (13) But now notice what happens in his 2002 message, after somebody has perhaps pointed out the false information. Now it mutates to "Sexual predators ... after they serve their sentences, are more likely to reoffend than other criminals." (14) By changing "sex offenders" to "sexual predators" (a term used in a law regulating civil commitment for mentally disordered people convicted of violent sexual offenses), Lockyer has made his second statement scarier and less clear than his first statement, especially for casual readers who tend to lump all sex offenders under the term "predators."

It is important to remember that even though this substitution may seem like a small one, both frightening statements still conflict with that U.S. Department of Justice Web site information. They also conflict with the authoritative psychologist Howard Barbaree, who noted that he had worked in assessment and treatment since 1976. "Generally in the literature, sex offenders have lower rates [of recidivism] than general offenders," he said. (15)

Is it unrealistic to expect Supreme Court justices to handle statistics better than a victims' rights organization or the California Attorney General? Perhaps it is—a doctoral student mentioned that statistics was the most difficult course he had studied, that statistics are not difficult to falsify, and that one can prove almost anything by manipulating them.

Is it unrealistic to hope the justices will check statistics they are given? If you don't think so, maybe after you read through the following metamorphoses and see how they magically and deceptively mutate to support the writer's point of view, you will agree that the justices should not rely on the accuracy of information in the arguments they receive.

First let's jump back to one of Solicitor General Olson's carefully crafted statements. "When they reenter society at large, convicted sexual offenders are much more likely to repeat the offense of conviction than any other type of felon," he wrote in 2001. (16) Of course, he hadn't said that recidivism rates for sex offenders were higher than the general criminal population. But it was close enough to create the same effect. Then, in Olson's arguments for Megan's law in the Alaska case, although he referred to the same study as in his earlier argument, he changed his wording slightly: "When they reenter society ... convicted sex offenders have a much higher recidivism rate for their offense of conviction than any other type of violent felon." (4)

Did this change have something to do with the addition of the word "violent?" But in contradiction to Olson's statement, in one of the very Bureau of Justice Statistics studies he cited, there on page one among the "Highlights" was: "Released prisoners with the lowest rearrest rates were those in prison for ... rape ... [and] other sexual assault." (16)

Olson did not quote this highlight. A look at the table to which he did refer yielded enough mentions of numerators and denominators to frighten the faint of heart. But for those who dared enter the tangle, the analysis did not support Olson's dire suggestions: "Of the 3,138 released rapists," the report stated, "more were rearrested for something other than rape ... than were arrested for another rape."

Olson presented another permutation on the high-recidivism theme in a different brief. But this one showed another slight but maddening migration: "Convicted sex offenders are much more likely to recommit sex offenses than any other type of felon," he wrote. (17)

What could this mean? How could other types of felons "recommit" a sex offense if they had never committed one in the first place?

In another part of the same brief by Olson, was his misleading remark that "within just three years of release, 7.7% of released rapists had been rearrested for rape." This ignored the fact that 7.7 percent is a remarkably

---

117

low rate—the recidivism rate for people convicted of general property and theft crimes is about 50 percent.

One more bit of information contradicting the notion that sex offenders are unusually incorrigible, comes from Eric Lotke, who traced this idea to a 1989 study by Lita Furby which looked at treatment of convicted sex offenders and found the efficacy of such treatment to be inconclusive. This was somehow translated in the public mind, Lotke said, into some very different ideas—"Nothing works," "They're incurable!" These conclusions were doubly distorted considering that the "high" recidivism rate Furby noted was about 13 percent, which, as mentioned earlier, is already far lower than the recidivism rate for general property and drug offenders.

Thus we see, in the Megan's law decision of 2003, a mountain of statistics that were, at best, unchecked and contradicted and, at worst, falsified and twisted.

Was this the best we could expect from the towering intellects we suppose justices and solicitors general to be?

Distasteful, unnatural, sinful, dangerous, immoral, or uppity

This chapter began by quoting Richard, who said the effects of Megan's law are similar to the effects of discrimination against African Americans and gays. Being black, LGBT and convicted are obviously three distinct situations and we cannot draw parallels between them 100 percent of the time. Still, some observers have concluded that convicted people suffer overly drastic consequences because of a sector of society that is angry about the trend toward tolerating people who used to be viewed negatively.

Criminologist Stuart Scheingold, for example, mentions that "criminals are among the last socially acceptable targets for venting our anger and resentments in an increasingly tolerant society," and he points to Kathlyn Gaubatz's research showing that "Many Americans have decided to tolerate behavior which they nevertheless find bothersome. Thus they go about their lives, still carrying the burden of feeling that their fellow citizens are engaging in activities which are somehow distasteful, unnatural, sinful, dangerous, immoral, or uppity. But they choose not to release that psychological burden into advocacy of prohibitions on these activities...[As a result, they have been] developing a pool of insufficiently actualized negative feelings, and ... they [have] needed some place to put them. What better place than in strenuous opposition to the acts of criminal offenders?" (18)

Thus, these observers say that convicted people—and we know that those convicted of sex crimes are always a particular focus—have become the fall guys for the public's anger over increasing tolerance and, as a result, are suffering more punitive policies, such as from the misguided designer law—Megan's law—that we are looking at here.

Although the Supreme Court's majority declared in its Megan's law decision that the law was not punitive either in intent or effect, the latter idea is absurd. I don't know of anyone convicted of a sex crime who has been hung from a tree or dragged behind a truck, but the Supreme Court briefs (and many reports published later) did document plenty of dire consequences for sex offenders arising from Megan's law, including murders, fire bombings and suicides. And clearly, the law has had a severe impact on finding a place to live and finding and keeping a job. In current times, it is hard to imagine anyone suffering from any current law more than people convicted of sex crimes are suffering from Megan's law and its sister laws.

In the face of this suffering, we can take heart in the knowledge that Jim Crow laws such as literacy tests preventing black people from voting were finally struck down in the last century by decisions holding that a law's claimed intent—"We are only trying to make sure people can read the ballot, your honor"—is not as important as its de facto realities. Maybe someday police registration for non-dangerous offenders will be tossed into the dust heap with Jim Crow laws where they all belong.

14. A life of crime

January 2003

ELAINE HALLECK

Kari Fernandez clicked the Back button, wiped off the screen, and took a sip of lime mineral water, licking the rim of the glass a little to taste the salt she'd rubbed there. She had made herself a Russian, as her father called it. It was her new drink now that they'd all given up Coke. Even Trevor was interested in this "health angle," as Tata called it. For him, the health angle included a lot of fruit, especially when he saw it stopped him from breaking out with acne.

"Everybody in this house is getting skinny," Tata had said, her voice a little edgy. She was talking about Kari and Danny, but Kari knew Tata was worried about Dad. Even Kari had noticed how thin he was. She wished he would get back to looking like he used to. As for herself, she was glad she'd managed to lose a few pounds. Trevor said she looked good, especially when she put on lipstick, which she hardly ever did because Dad and Tata didn't allow her to.

But when she finished sixth grade in a few weeks, Dad said she could wear it on special occasions, like to graduation parties. If I get invited to any, Kari thought. She didn't really have any friends now, certainly not a best friend like Ashley had once been. There was Esther in her Spanish class but she didn't speak English too good, and they didn't hang around together outside class. There were hardly any kids in the complex and the ones she saw weren't that friendly. There were just her cousins in Delaney when they visited, which was hardly ever. After Ashley and all that, Kari had changed schools. Then the list came out with Dad's name on it, and even though the other girls at school were making best friends like crazy, Kari was out of that loop. Sometimes she saw Trevor's girlfriend Suzanne O'Brien at baseball practice and Suzanne was nice to her, but that was different than having a best friend.

Trevor was out of the loop too, although he acted like he didn't care. He did, though—that was why he was happy he stopped having acne. A lot of girls still liked Trevor, though—they saw him as such a hottie. Especially Suzanne, who didn't seem to care at all about Dad's problem or even that Trevor was on probation. Maybe that was because they had known each other for such a long time and Trevor was basically a good kid, like Dad had always said.

Both Kari and Trevor still played baseball and Kari was almost the best one on her team. But still, after the games, nobody invited them over or offered to drive them home, except Suzanne's mother once in a while. And almost nobody, including Suzanne, could come in their house, because of Dad's parole rules. Anyway, Suzanne always had to go right home, and then after her father died, she completely stopped coming to baseball because she had a lot of brothers and sisters and had to help out.

Trevor's on probation, Kari sighed to herself. And all because of a nut. It didn't help that time all those cops came over at 6:30 in the morning and wanted to test Dad's DNA. She and Trevor had just been getting up for school, and Dad had invited the cops in the living room. Kari and Trevor hid behind the bedroom door, whispering. Trevor was upset. As soon as he heard the cops leave, he went in the living room and looked out the window.

"Kripe! There's five cars!" he said, looking around like he wanted to find something to throw. Meanwhile Polly and Tinkerbell were gabbing and whistling non-stop, like they had been the whole time the cops were there. They acted like they thought it was a big party. Dad went in the bathroom.

"One of the cars says 'SAFE.' That's for Sexual Assault Felony Enforcement! Everybody around here is gonna see them. Now they're really gonna think we stink. Kripe!"

Kari was amazed he only said "Kripe." But then he did something out of character for him—he pounded his fist on the wall. It was only once, and not very hard, but Kari had never seen him do anything like that. It made Dad open the bathroom door. He just stood there looking at Trevor and then he said, "Calm down. I'm sorry."

Trevor did calm down, and so did Tinkerbell and Polly, but to Kari, Trevor changed a lot that day. He seemed to have a grudge, to want to do something bad, to show them he didn't care, to spit in their faces. Maybe that was why later he got caught at school with a joint. That mystified Kari—she knew Trevor didn't smoke or anything. He must've had to beg somebody to let him have that joint. So then he had to go again to juvenile court and he got two years probation and had to visit a probation officer all the time.

Now it was Saturday and Kari was home alone using her computer. Usually it was locked in its cabinet, because Trevor wasn't supposed to use it. Sometimes Kari felt bad using the computer if Trevor was around, because he'd get mad and bug her to let him use it. They were still in the same, too-small apartment because the manager hadn't found them a bigger one. So if Trevor was home, and they felt cramped for one reason or another, they'd go out and play catch, which was how Kari became almost the star baseball player. They couldn't do any batting in the complex, just throwing and catching. There was a park they could have ridden their bikes to. But Kari didn't like going there anymore, not since the three white angels had disappeared.

That's what Tata called them — the three white angels. Tata talked like that sometimes, kind of sarcastic, when something was bothering her.

After the white angels, a guy came to school to pass out information about Stranger Danger—that's what the cop called it. Kari and Trevor used to like going to parks, but after Stranger Danger, Kari was too afraid. Now just looking at the park gave her the creeps. She figured there was nobody there except Strangers—and they must've been Strangers who didn't have cars, because whenever Kari rode by, there were never any cars in the parking lot.

She'd been chatting a little on this Saturday, but she was supposed to be doing homework. At least when you're chatting, nobody knows about that stupid list Dad's on. Kari was in a chat she'd heard kids at school talk about, but she didn't talk to any of them, at least she didn't think she did—she didn't even know what names they used there. Kari used a different name online, cariana90, and she didn't use her own picture, just a cartoon. Sometimes chatting was fun, but on this particular day Kari was bored with it.

The only interesting thing she noticed was somebody in the chat called "pretty pink teen." That's weird, Kari thought. Who would call themselves that? First of all, it was conceited, and second, nobody Kari's age called themselves "teens." Girls gave themselves names like "curtfanatic" or "ringsinger," not "pretty pink teen." And "pretty pink teen" was in glowing pink letters. Kari didn't even know how to make her name glow in color like that.

But she usually chatted with everybody she saw on the list, so she asked pretty pink teen where she went to school and told her she went to Wheeler. The answer was something stupid —"Hey cariana90 thanks for writing and you have a great day"—and pretty pink teen didn't answer Kari's question about school or anything.

So instead of chatting, Kari decided she might as well do her homework, which was a project about tuna. But then, while researching tuna, she instead started reading the latest on a news story that had caught her interest—she didn't know why. Maybe it was the guy's name, which was easy to remember—Ronald Rose. Or maybe it was because he did a sex crime, like Dad, although in Ronald Rose's case, he'd been convicted for using a date-rape drug and then videotaping himself with a girl while she was unconscious and naked.

Ronald Rose's trial had been big news a few months ago because he was a local guy and the grandson of a rich Hollywood director. And then, when he was on trial and things were looking really bad for him, he suddenly disappeared. He was under house arrest and just didn't come home one night. What had happened to him? The cops said his dog and cold weather clothes were gone from his house. One night when Kari was watching the news with Tata and Trevor, she saw how Tata was fixated on the screen when they were talking about Ronald Rose. That's when Kari picked up on the strange but true fact that she and Tata were both silently cheering for Ronald Rose to get away.

Well, believe it or not, the judge continued the trial after Ronald Rose got away and then they convicted him and even sentenced him—to 124 years in prison!

"He didn't even kill anybody!" Tata said. "In Mexico, they don't have life sentences. The system is bad and police beat people up or even kill them, and most people pretty much hate them. But Mexico doesn't have life sentences or executions either, at least not officially. It's a Catholic country."

"Hey," Trevor put in, "Did you hear about that guy Trevor Volpe who got 20 life sentences for sucking toes?"

Tata and Kari just looked at him. "Oh, come on, Trevor," Tata finally said.

"I swear to God!" Trevor defended himself. He looked at Tata with wide eyes then, as if he was waiting for her to say something about his language.

"Trevor, in this family we don't take the Lord's name in vain," she said, but then curiosity got the better of her. "Whose toes?" she asked.

"He worked in a camp and he sucked some little kids' toes and he got 20 life sentences in prison!"

"I'm sure that's not all he did," Tata said.

"It's all he did," Trevor insisted.

Later Trevor got on the computer. Usually all he did on the computer —which he wasn't even supposed to use—was write letters to Suzanne using a fancy gothic script. But this time, he got on the Internet and, fast as lightning, looked up the guy he was talking about so that he could show Kari.

"Look," he said. "There's his name, like mine—Trevor Volpe. That's why I remembered him. The cops said, 'Sexual attraction to children is something that doesn't just go away. He should be kept from the public as long as possible.' So he got 20 life sentences."

Kari studied the screen. "But look. It says 'State law requires a life sentence for each count of child molestation.'" Then she looked at Trevor. "But isn't that what they said Dad did? Child molestation? How come he didn't get life in prison?"

"No, it was 'lewd' something," Trevor answered.

"What's 'lewd'?" Kari asked.

"I don't know. He's a lewd dude."

"Don't say that. He's not."

"But you don't even know what lewd means. Anyways, it's a joke."

Kari had been disturbed upon reading over Trevor's shoulder about how his namesake Trevor Volpe the toe sucker had been hauled, sobbing, from the courtroom to serve 20 life sentences. But on this Saturday, that sad story wasn't bothering her so much, especially when she saw today's big news alert—Ronald Rose had been captured! In Mexico!

Mexico, Kari thought dreamily. Then her spirits sank as she read, horrified, about the messy scene at a taco stand in Puerto Vallarta—where was Puerto Vallarta anyway?—with tear gas and a bounty hunter named Dog and Mexican police. This circus ended a few days later with Ronald Rose's deportation back to California. Still, Kari dreamed about the seemingly exotic, probably faraway location. But apparently it hadn't been far enough away, or maybe Ronald Rose wasn't smart enough, because people said that he'd been surfing and hanging out with the tourists instead of laying low. And some of his hanging out buddies tipped the cops about him.

Now nobody was at home with Kari, so she couldn't share the news with anyone. She glumly imagined poor Ronald Rose, who might at that very moment be sitting in the same jail where her Dad had been those four awful days. Was it the same jail as the toe sucker too? Thinking about all of her heroes—some of them pretty unlikely heroes—sitting in jail together was too overwhelming. So, a little reluctantly, she turned her attention once more to the far simpler world of tuna, and when she found enough information, she shut down the computer and did some Spanish.

Yes, the 13-year-old Mexican American girl who didn't speak Spanish had taken an interest in that "foreign" language. And she liked it. Perhaps it was because her classmates were different from a lot of students. Some of them were kids from Mexico or even El Salvador or Guatemala who didn't speak English too well. Maybe they were taking Spanish because it was an easy A. Others just seemed to be outside of the mainstream, at least outside the opinion Kari had heard some girl say—that Spanish was "sucky."

In fact, Kari had gotten to be friends with another student in the Spanish class, a tiny girl who was named Esther, just like Kari's cousin, and whose hair and eyes were just as black as Kari's. Esther didn't speak English so good. She was from an area in Mexico called Los Altos—that meant "the high places"—from a village that Kari had given up trying to pronounce, much to Esther's amusement.

"Yahualica de Gonzalez Gallo," Esther had repeated giggling, with Kari trying to repeat it after her, about 20 times. Kari could say Gonzalez OK, and she had learned that "gallo" meant rooster. But she couldn't say the whole thing, especially the first part. Finally, she just started saying Esther was from Los Altos.

"What do they do there?" Kari asked one day when Esther brought some candy for everyone in the class. Kari tried one of the soft brown cubes with a nut sitting in the center and decided it was the best thing she'd ever tasted.

"Marijuana," was the one word Kari understood in Esther's answer. In Yahualica de Gonzalez Gallo, they grew marijuana.

"Marijuana?" Kari asked. "Don't they grow anything else?"

"No," Esther shrugged matter-of-factly. "Only marijuana."

Although they weren't in any other classes together and Kari didn't see much of Esther, she was Kari's friend—her only friend at school, in fact. Kari sensed it was because Esther was so different from other kids. She didn't care about things like Kari's dad being on a police list and on parole. "Well, they make good candy, anyway," Kari told Esther, wishing she could ask for another one.

"No," Esther said. "No es from Yahualica de Gonzalez Gallo. Is from here, from store of Mexico."

Later, Kari informed Tata about this store and got her to go there. It was called simply Super Mart, and was in a strip mall about a half mile from the big Ralph's. It looked and even smelled different from Ralph's— it wasn't so bright, for one thing—and Kari discovered she liked checking out the food. Kari and her grandmother tried to find the candy, but since Kari didn't know its name, it wasn't so easy.

"Tata, Esther's from a little town in Mexico with a funny name ... Yalica de ... Gonzalez Gallo. She says they didn't make the candy there, though. They grow marijuana, only marijuana. She said it's kinda high up in the mountains, in Los Altos, and nobody hardly goes there. I mean, except the ones who live there."

Tata looked at her sharply. "What did you say?"

"No, Tata, Esther doesn't grow marijuana," Kari tried to explain. "I mean, I don't think so. It was in her town."

"No, I mean what's the name of the town you said?"

Kari laughed. "I can't say it very good, Tata. Except the last part. It's like Yazalica ... de Gonzalez Gallo."

"Is it Yahualica de Gonzalez Gallo?"

"That sounds right."

Tata smiled a little smile. "That's where my parents came from. Yahualica de Gonzalez Gallo. It's in the center of Mexico. They said it was beautiful. They loved it. Well, except they left because there really wasn't anything to do, any work. It was pretty isolated and the roads to get there were bad."

They were in the fruit section and Kari suddenly came across the brown candy in cellophane-wrapped trays on a lower shelf. She looked at the label.

"Look, it is from Mexico. It's from Puerto Vallarta!" she marveled. The same place as Ronald Rose got caught. She asked Tata to buy some.

"I thought you were eating healthier," Tata said.

"Oh, well," Kari said, disappointed. "But it's made with milk. Maybe ... can we buy it for Dad then? It's his birthday pretty soon." Tata put the candy in their basket and Kari knew it was because Tata wanted her father to gain weight.

When they got home with the candy and other stuff, her Dad was there.

Kari immediately sensed that something was up.

Danny helped them put away the groceries and took the candy out of one of the bags. "What's this?"

"It's for you," Tata said.

"For your birthday," Kari sighed, realizing she should've put it away fast, so she could've wrapped it for later.

"Thank you. But what is it?"

"Mexican milk candy," Tata said. "You might as well open it and have some, now that you've seen it."

Dad eyed the candy hesitantly. "Well, it's better than my other birthday present." When Tata didn't answer, he added, "You know ... that I have to go to the sheriff station and register again."

Tata started removing the cellophane from the package. "Kari and I will have one, but the rest is for you."

As Tata got it open, Dad looked at the candy and said, almost to himself, "Something happened." Kari had been reaching out to try one of the delicious treats she remembered from when Esther brought them, but upon hearing this, her hand dropped.

She saw Dad press his lips together. "Go on princess, take one." Kari took a candy but didn't eat it. She was waiting to hear the bad news she was pretty sure Dad was going to say.

"Hijo, you take one too," said Tata. Kari had hardly ever heard her grandmother use this affectionate word, "son," to talk to her father, but lately, all of a sudden, Tata had been speaking a little Spanish to him, and he'd been answering her in Spanish.

This one word seemed to signal something to Dad, and so, while taking a slow bite of the milk candy, he hesitantly began his explanation in Spanish. Kari only understood the easy words: "mi foto," "mis datos," "alli"—over there. He gestured with his hand at some unseen area. From his worried look and the bits she could understand, Kari figured out that somebody had put up a photo of him, with his address, somewhere in the apartment complex. She also figured it was the doing of the apartment manager, and was connected to the cops coming that day with all those cars marked "SAFE."

"Dad, the candy is from Puerto Vallarta," Kari said. She still couldn't bring herself to try her beginner's Spanish with him, although Tata

126

helped her a little with her homework. "It's the same place they captured that guy."

"What guy?"

Tata said, "Oh, the one we've been watching on the news. He drugged a girl, and got away during his trial a few months ago. They just picked him up in Mexico. The Mexican police sent him back here."

"They did?" Dad said. "I thought Mexico didn't do that to Chicanos."

"Well, he's not Chicano. He's a regular gringo. A rich one, too. But I thought they didn't send anybody back here that might get executed or go to prison for life. And he got 124 years. But you know, hijo, in Mexico, a lot of times a law is something on paper. Just because there's a law, that isn't the way things necessarily happen."

Dad didn't say anything. But later when Kari was on the sofa watching TV, he sat down and asked Kari if she understood what he said to Tata, about his picture being on a sign outside. "I'm sorry, because it might affect you and Trevor and Tata," he said.

"It's OK, Dad," Kari said bravely, but at the end of her sentence, out popped a little half-sob that had snuck up on her. Dad put his arm around her, and that made her tears really start up, but she turned her head away from him so he wouldn't see and she managed not to sob again. "I don't ..." she swallowed and tried to loosen up her throat, "... really know anybody here anyway." But the fresh flow of tears that started up belied her words. Finally, she just leaned into her father's shoulder and said, "I love you, Papi."

"I love you too, Princess," he answered. "Someday when all of this is over, it will be OK."

But Kari wondered if it would ever be over. "Sometimes I think the only way is ... we gotta go somewhere else, far, far away," she said.

"I thought about moving to Mexico," Dad said. "But now I'm on parole. And Trevor's on probation. It'd cause a big alarm. Maybe when I'm off parole and things get back to normal."

Would things ever get back to normal? On TV, there was a lot about Catholic priests molesting kids, and there was the war in Iraq starting and people demonstrating, and on that very same night, after Kari went to get a tissue and blow her nose, they saw an ad on TV that showed a little girl holding hands with a man in an elevator and as the two of them get off, the little girl looks back for a second at a black lady who was in the elevator, and the girl smiles a kind of pitiful smile at her. Then the ad said that child abductions happened all the time and if you see something suspicious like that, you should call the police.

"Well, what if you're wrong?" Dad burst out. "What's suspicious about a little girl holding hands with a man?"

Kari knew he was saying that because he usually held hands with her when they were out walking. Maybe not that much recently—after all, she was 13 now—but there were times when they were very affectionate. There had always been those times.

Tata was sitting in the armchair by then, mostly reading her novel. But she saw the ad too. Using her sarcastic voice again, she said, "Well, finally a little equal opportunity!" Kari figured she meant the black lady on the elevator.

15. War on Crime

1939 to 2008

ALEX LANDON

"Some guys tell me they'd rather be in prison." Arizona attorney Robert Campos was talking about his clients caught in intrusive, Big Brother therapy programs and on "lifetime probation" (a scheme that seems to be a contradiction in terms, since probation by definition is a finite testing period to assess a person's readiness for unsupervised life).

How can such strange and disturbing things be happening in the Land of the Free? To find out necessitates a short trip to the past.

The late 1960s and early 1970s were times of conflict in the United States. The deadly War in Vietnam was raging and, closer to home, a war over the rights of African Americans seemed ready to erupt. Students were demonstrating against the war. Black Americans were demonstrating for civil rights, and riots that drew on their discontent broke out in major cities.

Social and legal currents were swirling every which way. A swell of court decisions put a moratorium on capital punishment and gave accused people protection against police who, before that, could do pretty much what they pleased. The early part of that turbulent era brought in Miranda warnings ("You have the right to remain silent"), the institution of public attorneys to represent the accused, and the curbing of police searches.

But many people didn't think these changes were positive, especially in view of the demonstrations and riots, which were seen as evidence of lawlessness. In the 1964 election, Barry Goldwater declared that an uncontrolled crime rampage was in progress. He didn't win the election, but his crime-mongering rhetoric affected the whole society and the victor, President Lyndon Johnson. By 1972, even sober skeptics such as James Vorenberg, who served as director on Johnson's "Crime Commission," seemed to have been convinced by official statistics that a frightening crime wave was indeed in progress. Whether the crime wave was real or not, Vorenberg noticed a change in people's mentality—the explosive growth of the security industry and the new popularity of German shepherds as guard dogs. (1)

Evidencing the schizophrenic clash between opposing ideas that was in progress, the death penalty was ruled unconstitutional by the U.S. Supreme Court in 1972, but was then gradually re-instituted by most states later in the 1970s.

Johnson, wanting to distance himself from the War in Vietnam, which he had expanded (provoking college students threatened with the draft to organize huge anti-war demonstrations), started a trend of declaring domestic "wars" on problems. Johnson was not one for crime mongering, but his people did come up with the opportunistic "War on Poverty" designed to mollify those who objected to the Vietnam War.

When Richard Nixon won the presidency in 1968, it was on the heels of his campaign telling people worried about crime to blame it on recent Supreme Court decisions curbing police abuses (such as failure to inform criminal suspects about their rights). Once in office, Nixon too wanted to placate people angry about the Vietnam War (as well as to squelch the "crime wave"). So now a new "War on Crime" soon became his rallying cry. [1]

P.O.s are God

Besides distracting critics of the War in Vietnam and hopefully decreasing crime and poverty, can you imagine another long-term result of this public-relations blitz of domestic "wars"? You may glimpse the answer if you recall that in the military world, accused soldiers endure a legal system that doesn't offer them as many protections as in the civilian world. That means that in a court-martial, the cards are more stacked against the accused person than in a regular court. And, although politicians don't want you to think so, the cards are already heavily stacked against accused people in court. No matter how rich the accused person—and most are not—the government is always richer and has far more teams of taxpayer-financed lawyers at its disposal.

So, by declaring "War on Crime," the government in effect declared war on Constitutional protections and stacked the cards more in its own favor. What then arrived in the civilian legal system in the wake of the "War on Crime," besides tough laws and money to enforce them, were exceptions to Constitutional principles, shriveled rights, and other distortions of important principles.

Unfortunately, decades after the War on Crime began, this is still what we see. In this book, we have already mentioned some of these distortions. When the attorney ironically said, "P.O.s are God," he was speaking about one such distortion, for obviously, parole and probation officers, like every other authority in the criminal justice system, were meant by the American founders to have limited—not God-like powers.

---

[1] The war theme became such a hit that, years later, a "War on Drugs" would once again take aim at crime. This new "war," in the mid-1980s, established mandatory minimum sentences for many drug crimes. Later on, judges, both liberal and conservative, would routinely slam these mandatory minimum sentences as grotesquely harsh. (2)

But the unfortunate reality is that they have given themselves God-like powers. This was illustrated in an appeals court decision in March 2003, that struck down a common practice in California's parole system, calling it unconstitutional.

The case involved a man who, as a condition of his parole, had been forced to sign a waiver allowing police to conduct searches of his home "at any time of the day or night, with or without a search warrant, and with or without cause." This all-too-common document is called a Fourth waiver, because by signing, the man was waiving his rights detailed in the Fourth Amendment to the Constitution, which protects us from unreasonable searches. The P.O. tells a person that if they don't sign, they will be violating one of the conditions of their parole and will be sent back to prison. Of course, the man signed, and later an FBI agent got the OK from the P.O., entered the home where the man lived with his sister, interrogated him, and got him to confess to a bank robbery.

But even though the court decision threw out the confession and the practice, a lot of damage was done over the many years Fourth waivers were used. And even after San Diego attorney Michael McCabe won this appeal in 2003, challenges to the decision would be coming down the pike. Along with these would come new unconstitutional measures too, because politicians and government authorities never seem to tire of devising ways to weaken rights—and they have plenty of taxpayer money to work on it. Forcing people to sign Fourth waivers is just one example of practices that have resulted from the erosion of rights and principles under the War on Crime. Two more examples are threatening to send people to prison to force them to enter psychotherapy and forcing people already in prison into psychotherapy. Both spit in the face of such principles as voluntary consent to medical procedures, therapist-client confidentiality and the Fifth Amendment's protection against self-incrimination.

Other examples of fractured principles are making people on parole and probation undergo lie detector tests—inadmissible in court under most other circumstances—as well as tests specific to sex offenses, such as the plethysmograph and Abel test. All these tests can result in self-incrimination, because they are given by P.O.s and other agents of the government who are hostile to the subjects or have conflicts of interest. And, as mentioned, none even conform to the simplest principles of accuracy. Independent experts see them as glorified Inquisition devices without a scientific basis.

Other unprincipled punishments carried out in the parallel universe that convicted people inhabit violate the Constitution's prohibition of ex post facto (retroactively increased) punishment. Some examples are the constantly-appearing and never-ending costs enforced by P.O.s—for lie detector tests, for psychotherapy, and so on.

A real Godzilla

And other strange birds fly out of the parallel universe created by the War on Crime: denying some convicted people the right to vote after they leave prison or finish probation; police registration of convicted people; denial of housing to convicted people; electronic tracking of convicted people. Such "tough on crime" laws seem to be the products of minds bent on finding harsh new punishments and control measures not specifically outlawed in the Constitution or Bill of Rights.

Besides these relatively unnoticed effects of the War on Crime, what have been some of the more tangible results over the years? In the liberal prelude to President Johnson's War on Crime, his Crime Commission Director James Vorenberg expressed a sensible perspective on prisons: "If we take a person whose criminal conduct shows he cannot manage his life, lock him up with others like himself, increase his frustrations and anger, and take away from him any responsibility for planning his life, he is almost certain to be more dangerous when he gets out." (3) Such insights had led the Crime Commission to make many intelligent recommendations.

However, with crime looming as a major issue, Vorenberg's views in the end did not come to fruition. The Safe Streets and Crime Control Act was passed in 1968 and pumped in more than $1.5 billion dollars in new federal money to the criminal justice systems of cities and states. Vorenberg mentioned a two-year period when federal money for the Law Enforcement Assistance Administration program shot up from $270 million to $700 million dollars. However, looking back in 1972 at the actual results, he lamented how poorly most of his commission's recommendations had been carried out by the states.

But at that point he expressed some optimism about California, which had by 1972 developed an extensive, alternative work-furlough program for prisoners and as well as a subsidy to counties, which kept the state prison population low by putting offenders on probation. Vorenberg wrote that the number of state prisoners had declined from 28,000 to 21,000 over the previous three years, that plans for new prisons were scrapped and some existing ones were closed!

Unfortunately, what happened next in California was that it fell in line with the foot-dragging states. This development highlights another key player in the War on Crime which until now has hardly been mentioned—the Victims Rights movement. Although the name "Victims Rights movement" has a grass-roots ring to it, in reality its main actors are special interests, politicians, government employees, entertainment figures and even, as we will be see ahead, tax dollars. Although, at least in the beginning, some groups focused on and seemed to involve ordinary victims of crime, often the Victims Rights movement does not truly represent victims, but rather exploits them in order to survive and thrive. So, although California began the War on Crime by making some effective reforms in its justice system, something happened a few years later that sent the state's system over a cliff. That something was the powerful union mentioned in other chapters—the California Correctional Peace Officers Association, or prison guards union.

Even in 1972, Vorenberg had already identified militant prison guards unions nationally as a primary force opposed to the rational changes his commission recommended. He mentioned cases of angry guards orchestrating prison escapes to dramatize their refusal to change. By 2009, California's early start on progressive changes had been stomped out by the California Correctional Peace Officers Association, who had started their dirty work around 1980, three decades earlier. Leonard Gilroy, writing for the Reason Foundation, has called this union "the biggest obstacle to ... meaningful prison reform." (4)

The effects CCPOA has had on California are dramatic. Over the three decades, the state's correctional system became addicted to money, huge quantities of it. The union exploded from 2,600 officers to 45,000. The number of people working in prisons shot up. Prison construction and guards' salaries shot up. In 1980, the average guard earned $15,000 a year. By 2009, one in every 10 guards made more than $100,000 dollars annually. (5)

After that initial, hopeful drop in the inmate population to 21,000 that Vorenberg mentioned in 1972, California's inmate population soon boomed under CCPOA's influence. By 2006, there were more than 172,000 inmates, about 200 percent over capacity. The corrections budget had shot up to $8.2 billion. (6) After a determinate sentencing law went into effect in 1977, the number of inmates skyrocketed. Another force that caused the inmate population and number of prisons to increase dramatically was California's three-strikes law, which CCPOA supported in a big way.

In fact, although CCPOA is not itself considered a Victims Rights organization, to get the three-strikes law and other measures passed, it leaned on Victims Rights groups, and even created one. It donated $1 million dollars to then-Governor Pete Wilson's reelection campaign after he agreed to support the Three Strikes law. CCPOA also teamed up with the father of a girl, Polly Klaas, who was murdered in 1993. This event, tragic for the family, turned out to be convenient for the union, because the Three Strikes law was easily passed in the furor over the murder. Polly's father went on to found a Victims Rights organization aimed at promoting tough treatment of offenders.

But the Three Strikes law turned out to be as tragic as Polly's murder, because by 2004, it had clearly not been effective in reducing crime. In fact, you could even conclude that it caused a rise in crime, because in states without Three-Strikes laws, crime dropped much more over a 9-year period than in states with such laws. More tragically, although it had been aimed at "violent" offenders, by 2004 the three strikes law was responsible for 354 people who were in California prisons for life for petty thefts under $250 dollars.

But the law was extraordinarily effective in one respect — keeping the prison guards employed. It is seen as a major factor in California's prison growth. Like many designer laws with catchy titles that are hatched under the influence of well publicized murders and raised under the wing of the Victims Rights movement, the Three Strikes law is a real Godzilla.

As mentioned above, the union influenced Wilson and later leaned on other governors, such as Gray Davis and Arnold Schwarzenegger, even though Schwarzenegger came into office promising to terminate the CCPOA's power. Nevertheless, legislators and corrections officials attempting to rein in the union have found in it an intimidating adversary. "Those who come forward [to criticize CCPOA] find themselves sent to a job in the prison's Siberia or fearing for their lives," said one would-be watchdog in 2006. (7)

But governors, legislators, and a murdered girl's father apparently have not been enough for CCPOA. It also created its very own Victims Rights organization, a Sacramento political action committee called Crime Victims United, which promotes and pushes tough laws that increase the prison population. Although this PAC's director, Harriet Salarno, said the PAC is independent from the union, financial records show that since 2004 the only group that has funded it is CCPOA. (8)

Victims groups that are not really run by or for victims form one hefty component of the Victims Rights movement. Another component is made up of groups that were indeed founded by the relatives of victims and once may have been grass-roots groups but, on closer examination, prove to have less than wholesome motivations. Over time, these organizations that were founded by victims' families often mutate into groups that can no longer be called grass roots.

Such organizations may become so preoccupied with their survival that they turn vampirish, so hell-bent on their aims or on revenge that they mutate into caricatures of their earlier selves. And in these altered states, they may spew out false information and statistics that, because the public naturally sympathizes with suffering parents and believes these groups are credible, are seldom questioned.

Blurred boundaries

There are many examples, but a well known one is the aforementioned California group founded by Polly Klaas' father. In professional-looking Web pages and newsletters, such groups typically pull false or unprovable information out of their hats and present it as fact. "There is not one documented case of a pedophile ever having been cured," a newsletter on the Klaas Kids website proclaimed, and "It is a ... fact that whenever a sexual deviant is anonymously released into the community, the probability is virtually guaranteed that the offender will revert to deviant behavior." (9) Groups like this could well be the reason that so many malignant myths have circulated about the "incurability" of sex offenders.

In 2002, about a decade after the tragedy in his family, Marc Klaas' organization was still in existence and, like other non-profits, solicited donations, including donations of used cars. Soon after Danielle Van Dam disappeared that year, perhaps to support the Van Dams, perhaps to infuse life into his organization, perhaps both, Marc Klaas showed up near San Diego on the Van Dam doorstep for a press conference.

"It can happen to anybody," he said to the assembled national media, "Every child is vulnerable." His statements spread panic by giving the false impression that extremely rare child abductions and murders were common—and, not incidentally, implying that organizations such as his were fulfilling a desperately needed service. Klaas then stayed on in San Diego to spar on the air with a no-holds-barred talk-show host, Rick Roberts, over the suggestion that something the Van Dam parents did had contributed to their child's kidnapping.

The Van Dam case provided a stage for many other less-than-salutary aspects of the Victims Rights movement. Besides attracting the ghoulish attention mentioned above, there was the following final, sorry chapter that makes the Van Dam case a classic in Victims Rights annals.

Sometime after the accused man's conviction, the case attracted high-profile talk show hostess and attorney Gloria Allred. Allred and the mother announced to the press plans to push for a law that would further extend the reach of the death penalty, as well as plans to sue the convicted man, by then on death row, and strip the remaining monetary assets from his estate. Later the mother appeared with the sympathetic arm of a California legislator around her shoulder as she fought back tears and promoted the law. Naturally, it would be called "Danielle's law." (10)

On this occasion, some of the less wholesome motivation behind the public relations posturing revealed itself. "Closure" or "to prevent it from happening to others" are usually cited as rationales when victims' relatives are utilized by politicians to promote designer laws. But in this news conference, when the mother spoke about the convicted person, she was surprisingly candid about what was driving her—revenge. "I only hope that when he gets to San Quentin [Prison] that the inmates there have the same hate and anger I have I hope he suffers 10 times the pain and fear we suffered." (11)

Anger and revenge as motivation seem to be openly acknowledged in the very name of an organization that is the iconic Victims Rights group: MADD, or Mothers Against Drunk Driving, one of the first Victims Rights groups, founded in 1980 in the wake of the War on Crime, by a woman whose daughter was killed by a drunk driver. But MADD also illustrates the excesses such groups can fall into after years of success and dogged fixation on their goal. A critic in 2002 described MADD as a rotund bureaucracy with lots of money and too little to do. Having effectively fulfilled its reason for existence (reducing traffic fatalities from drunken driving), the group had set its sights on a misguided goal—advocating random roadblocks that would result in many people being arrested for very low levels of alcohol, such as could occur after a single drink and were not particularly dangerous. (12)

Such myopia has infected many Victims Rights groups, including some that have met with more success than they probably dreamed possible when they began, success that in fact altered their very basis. One of the most successful anti-crime groups is one that has blurred the boundaries between grass-roots advocacy, entertainment and government. This is the National Center for Missing and Exploited Children, begun by John Walsh after the abduction-murder of his son in 1981. After founding the group, Walsh soon went on to host an extremely popular TV show, "The FBI's Most Wanted," a precursor of the reality-crime genre that mushroomed a few years later.

A couple of decades after its inception, the Center was still going strong, filling mailboxes with alerts on missing children. On March 8, 2004, the group had taken out a costly, full-page ad in People magazine on the topic of child sexual abuse. It depicted a white girl, a model about 8 years old, and claimed, "35 percent of these victims never report it," a statement impossible to be proven but unlikely to be questioned by a trusting public. Perhaps the most remarkable thing about the Center was reflected in its 2008 annual report, which showed how far it had come from its beginnings. In its thank-you section, the Center listed page after page of donors: businesses, individuals, foundations, police departments and so on. But in reality, these donors were small potatoes when compared to a single entry that appeared almost inconspicuously on the financial report page under Revenue. "Federal funds, $31,715,50," it read. (13)

You read correctly—the Center received almost $32 million dollars from taxpayers, almost 70 percent of its revenue.

So is the Center government or private? The Center seems a lot like a government body when you consider not only that it survives on tax dollars, but also that it frequently works hand in glove with police. In 2003 when, post 9/11, the Homeland Security Department deported 89 foreigners convicted of unspecified sex offenses—and one can only hope it wasn't for urinating near the border—there was Walsh in the limelight again, this time with Secretary of Homeland Security Tom Ridge, announcing "Operation Predator." (14) Ridge had been appointed by former President George W. Bush to head up the agency created to combat terrorism after 9/11. We have seen this unhealthy tendency to lump foreign enemies together with ordinary criminals before.

Walsh said he was sending "a loud message to pedophiles ... especially illegal aliens that come here, that molest our children, serve time in our prisons and then are released, that you cannot stay in the United States." However, since illegal aliens are normally deported after prison, the impressive sounding "Operation Predator" could only have been a streamlining of administrative procedures. Spokesmen indicated that was the case when they said the operation included "a single Web portal to access all publicly available state Megan's Law databases."

On the other hand, considering that the National Center for Missing and Exploited Children runs expensive advertisements in glossy national magazines, it seems more like a private advocacy group. But the ads contain misleading and alarming information that affects government decision makers, making the Center appear to be another strange bird that flew out of the land of the War on Crime. The suspicion grows that the Center in reality is a government body that spends tax money to influence the government to keep on giving it money. [2]

In sync with this apparent confusion as to the nature of the National Center for Missing and Exploited Children was a confusing image on the cover of its 2008 annual report. Perhaps to repair the near-exclusive focus of Victims Rights efforts on white children, or perhaps in response to the recent election of a black president, Barack Obama, the report carried a cover image of a pretty black girl. But it wasn't an image of a real girl, like on the group's ubiquitous mailbox flyers. Instead, the girl appeared to be a model, about 8 years old, posing with a long-stemmed plant, wearing a bare-shoulder summer dress, a fashionable hairdo, lipstick and eye makeup.

---

[2] Federal employees are restricted by the Hatch Act of 1939 as to participating in political activities. An Environmental Protection Agency employee, for example, may not be able to speak at a Sierra Club event. Such restrictions were instituted to protect against federal employees using their positions to influence funding of their offices. But because the National Center for Missing and Exploited Children is not seen as a government organization, it is not affected by the Hatch Act.

Was this supposed to represent a missing girl, an exploited girl, or simply an African-American, like the new president? And if the latter, were the bare-shoulder summer dress, fashionable hairdo, lipstick and eye makeup simply another attempt to keep federal funds flowing toward the Center? Had the Center's mission, like other Victims Rights groups, migrated from preventing crimes to insuring its own survival?

The contagiousness of injustice

We cannot leave this section on Victims Rights without mentioning another effort with show-business blood in its veins, one that breaks the mold by virtue of being founded by an African American — Oprah Winfrey.

Winfrey, "from her media mogul perch high atop any power list in the country," as Mary McNamara wrote, is an exceptional phenomenon by many standards, "her face smiling down from billboards, out from the television screens, up from magazine racks, her name emblazoned on bestselling books."

Of course, Winfrey's prominence in the Victims Rights movement is atypical because of her race. However, as McNamara also wrote, Winfrey "seems to transcend race or gender or class." (15) And the fact that Winfrey is unusual in the Victims Rights movement in terms of race may also be offset by another distinction—she is not a relative of a victim, but the victim herself. She started the "Oprah's Child Predator Watch List" and "Oprah's law" in her own name, because she was abused as a teenager by male relatives, she said. Another difference between her effort and more typical designer laws is that the incident that allegedly provoked her does not appear to be nearly as horrible as incidents that typically provoke designer laws—abductions and murders of children by strangers. In fact, since it happened between people who knew each other and probably in the home, Oprah's incident sounds like the kind of situation that the courts typically see.

"Oprah's Child Predator Watch List" offers $100,000 rewards for the capture of "predators"—a lot of money, even for a media mogul, and another atypical aspect of her activities. Winfrey testified before the U.S. Senate Judiciary Committee for the passage of "Oprah's Law," or the National Child Protection Act, which was in 1993 signed by President Clinton. So in this case there was no politician hitching his or her star to Oprah Winfrey, as in more typical designer laws that will be described later. Winfrey was star enough in her own right.

Those atypical aspects aside, there are still some aspects of Winfrey's efforts that bring them into the fold of typical Victims Rights campaigns. One of course is the main player's status as an entertainment figure. Another is a possible revenge motivation. Her revelations about the abuse she said she suffered were of a piece with the soul-barings that take place on her daytime talk show and others like it. Psychiatrists and psychologists may have some insight into what prompts people to talk about intimate topics in front of millions of people. Perhaps they are seeking social approval, which can be a powerful factor in helping victims get over bad experiences. It is also plausible that in many Victims Rights efforts, vengeance is a powerful motivator.

The financial health of Winfrey's Victims Rights efforts, which are probably due to her general business and show business savvy, is also not atypical of Victims Rights groups in general. Whether or not her Victims Rights activities are non-profit, many non-profit groups are non-profit in name only and operate with hefty budgets and generous salaries.

In another chapter we will illustrate how typical victims are sometimes swept off their feet by politicians who, in tandem with the media, manipulate public terror and disgust over a high-profile crime. Unfortunately, this type of drama is a lot more interesting to the public than contemplating the bad, but subtler, effects of the War on Crime and the Victims Rights movement: the war on constitutional protections, the fracturing of classic medical and legal principles, the creation of over- broad laws, the financial hemorrhaging of governments, the filling of prisons, and the deterioration of the lawbreaker's character.

In fact, probably many law-abiding people are not much bothered when a convicted person suffers the loss of some right or the perversion of some principle. After all, as that social worker in a therapy factory said, these are people who committed a crime so "Why should I worry about violating their rights?" However, if there is one thing readers should take away from this book, it is that we should all care. Why?

One reason is the statistics mentioned at the beginning of this book showing the surprising number of citizens who fall on the wrong side of the law—one in every 37 U.S. adults with "prison experience." All of us like to think "it could never happen to me"—I could never be accused or convicted of a crime—but these statistics show that it could.

A second good reason to care is the obscene amount of money being spent after a crime is committed instead of on effective prevention—in prenatal care, parenting education, schools, good nutrition in schools, and so on.

A third reason to care: most people have an innate sense of justice, which, when awakened with information, rebels at the idea that anyone should be in prison for life for committing a petty theft—a reality mentioned earlier in this chapter. Just so, our innate sense of justice is offended upon realizing that when people who have completed prison or probation are endlessly saddled with harsh consequences, the effect on their character will be bad, sometimes endangering both themselves and other people.

Here are two examples. In December after that summer of 2002, a man arrested for rape in Encinitas, California, told the woman he did it because he was a registered sex offender, and his life was already ruined. He had nothing to lose, he said. He planned to kill himself afterward. (16) In the same month, the Los Angeles Times told of gulags created for released sex offenders in marginal areas in Iowa—a phenomenon that would soon be spreading—where a man was forced by parole officers to live in a seamy motel, away from schools and public transportation that could take him to a job.

"It makes you want to reoffend," he said bitterly. (17) This illustrates that sometimes the welfare of convicted individuals is difficult to separate from the welfare of everyone else. In other words, people who have nothing to lose have few reasons not to commit a crime.

My last reason for all of us to care when some of us suffer injustice is the contagiousness of injustice. This fear that was well understood by U.S. founders when they established our Constitution and Bill of Rights with their dramatic emphasis on the rights of the accused and convicted.

The fact is that many people who made up the nation's founding population, and whose experiences drove the Constitution and the Bill of Rights, had fled from European societies where accused and convicted people were regularly trampled on. In fact, many of the founders had themselves been, in one way or another, on the wrong side of the law. They were political or religious dissidents, people deported from Europe's prisons, indentured servants—people who, in some important sense, were unsuccessful in their original societies.

In the 21st century, an era much enamored of police, especially the Hollywood version of police, to assert that America was founded by criminals may not elicit many cheers. But it was so, and the experiences of the founders led them to understand the tremendous, innate power of the government and to focus on protecting those accused of crime.

The contagiousness of injustice was eloquently voiced after an infamous era in an otherwise civilized society during which large numbers of people suffered extreme injustice—Nazi Germany. The spokesperson was not a philosopher. She had been a very young woman during the Nazi era, and a member of the inner circle of Germans in power—she was Gertrude Weisker, the cousin of Eva Braun, Hitler's girlfriend.

She made a curious statement, and one that was probably criticized for its insensitivity to those who suffered in much more tangible ways. Referring to all average Germans during the time preceding Germany's defeat, she said, "With the Nazi regime we felt ourselves in a big concentration camp." (18)

Closer to home, Benjamin Franklin brought his incisive wit to the question of freedom versus security when he said, "Those who would give up Essential Liberty to purchase a little Temporary Safety, deserve neither Liberty nor Safety." We would do well to remember that this applies even, and especially, to safety from crimes that cause panic.

16. That's the trouble with kids today

April to December, 2002

ELAINE HALLECK

When Kate noticed Danny's picture behind glass on the notice board near the office—the same notice board where she'd seen the other guy's poster earlier—she didn't know how long it had been there. She hadn't seen Danny or his family in a while. So she called their apartment right away, but nobody answered. It was around noon. Kari and Trevor were probably at school, Danny's mom was at work, and Danny was probably sleeping before his late afternoon shift. Feeling sick, she put down the phone.

She grabbed her keys and headed out into the bright sun. It was April but afternoons were already warm. She walked past the pool, mailboxes, and again, the offending notice board, perched incongruously in the midst of a cheery planting of yellow, daisy-like flowers.

Danny William Fernandez, she read again, Serious Sex Offender with his address and other details. The other man's picture wasn't there anymore. Had they run him out?

The manager, Mary Ann, was in her office, where a couple was filling out forms. Kate hesitated outside the door. Should she speak in front of the couple?

"Come in, Kate!" the manager called. Kate stepped in gingerly, aware that the manager's cheerfulness had a life expectancy of one or two seconds.

"Jerome and Linda here are doing some paperwork," she explained amicably. "What can I do for you?"

"It's about the picture of Danny Fernandez." Kate said, gesturing vaguely outdoors. Mary Ann stared at her wide-eyed. Kate swallowed and continued. "Do we have to have these pictures? It's not necessary. It's offensive. I know Danny. He's a friend. He's not dangerous. The other guy wasn't either."

Now Jerome and Linda were staring at her too, their brown eyes round. Linda's hand, which had been busily filling out forms, lay frozen on the manager's desk. She had on several beautiful rings that, on her dark brown skin, made her hand resemble some bejeweled robin that had been shot out of the sky and now lay inert.

The manager said, "OK, Kate, thank you. We'll take that into consideration." She hesitated and then added. "But you know, it's public information."

That didn't seem right to Kate—it wasn't like the manager had posted a page out of the telephone directory—but she could only sigh and ask, "What happened to the other guy? Did he leave?"

At this, the manager seemed to lose patience. "No, he's still here," she said in an incongruously musical tone, standing up. But she really couldn't go anywhere in the tiny, crowded office.

"Well, that's good," said Kate.

"A lot of people here have kids, Kate. That's why we put up those notices."

"I haven't seen very many kids. It's mostly Marines."

At this, a slight rustling came from Jerome and Linda, and somehow Kate knew that, even though they were dressed in regular clothes, they were Marines.

"We're both," Linda said. "Military and we have kids—one kid."

"Thanks for stopping in, Kate," the manager, still standing, said.

"Those photos make the place look bad. They're creepy," Kate added stubbornly. But she obligingly turned toward the door, as Mary Ann, like a herding dog, nudged her out, putting up the "Back in a Few Minutes" sign on the door and closing it behind Kate. "Almost lunchtime," she mumbled in apparent apology.

Kate stood there for a few seconds, smarting over her unseemly rejection, then started towards her apartment, when she heard a car honk lightly. An old silver Mercedes was idling outside the big, metal gate. Out of the driver's window came a waving hand, then a head. Sandra. Oh my gosh. In the flurry over Danny's photo, Kate had forgotten. Sandra was having a recital and Kate's Toyota was getting a tune-up, so Sandra was picking her up.

When Kate piled into the car about five minutes later, she noticed Jerome and Linda coming out of the office. They were walking toward their car, but both their heads were sharply turned toward the notice board.

"I like this car," Kate informed Sandra. Then she nodded toward Jerome and Linda in the distance. "I think I scared those people."

"The black couple?"

"Yeah. They were filling out a rental application and I went in the manager's office and complained about a sign the manager put up about my friend. Remember I told you about him? The one who got in trouble because of the young girl? It's a sign from Megan's list, like a Wanted sign. Serious sex offender in apartment T11. "

"That stinks. It reminds me of what people are doing to Muslims now. I've heard of people doing that to sex offenders in Texas. I thought a judge stopped it."

"I bet you didn't scare that couple, though," Sandra added. "I don't think black people like to see someone singled out for condemnation any more than Muslims do. They may be more afraid of the policies at your apartment complex than of Danny."

"Of course the manager said she did it to protect children. But that's B.S. I think the girl hurt Danny more than he hurt her," Kate blurted out. Sandra didn't reply. "Pretty radical, huh?" Kate admitted.

"Maybe you should talk to a few victims. Maybe you're only seeing one side."

"But there's no shortage of victim stories. They're spilling their guts every day on Oprah. Now everybody wants to be a victim." Kate remembered that Candace at the college was an Oprah fan, but she doubted Sandra was. And I don't even own a TV, Kate reflected. Oh, she had caught a bit of Oprah at her mother's house in Detroit. People were confessing all sorts of things on TV—and being praised as brave for doing it.

Sandra pressed her lips together and tilted her head and Kate could see she was skating on thin ice, straining another friendship. Already, Abigail —she of the Megan's law notebook—was acting noticeably cooler toward Kate than before, despite their common backgrounds in TV. Yet it didn't distress Kate much. She wondered if it should.

But she did care about what Sandra thought, so when she ran across something later that day, it led her to take Sandra up on her suggestion to investigate victims' viewpoints.

It was in a weekly newsmagazine she had at home near the top of a pile of reading material she'd been intending to get to. Kate had picked it up months ago, just after the discovery of Danielle van Dam's body in San Diego, and the arrest of the van Dam's neighbor as a suspect. The magazine was obviously related to the super hype about the case—its all-black cover and white letters screaming "Their Teachers Molested Them." Although Kate was a little ashamed of her interest in something so sensationalistic, she had taken the magazine.

In fact, she had started reading it. But it was so long and so depressing. It reminded her of Abigail's notebooks full of Megan's law information.

So she hadn't gotten around to reading the magazine. But after two more abductions of girls—and after Sandra had said Kate needed to learn victims' viewpoints—she resolutely carried the magazine to the beach one beautiful, misty morning, walked a short distance from the parking lot, crumpled down on the sand and immersed herself in the meticulous accounts of Karen, Sarah, Gary and Alejandra—people who, as teens, had been molested in some way, shape or form.

In fact, many of these ways, shapes and forms, seemed to Kate a stretch. She was just coming to the conclusion that none of them justified the grim, black cover with its suggestion of evil with a capital E, when she noticed in the near distance Mona bobbing along toward her, up and down the beach's sandy knolls. Kate had arrived early and Mona late. Kate found she had been reading for almost an hour. She stood and brushed the sand off her legs, leaving the magazine with its black cover facing up on the sand.

"'Their Teachers Molested Them.' My goodness!" intoned Mona as she walked up.

"It's not like it sounds." As Kate bent over and picked up the magazine, her yellow highlighter fell out.

"You're serious about this!" Mona raised her eyebrows.

Kate felt sheepish about the highlighter. "It's my new crusade to learn the victim's point of view. But so far I'm underwhelmed. For one thing, some of the molesters weren't even teachers. They were friends of the parents. A couple of the kids had a lot of affection for their molesters. Plus, there wasn't any violence or coercion. In fact, none of it was full- fledged sex—it was touching or back rubs gone erotic—stuff like that. One victim actually carries around a photo of her molester's baby daughter in her wallet to this day. Another one said she loved her molester, a woman who was a friend of her mother, and even had her in her wedding party."

"There was a lecture in medical school," Mona replied. "A doctor said it was tough to get a handle on molesting, because often the children like it. I'll never forget it. 'Children can be sexual too,' he said."

"I wasn't. I didn't have the slightest interest in boys until I was maybe 12."

"Well, I suppose that's who he meant. Didn't you tell me a lot of child molestation victims aren't actually children? They're teenagers or young teenagers?"

"Well, yes, and in the story, the youngest one was in fifth grade." Kate flipped and scanned the pages. "Yes ... Sarah. Her fifth-grade teacher reached under her clothes when she sat on his lap studying math. Then Karen. She was 13. A teacher kissed and touched her on a ride at Disneyland, in one of those House of Horror rides. Later she had a sexual relationship with a married woman who was a friend of her mother's and who more or less adopted her. Then there's Alejandra. She was 16. She says she fell in love with her married physics teacher and became suicidal after her mother found out about it and the police were closing in on him. And Gary. Oh—he was younger. He had sexy encounters with a nun when he was only in second grade. She was a close friend of his mother. That sounds pretty weird. But there were no threats in any of these, except the nun told Gary not to tell anyone."

"Come on. Are we walking south?" said Mona. Kate rolled up the magazine and soon the parking lot was a distant memory and the only signs of civilization were surfers and the occasional, jarring glimpse of the nuclear reactor towers.

"This is a famous surfing beach," Mona said. "A spot called The Trestles is internationally known. President Nixon gave part of the Camp Pendleton base to be used as a park down there where the base meets the beach. And farther down, there's a trail that leads to a remote area that's a nude beach. I used to go with my sister to a nude beach called Black's Beach in San Diego, before medical school. I've heard the one here is a hotspot for gay men. "

"Are we going there?"

"It's pretty far."

"I've never been to a nude beach," Kate said. "Well, I made one just for me—on a little island in Greece. But I don't know if I want to go to one now."

"It's a lot different from what you probably think. Or at least Black's Beach was. There were old people ... fat people ... people playing volleyball. It was actually less sexy than beaches where people wear bathing suits."

Well, well, Kate thought. Mona has—or had—a wild side. And as a slightly chubby person, she had probably qualified as one of those less sexy people at Black's Beach. Now her willingness to go there made her interest in a cause as unpopular as opposing the death penalty seem more understandable.

"Did I mention to you about the age of consent?" Kate asked.

"At the nude beach?"

Kate laughed. "No, in general. In the story." She shook the rolled-up magazine for emphasis. "The legal age of consent. I've been reading up on it. Alejandra was 16. If she'd lived in a lot of countries—like Canada, Austria or Germany, I think—the age of consent there is 16. It's 16 in a lot of states in the U.S. too. So if her story had been told, like, in Germany, it would've sounded way different. It wouldn't have been about molesting and predators and victims. Maybe it would've been about an affair and a broken heart.

"And in other countries ... Japan, Korea, Mexico, or a lot of South American countries ... I read the age of consent there is 13. So Karen, in the story ... she was 13. That sounds pretty young to us. But if she'd been Japanese, her relationship with an adult wouldn't have been a crime.

"And did you notice the cover?" Now Kate unrolled the magazine briefly to expose it to Mona. "All black, just like the cover in the other magazine with the article you showed me about that kid Jason. Black is the color of death, and despair, and evil. So ... something that's acceptable in some places ought to be viewed as deepest, darkest evil? And besides that, look who's complaining ..." Kate was minimally aware she was rambling on, but Mona's serene, neutral expression encouraged her to continue. "You don't hear girls in their teens or twenties complaining about men falling for them. It's only people like us that are almost over the hill. Do you think we're jealous? And we're in the majority now ... we're the baby boom ... women in our forties and fifties. I've always had a secret desire for somebody to call me 'baby.'" Mona's body language—little nods and uh-huh's—prodded Kate into following this new tangent.

146

"Why is that? Why do people in love use diminutives like honey and sweetie? I saw some articles during the summer, after Danielle. You know, the papers are full of stuff about sex crimes. These articles were on, like, the Community Page. They were written by ordinary women, I think—maybe teachers—they said 'inappropriate' and 'sociopath' a lot. They were criticizing girls who wear sexy clothes like padded bras and leather pants. They said they weren't blaming girls for attacks against them but I think they were trying to have it both ways, because they made a connection between murders of little girls and girls wearing sexy clothes. But, well, don't you think that when people come down so hard on girls being sexy, it's from jealousy? And besides, they're battling nature. It's natural for men to be attracted to smooth skin and full breasts—they're signs of fertility. It's a survival mechanism."

Mona finally made an objection, but she still seemed relatively accepting of Kate's rant. "But I don't think lowering the age of consent is going to go over," Mona said. "Especially now, after those three girls. Didn't you say things are moving in the opposite direction—that the age of consent is going up? I heard that some gay men were advocating man-boy sex. I imagine that's got some people upset."

"Yeah. I read an article by a criminologist who said that a lot of Americans have decided to put up with behavior that they still feel is unnatural. So they go around feeling angry, but they can't admit it, and they need some place to put their anger and criminals are the only socially acceptable targets. And that's what's behind the tough on crime movement. And you know what else? I think that September 11 is what is behind all the fear about the murders. In those articles, they said parents who don't let their girls wear sexy clothes are like F14s protecting the White House against terrorism."

"I saw something about girls and sexy clothes on Larry King Live. That was after those other two abductions—Samantha and Elizabeth. You knew about them, right?"

"How could I not know? Samantha was from Orange County. I don't have a TV, but you'd have to be living in a closet not to hear about it."

"You don't have a TV? You must be the only person in L.A. that doesn't. TV is king here. A lot of programs are made right here."

"Believe me, I know. I used to work in TV, remember?" To Mona's nod, she continued, "On Larry King, did they mention the 'sexualization' of young girls? That was another word in the articles—'sexualization.' I think that was the first time I ever heard that word."

Mona laughed. "I don't think Freud would like the idea that children get sexualized. He had ideas about Oedipus and Electra complexes—you know, sexual attraction between parents and their children—and oral, anal and genital stages. Well, none of that leaves much room for the idea that children were ever non-sexual to begin with! But Freud's ideas don't go down very well anymore. Behaviorism is in vogue here. It's more quantifiable—more of a science than an art, they say. In other cultures, people seem more accommodating of the idea that children experience sexual pleasure. In India, a mother will stroke her baby son's penis to calm him down."

"I had a friend in college from India!" Kate replied, eager to support Mona's idea with what she knew. "He was a big, handsome guy named Suresh. And he said he loved to go home to India because he could sleep with his mother! He said he would throw his leg over hers in the night! I think if that happened here, somebody would be calling the police." Then Kate remembered what Polly had said. "At the risk of sounding idiotic, though, I heard Freud was passé."

"Oh, I don't know about that," Mona said, sounding as if she knew very well about it. "I'm also pretty skeptical that padded bras and leather pants are causing girls to be murdered. There seems to be a general fascination with sexy clothes. Have you seen the full-page bra ads in the newspaper? Have you been in the bra department at Macy's? It's huge. They have one huge room after another. Bras, bras and more bras, every imaginable color, style and size. And in the dressing room, they actually have a sign saying men aren't allowed in!"

"Really?" said Kate. But as they continued walking, and visions of Macy's bra department faded from her mind, with nothing else to distract her except sea, sky and sand, her mind went back to the magazine.

"The more I think about this article," once again she twirled the rolled up magazine. "Their Teachers Molested Them ..." she scoffed, "the more I think that other people's reaction to what happened was what caused the kids' trauma—not just the events themselves."

"But are you being objective? You only read one article," Mona protested.

"Well, that's true. Okay, I guess I'm quick to take Danny's side. But everywhere you look you see people claiming the opposite—that the illicit sex or the crime, or whatever, caused the trauma. That's the standard idea in the public mind. I don't know if I'd ever find another article that supports my conclusion. And, of course, it's just my conclusion, from reading between the lines. I doubt these kids would agree with me, at least consciously, and in fact they said some things that support the standard conclusion." Kate unrolled the magazine and zeroed in on a quote. "He stole the innocence I had ... I should have waited at least till I was 18 and learned frfrom someone in a committed relationship." Kate rolled her eyes slightly and turned toward Mona. "Well, shouldn't we all have?"

"Well, context does have a huge influence on meaning," Mona stated. Kate wasn't sure if this meant that Mona supported or opposed her idea that the general reaction to a crime caused the trauma. But, encouraged by her tone, Kate continued reading. "It said Alejandra became suicidal after her mother found out and the police were closing in on the physics teacher. It wasn't until later—after therapy—that she said she felt cheated by the teacher."

"But wouldn't everyone agree that sex with a person your own age is ideal?" Mona said.

"Well, what bothers me is that it seems like someone—the therapist probably—painted a picture of a house with a white picket fence for Alejandra, like everything would be great if only she hadn't gotten involved with that nasty teacher. And she didn't even have sex with him! And besides, I was in a committed relationship the first time, but I still cried afterward—I wasn't a virgin anymore! And, who wouldn't feel bad with the police chasing the guy? And we have to keep in mind what would've happened if Alejandra had lived in Austria. Probably nothing. It was the police and her mother—and her therapist—who cheated her," Kate insisted.

To Kate's surprise, Mona now seemed agreeable to this, or maybe she just didn't want to continue arguing. "It's true that people don't get angry about plain old misfortune—it's when misfortune is considered as injury, especially when there's a sense of entitlement. When that girl said she felt cheated—that's entitlement."

Kate stopped to flip through the magazine and a small ocean wave came darting in and licked around her ankles. Her eyes sifted through text she had highlighted yellow. "Here. Gary says his 'trust issues' could be traced back to Sister Priscilla getting him to trust her. Then Karen said she hadn't let Carmen penetrate her, so that was why she didn't let later lovers penetrate her emotionally." Kate rolled her eyes slightly, then read on.

"But look here. First Karen says that when the relationship was occurring 'I didn't remember, then, ever feeling uncomfortable about it.' But then she changes her tune. She says the relationship was what later caused her to use marijuana and cocaine, to have an eating disorder and marital problems. She's blaming it for everything. But then, down here, she mentions what I think is the real reason she felt bad about Carmen. 'I had tons of friends but I was afraid if I let them know who I was, they would judge me and not want to be my friends.' She says all the kids in her high school were terribly shocked to find out the gym teacher was a lesbian, so she certainly didn't want anybody to know about Carmen."

"Socially constructed trauma." Mona pronounced the words carefully. "I think that's what you're talking about."

Kate wanted to turn this new concept over in her mind, but their conversation suddenly veered onto the alarming fact that a couple of guys sunning just ahead were naked. They turned back to the parking lot.

"I guess that old Black's Beach feeling is gone," Mona said. "I wonder how it is there now. I haven't gone in years. Maybe now it's a gay hangout too. And speaking of socially constructed trauma, and socially constructed acceptance too, I guess, that's Black's Beach all the way. You play volley-ball one time with a bunch of naked people and you stop worrying about where to look."

With that, the tank that fueled their discussions seemed to run dry, so during the remainder of the walk back to their cars, Kate was content to watch the tide recede from the damp beach and the long-legged birds run across the glassy sand looking for a snack.

*

Kate felt somber by the time she rolled in to Green Manor, and it didn't help that she anticipated passing the sign with Danny's picture, which that morning she had ruefully noticed was still there, although it had faded a bit. The long gate creaked open, and she could see the notice in the distance. But wasn't something different? Yes, it had definitely changed. As she got closer, she realized with a shock that it was now a smiley face. She stopped. Underneath the smiley face, something was printed—HAVE A GREAT DAY—in a strangely incongruous, super-ornate Gothic font.

She almost laughed out loud, thinking immediately of Trevor and Kari. The smiley face on white paper had been glued to the outer side of the glass, completely blocking the poster of Danny underneath. As she sat there for a few seconds, incredulous, she noticed in her rear view mirror that the manager had come out of the office. She seemed to be glaring at Kate. Kate let up the brake and moved on. But then she noticed that Mary Ann was walking along behind her car. So she stopped again, rolled down her window and turned her head to face Mary Ann.

"I suppose you think that's funny," she said. Kate noticed Mary Ann had on an unusual quantity of bright red lipstick today and it was seeping out of the corners of her mouth.

"Well, yes, a little," Kate confessed, apologetically.

"Just so you know, it's all been recorded on our security cameras."

"Well, I didn't do it," said Kate. "But I'm happy somebody did. Can't you just take it down?"

Kate wasn't sure what she meant should be taken down—the smiley face or Danny's picture under it. But it didn't matter because the manager abruptly turned and walked away. Kate's heart pounded as though she were guilty. Oh of course, she thought, we can't not have security cameras. There are far too many important people here. I'm sure Osama bin Laden himself is after somebody in this apartment complex. Then she realized that with all the military people living there, her ironic assessment might just be correct. But she didn't want to pursue that line of thought, so she drove to her little garage and got out of the car, noticing she had deposited a lot of beach sand on the floor under the driver's seat.

As she walked up the concrete stairs to her apartment, she kept stepping on bits of packing material. Somebody must be moving into the empty apartment next door. As she turned, key extended, toward her door, she stopped in surprise for the second time in just a few minutes.

A gold spray-paint scribble defaced her door. Her blood began to race again. Who could have done that? Had it been a random thing or did somebody dislike her? Could it have been Trevor and Kari? But no, they seemed to like her. Had it been that way this morning when she left? Surely she would have noticed.

She let herself into her apartment, feeling almost queasy from nerves, and absentmindedly attended the little, blinking red light on her answering machine. "Hi Kate. This is Liam Michalewicz—Bart—your cousin. Thanks for calling, and yes, I'd like to see you. Could you have lunch sometime?"

Good old Bart—oops, Liam. Where had he come up with that name? —from that Irish movie star? Well, it was better than Osama. Her cousin Bart had always been a very quiet guy, quieter than Kate. In fact, Bart had been painfully quiet. This, together with being very tall, very thin and very blond, made him quite noticeable, something Kate was sure was unwelcome to such a retiring soul. She wasn't sure what he was doing here in Los Angeles, or even what his background was, as she hadn't seen much of her father's side of the family since she was a kid. They were a cantankerous Polish clan and usually deep into some dispute or another. Kate knew Uncle Mickey was a policeman, and she even thought Bart, or Liam, may have been one too. Police work seemed a particularly bad choice for him. Maybe it was that he had always been a bit of a social clod, and Kate thought that a policeman, at least a good one, ought to be congenial. Bart's message, just now, was one of the most congenial things she'd ever heard come out of his mouth. Maybe he'd changed. Maybe his personality changed when his name did—Bartek to Liam. Kate didn't know when that had happened—probably recently, since Uncle Mickey had mentioned it in his letter.

Kate called Liam back almost immediately, since he'd left his office number. A receptionist answered, "Tower of Hope." Kate was so taken aback by the name—Tower of Hope??—that she blurted out, "May I please speak to Bart Michalewicz?"

The receptionist said nothing, so Kate quickly corrected herself. "I mean Liam! Liam Michalewicz!"

"Um, you mean Mickey Michalewicz, right?" the receptionist said, pronouncing the last name, correctly, just as Kate had—"mi-ha-LEY- vich."

Now Bart had taken his father's first name? "Well, I suppose so. There can't be more than one Michalewicz in an office," Kate said.

"Yeah. Everybody just calls him Mickey," replied the receptionist in a friendly voice. "May I ask who's calling?"

"Kate Michel." She paused, and then added, "So it's not Bart? Not Liam?"

"Nope! Just Mickey!"

Since they seemed to be getting on well, Kate added, "You pronounce the name very well. It's my name too, sort of. I'm his cousin. My dad changed our name, though, to Michel. It's easier."

"Yeah. We get a lot of calls for him from the courts. They really massacre his name. So he's trained people to just ask for Mickey."

The courts? Bart-Liam-Mickey got calls from the courts? "If you don't mind my asking," Kate added, "What does Tower of Hope mean?"

The receptionist hesitated again. "I mean," Kate put in, "I obviously know what a tower is, and I know what hope is, but why is this business named Tower of Hope?"

But the receptionist still seemed confused. "Well," she finally began, in a sweet, lilting voice, "We offer sex therapy. And I guess we offer our clients hope. I'm sure Mickey can explain it better. Shall I put you through to him?"

As Kate's call went on hold, at first she was confused too. Wasn't sex therapy like Masters and Johnson? What could the courts have to do with that? And she hadn't been aware that sexual problems were considered terribly hopeless. Then it hit her square in the gut: Courts. Sex therapy. Mickey. Danny mentioned a Mickey. Can my own goofy cousin Bart be Danny's stupid therapist? The one who'd invited her to ante up as Danny's significant other? Unaccountably, fear gripped Kate's stomach as she wondered if Danny had mentioned her name during therapy.

She almost slammed down the phone. In fact, she would have, except at that moment, Bart picked up. "Kate?"

"Bart?" she blurted out. "I mean, Liam? Or Mickey? What should I call you? Uncle Mickey said you'd changed your name to Liam."

He laughed. "It's a long story. Call me Liam. Mickey is just for convenience. But how are you?"

He certainly sounded a lot more composed than Kate felt and a lot more suave than the teenager she remembered. Kate's mind was racing, this time from fear that Danny had mentioned her name, and it suddenly threw out a solution. "I'm fine thanks. And you know what? I changed my first name too—to Kathy."

"Kathy?" Liam said. "The secretary told me Kate."

"Well, I didn't want to confuse you. I didn't know if you'd pick up if I said I was Kathy." She laughed nervously. "I've always liked that name. So when I moved here to California, I thought, now's the time for a change!" If Kate had had the time to think clearly, she would have been slightly ashamed at realizing that she had always hated the name Kathy and she used to stop people from calling her that.

"OK. How long have you been in L.A.?"

"Are we in L.A.? I live in Orange County." Better skip the joke about behind the Orange Curtain, Kate thought. Who knew what her cousin's political persuasions were? She already felt as if she were talking too much. "You know I teach at Orange Grove Community college?"

"Yeah. Then we're not too far apart, at least our offices. I'm in an area that's a little downscale. It's tough to find an office," he apologized.

She let that slide, but made a mental note to expect Bart's office to be a dump. That was strange, though. It seemed to Kate that there were oodles of For Rent signs, especially in the economic downturn after 9/11. And she wondered where in Orange County one could find something described as "downscale." But these thoughts were just a passing blur as she began grappling with the reality that it looked like she was going to have lunch with a guy Danny called "Asshole." She hoped her newly acquired name wasn't going to trip her up. And him a therapist! Wouldn't he see through all her nervousness?

Kate and her cousin set a date for their lunch, arranging to meet at a restaurant midway between the college and Bart's office. Kate certainly didn't want to go to Bart's office, not because it was downscale, but because she had the horrifying thought that she could run into Danny there. But hadn't Danny said his regular appointment was at night?

Kate sincerely hoped she'd feel calmer in a week.

She wondered if she'd tell Bart she had a friend in one of his groups. To this question, her mind immediately screamed No, No, No! She wondered if she'd tell Danny, if she saw him, that she was having lunch with his therapist. To this, her mind firmly intoned, Not a good idea. She remembered Danny telling her about some kind of truth-extracting arrangement he had with Bart. So confiding in Danny was out—who knew what he'd feel obligated to say to his therapist? With a shudder, she remembered the difficult times she'd had during primary school about having to go to Confession to a priest, the Inquisitorial stipulation that she tell all, or else incur the wrath of Hell all the more for having left something out. In fact, now that she thought of it, she knew Bart had been through the same school system. Maybe that was how he came up with his truth regimen.

Considering her long walk almost to the nude beach that day, the smiley face on Danny's Wanted poster, the confrontation with the manager, the defaced door, the surprise conversation with Danny's torturer, and her sudden name change, Kate needed a nap. But just after she dozed off on the sofa, a thump and crash outside made her remember the graffiti. She jumped up, flinging open her door, and immediately felt ashamed when confronted with her new neighbors in the process of moving.

"Oh!" Kate said, still woozy from sleep. "You look familiar!"

The woman looked steadily at Kate and said, "Oh, yes. You came in the manager's office when we were there. We're sorry about the noise. And the mess. We're Linda and Jerome Daniels and that's our daughter O'enn." Somebody who might have been Jerome was passing them, carrying a pile on his head from which a blanket hung, half covering him. A girl was kneeling on the landing, picking up books and pots that had fallen out of a box and made the noise that awakened Kate.

"I'm Kate Michel. No problem about the noise. I have this graffiti on my door so I'm a little nervous."

"I noticed it," Linda said, biting her lip. "It wasn't here when we looked at the apartment."

"I didn't even know your apartment was empty. It has two bedrooms, doesn't it?"

"Yes," Linda said. "Actually, we almost didn't move in because they put up the sign about your friend. We didn't like them doing that. But we were staying with friends and we're desperate to get O'enn settled in school. We might only have a few weeks together before Jerome goes to the Middle East."

"Well, like I said, he isn't dangerous, so don't worry."

"No, it's not that, although it crossed our mind. Mostly, we just don't like the idea they put up notices about people who live here. I'm from an all-black town in North Carolina, and I never heard of anything like that. Except maybe 50 years ago."

"100 years ago. 200 years ago," said Jerome, as he emerged from the apartment and passed Kate and Linda. "We should make a petition against it." He threw these comments over his back as he disappeared down the stairs.

"Jerome's from Atlanta," Linda explained, smiling. "He's uppity."

"Well, I'm from Detroit, which is mostly black too. They have Megan's law, I suppose — all the states do. That's what's behind these notices. But I never heard of it when I was there. I think it's way bigger here than in Michigan. Plus, for months Danny and his family have been wanting to move but the manager says there are no two-bedroom apartments. And now she's rented this one to you. It's certainly not your fault. I'm sure there are other vacant two-bedroom apartments. But she probably won't rent any of them to Danny. She wants them to leave."

"That's housing discrimination. Isn't there a government agency he can complain to?" Linda asked.

"I doubt it. A government agency started the whole thing." Kate paused to take a breath. "A petition is a good idea, except ..." she hesitated and looked at her defaced door, "you and Jerome are almost the only people I know here, except Danny. I guess he'll sign it. But I don't know if anybody else would. And I don't know why this graffiti happened to me. A while ago, I watched some women harassing another guy who the manager posted a sign about. I don't think they lived here, but maybe they were mad at me and that's why I got the graffiti."

Linda, looking steadily and seriously at Kate, sighed almost inaudibly. Kate imagined she was wondering if she should have moved into this hornet's nest, especially with her husband leaving soon.

"Don't worry," Kate said. "Nothing's going to happen to you."

"Yeah, well, I just hope nobody puts a burning cross out here," Linda replied.

Kate almost laughed, but realized that something similar had passed through her own mind.

The next day, Kate called the apartment office. But when she asked if the door could be repainted, the manager said Kate had to do it at her own expense.

"But it was vandalism!" Kate protested.

"Just like the smiley face pasted over our warning sign?"

"I didn't do that either!"

"We know you didn't. We have the photos. The point is that some people commit vandalism and then expect us to clean it up."

"Who pasted over your sign?"

"Two kids — a boy and a girl, we think. They looked around 13, 14. They were wearing big Mexican sombreros, so we're not sure."

Kids in sombreros? Again, Kate thought of Kari and Trevor. Who else would cover up Danny's Wanted poster?

"You must have an idea," she said to Mary Ann innocently.

"Yes, and they will be dealt with," Mary Ann replied.

Now Kate was getting angry—and thinking harder about the petition that Jerome had mentioned.

*

"Kathy ... Kathy ... Kathy ... Kathy ... Kathy," Kate repeated aloud in the morning as she drove to work a week later, ruefully using the repeat-it-five-times technique she told her students to use to memorize information for art history exams. And don't even get near the topic of Danny and all that. This is just my goofy cousin that I used to have good times with—although when she tried to think of some, she really couldn't. All she remembered was seeing The Endless Summer at a theater in the Fisher Building with Bart and his brother when they were all teenagers, and thinking the movie was endlessly boring. Bart seemed to enjoy it, but since he never said much, it was hard to know. Maybe his attraction to the endless scenes of waves and rapturous surfers explained why he'd ended up in California. Kate didn't know what explained her presence in the Golden State—and she was starting to hope she hadn't "ended up" there.

At the last minute, Bart called Kate's cell phone to say he had a little emergency, was running late and would Kate mind driving to his office. She agreed reluctantly, keeping it firm in her mind that Danny's appointment was at night. When she drove to Bart's office, it was already near 3 and she saw it was indeed in an area that, while not exactly 'downscale,' was non-descript and depressing—a combination office center and strip mall almost hidden in the shadow of a couple overarching freeway ramps. The mall had an adult video store as well as something called Patty Pants Gentlemen's Club. It would have been hard to find a less ostentatious location in Orange County for such an ostentatiously named business as "Tower of Hope."

But soon Kate started to understand Bart's difficulty in finding a rental.

Passing through a covered landing outside his office, she came upon a knot of smoking men—probably clients taking a break, she realized. Then her heart thumped.

Clients! Sex offenders! And Danny could be here! What if he came early on this one day? Kate looked nervously at the sun and saw that it was still safely situated well away from the horizon. She was surprised at her silly reaction. Regardless, she seriously considered leaving, and telling Bart she'd had a flat tire. But the men had seen her and, although they were barely looking at her, a college professor should not be seen doing about-faces in sleazy parking lots.

Inside, she was spared much time in the waiting room, where a television played for a lone man who stared at it. The receptionist sat behind glass, although she still seemed friendly. She immediately showed Kate out of the waiting room and to Bart-Liam-Mickey's private office.

The door was open and, inside, a figure silhouetted in the glare of a window could be seen standing next to his desk and computer and putting on a suit jacket.

Oops—Bart isn't skinny anymore. In fact, as he turned toward her and her eyes adjusted, she saw further that he hadn't aged well. Could this tall and almost portly middle aged man with a bulbous nose the same shade of red as the rest of his face be her cousin whom she remembered being, while not exactly gorgeous, pleasant looking?

"Kate!" he exclaimed, with a brief hug. "Good to see you, kiddo! Sorry about being late. I had a little emergency. Thanks for coming over. How about if we go in my car?"

"OK," she said, realizing in the back of her mind that Bart had apparently forgotten her new name. And what about that "kiddo?" Wasn't she actually six months older than him? And that red nose and face — does he drink too much or what? She pondered how to remind him that he should call her Kathy. Of course, her insistence might ring false and if he was psychologist enough to detect that—he, the famed extractor of truth —then maybe her ruse would be exposed.

But Bart diverted her attention from this worry with an unexpected revelation. "Hey, sorry about this," he said, pointing to his head. "I just had hair transplants." Squinting at his hulking silhouette, Kate saw he was indicating a series of little scabby knots of hair near his hairline. She hadn't noticed them in the glare, but now that he had pointed them out, she was disconcerted by them—and by the Patty Pants sign visible through the window directly behind his head, integrated with a curvaceous pink derriere. All of this seemed to notch down the stature of the famed interrogator.

Kate searched for an adequate response. "Oh really?" she said.

"Yes, really," he said flatly.

"Well ... is my car OK out there," she flashed him a little nervous smile, "with only Patty Pants to protect it?" Bart assured her it was.

"What was the emergency?" Kate ventured as she settled into Bart-Liam-Mickey's Lamborghini, realizing belatedly that if he was regularly parking his stupendous ride here, surely no thief would molest her bottom-of-the-line Toyota.

"You don't want to know. We had to do some testing on a man involved in a child protective services case."

"Why don't I want to know?"

"Oh, a lot of dirty details. I'm a social worker, but I don't do the type of work most people think of when they hear 'social work.' It's pretty easy to get burnt out. And today I was pressed for time, which is why I ran late."

As Kate was sitting quite close to Bart in the tiny car, she noticed that he reeked of espresso and, for no reason she could fathom, it disgusted her. "Your receptionist mentioned that you work with courts," she hinted, realizing belatedly that she'd gotten herself squarely into the topic she'd planned to avoid. But I will steer clear of the slightest mention of Danny or anybody like him, she promised herself, sensing that her curiosity had already eroded her resolve.

"Well, this was a little different. There was insufficient evidence to generate a criminal charge. The court isn't involved ... yet."

Kate mulled that over. She realized it couldn't have been a case like Danny's, which definitely involved a criminal charge. This sounded voluntary. But why would somebody volunteer to have the kind of tests Danny mentioned that "Asshole" gave? Finally, she couldn't resist a question.

"So you did a psychological test on somebody suspected of ... being an unfit father?"

"More or less."

"Hmm." Kate pondered that as Bart made a u-turn on a left arrow, a quirk of California roads she couldn't get used to. In the silence, she noticed that she was hugging the car door, straining to put a little more physical distance between herself and him. Was it the espresso smell? But she liked coffee! She observed her emotions and realized she was getting ever so slightly riled up. She had to be careful.

"You're saying 'hmm' like that's a strange idea," Bart commented after he'd executed the u-turn.

Kate glanced at him, feeling more perturbed. He was impassive, staring ahead and seemingly deep in concentration on the road. She imagined his reaction was typical for a therapist — she'd been in therapy once — but this had an inquisitorial feel, as if an overhead spotlight had clicked on. "I say 'hmm' when I'm thinking. I guess you mean there wasn't enough evidence to take the guy to court."

"We see a lot of deniers in this type of situation."

As her anger mounted, her resolve to avoid mention of anyone like Danny faded. I don't have to mention Danny specifically, she rationalized to herself as she plunged on. "So ... you're sort of on a fishing expedition and you expect them to be lying. What sort of tests are they?"

"Nothing you've ever heard of. They're only used in the field of sex offenses."

"Try me," said Kate. "I used to be a news researcher. I've heard of a lot."

"One is the plethysmograph. It uses sexual stimuli and measures changes in the penis. The other is the Abel test. It measures reaction time to sexual photos. Not exactly cocktail party topics."

Kate laughed. "Was that a Freudian slip?" Bart gave her a deadpan look—just like the old Bart she remembered. She continued, "You said 'cocktail.' You were talking about testing penises."

"Oh," he said flatly.

"Sorry, I'm a fan of Freud," she said, momentarily marveling that here they were, she and her cousin, calmly discussing penises. She thought about reminding him that he'd brought up the risqué topic.

"My work doesn't draw much on people like Freud. In fact, we throw up our hands at him. We use CBT. Cognitive behavioral treatment."

"Oh. Like Pavlov's dogs. Behaviorism is a little mechanistic for me."

"That was only the beginning—the 'B' in CBT," Bart countered, "back in the dark ages. We use it in aversive conditioning tasks. But now, of course, we've added the 'C,' for cognitive. We employ a lot of peer pressure—the other guys in the group telling someone that what he said was BS."

"Maybe they should call it CBST." Kate thought her little joke was outstandingly clever and she had to suppress several outbursts of giggles. But it produced no discernible mirth in Bart's stern visage which, she was starting to realize, reminded her of a balding Chewbacca from Star Wars. But Freud and Pavlov were tangents. And Bart's reminder about "peer pressure" started to kindle Kate's temper again. She returned to her earlier point. "So why would somebody take one of your tests if they weren't forced?"

"No. They want to. They're trying to clear themselves. They're not my usual type of client, but it's quite common. Somebody is accused of molesting his daughter. Or it could be an uncle, or family friend, or a coach. But it's just the mother's or the child's word against his. So he's trying to establish that he doesn't have deviant tendencies."

"What an ordeal. But ... when the results aren't favorable to the man, which it sounds like they aren't a lot of the time, then I suppose confidentiality isn't a concern in your type of social work?"

"Confidentiality? No. I consider my obligation to be to the public —public safety. Most of my clients are convicted of sex crimes. I don't concern myself with their rights."

By this time they had parked and were on their way into the restaurant. "You're following in Uncle Mickey's footsteps then?"

"How so?"

"He was a policeman. You said 'public safety.' Don't police usually work in 'public safety' departments?"

Bart more or less let that drop. "Kiddo, you're the only person I've ever met who's been worried about my clients' rights. Most people are astounded I can treat them like human beings. How'd you get so interested in this, anyway?"

At that moment, the waiter came for their order. She and Bart-Liam-Mickey made their selections—wine and spaghetti for him and a club sandwich and smoothie for her. By then she had an answer ready.

"I don't know that I'm so interested," she said, again feeling clever that she had zeroed in on his "so" just as he had on her "hmmm." "You know I was in television for 30 years?" She didn't know if any more news about her career had reached Bart via the family grapevine than had reached her about his. "Sex crimes are in the news a lot. I'm a researcher at heart."

"I think I knew that. WXYZ, right?" Kate nodded. "But now you're teaching ... what?"

"Art history."

"Oh," he said in a tone that could have reflected either relief or disappointment. "Well ..." he took a sip of wine, "I'm in the news from time to time. Two reporters have called me recently. One came out and took a picture of me at my computer—but you couldn't really tell it was me. It was sort of a profile."

Kate wondered if the Patty Pants sign had been in the background. "Related to Danielle and Samantha and all that, I suppose," she said.

"More or less. There's a lot of interest in sex crimes now. The scandal about Catholic priests. Those murders. Elizabeth Smart's disappearance."

"Do you mind the media's interest in you?"

"No. It builds my credibility. I can always use more of that. It's good for business. But, like I said, it's stressful too."

"The business or the media?"

"Both."

"You know, I don't even remember hearing if you have kids." Kate seemed to recall that Bart had gotten married but she didn't think it had happened in Detroit or she might have been invited to the wedding. Asking about kids was a good way to broach the subject tactfully, she congratulated herself.

"I used to be married," he said. "No kids, though. What about you?" Kate updated him as briefly as possible. She didn't like talking about her marriage—it seemed so long ago. It crossed her mind that Bart's transformation from Bart to Liam could have been part of a divorce.

"Well, if your job's stressful, do you ever think about doing something else?" she asked.

"Every day."

"Well, obviously, without kids, it's not so hard. I left my first career in television, even before my daughter Corey finished college. I liked the research in television, but I didn't like what they did with it. Maybe you could go back to school."

But Bart shook his head no. "I already did that... when I stopped being a probation officer and got a Master's in social work. Maybe I've gotten lazy. Or maybe it's too late. It wasn't that easy to get where I am and I think a lot of people would envy me. And... besides, I'm not willing to go back to eating peanut butter sandwiches."

As they dug into their lunches, Kate was tempted to point out that peanut butter sandwiches were good for you. But a piece of bacon escaped her club sandwich and bounced to the floor, distracting her, so she let her comment drop too. She felt a little sorry for Bart, like he was caught in a bad cycle. She felt even sorrier for him because, there at the table, she had a closer view of the bloody tufts of hair that comprised his hair transplant. A couple of them had little band-aids on them. Maybe the transplant had something to do with the divorce too. At the same time, Kate was close enough to smell that Bart was now, naturally enough, emitting a strong odor of garlic. For dessert, he ordered another glass of wine and an espresso.

"Do you have a significant other?" As soon as Kate said it, she kicked herself mentally for using the same term Danny said Bart used. In fact, Bart now shot her a piercing glance over a sip of espresso, as if he was reading her guilty conscience. But then Kate chided herself for being paranoid. Come on, she told herself, my goofball cousin is no psychic.

"No," came his answer, followed unexpectedly by, "How do you think women feel when they find out I treat sex offenders?"

Although Kate recalled him saying, a second ago, that he was respected, she saw his point about his social life. She murmured something vaguely soothing. Yes, she reflected, his choice of professions really cements his nerdiness, and it even adds a dash of the unsavory. Then Bart asked Kate the reciprocal question and she explained her current lack of a significant other. Of course, there was Danny, but that wasn't going anywhere, and Kate was still resolved not to touch the topic with a 10-foot pole.

With Bart-Liam-Mickey's non-stop ordering of wine and espresso, the lunch seemed to go on and on. Kate hoped a person his size could drive after imbibing three generous glasses of wine and, by the time they peeled into his parking lot, she could have used a glass too.

"Are they strict here about drinking and driving in California?" Kate asked, wanting to jump out of the Lamborghini and kiss the ground when Bart finally stopped it in his office parking lot. She wondered if combining espresso and wine made you an alert drunk.

"Yeah, sometimes. But if I got stopped, I could probably flash them my union card. I belong to the same union as correctional officers, ever since I worked as a probation officer."

Kate didn't like the sound of it, but she didn't comment, sensing that such an affiliation made her Pollyannish suggestions for a change of profession all the more unlikely.

They said their goodbyes there in the parking lot—no hug this time —and she wondered if they'd see each other again. Her family, especially on her father's side, was so cold, and she was afraid that she, shortened name and all, had inherited the Michalewicz rancor. Poor Bart certainly had. He seemed to be suffering from a big case of middle-age anxiety too.

As he walked off toward his office, Kate opened her trunk to make sure she had some books she needed the next day. Then she glanced up and was taken aback by the sky. The sun was getting low, and it was partly hidden in some peach clouds set off by the Patty Pants sign, now glowing fluorescent hot pink — almost the same color as the hot pink rugby jersey Kate was wearing. The sign was set off by some wispy lavender clouds the same color as the horizontal stripes in the jersey, Kate noticed. She looked up at the dark arc of the freeway overpass framing the whole vista. It was a dramatic view.

"Nice neighborhood, huh?" said a pleasant male voice from a little distance off. Kate turned and saw a clean cut, good looking, smiling man leaning against the open car door of a car with a bright orange surfboard on top. The only thing that marred the scene was that he was having a cigarette.

Kate didn't know if he was being sarcastic. "It's pretty now," she answered.

"I agree," he said. "I was just meditating on it. If you can call this meditating." He held up his cigarette. "Are you going to be a therapist with Mickey?" Kate looked at him in surprise.

"Sorry to be nosy, but when I saw you earlier, I figured you were a therapist. You look like a therapist."

"In this shirt?" Kate asked, thinking her bright jersey too flamboyant for a therapist. The man shrugged. "No. I'm Mickey's cousin," Kate continued. She figured he must've been one of the men on the landing. Shouldn't she feel nervous about being in a sleazy parking lot with someone she now assumed was a sex offender? But, no, this smiling man with the surfboard didn't look very menacing.

He seemed to read her thoughts. "I've often wondered why Mickey chose this location. It's like he's trying to trip us up. He gives us a lot of rules against doing anything risqué. And then he puts his office in this sleazeball plaza."

Realizing that this guy, like Danny had said, was "on a short leash," made Kate's nervousness evaporate. Somebody on a short leash was not about to mess with her. Then her nervousness began to inch up again as she asked a devious question.

"How long have you been coming here?" Her real motive, of course, was to find out if he knew Danny, whom she was always worrying was about to get thrown into prison by this demon she now recognized as her cousin. She dared not ask about Danny directly, although she was starting to wonder why she need feel so nervous. She hadn't done anything illegal.

This back-and-forth cycle—relax, confide, worry, relax—was weighing on Kate after several hours of engaging in it. But what the man said next put her once again in relax mode.

"Too long. Actually, this will be my last time. I cussed him out. With my P.O.'s blessing. I got a better therapist. I'm out of here. I had a last session today with one of his underlings. He goes through them fast. That's why I thought you were a new therapist. You look calm."

Calm? How could he think she was calm when inside she was a raging mess of emotions? Kate might have marveled further at the idea, except that now she was preoccupied by the realization that this handsome guy wasn't on such a short leash after all. "You cussed who out?"

"Mickey. He's borderline abusive. He makes you feel like all you ever think about is sex. And he takes advantage of people's legal vulnerability. He's a bit of a sadist too. I wish probation would get wise to him." He pointed behind himself, to Mickey's Lamborghini. "Obviously, he has a steady flow of clients. Most of them don't know how to get away. I was a police administrator before my offense. Now I'm an accountant. So I have a little more understanding of things. Sorry, I shouldn't unload all this on you—and you're his cousin."

The man was smiling all the time he talked and it went a long way toward diluting the rancor that his words might have otherwise conveyed. And now he smiled even more broadly. "But I'm so happy to be rid of him, I don't even care if you tell him."

Hearing this, Kate's resolve not to confide in him about Danny evaporated like dew on a desert flower. "I'm not exactly sympathetic to ... Mickey. I have a friend who comes here. It's a coincidence, but Mickey is his therapist, and I didn't mention his name to Mickey. But I'm curious if you know him. His name is Danny Fernandez."

"We don't know people's last names, and Mickey handles 150 bodies a week. So no, I don't think so."

"Bodies?"

"That's how Mickey puts it. It's police talk. It's terrible, isn't it? Sorry."

"What was your offense?" As soon as Kate said it, she was shocked at her own audacity.

But the man didn't seem fazed. "My victim was my daughter, when she was 16. I touched her once on her outer clothing and once on her inner clothing. I was already divorced from her mother. I was a sex addict — escort services and that type of thing. Now my daughter is over 18. We're reconciled. I'd like to get married again."

Kate noticed there was none of Bart's self-pitying "Who would have me?" even though this guy probably had more reason for it than Bart. "This is like a confessional," she said, suppressing a smile. "Bless me father, for I have sinned. I disobeyed my parents twice."

"Oh, you're Catholic too!" He smiled broadly. "The silent warriors."

"I was raised Catholic," Kate said. "Twelve years in Catholic schools. With nuns."

"If you're raised Catholic, you're always Catholic, don't you think?"

"I don't know. I think I'm a fallen away Catholic. In my last few years at school, the nuns talked about love, not Catholicism per se. Love God and love your neighbor as yourself. That's what I practice."

"Mickey never talks about love. He'll never allow that anything we did might have been motivated by love, even misguided love. He calls it gratification. In his mind, sex and love are like oil and water—they don't mix. But I know I loved my daughter. I shouldn't have done what I did, and I hurt her a little. But it was more what came later that hurt her. Her mother hates me. Mickey would call what I just said denial."

He took a last puff on his cigarette and threw it to the ground—the smoker's habit Kate most disliked. He must have seen her eyes follow his cigarette butt.

"I want to quit smoking," he said. "It clashes with surfing."

But Kate's mind was on another track. "I'm so worried my friend won't get through his five years of probation. Can it be done?"

"A lot of people have done it. A lot of people fail and sometimes it's not really their fault. He needs an excellent relationship with his probation officer. And to pay all his fines. And attend therapy."

"Somebody at the college where I work teaches yoga to quit smoking. Do you have a card? I can e-mail the information to you." Kate didn't know exactly what had gotten into her, with her rash offer of future contact. Maybe she could share this guy's savvy with Danny, she told herself. But she didn't have time to further analyze her motivation as she examined his simple card. Michel LeDuc. Accountant, Enrolled Agent. "Michel? Your name is Michel? That's my last name!"

"I'm French Canadian. People here laugh at my name. I'm forever saying 'With no e at the end, it's a man.'"

He was very much a man, Kate was starting to notice, with reddish brown hair that might have been tinged with grey, a healthy tan, a slightly rough-shaven face and a wide, flashing, devilish smile.

*

"I like this beach," Kate told Mona. They had come to San Onofre beach in the early morning, ready to once again dare the possible dangers of the nude beach. Kate considered whether she should remove the electric pink jersey she was wearing over a tank top but decided it was still too cool. "It takes longer to get here, but it's more peaceful than beaches farther north." She narrowed her eyes to follow a surfer in the distanc walking toward the sea. "I met a surfer the day I went to have lunch with my cousin."

"Were you at the beach?"

"Far from it. We were in a parking lot under a freeway overpass. He had a surfboard on his car. He's in one of my cousin's groups too. Or was."

"This is your cousin who's the ... therapist or something?"

"Yeah. More like 'or something.' He's half cop, half therapist. Coincidentally—extremely coincidentally—he runs Danny's group therapy."

"Wait. I'm confused. You met a surfer in a parking lot ... while you were having lunch with your cousin? And Danny ... works for your cousin? And you're going out with the surfer?"

Kate laughed. "No. It's confusing. It turns out that my cousin, who's a sort of therapist, owns the business where a judge made Danny go for sex offender therapy. I met the surfer after I had lunch with my cousin, outside my cousin's office. He used to go for therapy in my cousin's business. And we're not going out. I have his card, though. He told me some things I thought could help Danny. Well, he's good looking, that's for sure, but I haven't contacted him."

"Oh," said Mona. She hesitated. "But ... if you go out with this surfer, that would make two sex offenders in your life."

"Well, Danny isn't exactly in my life."

"You said you were interested in him. And now this other guy too. I'm a little worried."

"What if I bump one of them off?" At this, Mona just looked at Kate, so she relented. "Yeah, I suppose you're right. And now, Danny has said little things to me that are like … what they add up to is that he did it. When I told him that I'm upset that he lied to me, he said, very matter-of-fact, 'You can understand why, can't you?' And yeah," Kate shrugged, "I can, but still … it changed something now that I know he lied."

"But didn't you say before that you thought there was a good chance he was lying?"

"Yeah," Kate sighed. "It's funny, though—I never even thought Danny was that good looking. It's a mystery why I got so interested in him. It's not like I went out looking for him. It seems to me to be the other way around. Like there was a plan and I fit into it."

"Whose plan?"

"Well, God's I guess. When there are big coincidences like that, sometimes I think I'm not the one in charge."

"Are you sure it's not the devil?" Mona smiled.

"Do Jewish people—or Unitarians—believe in the devil?"

"I'm practically an atheist. Atheists are even less likely to believe in the devil than God. But anyway, what do you say your role in the plan is?"

"Well, to help." Kate felt sheepish admitting it.

"To help?"

"Well, yes. What's so bad about a person wanting to help somebody? Isn't that what we're supposed to do?" She knew she sounded defensive.

"Well, just be careful."

Kate didn't know whether she was more crestfallen or irritated. But, admitting the possibility that Mona was right, she said, "OK, I will." Then she changed the topic. "Hey, remember that magazine article we were looking at? And remember you mentioned … socially constructed trauma?" Mona nodded.

"Well," Kate continued, "Later I thought about something else—those two teenagers in Antelope Valley last fall. Did you hear about that? That was the opposite—socially constructed acceptance."

"The girls who were kidnapped in a lovers' lane and then rescued?" To Kate's nod, Mona added, "Yeah, I saw them on the Today show afterwards. They were amazingly calm. They both had on a little bow above their hearts, which I think came from a support group that helped them."

"Well," Kate went on, excited to relate her new realization, "You know I don't have a TV, but in the papers at first they used standard procedure and didn't publish the girls' names. But after the Today show, the L.A. Times stopped that and said the stigma of rape must be fading. The thing is, the girls were rescued in a big blaze of gunfire and their kidnapper was killed. Then there was a welcome back party with deputies, their families and everybody cheering and crying. And a writer said that when something is talked about a lot, a social norm of support is created. Well, these two girls practically became celebrities.

"And the whole issue of violence ... you know how people say sex crimes are violent and they cause trauma because they're about anger or power—and it doesn't matter whether or not they involve any force or threats! Well, in this case, the crime actually did involve violence real violence. The guy used a gun! He tied them up with duct tape, and he raped them. But later, they seemed OK. And people say the victim's life is ruined, because of the shame, if anybody finds out. But in this case, tons of people found out. So don't you think it shows that secrecy causes the damage? That it's better if people do find out about it, so that you get that social norm of support?"

"There's something to that," said Mona. "Maybe it could apply to the Catholic priest scandal. All the years of secrecy and cover-up had a bad effect on the victims. But I don't know if it applies to all situations."

"You know what else?" Kate put in. "OK ... they say that handling the victim with kid gloves after a sex crime is to protect them. Well, I think there's more than meets the eye there. In fact, now I don't think that the real idea is to protect kids at all. Remember in the story about the teachers, I said that I thought that the real culprits, the ones causing the trauma the kids said they felt, were the adults who were supposed to be helping them: the police, and their parents and therapists?"

"Yeah?" Mona said.

Kate plunged ahead. "And, you know, there's that other thing we talked about—the age of consent going up. Everyone says it's supposed to protect kids. But other things are happening that don't jive with that. Have you heard of the 'children as molesters' movement?"

"No," Mona answered, a touch of tell-me-more in her voice.

"Well, serious sex offenses are being defined down. For example, sex play between brothers and sisters—it's very common. But now it's being turned into a serious crime. I've read about boys accused of silly things: mooning or laying on their sister in the bathtub. A teacher or social worker finds out and the kid gets dragged off to court. A boy committed suicide in a California juvenile sex-offender institution because he couldn't get out unless he confessed in therapy to a crime he supposedly committed when he was 11.

"Do you realize we actually have juvenile sex-offender institutions in California? No wonder California has such a huge budget! What's more incredible is that right now there are 21 states that execute people convicted when they were 17 or younger."

"I know about that!" Mona said enthusiastically, on home turf discussing the death penalty and tiny little people. "There's been a trend in the United States toward prosecuting children as adults. Laws like that were passed in a lot of states in the 1990s. In California, we passed one with in 2000—Prop 21, I think."

Kate was warming up now as her and Mona's agreement built. "Well, do you know what happened in Florida? I read that a 12-year-old kid got a sentence of life without possibility of parole. And a 15-year-old retarded boy was prosecuted as an adult after his first crime, which was stealing a couple dollars in lunch money. And there was no weapon and the victim wasn't physically harmed and the kid's mother had died, but he spent the next Christmas after his mother died in an adult jail."

"It's like out of a Dickens novel," Mona agreed.

"But how can people on one hand claim to be so vigilant in protecting kids from being molested and from trauma? And then, on the other hand, we send them right into the jaws of traumas like execution and jail?"

It was a rhetorical question and Kate didn't expect an answer, but she let it hang there in the air a second, then went on.

"I ran across something that I think explains it. You won't believe it. You might think I'm crazy ... maybe I am. These two anthropologists studied a subsistence fishing society in the South Seas, and they noticed that the little kids were really good at supposedly difficult adult tasks. So they realized that little kids don't lack ability. And they compared that with European-type societies where kids have a long period when they're not considered good for much—all those years when kids are useless because they're supposed to be getting an education. They're not even allowed to work. And the anthropologists said that our society does this for a reason—but it's not that adult tasks are too hard for kids. You know what they said? That it's to prevent the kids from competing with and threatening adults!"

Again, Kate was watching Mona's expression, which seemed to give her the green light to continue. "Doesn't that explain a lot of things?" she went on. "Like about the age of consent going up? Think about it. Look who's in charge now—us ... baby boomers, people in their fifties who were born after World War II. We're a big demographic bulge, including a lot of politically active women—the so-called feminist majority. So what are we doing while we're in power? We change laws. We make the laws stricter about who young girls can be sexual with. We decide that kids can't even be sexual with each other. We start executing teenagers who commit crimes. We put them in jail. Is that protecting kids? Obviously, no! What's really happening? We're jealous of them!"

As she had been building to her point, Kate's gaze fixated on a spot near the edge of the ocean. There, where the water met the sand, a bright orange blob had materialized alongside a bright orange surfboard. As the last pronouncement issued from her lips, the blob became a man—a surfer in an orange wetsuit. He tucked the board under his arm and began walking. Coming closer, Kate saw he seemed to be looking directly at her. A big smile appeared on his face as he headed right for them.

17. Sounds good

2002 to 2009

ALEX LANDON

"Once the box is opened you can't shut it. No one is going to say it's too expensive."

It was 2008. Megan's law, the Amber alert, Danielle's law, Jessica's law and their ilk had already come and, unfortunately, not gone, when Eric Janus, Dean of the William Mitchell College of Law, made the above observation about the dismal repercussions, especially financial repercussions, of these designer laws. (1)

Yet a few people around that time were heroically trying to close the seductive Pandora's box.

In September, 2009, the U.S. Ninth Circuit Court of Appeal made a ruling that nixed part of a 2006 national law. (2) That law had retroactively required teenagers who committed a sex offense, even at the tender age of 14, to register with police every 3 moOnths for 25 years—and suffer all the results of untouchability illustrated in this book. It was another sorry example of classical principles trampled in the cases of people convicted of sex offenses, flouting the longstanding idea that juveniles are not as capable of reasoning as adults and so should be protected from harsh consequences of lawbreaking.

When the decision to spare teenagers was made, it was based on the Constitution's prohibition of ex post facto (retroactively increased) punishment. Those key phrases—"ex post facto" and "punishment"—highlight how different the 2009 conclusion was from the one about Megan's law that was reached by the U.S. Supreme Court in 2003 and mentioned in another chapter. (3) At that time, the Supreme Court had declared that registration for people who were convicted before Megan's law's passage could not even be classified as "punishment," so of course it couldn't be a violation of the Constitution's ban on "ex post facto punishment"—or, for that matter, cruel and unusual punishment either. The 2009 Court of Appeal decision was a rational interlude in a generally irrational trend. There have been other rational interludes. In 2002 the Supreme Court nixed the execution of the mentally retarded, based on the Constitution's Eighth Amendment ban on cruel and unusual punishments. And in 2005, the high court threw out the death sentences of 70 people who had committed murder when they were teenagers, declaring that executing juveniles was unconstitutional. (4)

Another positive change has been the toning down of a few of the outrageous claims made by politicians. By 2009, seven years after the panic during the summer of 2002, California's new Attorney General Jerry Brown had produced a report on Megan's law that was a mere six pages long—a model of terse and sober prose in comparison to the ballistic misinformation during former Attorney General Bill Lockyer's earlier term in office. (5) Of course, by 2009, Megan's list was on the Internet, so perhaps Brown was painfully aware of how easy it is to fan the flames of public fear into a full-blown panic and how readily the public follows when trusted leaders point the way.

Another welcome change has been that in recent years even the mainstream media—especially print media—have occasionally said goodbye to some myths of the past. For example, attorney Todd Melnick in 2008 was quoted in the Los Angeles Times pointing out that, "Five years ago sex crime recidivism was thought to be 50 percent or higher. Now we know it is closer to 3 percent, particularly for older men." (6)

In addition, in various states, there have been challenges to laws on sex offenders—more precious moments of reason during the long, hot decades of panic and overreaction.

Many more challenges such as these could eventually bring laws on sex offenses into the more rational universe where important ethical and constitutional principles are observed. But it will be a long road. For people convicted of sex crimes, the situation remains grim, and the forces arrayed against them are not only undaunted, but still passing bad laws with gusto.

"There oughta be a law"

However, it is not only sex crimes that get this harsh reaction. We see a toxic atmosphere around other types of crime too.

Here's an example. In 2005, 11-year-old girl, Maribel Cuevas, spent five days in Juvenile Hall, 30 days on house arrest wearing an electronic tracking device, had to hire a lawyer and faced up to four years in custody. Why? Maribel was being charged with felony assault—for allegedly throwing a rock at a boy. (7) Maribel's treatment was made much more likely by the passage some years earlier of Proposition 21, which had weakened the juvenile court's ability to take a protective role, parens patriae, so called because it is like the role of a parent. Proposition 21 had seriously stacked the cards against kids by giving district attorneys the right to charge them in adult court, a major departure from the past, when more emphasis was put on rehabilitating youngsters.

As another example of the growing harshness toward all types of crime, compare two cases of vehicle wrecks, separated by about 50 years, which both involved multiple deaths and elderly drivers.

One happened in 1956, well before the War on Crime got rolling. A train had derailed near Los Angeles and 30 people were killed. The train's elderly engineer admitted he was at fault for driving too fast. He was never charged with a crime.

Contrast that with 2003, after the War on Crime and Victims Rights movement had been rolling along for decades, when 86-year-old George Weller drove his car through the Santa Monica farmers market, killing 10 people and injuring many more. He said he got his gas and brake pedals confused. In this meaner, harsher era, this elderly man was charged with 10 counts of vehicular manslaughter and faced 18 years in prison. In 2006, at 89 years of age, he was convicted, sentenced to five years of probation, and ordered to pay about $107,000 dollars in fines and restitution.

Unfortunately, many of us have grown accustomed to such harsh consequences for crime. We do not have long enough memories to know that things have not always been like this. Neither have we looked outside the United States enough to realize that laws are much less harsh in many countries we consider advanced. Instead, reared in our perhaps excessively law-abiding or fearful culture, we are accustomed to thinking that, when any problem raises its ugly head, "There oughta be a law."

But is there such a thing as too many laws? Californians at times must have thought so, because they voted for a "sunset law," which told state legislators to periodically reconsider and vote upon existing laws. And people also voted in "term limits," a law reducing the number of years legislators could hold office. Both aimed to rein in laws and lawmakers run amuck.

But when it comes to trimming down excessive laws, lawmakers have obviously not taken the lead. What would they do if they didn't argue about proposed laws? Would they have jobs? And even if term limits keep a person from holding office very long, who is to say that fresh, new legislators create fewer or better laws than stale, old legislators? Experienced legislators, once they realize that many laws that "sound good" often have dreadfully counterintuitive results, sometimes do speak out against bad proposals. But normally they do so only if they are not running for re-election.

An excellent example of lawmakers running amuck—and a really low moment in regard to sex crimes—came in late 2003, when former California Governor Gray Davis was squirming in the vise-like grip of Arnold Schwarzenegger, who was getting ready to terminate Davis from office and claim the throne for himself.

In that year, the public had still not recovered from the summer of 2002—a terrifying summer made much more so by media moves that might have been scripted by Hollywood. So, with Schwarzenegger's hot breath on his neck, Davis tried to take advantage of this lingering fear. No doubt hoping that his feminist constituency as well as the child-abduction-addled public would applaud him, Davis championed the extension of California's Megan's law, which had been about to sunset. (8) He even called the legislature back in a special session just to extend Megan's law. And, whether legislators were yearning for a vacation or really in favor of the law, they extended it by an overwhelming—in fact, unanimous—vote.

But Davis wasn't finished milking sex crimes. Of 12 crime bills he signed during the final months before the referendum to oust him, 11 dealt with sex offenders, mandating stricter punishments, public notification and surveillance. However, just as President Johnson's War on Crime didn't erase his record on the Vietnam War—the war helped torpedo his presidency—Davis's machinations didn't save his neck either. The history books tell us Davis's fate. But unfortunately, history books don't tell us about the long-lasting bad effects of those 11 laws Davis signed.

18. Homeless

Fall, 2002 to February, 2003

ELAINE HALLECK

Sometimes Pera Fernandez thought about the time when Danny and the kids had moved out of their first house and into a new apartment. Now, it seemed to her like all that had happened in another country, in another life. But in reality, it had happened just two years previously.

Oh, Danny said he moved because he couldn't stand living next to that family, with everything that was happening. But, besides that, it must've been because of all the cops that had been in and out of that house.

And now the cops had been in and out of Pera's apartment too — the one she was sharing with Danny, Trevor and Kari. And so Pera came to realize that no one could ever feel really at home again after five cops show up at 6:30 in the morning, even if two of them were ladies. It became impossible to relax. People talk about feeling violated by a break-in or even by storm damage. But cops were just as bad.

"Tata, even Polly and Tinkerbell haven't been acting the same," Kari complained.

"Hijo, I thought it was illegal," Pera told Danny. "On television, they always have a search warrant."

"I had to sign a paper with my P.O. It gave them permission to come in and search whenever they want."

"Do they have to put you in handcuffs? And why did they need five police and all those cars?

"It's a good thing Trevor didn't see," Kari said.

At the mention of Trevor, everyone went silent. He wasn't at home at that moment. He had ridden somewhere on his bike ... probably to Suzanne's. He was spending a lot of time at Suzanne's helping out, cutting grass and the like. But he was a worry for them all, always seeming to be the edge of ... nobody was exactly sure what. He wasn't loud and he didn't have a bad temper. In fact, most people described him as a sweetie. But Danny always kept his motorcycle keys in his pocket, or under his pillow when he slept, because he was sure Trevor was going to take it for a ride the minute he got a chance. After all, he was 15 and was taking driver's training. And sometimes he did things that were very surprising, although never exactly criminal, and later when you told him that he shouldn't have done whatever it was, he admitted that he was wrong and said he was sorry.

The latest thing, of course, was sneaking out to cover the sign saying Danny was a sex offender. Well, Trevor and Kari did it together, but because Trevor was already on probation, all the blame fell on him.

Danny had been speechless over that incident. Pera thought he was secretly grateful, because he was afraid he was going to suffer even worse public exposure. He said there was one guy in his group who was having a terrible problem in his neighborhood—everybody had a sign on their lawn saying he should get out.

At first, all that happened was that the manager removed Trevor's sign—although it took a lot of scrubbing. Pera wondered where he ever got the idea to use evaporated milk to stick his sign up?

But later his probation officer came out to the apartment. He was an older guy with dark, greying hair and a mustache, and he seemed kind of nice. No handcuffs that time. He sat down and asked about their family situation, but he seemed to already know about Danny.

Finally he said, "I was going to look for some Mexican sombreros. Can I say I didn't find any?"

Pera, Danny, Trevor and Kari just looked at him—and not at each other. "Yes," Danny finally mumbled. Later, Pera saw Danny stuffing the hats in the trash bag. He couldn't very well take them out to the dumpster uncovered, now that he knew there were cameras.

The worst thing about that incident was that somehow, because of it, the manager got in contact with Danny's P.O. Now she would be calling his P.O. up all the time. In fact, at Danny's next appointment, sure enough, the P.O. mentioned that a day care center was starting up right in the apartment complex. And the city might pass a law that anyone who committed a sex crime couldn't live by a school or a park. And if the law wasn't passed, the P.O. could just make that a rule in Danny's case. What it all boiled down to was that Danny might have to leave.

"But we were here first," Pera told Danny one Saturday morning when the kids were at baseball and Danny was putting a small chain and padlock on Kari's new computer hutch in the bedroom. "Besides, I didn't think it was allowed to run businesses out of here. I met a guy who wanted to have an Internet business and the manager told him no. A day care center would be even more noticeable."

"She's probably making a special exception for the day care center," Danny said. "She's wanted me out for a long time. Maybe I'll go and live over at Chucho's. Then I'll have to go register again." Pera noticed that he didn't have a complaining tone of voice. He seemed to have accepted it.

But she hadn't. "What? And leave us here?"

"Sounds like a bad idea, doesn't it? But I'd come over here all the time."

"Hijo, Trevor needs a father—you know that. And Kari would be brokenhearted. And, who knows what's near Chucho's house. Besides, hijo, they shouldn't be breaking up your family. That's the opposite of what should happen. A person's family is what keeps them, you know ..." Pera's voice trailed off, and she knew that she was the one who sounded whiney.

"Believe me, I know. But Trevor might do better without me around. He's good with you. With me, he's got an attitude."

Danny had something there. They all knew that a lot of Trevor's problem was that he felt bad about everything that was happening to Danny. So maybe if Danny weren't around, and the cops weren't coming over, and there was no sign about Danny, Trevor would settle down. And Chucho was more or less family, even though he wasn't Danny's real father.

But all this was killing Pera. To her, everything that was happening to Danny — wasn't it all because of the three white angels?

Once Danny told Pera that she shouldn't talk like that — "the three white angels." After all, Patty, his kids' mother, was white.

Pera realized that if the reaction to the three white angels hadn't caused Danny such problems, then she really wouldn't have cared much that it was white girls who were picked to be angels when disappearances of kids who weren't white had been ignored, or that everyone made it seem like there was a crime wave of kidnappings when really there wasn't. But all Danny's problems made it seem as if there was a war against Danny that would never end.

Pera knew that most people probably thought that it doesn't matter if, after some kids die, they get a lot of publicity and others don't. None of the children, whatever race they are, are going to come back because of the publicity.

But it does matter, Pera decided. Because the publicity has a lot of effects on the rest of us. Look at what happened after the three white angels. First, there was that "Stranger Danger" program—it had scared Kari to death. It scared a lot of people to death. Nobody was going to parks anymore. They were as empty as the ocean was after the movie Jaws. Everybody was suspicious.

Next, they started putting up cameras at the big intersections. They said it was to catch people running the light. But Pera knew it was also because of the three white angels and probably 9/11 too. Who was to say the police wouldn't use those tapes to check people's movements if there were a crime or another attack? Everywhere you looked, there was fear.

And then there were the TV shows, picking up where the news left off. In the fall after the white angels disappeared, prime time was full of white angels and police stories, mostly made-up ones, although sometimes you couldn't tell which were real and which were invented. Pera remembered one "CSI: Crime Scene Investigation" and several "Law and Order" shows and one called "Special Victims Unit" that all had pedophiles and serial sex killers and little kids being kidnapped.

Well, naturally—all those shows were made a few miles away from where the real-life drama of the three white angels had happened. It was like California was ground zero of little girls disappearing. Hollywood was blowing up these local crimes and spreading fear all around the country and probably the whole world. Now that Pera thought about it, these programs seemed kind of sick or immoral. They took something that was really horrible, but really unlikely to happen, and created a feeling of fascination around it. People would be sitting around eating potato chips and watching these shows and, in this passive frame of mind, they'd start thinking that a lot of sicko pedophile murderers were running rampant. Or—you know what they say about copycat crimes—they might even start thinking about committing the same kind of crime.

But there was something even worse—something that was so disturbing that it was almost unbelievable. The true trend wasn't stranger danger or a "crime wave" of children getting murdered. It was actually a wave of people getting their lives messed up by the police.

Pera hadn't learned this surprising fact all at once. No, it was after months of talking to friends, and opening up about what was happening to Danny. Then she started to realize that practically everybody she knew had a similar story in their own circle—some cousin, or brother or old friend—who had been accused or convicted like Danny. In some cases, Pera had known these friends for years, yet they had never told her their stories. Probably it was too shameful. But as soon as she took a chance and told people about Danny's problems, she almost drowned in a flood of similar stories. It turned out there were a lot more people like Danny than Pera had ever realized.

Probably the first one to come to light was Danny's friend Jorge, whom he had known for years. Danny never realized until that summer that Jorge had a problem like his. People just don't talk about it, except to somebody in the same boat. Jorge told Danny that, after the second white angel went missing, the police gave him lie detector tests and searched his place too. And when, on account of the angels, they put the Fernandez's house on the Internet, Jorge's was on it too.

Another person was Sandy. She and Pera had been going out to Coco's for pie after church for years. After Pera told her about Danny, Sandy said, "That sounds like the jam my brother got into."

"He's such a sweet guy," Sandy explained, but he had a drug problem. He was divorced and did something with his teenage daughter. Sandy didn't know exactly what, except she was pretty sure it wasn't intercourse. His ex-wife called the police on him. When that happened, he was so worried as he waited for them to come and arrest him that he went to a therapist.

The therapist told him to turn himself in and confess. The therapist even made the call to the police from his office and testified for Sandy's brother in court. And in spite of that—or maybe because of it—Sandy's brother got 40 years in state prison. 40 years! Even a lot of murderers don't get 40 years. Pera thought that was some lousy help he got from the therapist, although of course she didn't say so to Sandy, and it didn't seem to have crossed Sandy's mind. Pera thought that Sandy's brother would've been a lot better off getting a lawyer—like Danny had—instead of a therapist. In fact, she couldn't imagine what had possessed him to call a therapist. Maybe he had the idea that a therapist was supposed to be a form of salvation, a rock in times of trouble. Almost like God, or a priest.

In fact, Pera thought that Sandy's brother should probably have called a priest. At least a priest wouldn't have made him turn himself in! Pera knew a lot of people didn't respect priests any more. All you hear about them now is that they molest children. Well, maybe some of them did, but Pera knew priests who were good people. And at least a priest wouldn't make things worse for a person who came for help.

The next person was Maureen at work, who told Pera that she and her husband had a friend who turned into kind of a phantom after his ex-wife said he did something to their little girl who was only 7. The man always insisted it wasn't true and it didn't even go to court. But he wasn't allowed to see the daughter anymore. And he never had a good job after that, maybe because he kept moving around to follow the ex-wife, who was always trying to hide from him. When the girl got a little older, he wanted her to know he didn't molest her, so he kept trying to find her. Pera told Maureen she bet Danny would do the same.

It got so that any time Pera got up the nerve to tell somebody about Danny, she wasn't surprised when they came back with a story about somebody they knew.

Next was the secretary at work, Patricia. She told Pera she had a "very immature" 21-year-old grandson who was in county jail because of something with a 13-year-old neighbor.

"She's been after him forever," Patricia said.

For weeks, Patricia had been on pins and needles, getting calls from her grandson from jail. He didn't have money for bail. Pera knew how that was. The prosecutor, who was a lady like in Danny's case, was threatening the grandson with six counts and eight years of prison for each one. This was right during the panic about the white angels in Orange County, which was where Patricia's grandson lived.

"Get this," Patricia told Pera one day. "He's going to have to pay restitution for being in jail—$200 dollars to $10,000 dollars. I knew the prison system was for the birds before, but now I know it for sure." Patricia also told Pera about her cousin. When he was almost a teenager himself, his girlfriend's parents turned him in because she got pregnant. After he got out of prison, he married the girl and was a good father to the baby, but he had to register for all his life because of Megan's law. One day, somebody figured out he was the dot on the new Web map, and people threw rocks through his window and put up posters about him.

That scared Pera. All of these things scared her. Something crazy was going on. On one side, a lot of ordinary people like Danny were being accused and suffering for something they did that sounded sort of like child molesting, but really wasn't as bad as that. Or maybe they hadn't done anything at all. But generally, no one realized how many people were in this situation, because the people in trouble were too ashamed to tell anybody. Pera certainly hadn't been aware of how many people were in Danny's shoes before his problems turned into one of the biggest headaches of her life. But still, nobody was talking about it.

On the other side, what everybody was talking about was children getting molested—priests, for example, were supposed to be molesting kids like crazy. It was in the news constantly, along with accounts of every little thing happening in the cases of the three girls. This was the only side most people were hearing. And so life was miserable for people like Danny.

But Pera didn't give up. She kept saying the rosary and thinking about St. Paul's advice, to always give thanks, always keep on praying, no matter what. So she did. Even after Danny left his kids in her care and went to live with Chucho.

*

One Saturday when Danny was at Pera's apartment, his friend Kate came over carrying a nice big birdcage she'd found in the dumpster. Trevor and Kari helped her carry it up from the trunk of her car, which was also very big.

"This is great, but where can we put it?" Danny said.

"You better hang it," Kate suggested. So out came the hammer and nails. When they were almost finished, they started talking about Kate's petition to take down the sex-offender signs in the complex.

"Not many people signed—about 50," Kate said, "But at least they took down the sign about Danny. But then you're not living here anymore. I don't know if they'll put up more in the future. Of course, the other guy that they put up a sign about signed our petition. And his wife. There's not that many black people here, but most of them signed. And a lot of Hispanics. And some plain old white people too. But I think all the people who gave me a hard time when I came to their doors were white. That wasn't fun."

"Thank you," Pera said.

"I'm not sure why I got so interested in it. My neighbors encouraged me, though—Jerome and Linda. All of us took the petition around together. Even their daughter came. I never would've had the nerve otherwise. Mary Ann, the manager, is furious at me. She even called me one night."

"Well, she started it," Pera said, getting a little worked up. "She should realize that some people would object. And she shouldn't be calling you up and bothering you."

"Jerome said her campaign against Danny could descend to the mentality that in the past caused his people to be lynched."

"Kari said she saw a sign in somebody's window that said, 'Leave Our Neighborhood Now Child Molester,'" Pera told Kate.

"I saw that when we were going around with the petition. I didn't want to knock on that door. But Jerome did. He has a degree in community organizing. The guy with the sign kept saying he had checked with the police, and it was legal. Jerome told him, 'It may be legal, but that's not the point.' He was very polite. He said, 'Sir, with all due respect, I suppose if you put a sign up that said, 'Leave Our Neighborhood Now Nigger,' that would be legal too.'"

"What did the man say?"

"Nothing."

"But is that legal?"

"Well, it's just words," Kate said. "Later I'll show you the Megan's law Web site. It says harassment or discrimination are illegal. Maybe that sign could be seen as housing discrimination, but nobody's complaining. The victims, like Danny, are too afraid and ashamed."

Kate glanced at Danny who by then was busy in the toolbox and didn't seem to hear. "It's so much like the signs the cops themselves put up. Jerome said that in the Old South, the cops were in on the discrimination too. The cops were in the Ku Klux Klan. And a lot of discrimination was legal then—like laws to prevent blacks from voting."

"What's 'nigger'?" Kari asked.

Now Danny perked up. "It's good you never heard it, Princess. It's sort of like 'negrito.' You know, what Chucho used to call me, when I was a surfer. But it's a bad word. Nobody says it anymore."

Trevor went outside, and Danny asked Kate if she could help Kari with some homework on her computer in the bedroom. When Kari finished, as she rummaged in the closet for her baseball mitt, Kate looked up the official California Megan's law site and showed Danny and Pera three reports.

"Listen to these headings in the 2001 report," Kate said. "They make Megan's law sound so cheerful—'Only a Call Away,' 'A New Era of Access,' 'Looking Ahead,' 'Success Stories.'

"And this is the part that really gets me. It says it's illegal to use the service to discriminate or harass a registered person. But then—right here in these stupid 'Success Stories'—they show that it is being used for discrimination.

"Look. They don't use names—here it says a 'movie theater staff' member' and here's a 'real estate agent,' and a 'manager in a laundromat.'"

"Did any of them lose their jobs?" Danny asked. To Pera, he sounded nervous.

"Well, I'm sure the real estate agent lost his client. It says this other man was 'relieved of his volunteer status.' Then ... here in the 2000 report is a guy who didn't get hired as a Santa Claus. They actually admit it. And here's a soccer coach. Somebody identified him and there was an investigation that showed that he didn't molest any kids on the team. But, look, it says 'At the request of the soccer league officials, the convicted sex offender resigned as coach.' If that isn't job discrimination, I don't know what is. Don't you think the attorney general should be ashamed to admit on his own Web site that Megan's list is causing the discrimination he says is illegal?"

Danny and Pera were now scanning the "Success Stories" along with Kate.

"Do you notice anything?" Kate said.

"What are 'hits'?" Pera asked.

"It means that somebody found the person they were suspicious about," Kate said.

"But why were they looking up those men? Did they do anything wrong?" Pera asked.

"That's what I mean. That's what my friend noticed when she was looking at these reports. In most cases, no. They weren't doing anything wrong at the time people were looking them up on Megan's list, not even breaking their probation rules, which sometimes say they can't be around kids. But somebody checked up on them just the same. It was checking up for the sake of checking up.

"In the stories where somebody was actually doing something wrong, sometimes their crime was not registering. But you can understand why they didn't, because look what happens when somebody gets a 'hit' on them. They lose a job or something—they lose something big!"

Kate seemed to be getting worked up and Danny seemed to be getting more worried.

"My lawyer told me if I don't register, it could be a third strike," Danny said. "I could go to prison for life. I already registered at Chucho's."

"So registration is yet another obstacle in your path—another chance to screw up. It's like those stupid traffic stops to find drunk drivers. They try to get you coming and going."

Danny began looking so serious that Pera wanted to change the subject. "Where are Trevor and Kari anyway?"

"Playing ball," Danny said.

"Did you see Kate's new car?" asked Pera. "Well, it's not exactly new, is it?"

"No, it's an '87 Mercedes I bought from my friend Sandra."

"It's a new old car," Danny said lightly, and Pera was glad to see him cheering up.

"Let's go look at it," Pera suggested.

"It doesn't look old," Danny said a few minutes later as they stood near the apartment gazing at the car. "It's in good shape. It's big. It's beautiful. How much was it?"

"Only $2,000 dollars. I didn't really need it. I still have my Toyota, and that uses a lot less gas. This one is a real hog. But Sandra was getting a new car and I liked it. There's nothing wrong with it. It's just old. It's getting hard to find parts, Sandra said. But Germans build these things like tanks."

Danny kept staring at it. "Yeah, it's nice. It would be a good family car. I could sleep in it, when I'm homeless." He was suddenly serious again, and so were Pera and Kate. Just then, the trunk of the car began to slowly open. But hadn't it been locked? They all stared, mystified.

After it fully opened, Trevor and Kari got out. "It's big in there," Trevor said, a little sheepishly.

"We were pretending we were *ilegales*," Kari said.

"That's not a very good thing to pretend," Danny told them.

"We don't have to pretend," Trevor added. "We are." Danny looked at Trevor. But he wasn't mad.

Pera went indoors with the kids. Later when Danny came back in the apartment, he told Pera he was thinking about selling his motorcycle and buying the Mercedes. She asked him if he could he afford it. He said Kate would let him have it for monthly payments of $100 dollars. He seemed happy, so Pera was happy.

But he said the manager, Mary Ann, walked by when he and Kate were outside, and gave them a dirty look.

"Now what's gotten into her?" Pera sighed. "Isn't she satisfied that she got rid of you? Can't you even visit here?"

19. Sting of the thought police

March 2003 to 2010

ALEX LANDON

On January 30, 2007, Matty Nash, drummer and founder of the popular rock group Mutaytor, baited by a popular NBC exposé television show, is lured to a Long Beach, California, decoy home by online promises of sex with a—fictitious—teenager. He is exposed on the show's cameras and then trapped by police. He later pleads not guilty to a felony charge and his career implodes. (1)

On May 4, 2009, in a San Diego courtroom filled with supporters of former assistant secretary of the Navy, lawyer, and decorated war hero Wade Sanders, a judge sentences him for possession of child pornography. The handsome 68-year-old calls his conviction "the hardest moment of my life" and says his years commanding a Swift Boat in Vietnam's Mekong Delta were "a walk in the park" in comparison. (2) Sanders had accepted solicitations for free downloads of child pornography from FBI agents posing as porn distributors. Despite having no earlier offenses of any type, Sanders receives over three years in prison. Your federal tax dollars at work.

Sadder yet, on November 5, 2006, after another baiting by those responsible for the aforementioned TV show, Texas assistant district attorney Louis Conradt, Jr., who did not go to any house where any fictitious teenager awaited, is nevertheless about to be served with a search warrant at home based on his alleged communication with a—fictitious—13-year-old decoy. He shoots and kills himself as police enter his house and the show's camera crews wait outside to film the scene. (3)

These three tragedies are all-too-familiar examples of people cut down in their prime by an illogical neo-Prohibition crusade that has its origins, yet again, in high-profile but low-level crimes manipulated by politicians. Later, in Chapter 21, we will look at what was considered a crowning moment in that crusade.

But first let's examine these stings. Such elaborate, high-stakes fictions that focus on crimes against children and yield stunningly harsh consequences have been getting more common. They may be carried out by vigilante groups, TV shows or, more commonly, by police and the FBI. The stings are labor-intensive setups that aim to entrap people based on their thoughts, intentions and speech (although the stings may not meet the strict legal definition of entrapment).

The stings generally focus on pornography or on chats and e-mail that are said to constitute "solicitation." It is a strange fact of life in 21st century America, that in many jurisdictions, a solicitation, especially if done online, with the belief that the other person is a minor, is a crime, whether or not the other person actually is a minor. This is the type of ethereal misdeed — thought crime, some may say—that was supposedly committed by Louis Conradt when he allegedly asked for an indecent photo of the decoy "13-year-old."

As for stings focusing on pornography, the one on Wade Sanders is typical. Here again, we see the flimsy nature of these stings, because Sanders never actually received the pornography offered by the FBI. Nevertheless, his willingness—his "OK"—was used as justification for a search warrant to examine his computer, where child pornography was found. It is another strange feature of modern life that the mere possession of child pornography—as opposed to creating or selling it—has very severe consequences. In Sanders' case, he had a spotless record before his misstep. Nevertheless, he was sentenced to a long time behind high walls and razor wire.

Real money vs. "thought crimes"

Such punishment could be considered cruel and unusual because possession of pornography generally entails just that—possession, not creation or selling. The person has done it out of curiosity, or perhaps voyeurism or loneliness. He doesn't act on it or do anything with it.

Of course, you might not think so if you had slogged through a 2,000-page pornography report produced in the 1980s by Edwin Meese, former President Ronald Reagan's Attorney General, who claimed there was a link between some pornography and child molestation. (4) Despite the sheer weight of all those pages, we must be very cautious about such claims. Keep in mind the old joke that drinking milk causes heroin use, since all heroin users started using milk before they went on to harder stuff!

Another reason to be skeptical about so much hard time for mere possession is that in the age of computers, pornography is very easy to obtain —just a click away. And free pornography? By removing the cost, a substantial impediment to acquiring pornography in the real world magically evaporates.

For all these reasons, strict sentences are not appropriate for possession of child pornography, which is relatively effortless and innocent. In contrast, creating and selling child pornography are crimes for which strict punishments are justified.

In the other case of smoke and mirrors mentioned above, Matty Nash didn't have sex with or even kiss the phantom "girl" at the house, but merely showed up seeming eager to do so. Who knows—maybe he would have had second thoughts, like the lead character in the movie American Beauty when he finally had his teenage prize in hand.

An important point about the stings mentioned above is that desires, intentions and speech (legally, images are considered speech) are not the same as acts and should not be judged so in a court. Many of these extreme prosecutions happen at the dividing line between thoughts and actions. That means tremendous and expensive resources are being devoted to controlling something that is quite ethereal. Compare the excessive spending on such flimsy goals to some of the expensive, ill-advised wars begun by our leaders in recent years. In fact, both brands of excessive expenditures may have originated in the same mentality. Perhaps as you read on, you will agree.

Yes, the "crimes" may be insubstantial, but the money spent setting up and punishing them is all too real. Investigation and prosecution of possession of child pornography have gotten truly out of hand, and even some staff members of the U.S. Sentencing Commission seem to realize this. In 2010, a few of them came to California and talked about the possibility of relaxing sentencing guidelines for child porn possession. Let us hope this happens at some time in the near future.

It may be instructive to compare the climate around child pornography to that of adult pornography. After years of clampdowns, the relationship between adult pornographers and authorities is more or less stalemated, as long as producers keep behind a line drawn decades ago by the courts, which decided that "community standards" hold sway.

The way this standard is applied in film, is that permissible movies must have a plot line, however thin it may be. Perhaps the best known in the genre was "Debbie Does Dallas," in which a cheerleader takes on a football team —not exactly a profound plot line, but sufficient to avoid prosecution. As for other art forms, there is the rare bird that squawks at materials deemed "obscene," such as former President Bush's Attorney General John Ashcroft, who in 2003 curtained a partially nude statue of the Spirit of Justice in the Great Hall of the Department of Justice. Ashcroft also initiated a crackdown on adult movie producers in Washington, D.C. (5) But generally, the trend has been to relax prosecution of adult pornography.

Child pornography of course shows no such liberalizing tendency — it is never seen as acceptable. Apparently, some people believe that no view of a child's body can be anything but sexual—as was evident in 2010 in the outraged reaction to proposed full-body security scans of children (and adults) at Heathrow airport. (6) However, the relaxation in recent decades on adult pornography should give us pause. In 2010, even TV shows such as "South Park" were using language that could have gotten Lenny Bruce busted in the 1950s.

What we need to do is stop the ruinous spending on prosecution and imprisonment for low-level crimes, whether for child pornography possession, "soliciting" minors on the Internet, or for the many other minor crimes mentioned in this book. We must awaken to the reality that something is very wrong when we spend real money recklessly on "thought crimes" at the same time as we let our school systems hemorrhage, lay off teachers and shut down school programs such as art and music — the disciplines that make life worth living.

20. The land of the free

January, 2003

ELAINE HALLECK

"Look, Trevor. They got her," said Kari Fernandez. Trevor shifted under his covers.

"Trevor, wake up. She looks like Mom, doesn't she? She's pretty. Look at her hat."

"Why can't you let me sleep?" Trevor said in an indistinct moan. "We need a bigger apartment."

Kari looked over at his flattened form, with only the rounded back of his head and a few tufts of dark blonde hair visible at the edge of the blanket. Then she glanced at Tata's bed, its bedspread neatly arranged over the pillows, with her blue rosary on top. She must have forgotten to hang it over the crucifix on the wall, where it usually was. It was Saturday, but she was already at work.

Now, despite his complaining, Trevor turned over, raised his head and looked, bleary-eyed, at the computer screen.

"You're obsessed," he observed.

"Obsessed?" Kari paused, then added weakly, "I am not."

"Why don't you just chat like everyone else?"

"It's more fun to look up interesting stuff. Kate showed me how."

"You were obsessed before that. Remember Ronald Rose?"

"Yes! And now, here's another one! But it's a lady, Nanci Dion. She's from Utah or Arizona or somewhere. She stole her kid from the father and ran away. They been looking for them for days. Now they found them—here! Or near here. They did an Amber Alert."

"You're obsessed," Trevor repeated. "What's an Amber Alert?"

"It's like they put it on the radio and on the freeway and ... everywhere ... that you're bad and you escaped, and everybody should look for you."

Trevor came over near the screen. "That sounds pretty bad. What'd you say she did?"

"She kidnapped her kid. Look, here's a picture of them. They found them in a state park by San Diego. You think they were on their way to Mexico?"

"How can you kidnap your own kid?" Trevor asked.

"I don't know," Kari admitted. "But don't you think she looks like Mom?"

"A little."

"What if Mom kidnapped me?"

"You're obsessed, Kari. Mom isn't going to kidnap you. We don't even know for sure where she is, until next time she calls. Maybe someone kidnapped her!"

"Who would do that?" Kari asked, before she realized Trevor was joking. After a few seconds, she said, "Trevor, do you think Mom would want to kidnap me?"

"I don't think so." But when Trevor saw how sad Kari looked, he added, "She has too many problems of her own to think about kidnapping us. But she loves us."

"Yeah, she does. When she took us to Disneyland last year, she told me she loved us. Anyway, if she did kidnap me, I bet it would be fun."

"Hey, how come you got lipstick on? You look nice."

"Why not?" Kari shrugged.

"When you're in your sweats and on the computer?"

"Well, Tata bought me some, but Dad won't let me wear it. I'm just practicing."

"Is Dad here?"

"Of course. He's sleeping on the couch."

"Did he get the new car yet?"

"You mean the old car? No. But I think he's getting it today."

"Does he still have the motorcycle?" Trevor came over and sat down on the bed by Kari's little computer hutch.

"I guess so. How else could he get here after work last night?"

"Hey, let's look up Yamahas. Let's see how much he can get for his motorcycle." He began to search.

"How'd you learn how to use a computer so good?" Kari asked him.

Trevor said nothing and kept searching. He brought up a page full of motorcycles for sale. "Sweet. Look at that one. It's like Dad's except it's red."

Kari knew Trevor wasn't a liar, so she asked, "How could you have been using my computer? I keep it locked."

"Not always. Sometimes you leave it on."

"But you're not supposed to. What have you been doing?"

"Nothing. Stuff like this. Chatting sometimes."

"With who? Suzanne?"

"Are you kidding? Not any more. Their computer broke. They can't even afford antibacterial soap since her father died."

"Then who do you chat with? Kids from school?"

"A little. I don't know who they are half the time. I chat with someone called Pretty Pink Teen sometimes. Don't tell Suzanne."

"I saw Pretty Pink Teen in the chat room. She didn't wanna chat with me."

"She probably just likes guys."

"Yeah. That name—it sounds like she likes guys."

"Yeah, and she only likes older guys. She thinks I'm 20. I lied."

Kari was shocked. Trevor didn't usually lie. "Why'd you tell her that?"

"I don't know. She said she was gonna send me her picture, and she sounded like she was kind of ... a hottie. I think she was hoping I was older, so I told her I was. Hey, what time is it?"

"Quarter to eight."

"I gotta go to Suzanne's."

"So early?" Trevor stood up, then bent over to kiss Kari. He was aiming for her mouth, but she turned her head so he kissed her on the cheek. "Ay, Trevor. You better brush your teeth before you go. Your breath doesn't smell too good."

Trevor brushed his teeth and got dressed.

"So is she pretty Trevor? Miss Pretty Pink."

He hesitated. "Well, yeah."

He went in the kitchen. Kari heard him quietly open the refrigerator door, so as not to wake Dad up. He was getting a glass of milk for his breakfast. He was gone within five minutes. As she sat at the computer, looking at the picture of poor Nanci Dion getting dragged away by cops, she thought she heard the sound of a motorcycle starting up, and then driving away. She decided she better get dressed and check.

*

In the darkened living room, Kari saw a big lump under a blanket on the sofa. The lump was her Dad. She looked around and didn't see his motorcycle helmet anywhere. She looked for his keys and spotted them on the end table next to his sofa, not under his pillow. But was there one missing? She wasn't surprised when, after quietly taking the keys and slipping out the front door, she didn't find his motorcycle parked in their carport below.

Kari stood in the empty carport, staring off at the hills behind their apartment. They looked so inviting in the cool morning sun. The neck-high bushes scattered here and there were a sparkly mix of browns and bluish-greens, still moist from the rainy winter season. She remembered how endless and scary the chaparral had seemed after Rikki got killed, and the idea of coyotes was fresh in her mind, but she hadn't seen any coyotes for a long time. If you just kept walking straight, what would you come to? She wanted to wander out there, through one of the gaps in the wood fence, and see if she could find some flowers to pick. It was February, almost time for flowers. What was there to stop her? Her Dad would sleep until at least noon, and Tata wouldn't be back until two.

Kari thought she should probably go in and tell Dad that Trevor had taken the motorcycle. But won't that just make him lose sleep worrying?

She didn't think about Trevor's cell phone, which she could have used to get him to come back. She put Dad's keys safely in her pocket, and turned sideways to get through the fence.

She didn't know exactly how long it was before she came back. She was carrying some long, skinny branches from a eucalyptus tree, with their slender, pointy, blue leaves and a lot of little blue things, like hard buds, growing in bunches. She almost hadn't taken them, because just as she was stripping them off a bigger branch, she noticed some people quietly sitting in the shadow of another little tree some distance off. They seemed to be watching her. But she finished and walked in the opposite direction, back the way she had come. Then she realized they must have been ilegales. She could have tried her Spanish on them!

After squeezing back through the space in the fence, she noticed several men standing around in the sun outside her apartment. Cops. Again. A couple of them were ladies. They didn't look very nice, even the ladies. They were fat. They seemed to be looking at the carport, at the apartment. One was talking on a radio or a cell phone.

Kari stayed standing by the fence in the shadow of a tree and some bushes, feeling like an ilegal herself. They hadn't seen her. She realized she was more afraid of them than she had been of the ilegales under the trees a few minutes ago.

"Is he in there?" Kari heard one of the cops say. "Where's the vehicle?" When they finally started up the stairs toward the apartment, Kari thought about her Dad sleeping indoors and she instinctively left her cover and walked toward them, trailing her eucalyptus branches on the ground. "Jack!" one of the lady cops said to the man farthest up on the stairs. "Wait up." Then she said to Kari, "Do you live here?"

Kari didn't answer. She wanted to. She wanted to say something smart, like, "Good morning to you too!" but her mouth seemed to have frozen.

"I think we got ourselves an alien," one of the men said.

An alien—Kari thought, a space alien? Do I look that bad? "I'm not," she said. "I'm from here."

The lady looked at the eucalyptus branches. "Where did you get those?" Again, Kari wanted to say something smart, like, "From Mars." But instead, she said, "Back there. I was taking a walk. I'm gonna make ... an arrangement."

"An arrangement," one of the men cops said. "You know it's illegal to take plants out of the parks."

"Don't worry," said the lady, looking at Kari. "Do you live in T11?" When Kari nodded, she said. "Why don't you wait out here with me while they go inside?"

"Why are they going inside?" Kari asked. But the group had resumed its slow advance up the stairs. The first one knocked on the door hard.

Nothing. "He's sleeping," Kari said. They knocked again and finally the door opened and Kari saw Dad, in his green plaid undershorts and shoes with no socks, open the door. He was buttoning his shirt.

Here the dumb cops were again, catching people in their underwear. She didn't know if she was mad or afraid—probably more afraid than mad —but she began to cry.

"Don't worry," the lady cop said.

"I wanna go in."

"No, wait out here with me."

"No, I wanna go in," Kari said, and started up the stairs, crying harder than ever. She dropped the eucalyptus off the side of the stairs.

"Hey!" said the lady cop.

"Let 'er come in. It'll calm things down," said one of the guys at the top of the stairs. "I want you sitting down," he said to Kari as she passed. "And no getting up."

Kari sat down in an armchair while they put handcuffs on Dad and had him sit down on the couch. "It's for your own protection," someone said. Dad looked terrible and he didn't say anything to Kari. The sheet was over Polly and Tinkerbell's cage, and from inside Kari heard one little peep and a rustle.

"Why are you in your underwear with your young daughter in the house?" one of the cops said.

"They're shorts. I was sleeping under a blanket. She wasn't here."

"They're his golf shorts, man!" said another cop.

"Why are you sleeping here? You're not registered here," the first cop continued.

"Most of the time I live with my stepdad. I came here last night after work because I have to take care of some things here today."

"Who lives here?"

"My mother and my two kids. I lived here myself until a couple weeks ago. My P.O. told me I had to move because there's a day care center near-by. I already registered at my new address."

"That's the point."

Another voice interrupted them. "Jack, the computer's in the bedroom."

Kari looked at the cop standing framed in the door to her bedroom. Why did he say "the computer," like he already knew they had one?

*

When the cops finally left, Danny still looked terrible. Kari got him a glass of milk.

"What time is it?" he asked.

Kari picked up his watch from the end table, near where his keys used to be. "Quarter to eleven. Dad, are they coming back?"

"It sounded like it, didn't it? Dios mio, the last time it took them five months before they finally arrested me." He was silent for a minute. Then he stood up. "I'm gonna call my lawyer. I hope he's in today."

Kari didn't want to just sit there listening, so she took the sheet off the big new birdcage. Then she went over to the refrigerator, got out some eggs and started to make them some fried eggs. But she did it very quietly so she could hear her Dad a little. As she cracked the eggs, she remembered the cops finding that photo a few minutes ago, the one Ashley took of her so long ago, in the push-up bra, and her stomach jumped.

Then she heard Dad, who had apparently gotten through to the lawyer, speaking. "It was already on. First they looked on it. Then they took it." He was talking about the computer.

"I told them I didn't know where it came from. I don't have any idea how to use a computer, or any desire. That's the truth. I told them it must be my son's. That was the truth too. But then I felt bad. He's already in trouble." There was a pause.

"Well, then I said it's my daughter's computer and I always keep it locked, so my son can't use it. I tried to at least give them some doubt." Another pause. "My son's fishing knife. That seemed to really upset them, even though it was in his tackle box in the closet. They went through all the closets. They found a sexy picture that Kari's little friend took of her a few years ago. Kari told them her girlfriend took it. I don't know if they believed her." Another pause. "No, she had underwear on."

Another pause. Dad said some things Kari couldn't hear because the eggs were starting to hiss and pop, and suddenly she remembered the eucalyptus and the keys in her pocket and ... the motorcycle. She went outdoors to pick up the eucalyptus and when she came back in, she put Dad's keys back on the end table. He was off the phone then.

"Where's Trevor?" he asked, although he was staring at the long strands of eucalyptus dragging on the carpet like he was trying to figure out why she was holding it.

After Kari told him about Trevor, he didn't say anything. She gave him some eggs, salt and pepper, and a fork and he started to eat the eggs, mechanically. Kari ate hers too, and after they both finished, she said, "Dad, I forgot. We can call Trevor on his cell phone and tell him to come home."

"Yeah," he agreed. But he didn't make a move.

"What'd the lawyer say?"

"Not much. He said there's nothing he can really do, unless they arrest me again. Maybe he could call my probation officer, but I'd have to pay him. He was surprised there were so many cops. He said they must not have had anything else to do at the station. He said the cops have too much money."

He took his fork and scraped some egg yolk off the plate and ate it. "He said it doesn't matter what kind of pornography it is — children or adults. Even if it's adults, they'll say it shows unhealthy tendencies. The only hope for me is if they believe it's Trevor's. But then Trevor's going to get in trouble. Well no, I don't know. Maybe Trevor wouldn't get in trouble, because Trevor's offense wasn't a sex offense and ... well, I don't know if he could get in trouble for the child pornography, since he's a child too." Kari went to the bedroom and picked up Tata's rosary and got on her knees and said some of it. When she came back out to the living room, Dad was on the phone.

"It doesn't matter. You'll learn. I want you with me." Pause. "No, you stay there. I'll come over later to pick you up, after I get the car. I don't want you getting caught on that motorcycle."

He hung up, sighed, and looked at Kari. "He said he got the pornography. He said he told you this morning who it was from. Pretty Pink Teenager, or something. He said maybe it does have kids in it. He said he was going to throw it away, but he didn't have a chance, and then I moved, so he didn't think it mattered."

"Did he say he was sorry?"

"Of course." He looked through his phone book and dialed the phone, saying, "I'm calling Kate about the car. Then I have to call Tata."

Kari got a glass of milk and went back in the bedroom. She looked at the spot where her computer had been, empty now and a little dusty. Books and boxes and bags were still laying around where the cops had left them. She got on her knees and started saying the rosary again, leaning against Tata's bed. She cried a little and fell into a light sleep, still on her knees.

After a while, her Dad came in. "Princess, do you want to come with me a little later to Kate's?" Then he seemed to notice that she was on her knees. "You keep praying. When you're finished, put some stuff in a bag, like you're going away with me on a vacation for a couple of weeks."

"Going away?"

"Yeah, like we're going to Delaney. Don't take too much. But this time, take anything that's really important. Like your picture of Mom. Pretend like maybe you're not coming back. Because maybe we're not coming back."

*

On the way to Kate's, Danny was carrying the big birdcage, which wasn't easy. Kari had the aquarium with Eenie and Meenie in it. She wasn't quite sure why they were taking the animals to Kate's again, but she had pretty good idea. It looked like their animals were going on a little vacation too.

"Don't they ever rest?" her Dad grumbled, looking up at the sky. Until he said that, Kari hadn't even noticed the loud helicopter noise. As the roar of the engine and thub-thub of the rotors got louder, she heard an announcement over the bullhorn. As usual, she couldn't make out the words.

"It's like there's a war around here, there's so many cops," Dad said. "All the soldiers living around here too. We might as well be in Iraq." One of the parakeets squawked from under the sheet.

"Dad, listen. I think the bird said 'Iraq.' Don't say it too loud, Dad. Kate's neighbors are military. The ones who helped with the petition."

On the way to Kate's apartment, Dad mentioned that Kate had washed the car. It looked nice. He talked to Kate inside while Kari sat out on the balcony in a lounge chair in the afternoon sun. It felt so good, she almost fell asleep again. But the helicopter kept circling around over the chaparral where she had gone that morning and the noise kept her awake. The sound was creepy. She hoped they weren't looking for those people she'd seen, although she didn't know why she should be worried about them. At least they seemed peaceful and sort of shy, which was more than she could say for the cops.

"Kari!" she heard, in a strange, very loud hiss. She sat up and looked around.

It was Trevor, from just below the balcony. He was all messed up and looking around nervously. He didn't seem to know what to say.

"What happened to your jacket?" she said.

"Shh! I wiped out on the bike!"

"Where is it?" she whispered, leaning over the edge of the balcony.

"Back there!" He pointed toward the hills, where the noise of the helicopter still continued.

"What were you doing back there?"

"I came home, but when I got here, I forgot the code to get in. I saw the helicopter, and, I knew they were looking for me. So I tried to get away."

"You were riding around on the motorcycle out there?" He nodded. "Trevor, I don't even think they're looking for you. The cops that came this morning hardly said anything about you. They were looking for Dad. And those cops," she pointed toward the chaparral, "I think they're looking for some ... aliens."

Trevor was as nervous as a cat on the Fourth of July, and dirty too. Kari wondered if the helicopter noise was getting louder. She thought about telling him to go in Kate's garage and get in her car, since they were buying it anyway, but it was probably locked.

"Trevor, are you coming with us—to Mexico?" When the words "to Mexico" came out of Kari's mouth, she couldn't stop herself from sounding excited, as if she had said, "to Disneyland?"

Trevor didn't answer. "Go back home and pack," Kari commanded him. "I already did."

That seemed to loose Trevor's tongue. "I'm never going back there. And I don't wanna go to Mexico. I'll live at Suzanne's. And what about Tata? We can't leave her here."

That was true, Kari thought. But, still, she said, "Come on, Trevor. It'll be cool. Mexico is the land of the free. Maybe Mom will come. Maybe Tata will come, later. Right now, she can live with Chucho. She's got Chucho."

Dad slid open the sliding glass door and stepped out on the balcony. Kari saw he was holding some new keys.

21. Crusade

March 2003

ALEX LANDON

It is March 2003, just after the much-heralded reemergence of Elizabeth Smart, one of the trio of girls abducted in the preceding Summer of the Abducted White Girl. Within days, Elizabeth's politically adept father makes headlines as he begins a lobbying crusade in Washington D.C. to extend the Amber Alert—although it is reported that the Amber Alert had not played any role in his daughter's recovery. (1)

Unfortunately, it is not surprising how the crusade played out that March. In yet another example of the mentality of deception that characterizes the War on Crime, Elizabeth's father Ed Smart appears on a TV show saying his opponents in the discussion about the proposed law were "hurting children."(2) Probably as a result, there is not much debate in the House or Senate and the bill passes overwhelmingly, with many other measures rolled up with it in what becomes a behemoth bill, the Protect Act.

One part dramatically worsens penalties for mere possession of child pornography. Other attached measures expand wiretapping and monitoring of communications in all child abuse cases. Many people, including Matty Nash, Wade Sanders, Louis Conradt, Jr.,—the men mentioned in a previous chapter who were busted some years later for thought crimes —would have been well advised to take note of these sections, but who has time to pay attention to the flood of laws emanating from the capitol?

Fear-fried judgment

Other parts of the 2003 Protect Act ban computer-generated (animated) child pornography; establish a "two-strikes" mandatory life sentence for anyone convicted of a child sex offense who has a previous child sex offense. The act includes a measure authorizing lifetime parole for sex offenders. A Department of Justice press release about the Protect Act claims a "high rate of recidivism for such offenders" justifies this lifetime parole. (3) Another included measure eliminates the statute of limitations for sex cases involving children. The Protect Act also makes it easier to prosecute those who travel overseas for sex with "minors" (as defined in the United States), and it nudges higher—to 21, not 18—the age at which a "child" is finally seen as an adult.

There is also a "determinate sentencing" law that bars judges from softening sentences for sex offenders. Even the stern U.S. Supreme Court Justice William Rehnquist—normally a tough-on-crime figure—takes the unusual step of warning Congress against this law. His warning is ignored. (4)

Ed Smart, Elizabeth Smart and Donna Hagerman Norris (mother of Amber Hagerman, after whom the Amber Alert was named) soon join President George W. Bush in the Rose Garden of the White House as Bush signs the bill.

"No child should ever have to experience the *terror* of abduction," Bush says during the signing. The italics are mine. I use them because March 2003 is the same month Bush launched the invasion of Iraq, which he held responsible for the 9/11 terror attacks just 18 months earlier. Besides apparently linking child abductions with possession of child pornography and even with a judge's right to adjust a sentence, Bush was using the fear-fried judgment that grew out of 9/11 and connecting child abductions to terrorist attacks. He was living in the same logic-free parallel universe he inhabited when he linked the 9/11 attacks with Iraq and with the right to torture prisoners of war held at Guantanamo, Cuba.

An important postscript: although the Protect Act passes the Senate without a single dissenting vote, in the House the handful who vote against it are overwhelmingly black.

Surely these 16 African American representatives' "no" vote on the Protect Act reflected something important in their experience. Surely Reps. John Conyers, Elijah Cummings, Danny K. Davis, Barney Frank, Jesse L. Jackson, Jr., Stephanie Tubbs Jones, Barbara Lee, John R. Lewis, Bobby Scott, Edolphus Towns, Maxine Waters, Melvin Watt and the few others voting "no" well understood something about the power of the state, the power of distortions, stereotyping and witch hunts, something that was also part of the experience of the nation's founders but that nowadays is often too subtle or dangerous to say plainly, something spelled out in an elaborate, archaic hand on papers now yellow with age: in throwing principle and logic to the winds to squelch criminals, in criminalizing behavior that is common, a government sometimes takes steps that it should not, and must not, take without harming us all.

22. On the road again

January to November 2003

ELAINE HALLECK

Kate Michel looked at her watch and sneezed for the millionth time. 3:10 a.m. Thank goodness there was hardly any traffic. Otherwise, it might have been more than just a little dangerous to do what she was doing—driving herself home from the airport so tired that she had to sing loudly to prevent herself from falling asleep, and hoping she didn't run out of tissues to stem the rush of what was flooding from her nose and eyes. Somewhere between Atlanta and Los Angeles a perfume had started coming out of the ventilation system and, although she had been half asleep, she was awake enough to hear a lot of people besides herself had begun sneezing.

Going to Italy at 21 and starting from Detroit was one thing, but going at her age and starting from Los Angeles added difficulties she hadn't counted on.

But this time had been more purposeful than in the past, when she went to Europe as a semi-vagabond. One, this time had been an opportunity to see Corey, who was working as a flight attendant, even though she saw Corey for all of one day in Rome.

But what a day. Corey had never seen Rome before, so Kate got to show her a few of the magical places she remembered from when she was Corey's age—the deserted, ruined Palatine Gardens, the Bernini turtle fountain that you stumbled upon almost accidentally in a small plaza, the Michelangelo statue of Moses.

And then it was off toward the north by high-speed train to Padua, although without Corey. Kate felt sad after saying goodbye to her at the train station where Corey was meeting up with somebody to go hiking for a couple of days. But then she relaxed into the rhythm of the train, relishing the thought of finally having a first-hand look at the Arena Chapel with its fresco cycle, including The Lamentation of Christ, the subject of her dissertation, and the principal purpose of the trip.

And as an unexpected side benefit, what a relief it had been to have a few weeks' respite from Danny's drama—and her own, as she watched his from afar. Was Italy really a more peaceful place than California or did it just seem that way? You didn't exactly find peace by staring at the Lamentation—Giotto was an early Renaissance artist known for his emotional representations. And the scene of Jesus' dead body being tended by his mother and friends after his execution was hardly soothing.

But maybe it was the large-scale drama and trauma Italy had seen over the ages that made it seem as if 21st century Italians took things in stride more than Americans did. One mundane example: Kate remembered an article from the previous year that—in sync with the never-ending panic in California over child molesting—described the "predators" and "deviants" one might find on L.A.'s buses and subways committing such atrocities as groping, bumping and grinding. If a teenager were the object of these actions, the offender could end up on Megan's list for life. These pests were people you could have an Amber Alert on in a few years, declared a transit official. They were people caught in the grip of "desire for power and control," a psychologist assured readers, a desire that sometimes had to be cured by "libido-quelling drugs."

And how did they handle these atrocities in Italy? When somebody goosed the very blonde, very pretty Corey while "helping" her with her backpack at Rome's Leonardo da Vinci airport, it brought to Kate's mind the fate of apprehended "deviants" in Los Angeles. In Italy, by comparison, "deviant" applied to gropers would be an oxymoron, since by all accounts the country was the capital of gropers. Could a whole nation be deviating? Later, when Kate and Corey witnessed somebody apparently grabbing a squeeze in a crowded bus, the signora had a screaming fit, illustrating to Kate that handling things this way—the powerful way—was better than being a shrinking violet, and letting the police do Amber Alerts and send the groper off for brainwashing and libido-quelling drugs.

Kate was beginning to feel like she could use some libido-quelling drugs herself. As she drove along, marveling at how much traffic there was in the dead of night in L.A., she wondered when she would see Michel again. While things with him had progressed to the "in-my-life" stage, they were also firmly in the "just friends" stage. This was probably because of Michel's therapy, but it was a two-way street, as Kate didn't want to be drawn into his group therapy as a "significant other." Neither did she view his offense with his daughter as negligible, even though it had happened a few years ago and he was open and humble about it. However, he and Kate never discussed romance. Maybe now that he had this new therapist, whom he liked better than her weird cousin, the leash would lengthen.

But for the present, their get-togethers were centered around the beach. "I'm a surfing fool," Michel admitted. "It's so relaxing." Yet he brought her little gifts—granola bars, carry-out cappuccinos, even a shell necklace that he said he'd had since he was a Hawaii surfer—so she was confident he liked her.

One of the reasons Michel had been wedded to the San Onofre beach was that it was one of the only places he could go where there weren't any kids—the nudity and gays meant that it didn't attract many families. Under Bart-Liam-Mickey's idiotic rules, Michel couldn't go to beaches where kids typically went. He couldn't even go to church! And, coming from a small maritime community in French Canada where everyone was stoically Catholic, Michel missed church. He had insisted Kate send him a postcard of St. Peter's in Rome.

"You can't go to church?" Kate had asked. "What about freedom of religion?"

"Freedom of religion—I don't think freedom of any kind ever crossed Mickey's mind," Michel said. "But he's history now. He went overboard, but, well, I shouldn't have done what I did with my daughter."

That night, still making her way home along the freeway, and absently comparing it with the Italian freeways she had glimpsed from the train, Kate briefly thought about Danny, and wondered if he could go to church. Thinking about Danny made her realize that recently she hadn't been thinking about him much. Like Italy, Michel was helping Kate detach from Danny. At least she hadn't had any sleepless nights recently thinking about him—the flyer with his picture, his money worries, his problems with Trevor, whether he would get busted by his therapist, or even by an alcohol roadblock, and have a third strike. She thought Danny was still drinking a little more than he should, but considering all his worries, it was a miracle he wasn't worse. With his world bristling with cops, rules and hostility, it wouldn't take much for him to get in big trouble again.

The last time she saw Danny, when he bought the car, had been worrisome. First, he came over with all his pets, after asking Kate on the phone if she could pet-sit again "sometime." He said was planning a vacation with the kids, probably to Delaney. She didn't realize "sometime" meant that very day. But she didn't have the heart to tell him no, that she was leaving in a few days for Italy. In fact, he seemed so worried that she didn't even tell him about her upcoming trip. She just decided she'd ask Sandra to help out, or maybe Linda and Jerome. Jerome, after all, had left for parts unknown in the Middle East, so surely Linda and O'enn had room for a birdcage or an aquarium with two hamsters.

Kate and Danny had done the deal on the Mercedes in record time and, although Kate was only asking $100 dollars a month, Danny had insisted on giving her $500 dollars up front, "for the first five months," he said. It had been a strange afternoon, with helicopters making a lot of noise outside—probably chasing illegals in the hills behind the complex as usual—and Trevor showing up below Kate's balcony, looking as if he'd had a fight with a wild bear.

The pet-sitting included the food, although Danny had forgotten to bring it that day—he seemed so distracted—so for his first run in his new-old Mercedes, he'd driven the short distance to his apartment and back with the bags of hamster food, cedar chips, birdseed and gravel. For some unknown reason, when they set out, Trevor wanted to ride in the trunk, so Danny let him, and then Kari wanted to get in too. So Danny gently shut the trunk on them, checking with Kate how to pop it open. When he arrived back ten minutes later, Kate walked downstairs to meet him. She didn't know if the kids were still in the trunk—she imagined not—but on the front seat something new had already appeared, a gold- edged Bible.

As she pulled into Green Manor, still swabbing at her nose with a tissue, she wondered how Danny and his family were. She was desperate to sleep, but she thought about Sandra's car—Danny's car now—and decided to swing by his apartment, just to make sure all was well. She knew she shouldn't, and she felt sneaky—even sneakier when she passed an expensive-looking black sedan parked along the edge of the parking lot, with its lights out but the motor running. She couldn't see through the windows because they were covered with dew in the ocean-damp night. The car scared her. Were they criminals? Cops? She turned a couple more corners and then coasted by Danny's apartment.

The carport was empty. The apartment was dark. It was about 4 a.m. Well, surely everyone was sleeping inside. But shouldn't Danny be home from the late shift by now? And then she was past and couldn't be sure, but it seemed as if the windows yawned back at her curious eyes appearing awfully empty, as if maybe the curtains were gone.

*

You'd think that nothing at all has changed, Kate grumbled to herself as she sped south on the freeway a couple of months later. The way these people talk, it's like southern California is the center of the solar system.

Ever since she'd gotten back from Italy, she felt so much less burdened by the horrific way things were unfolding: the excesses Danny had been subject to, jolted further up on the trauma-meter by the kidnappings of the three girls, the capture and trial of suspects, the clamor of the media and politicians for tougher and tougher measures against sex offenders, and the near-vigilante spectacle of people camped outside the trial of Danielle's accused killer. And in the background, forming a warlike bass beat, was the inexorable launch of the war in Iraq, which practically had Kate covering her eyes.

She'd only been in Rome and Padua three weeks, but it was long enough to make it clear to her that the universe was a lot bigger than all this. She hadn't read a newspaper the entire time, and the world had carried on without her attention. The double fury in Southern California and Washington, D.C., which seemed to ramp one another up, was really just a tiny blip in life. It certainly wasn't the monster that sometimes seemed like it would swallow her up.

As usual, the traffic was like something from a set of The Road Warrior. It was around one in the afternoon. Kate knew it would already be dark before she and Mona finally arrived in Ensenada, in Baja California, Mexico, later that day.

To distract herself a little from the people tailgating at 80 m.p.h., Kate had been doing something she knew she shouldn't — listening to talk radio. What a dose of reality!—or at least the mediated version of reality. Now a couple of guys were carrying on about Governor Davis, who seemed to be in a serious tailspin, thanks to these guys and others like them. As a newcomer to California, Kate didn't much care one way or another about the governor, although at first she had felt positive about him after reading he was a favorite of women and environmentalists.

She'd heard this talk show a little before, enough to know their outlandish approach. And here they were calling Gray Davis "Gumby" and starting up petitions for a recall election. Well, at least it was better than talking about the three abducted girls. But sometimes Kate thought that, far from reporting news, these guys were actually creating it. They seemed like demagogues to her. Although she wasn't a participant in the media anymore, she was still an avid follower of print news, which she considered slightly less irresponsible than electronic news. Now, just as when she'd grown disgusted with her long-ago news writing job, she was once again seeing what most of the media did in a new and jaded light. Gone was all but a tiny trace of the idealism she had brought to journalism as a very young woman just out of college—the feeling that journalists were engaged in the noble project of bringing abuses to light. Maybe they had done so with Watergate, but Kate thought that now, over thirty years later, they had coasted for far too long on the laurels they had received over exposing Nixon and his dirty tricks. Rather than improving people's lives, they seemed to be ruining them.

The most curious thing about today's radio show was that before she left for Italy, these devils had been talking the same way—as if all the world's attention were riveted on California. But that was before Rome, before Giotto's paintings had opened a window toward something a lot bigger—maybe even eternity. Now that she was back, her eyes newly dazzled, here were these two talk-radio guys—still mucking around in the same stinky sewer. What was wrong with them?

Kate was on her way to pick up Mona at her sister's house in San Marcos, where Mona sometimes stayed during the work week, so it was natural to wonder what Mona would have said about all this. Kate knew that Mona was no fan of Davis'—she'd lamented before that he was a big supporter of the death penalty, plus a serious tightwad in regard to clemency and pardons.

"And he's supposed to be a liberal! A Democrat!" Mona had complained.

Kate knew that a lot of politicians were afraid to risk leniency toward criminals, because if their judgment proved wrong, it could backfire. How well she remembered 1988, when George Bush the father had surfed the huge wave of anti-crime sentiment that politicians had been building for years. Bush Sr. had run a vicious campaign against Michael Dukakis based on the fact that a man named Willie Horton had, on Dukakis' watch, committed a new violent crime while he was AWOL from a Massachusetts prison furlough leave. Bush's "Willie Horton" ads—featuring a prominent picture of the African American—had been thought responsible for Bush's victory and, in fact, was one of the principal outrages that soured Kate on her TV job.

Gov. Davis must have taken the lesson from the Willie Horton incident to heart, because never during his tenure did he show any leniency or commute a death sentence, Mona had pointed out.

"When he was governor, Ronald Reagan commuted 575 death sentences!" Mona had exclaimed. "And he was supposed to be a conservative!" But that was before Willie Horton. On the other hand, she hotly pointed out, the so-called liberal Davis not only was in love with the death penalty, he'd also rejected parole for murderers each of the 190 times his own board recommended it.

The miles ticked by. Kate was glad she'd chosen this inland freeway and not the one along the coast, which probably would have been prettier but more crowded. As she careened south along the curves through the low mountains and far suburbs northeast of San Diego, she thought about Mona's newest stories from the prison, which seemed to buttress their budding theory that some version of feminism was driving the arrests that were filling prisons.

For example, Mona had told her about a short, slight, graphic designer named Zork — his artistic name and nickname. On her patients' intake sheets, she could read the charges leading to their incarceration. Zork's was domestic violence. So Mona had asked him if the violence was against his wife.

"He said, 'Yeah, but it wasn't exactly violence,'" Mona explained. "So I thought, Aha! Denial! He said he'd had too much to drink and they had an argument and he yelled at her. She got scared and called 911. He said it happened twice before, but the other times he always left before the cops came."

"He didn't touch her?"

"He said he didn't. He said she just gets scared easily and likes to call 911. He said the last time it happened, he was sick of it, so he didn't leave. So now he's in jail. They talk on the phone every day, and she cries and says she's sorry."

"When he gets out, are they getting back together?"

"He said he doesn't trust her anymore. He wants a divorce."

"Sounds like being able to call 911 is kind of like having a gun in the house. If there were no 911, maybe the consequences of their argument wouldn't have been so severe. Maybe they wouldn't have broken up." Mona had looked thoughtful. "You know, there are so many people in California who moved here from somewhere else. If her family had been near, she could've called them or gone to stay with them if she was scared. Her family could've put things in perspective for her. On the other hand, I talked to another patient, another young guy named Tom, whose own mother turned him in for domestic violence! And it wasn't such clear-cut domestic violence either. His girlfriend got mad and slammed a telephone into his ear with a body pillow. He said it hurt a lot and he hit back reflexively—he was a wrestler in high school—and he gave her a black eye. He said he was going for her stomach and she ducked. He told me he never would've tried to hit her in the eye. His mother was in the next room drinking coffee. She called 911, and that was the last light of day Tom saw for eight months. And when his girlfriend testified in his favor, the judge said he didn't believe her and her opinion was irrelevant!"

Then Mona had launched into another story about a man named Roman from Lithuania. His wife was Lithuanian too, and they had three kids.

"He told me they moved to the States before they were married, 10 years ago. Now they own a restaurant. But that's practically down the tubes since he got arrested. He said his wife was trying to manage it alone, but they've had to close it twice.

"Why's he in jail?"

"He said he and his wife had an argument one day, and a neighbor woman was there. He grabbed his wife by her upper arms and sat her down in a chair. He demonstrated for me, with an invisible woman. So the neighbor called the police. When they came, his wife didn't want to make a complaint, but in California, there's a zero tolerance policy toward domestic violence — it doesn't matter what the wife wants. I guess that explains why Tom's girlfriend's testimony in court didn't matter. It's amazing when you think about it. The opinion of the victim doesn't count."

"Well, the big demand of the women's movement was for cops to get tough on domestic violence," Kate said.

"Yes, that's my point. But, again, doesn't it make you wonder exactly who the women's movement is? In these cases, what the state wanted won out over what the women wanted!"

"Well, you know what they say," Kate had agreed. "When you create a law, you create a machine. So you'd better be sure you really want that law."

"The famous statue of Justice has a blindfold over her eyes. Justice is supposed to operate inflexibly, without considering individual circumstances, sort of like a machine."

"Hmm," Kate replied thoughtfully, then remembering the time her cousin Bart the Inquisitor had chastised her for that absent-minded utterance. She wanted to joke to Mona that she sounded like an anarchist. But Mona had already launched into yet another story.

"I talked to a Mexican guy from Tijuana. He was so cute. He didn't speak much English. His charges were 'Terrorist Threats Against a Child Under 5 Years.' I showed him the words on my computer. I figured he must understand 'Terrorist'—if he could read. He said he's divorced, his wife had a boyfriend, he went to the house to see the kids, she wouldn't let him in, so he kicked the door and a neighbor called 911. He had another charge, something like Destruction of Property under $500. He got six months. Seems kind of extreme. Plus, again, his wife didn't want to press charges. I think they're both undocumented. They just wanted the police to go away. But it was the neighbor."

Kate had wondered if any of these guys had had lawyers. The charges all sounded pretty dubious. Mona said they'd had public defenders and sometimes they talked about them as if they thought they were practically in cahoots with the police. Kate hadn't realized it at the time she knew Danny, but now she was beginning to see that he'd done a very good thing by getting a lawyer, although he had to pay through the nose for it.

But all that with Danny had happened so long ago, before she got back from Italy to find he had suddenly dropped out of her life. And Danny seemed even more remote now that Michel, and other things, were intervening. Thankfully, Kate felt less responsible for helping Michel than she had for helping Danny, probably because Michel was savvier about knowing what to do.

*

The first leg of her trip over, Kate arrived at Mona's sister's house. When Mona got in Kate's car, it was as if the two were already on the same wavelength. Mona immediately asked if Kate had heard from Danny. "No, nothing," Kate admitted. "I've called his job. They just say he's not there. The second time, I tried to ask more and they got rude. I don't know how to get in touch with his mother or where she is. Their apartment is still vacant."

"Tell me again—you saw his picture on a postcard?"

"His and Kari's! It was after I got back from Italy. You know, I started checking out those things that come in the mail. They used to be on milk cartons. 'Have you seen me?' Well, in their case, it was 'Have you seen us?'

204

And there they were—both of them—on a flyer in my mailbox! The guy committed a minor crime and now his name is totally mud and his life is ruined. And Kari's picture too! It didn't say much else, just their names and the city and the date, January, 2003."

"So what happened to them? Did he kidnap her?"

"No! That's ridiculous! Who knows why they came up with that? With the same logic they use about everything else," Kate complained. "But you know, after I saw their pictures on that postcard, I started collecting them. Pretty soon, I had six, and five of them were for people who are related to each other—same last name. They're parents who 'kidnapped' their children!'"

"It's child custody disputes," Mona said. "Divorced parents get desperate because their ex won't let them see the kids."

"But the organization that sends out those cards didn't start that way. The guy who started it was the father of a kid who got abducted by a stranger—a very rare thing. That happened, I don't know, decades ago. Now that the group has gotten rolling, it looks like they ran out of abductions. So they're branching out to parents who run away with their own kids."

"Did I tell you about that friend of mine from Detroit?" Kate continued, thinking of beautiful Marlene and her little daughter Eve. "She was the one obsessed with 'pervs' and Alaska's Megan's list Web page. She and her daughter ran away from her husband in Detroit and came here. Then she had to go back because she was getting threatening letters from the courts. Next step for her was an Amber alert. There were mothers and kids on those postcards—not just fathers."

"Live by the sword, die by the sword," Mona said.

"Anyway, I want to ask the manager if Danny and his mom left a forwarding address, but for once she'd probably say it was private information. Maybe I'll never know what happened."

They drove in silence for a few minutes. "What about your husband?" Kate suddenly remembered to ask. "I thought he was coming."

"He's already in Ensenada. He's diving today with some friends, at La Bufadora, about a half an hour south of Ensenada. I might go too, if we ..."

The car windows were open a bit for a little cooling air, already necessary in March, when suddenly, two black jets screamed in just overhead, drowning out the end of Mona's sentence. In unison, both of their hands shot out to roll up the windows.

"Yow! What's going on?" Kate almost shouted.

"We're passing Miramar Air Base! They're practicing!"

"It's like a war here!"

"Well, there is a war, but it's not exactly here. This is how they're going to be flying around in Iraq in a few days. Scaring the crap out of people."

The high pitched screams had subsided as the black jets became distant black specks.

"They must have been like five feet above us," Kate grumbled.

"I suppose they have to be low since they're landing so close. I think I have PTSD."

Kate glanced at Mona. "Post-traumatic stress disorder?" Mona nodded, smiling. They drove in silence again.

"I just hate this war and everything connected with it," Kate said. But she knew she was preaching to the choir. "Sorry," she suddenly added, "What were you saying about Joe when we were so rudely interrupted? That he's driving near Ensenada?"

"No, diving—scuba diving. Well, he's driving too. Anyway, if I have time after classes, I'll do some diving too. It's a beautiful place when it's not rough—the ocean hits some rock cliffs there and sends up a big spray. He'll come up to Ensenada at night and stay with us, in the same house where we're staying. Do you think you and I will be in the same class?"

"It depends on the placement test. My level should be pretty good, unless I've forgotten a lot. Did you see that?" Kate asked, nodding toward the right.

"What?"

"That big black billboard thing we just passed. It was all lit up with capital letters. It said CHILD ABDUCTION. It was an Amber alert."

"Are you serious? First we have to deal with screaming jets and now an alert? Is this one of those new red or yellow alerts about terrorism?"

"No," responded Kate. "This is like an all-points alert they do after a child has been kidnapped. Who knows … maybe they do it after a kid has been kidnapped by their parents, like we were just talking about."

"What did it say?"

"All I could catch was "BROWN TOYOTA." I couldn't get the license plate number. Anyway, who could remember it? Thank goodness my Toyota isn't brown. And you're kind of short, Mona. Sit up tall so nobody thinks you're a kid I'm abducting. A lot of these drivers would be thrilled to catch a child abductor. This freeway is already like a video game half the time. What are you supposed to do if you think you see them? Make a citizen's arrest? This is ridiculous!"

Fuming, Kate drove on. The thick stream of traffic now seemed more menacing than before. "Did you hear that Elizabeth Smart just turned up, and she's OK?" she asked Mona. "Maybe that's why they're so geared up to do Amber alerts."

"Look," said Mona, "See that little, dark brown car up there with two people inside? That could be it!"

"Is it a Toyota?" Kate asked.

"Who knows?"

Kate was angry, but she was thinking clearly enough to wonder if something like this could have happened in January to Danny and Kari, if he had gone to ... But no, that couldn't be. He said he was going to Delaney. And in Sandra's silver Mercedes! She found herself slowing down. She didn't want to be anywhere near that brown car. It pushed ahead, out of sight. She wished it godspeed. Let them get away, she prayed silently, not thinking what an outlaw her wishes made her.

But they, whoever they were, didn't get away. When Kate exited the freeway 20 minutes later, veering off on the last exit before she would have driven into Mexico and heading for the long-term lot where they would park before walking across the border and catching a taxi to the bus station, traffic had slowed to a crawl.

"There must be a light out," Mona said. "Or an accident."

But it wasn't a light or an accident. As they inched forward on the service road, they stared at a conglomeration of odd vehicles off the left side of the road. Two plain white vans, several marked sheriffs cars, and a bunch of uniformed men clustered around a big towing vehicle containing not just one small brown car, but two. One looked like the dark brown car they had seen some miles back. The other was a golden tan color, and badly crushed at the rear.

"Oh my God," breathed Mona.

"Remember, Mona, you're an atheist."

"An agnostic." Mona paused. "It's got to be ... why else would there be all those sheriffs cars? But they can't both be the car they were looking for in the Amber alert."

"Let's hope at least one of them was! And that nobody got hurt or killed. I guess the thinking is that getting abducted is a fate worse than death, so if people die in a car crash, it's better than letting the bad guys get away." Fifteen minutes later, when Kate and Mona walked along the gated, fenced footbridge leading into Tijuana, Kate carried a backpack and a small bag, while Mona dragged a wheeled suitcase. Tijuana, in contrast to San Diego, seemed to Kate a mass of disorder, but so much happier, so much brighter. Que alivio—what a relief—Kate thought, already trying to get into the Spanish-speaking frame of mind, as she settled in next to Mona in the back seat for the short taxi drive to the bus station. Then she almost felt something like a vise loosening around her head—the same feeling, although more pronounced, that she'd gotten in Italy, as if she were free at last, free at last.

"I think the thing I like best about Los Angeles is that it's so close to Mexico," Kate told Mona.

The mesa was hot, dry and almost crackling on an autumn day a few months later. Kate sniffed the air suspiciously, then continued walking rapidly. The wind blew a strand of hair into her eye, so she stopped in mid-stride to clear it, then continued along the edge of the deserted, two-lane asphalt and gravel road to nowhere. She was heading toward something that appeared to be a lookout. She glanced at her watch. Mona would be off work in 45 minutes. Then they were off for Ensenada again. Hurray! She stopped at the lookout and gazed west. The surrounding high mesa went on as far as the eye could see, a mix of browns, dusty greens and drab golds. The only break was the group of gray buildings in the far distance—a state penitentiary. It was completely separate from the county prison complex where Mona worked, which, although it was much closer to where Kate was walking at the moment, was at the moment out of view behind a bushy knoll.

She had deliberately come early, the goal being to miss the crush of freeway traffic. With the three-hour drive from Orange County behind her, this walk was to get the circulation going in her legs and derriere. When Mona got off work, it would be just a 20-minute drive to the border and then another weekend immersed in Spanish.

Kate had become unaccountably enamored of Spanish. Not many of her friends could understand her desire to learn it—except of course for Sandra, the linguist. In Los Angeles Kate hardly ever found opportunities to speak Spanish, even though she was surrounded by one of the biggest concentrations of Latinos in the world. But the Spanish-speaking culture was so separate from hers that she sometimes considered hiring a maid just to have somebody to practice with.

From her perch on the high mesa, Kate sensed the freeways miles away, surging relentlessly forward like great, restless snakes. She and Mona would soon join that surge.

Resuming her walk, Kate remembered the last time they had joined the throng of cars heading toward Mexico, the day of that freeway hunt in March.

When she had gotten home later the following week, she collected the pile of newspapers that Linda had kept for her and plowed through them, looking for information on that day's dragnet. She found a small article, and followed it up on the Internet.

Yes, there had been an Amber alert in Southern California that day, at more or less the same place and time as she and Mona had been. It was for a 12-year-old Latina girl who supposedly—now Kate always said "supposedly," knowing what happened to Danny—had been kidnapped by a man who knew her family. Now the car was reported to have been a brown Datsun, not a Toyota.

Kate shook her head in disbelief. Not a Toyota after all. What about those two, crushed brown cars?

A newspaper photo showed the girl—chubby and dark—and standing in three-quarter view in a white sweater and slacks in front of a Playboy bunny logo, looking quite unlike a Playboy bunny, but so goes the pre-teen imagination, Kate reflected.

The newspaper was dated March 15, the day after Kate and Mona's harrowing freeway ride. There was no report that the man and girl had been apprehended. Then the story dropped like a stone out of the media. But another story did not disappear. It appeared again and again in the papers. It was about the reappearance of Elizabeth Smart, one of the three girls abducted the previous summer. A lot of people had given her up for dead, but suddenly she turned up safe, and there came a harrowing account of how she had been held captive all that time.

Next, after this harrowing experience, her father showed up in Washington D.C, pushing for a bill that would do many things—for one thing, extend the Amber Alert. A few people complained that the law bundled together too many dubious laws, all of them aimed at sex offenders. But with political adroitness and media savvy suggesting the involvement of wider forces, the father materialized on a national TV show and said his opponents were "hurting children." So the bill flew through the Senate and House and, in almost the same breath, President George W. Bush began the Iraq invasion and Ed and Elizabeth Smart, father and daughter, joined him in the White House to sign the bill. It was called the Protect Act.

Kate watched the development of the Protect Act and the Iraq war over a few days that seemed like eons, silently intoning "No, No, No." Wasn't the Protect Act Bush's way of diverting attention from the war and of directing attention to something everybody wants—protecting children, especially photogenic blonde ones? I can't be such a bad guy, Bush seemed to be saying, if I'm protecting innocent, little victims from madmen—just as I'm doing in Iraq.

Still observing the panoramic view from the little lookout with the penitentiary in the distance miles away, Kate felt so disgusted that she stopped, picked up a small rock, and hurled it into the bush. She'd never been able to throw, and the rock bounced a short distance off, as ineffectual as her silent protests.

Someone, somewhere must have been monitoring her near-seditious thoughts, because seconds later, a nondescript hatchback emerged from the bend in the dusty road. As it got closer, Kate was suddenly aware that she was in an isolated spot, even though she was within a half mile of one formidable security nexus and within two miles of another. But besides the distant buildings—four huge prisons bristling with guards, razor wire, turrets, guns and cameras—there was nothing here but mesa, brush, herself and the approaching car.

The car stopped next to her in a little burst of dust and Kate looked through the open passenger window at the driver, a sandy haired man inclined sideways across the seat so he could talk to her.

"What's up?" he asked.

"What's up??" she repeated idiotically.

"What are you doing out here?"

"I'm exercising. I'm picking up my friend who's a doctor at East Mesa." And why are you asking, she wanted to add, it's a free country. But he spoke with the voice of authority and it was clear he was a guard, even though he wasn't wearing a uniform, and it was clearer which way the wind was blowing, so she meekly obeyed his instructions to head back to the parking lot. After the hatchback was again out of sight, Kate's sole act of insurrection was to pick up another stone and throw it.

As she trudged gloomily back, she thought about how the year—and the war in Iraq—had worn on after that Amber alert and its depressing aftermath in the spring. She had later seen that Bush wasn't the only one calculating how much gain he could wring out of sex crimes. The topic was apparently a deep well of political benefits. One person who clearly realized the benefits was the Governor Davis, who, as autumn drew nearer, was thrashing around like a drowning man, seeking support wherever possible. When he finally threw out some eleventh-hour leniency to murderers and agreed to parole four, it was clearly a calculated move—three of the four murderers he pardoned were battered women who had killed their abusers. He was playing his feminist ace.

But he had been voted out anyway that October 7. Still, as the legacy of his battle with Schwarzenegger, he left a new bunch of stricter laws against people like Danny and Michel.

Oh, what am I thinking? Kate remembered abruptly. Those new laws won't affect Danny. Once again, she let relief flood through her, just as she had during the late spring at the moment she pulled the postcard from Kari out of her mailbox and saw, on the front, a marlin leaping triumphantly over the words "Puerto Vallarta, Mexico."

Was it some sort of cosmic coincidence that two postcards extracted from her mailbox had brought her news about Danny, first that one reading "Have You Seen Us?" and then the one from Kari? There was likewise some cosmic justice, Kate thought, that Davis would end up in exile—if only figuratively—just as Danny had ended up in actual exile from his country. That Davis had been unable to use fear of sex offenders as a life raft was a little perplexing to her. Many politicians before him had done it successfully and many would do it later. Maybe his disapproval rate was just too high—65 percent at one point—or maybe it was that he was so obviously calculating, or maybe it was the earlier electricity crisis. Or maybe the wrath of God.

*

"Welcome to California," Mona said. A couple hours had passed, and Kate had just been ticking off her complaints against Davis.

"No, California's back there." Kate smiled, pointing vaguely toward the back of the bus.

Mona smiled back and then, with mock-cautiousness, craned her neck off to the right and stole a look beyond the flimsy-looking guard rails and down the sandy, Baja California cliffs that fell away at their right to the ocean far below.

"Well, that's clear," she said as she momentarily covered her eyes in feigned terror. "You don't see anything quite like this north of the border." Possibly, she was referring to the car wrecks that littered the breathtaking drop.

As Mona began reading a medical journal, Kate too stole a peek down the steep incline and had a momentary image—more like a hallucination of a wrecked, silver Mercedes lodged behind a large bush. But then she reflected that this Mexican coastal highway wasn't on the way to Puerto Vallarta.

Furthermore, according to Danny's mother, when Kate finally got her number and called her, Danny and Kari had in reality not even gone to Puerto Vallarta. The Puerto Vallarta postcard might have been a decoy in the unlikely event that Kate's mail was being checked, but basically the postcard was to inform Kate how to contact Danny's stepfather for further car payments. Kate didn't think she'd be doing that.

Danny's mother hadn't said exactly where Danny and Kari had gone, and Kate didn't ask, but it was clear that Pera had been in touch with them, because she let drop the mind boggling news that Kari had slept in the trunk for the entire ride south through California, only getting out after they were safely across the border. "He said he was afraid he was going to get picked up." Pera added that Trevor hadn't gone with them.

"Well, it wasn't easy to decide, but in the end, Trevor stayed here with me and Chucho. It's been OK so far—his P.O. says the next step for him is juvenile prison, but he hasn't gotten in any more trouble. Most of the time, he's over at his girlfriend's house. She's a good influence. I don't know why a girl like that isn't put off by all the trouble Trevor's been in. Maybe she knows he's basically a good kid."

As Kate ruminated and the bus sped on, Mona began to doze over her journal and Kate's thoughts turned back to California politics. At the moment, Davis was still officially the governor, until inauguration day, at least. He was in his lame-duck period.

But already, even before he took office, Schwarzenegger had been suffering his own "sex crimes" scandal, a storm of criticism claiming he behaved crudely at the gyms he used to frequent. The female heavyweights were hammering him. Joyce Brown, a radio advice psychologist, had written that his long-ago advances toward her "were a lot about power, not about sex," almost on the same day as feminist luminary Susan Faludi commented that with Schwarzenegger's style of unwelcome advances, "Sex isn't even the prime object here."

How familiar all of that sounded to Kate. She knew Mona would have an opinion on this. Hadn't she been part of that long ago chorus of comments that sex crimes are about power? But such weighty thoughts soon slid away. Instead, thought about what fun it was to head south along this spectacular coastline dazzled her. Mona was deep into her nap, the open medical journal sliding perilously down her lap.

"How's the surfer doing?"

Kate started. She looked at Mona, who had suddenly revived and was looking at Kate alertly. The magazine was grasped safely in her hand. "Fine," Kate answered, still feeling embarrassed at the idea the Michel was the second sex offender she'd been interested in, although Mona hadn't mentioned it. "He's going to church!"

"Is that new?"

"Yeah. His former therapist, my idiotic cousin, wouldn't let him. He couldn't be around kids. Or maybe it was his probation officer. Anyway, with his new therapist, everything is better. Now he says he's glad he's in therapy. I go to church with him sometimes."

"That must be why I haven't seen you at the UU congregation."

Kate admitted it was the reason. Church, she had to concede, was not a much more standard date than the beach. But she enjoyed both and they filled the bill as low pressure ways of getting to know Michel. She was a little worried that eventually Michel wouldn't be able to surf, as some local city governments were discussing making all parks off limits to sex offenders.

Kate pulled out the Tijuana newspaper she had brought, smoothed the front page, and saw a story about a drug killing. Every time she got her hands on a newspaper here, there seemed to be something about drug violence. Ditto for every time she heard something about Mexico in Los Angeles, for that matter. Yet when she talked to people in Ensenada and Tijuana, drug violence didn't seem to have registered as a source of big-time worry. Kate wondered if the topic was another creature of the media, like the dangerousness of Detroit or the liberalism of California.

Later, Kate mentioned the headlines about the drug murders to Pati, the housewife in Ensenada who was putting them up in her house. Yes, it happens, she answered in Spanish, but not usually to people who aren't involved in drugs.

When Kate asked her if she thought the police should clean up the drug trade, Pati was indignant. "The police? They're worse than the criminals."

"Mexicans hate police," Mona said later when she and Kate were lolling around on a boardwalk south of Ensenada where Joe and his friends were diving. "They hate the government too. I think they generally hate authority."

Kate decided she must be right, judging from an elaborate altar to Pancho Villa she soon saw on the boardwalk. It was decorated with crepe paper, a framed photo and an assortment of marigolds and sugar skulls that somebody had put together not far from the heaving sea. It was around Halloween and Day of the Dead. Apparently, people constructed ad hoc altars to commemorate respected figures — even that hybrid outlaw-hero Pancho Villa.

"I thought he was basically a bandito," Kate said quietly to Mona as they mulled around the altar.

"Apparently somebody here likes him," Mona shrugged. "Maybe he was like Robin Hood."

On the Sunday morning that Kate was planning to return to Los Angeles with Mona and Joe, she woke up to find the little landing outside her bedroom sprinkled with black flakes. She touched one with her toe. An ash. She didn't have much of a view from the porch but what she could see of the blue sky didn't look quite right.

In the dining room downstairs, Mona and Joe were already watching television with Pati. "There are wildfires all over," Mona informed her, in slow Spanish. They were supposed to be practicing Spanish all the time while staying at Pati's. "I think they're worse in California. They might close some freeways."

Closing freeways was a radical move for California. Kate was alarmed. They had a six-hour drive ahead of them, a lot of it on California freeways, apparently right through the heart of fire country. Should we stay in Ensenada a day longer? But Joe and Kate had to work the next day.

"If they close freeways, maybe nobody will be working tomorrow," Joe said. "It sounds pretty serious." On the other hand, Joe was a doctor like Mona, so he was one of those people that should be working, come rain, sleet or—fire.

"It's a little apocalyptical," Kate observed after returning to the dining room from another sky check. "There are ashes fluttering down everywhere. I think I see some smoke."

Pati was in the kitchen, so they had switched to quiet English. The TV channels they were watching for fire news, strangely enough, were all from the U.S. and all in English. Ensenada was basically a sleepy port town without much in the way of media.

"Pati, do you think they'll close the roads between Ensenada and Tijuana?" Kate asked, changing back to Spanish.

Pati smiled. "They never close anything in Mexico. Even when they had the big earthquake in Mexico City in 1985, the government didn't do much. I lived there then. We didn't need the government," she said in a scoffing tone. "Government authorities stole some of the relief supplies! But the ordinary people were fine. There was no looting and disorder. Many people brought baskets of bread into the city."

Finally Kate, Mona and Joe made the decision to travel back to California as planned. Pati and her husband were going to visit his parents in another city that day, so staying in Ensenada would have meant finding a hotel.

So they retraced their earlier route and headed north that afternoon on the pretty coastal highway. Traffic seemed normal, although light.

"We have our systems in the States. We're great engineers, great planners," Joe reflected as they drove along. They were all glancing uneasily at the occasional plume of smoke rising from somewhere east in the hills of Baja. "Here they do everything on a smaller scale, a human scale really. A lot more depends on the individual. People don't rely on the government."

Unaccountably, Kate thought about the monumental statue of Justice wearing a blindfold and holding scales. Was the justice system an automaton like everything else?

"I like all the kissing that goes on here," Joe continued. "I get to kiss all the women. You see couples making out a lot too. You don't see that at home. When my cousin and his girlfriend from Poland visited me in San Diego, he told me he was shocked at the lack of affection. When he and his girlfriend kissed in public, cars would honk at them."

As they approached the San Ysidro border station to enter the States, they could see it was as busy as ever, with lane after lane of idling cars waiting to pass the U.S. checkpoints before they would be swallowed by the I-5 freeway. There was one big difference from a normal Sunday, however, and that was the blackness filling the afternoon sky north and east of the crossing.

"Looks like it's coming from where I work—where the prisons are," Mona solemnly observed.

Kate was with like-minded friends. She was returning to happy prospects with Michel. But her mood about crossing back into her own country that day was a stark contrast to her mood when she had crossed in the other direction the previous week. It wasn't just the skies that were already, at 2 p.m., as dark as dusk on a stormy day. It wasn't just unease about her long-term future as the companion of someone who was being made into an untouchable. It was sadness at leaving behind the happy country of chaos and kisses.

She thought about the last line in Kari's postcard, neatly lettered in her still childish hand. "We're in the Land of the Free now."

23. But Grandma, you have such big teeth!

2003 to 2010

ALEX LANDON

After former California Governor Gray Davis was voted out of office in 2003, his replacement Schwarzenegger didn't do any better than Davis in regard to crime and prison policy. When the Governator entered office in 2003 after chasing away Davis, it was after promising to get the budget in order, reduce the prison population, bring down the high recidivism rate, and terminate the prison guard union's political influence. (1) Despite Schwarzenegger's vows to take on the entrenched "tough-on-crime" interests, he failed miserably. In fact, in another perfect example of a horrible designer law, Schwarzenegger not only abandoned his promises, but actually signed on with those "tough-on-crime" interests. This happened just before the fall of 2006 when "Jessica's law" was proposed as a voter's initiative. And true to the designer-law template, Jessica's law would be championed by yet another politician whose star was hitched to a gruesome crime.

There had been intimations of something like Jessica's law long before it actually materialized in California. Gulags made up of former sex offenders suffering super-strict residency restrictions had already been forming elsewhere. Some of the most notorious were in Iowa, where parole officers had forced convicted people to live outside cities in cheap motels far away from schools or parks where children might be—and far away from education, jobs or public transportation to get to them, destroying much chance of their successful assimilation into normal society. (2)

In summer of 2006, a California politician brought Iowa's folly to California. Jessica's law (as Proposition 83) was put on the California ballot by legislator Sharon Runner, who was running for re-election in her district. The proposed law was a many-tentacled monster, including strict no-live zones such as in Iowa, more psychological evaluations for convicted sex offenders, harsher sentences, GPS monitoring for life, and in general many more hoops for convicted people to jump through.

Like Little Red Riding Hood checking out the wolf wearing Grandma's nightgown—But Grandma, you have such big teeth!— voters had to consider whether to embrace Jessica's law. And what was there to stop them?

The long-dead framers of the Constitution, with their determination to protect even those convicted of crime, seemed a quaint anachronism to many voters. No powerful anti-Proposition-83 groups would form. On the

216

contrary, a stampede of politicians—including Gov. Schwarzenegger, who was up for re-election and seemed to have forgotten his promises to improve the justice system—hoped to coast into office posing as brave predator slayers. They were hoping voters wouldn't be able to resist the seductive title of their re-election vehicle: "The Sexual Predator Punishment and Control Act: Jessica's Law." Who wouldn't want to control "sexual predators"?

The ultraconservative Runner had first proposed Jessica's law as an Assembly Bill and then, after her fellow legislators read and killed it, she paid signature gatherers to get it on the ballot. For skeptics, Runner's husband resuscitated that old argument that needed a stake through its heart—sex offenders have an "incredible" re-offense rate, he claimed. "Incredible" was a bit hazy, but who had time to do any research to check it out, especially when the claim came from someone in a respected role? "Why would he lie?" the average person might ask themselves, blind to the average politician's burning desire to get elected and re-elected, even at the cost of truth.

The stampeding politicians attracted ill-informed people—people inflamed by "predator," which was repeated as if it were an accurate descriptor of something besides an animal. This conjured up the Nazi era when other terms from the animal kingdom—"Parasiten" (parasites) and "Schwein" (swine)—were used to dehumanize people.

Such linguistic manipulation fosters the subtle racism behind designer laws—proposals hastily conceived after statistically rare, but high-profile tragedies. We had Megan's law, the Amber alert, Danielle's law, now Jessica's law ... all named after white children, even when similar crimes happened around the same time to children of color.

The law's promoters threw $150-a-head "Jessica's law" fundraisers—titillating spectacles for which they brought Jessica Lunsford's grieving father in from Florida. Photos of Jessica smiling from beneath her fuzzy, pink hat were prominently featured. California has the nation's largest, most diverse population, so it should have told us something that politicians had to go so far away to find ingredients they thought would inflame voters.

A bunch of silliness

Meanwhile, a more sober view was starting to take hold in Iowa, where prosecutors with experience in how the gulags worked had just published a damning putdown of no-live zones, calling them useless and counterproductive.

And GPS monitoring, although it intuitively "sounded good" to many people—especially in a high-tech-happy era—was in reality a false hope too. Yet hardly a soul could be found to point out how untested and costly GPS monitoring was, certainly not heavyweight politicians such as Schwarzenegger and Attorney General Jerry Brown, who had both signed on as supporters of Jessica's law.

But former Los Angeles County Dist. Atty. Steve Cooley, once co-chair of the Proposition 83 campaign, made a startling statement, speaking out against no-live-zones and GPS monitoring. "What documentation is there that this works at all?" he queried. Still, Cooley officially remained a supporter of Jessica's law. But one lonely district attorney clearly spoke out against the measure—San Mateo County's James P. Fox. Fox had a safe seat, and could afford to call the no-live zones "a bunch of silliness" that "would give people a false sense of security ... The vast majority of child molesters are not strangers; they are family members or family friends."(3)

Consultants explained the abundance of Jessica's law supporters and its dearth of critics by saying it was political suicide to be against such a measure. Any candidate who didn't support it would be ruthlessly attacked as a friend of child molesters, these analysts pointed out, evidencing the old, militaristic War on Crime mentality. (4)

Perhaps Proposition 83 backers thought they could also count on support from women who remembered that long-gone era when sex-crime convictions were scarce (unless they were against people of color). But I was encouraged when, after giving a speech against Jessica's law, a woman came up to say she was moved by my example of the young sailor or frat guy who gets drunk and sexually assaults a woman, goes down on a felony, and would have to wear a GPS bracelet for life and be prohibited from living where he can find a job. She agreed that the proposal went too far.

And when the audience learned that nationwide, one of every 37 living adults has been in prison and in California one of every 135 men was on Megan's list, my audience became more suspicious of Jessica's law.

It was instructive to notice that, in a straw vote after my talk, all the people of color in the audience nixed Proposition 83.

But it didn't work out that way in the November election. Jessica's law was approved by 70 percent of California voters.

The Pandora's box

Some longtime Californians face the results of many voter initiatives with a heavy heart. With Jessica's law, it was encouraging to know that 30 percent of voters recognized a bad law despite the irresponsibility of so many politicians. But dealing with the results of the vote still lay ahead, and when they came, they were not pleasant.

By 2007, the first year after Jessica's law no-live sections took effect, the number of sex offenders who listed themselves as homeless had risen by 44 percent. (5) Naturally, when people are homeless, they are more dangerous and harder to track, so, clearly, the law was already proving counterproductive in achieving its stated aim of "protection." In addition, the parole department was sending parolees back to prison on technical violations related to their residence location, so the law was turning into yet another hoop for parolees to try to jump through—a hoop that would inflate "recidivism" statistics.

By June 2008, among sex offenders on parole—the only people for whom Jessica's law's residence restrictions were consistently enforced— the number listed as homeless went from 88 in November 2006 to 1,056 —a whopping 1,100 percent increase!

However, in general, the residence restrictions were so unclear—the law didn't specify whether the provisions were retroactive or only applicable to new offenders—and were so stymied by court challenges, that residence restrictions were hardly being enforced. In San Diego County more than 70 percent of registered sex offenders were violating Jessica's law by living too close to schools and parks. In contrast, Iowa legislators, who by 2009 had a little more experience with residence restrictions, were able to wrestle that Pandora's box closed a bit, and had done away with the no-live zones except for violent sex offenders. (6) Sadly, for political reasons that will soon be clear, the possibility of California doing the same seemed to become more and more remote each day.

A stillborn law

The situation with GPS was worse. In 2009, about a year into an economic crisis that people likened to the Great Depression of the 1930s, California's budget was in one of the rockiest chapters in its rocky history. The GPS part of Jessica's law—the supremely expensive part—had supposedly been in effect for three years, but in reality it was hardly being carried out.

"I'm not aware of any sheriff in the state doing GPS," said Jim Denney, director of the California Sheriffs Association. "There is no local funding tied to Jessica's Law." (7)

This combination of no funding plus general economic malaise upended the GPS part of Jessica's law, making it dysfunctional. Those supporters of GPS, including Governor Schwarzenegger and Attorney General Brown, like typical California dreamers, had blithely dismissed the funding problems when people were voting on Proposition 83 in 2006. Apparently, they didn't want to appear soft on crime and hoped that a money fairy would appear, and it would all work out somehow.

But by 2009, the money fairy was apparently on unemployment like a lot of other people. Schwarzenegger was slashing education, mental health and even police expenditures—he wasn't touching prison spending, though—in an effort to bail out the sinking ship of state. Yet huge sums of tax dollars continued to be spent on non-dangerous, low-risk offenders. By September, Schwarzenegger was also dealing with a three-judge order to reduce the number of people in the state's extremely overcrowded prisons by 40,000 people. You might think he would have been happy about this great opportunity to reduce spending—as he had promised just a few years earlier—but instead he was dragging his feet.

Even back at election time in 2006, California had been in serious debt, so shortly after Jessica's law was passed, in an attempt to jolt some life into this stillborn measure, Schwarzenegger had set aside $106 million for the GPS tracking of just 6,622 people—only people on parole, and not the tens of thousands of others on Megan's list, as Jessica's law had mandated. Nobody seemed quite sure where even this relatively small amount of money was going to come from. By 2008, California's legislative analyst estimated that costs from Jessica's law would rise to several hundred million dollars annually over the next several years. (8) However, extrapolating from the cost of doing GPS just on paroled people, the expense of electronically tracking everybody on Megan's list would have been even higher than that figure, amounting to a staggering $1.05 billion dollars annually. (9)

Yes, that was billion, not million. To get a grasp of this figure, consider that in a recent year, the California Controller's report had showed the total expense for the entire operation of California, including education, highways, health, prisons, the governor's parties—the whole ball of wax—was $209 billion dollars. So only doing GPS on everyone on Megan's list would have meant spending a significant chunk of that figure.

But the state was already badly in the red. Obviously then, Jessica's law was limping. In fact, the whole teetering edifice of measures aimed at keeping tabs on tens of thousands of people convicted of both high- and low- level sex crimes could barely be enforced.

That didn't stop some people from trying. And somebody apparently tried in the case of Phillip Garrido, a California man who had been convicted decades earlier of a sex offense and would in 2009, just three years after Jessica's law passed, be accused of abducting a girl, Jaycee Dugard, and keeping her for years as a sex prisoner in his backyard. But before Jaycee was found, during the time that Jessica's law was ramping up and while Garrido was holding Jaycee prisoner, it was reported that officers checking on convicted sex offenders had come to Garrido's front door, asked a few questions, and then left, unaware of anything amiss.

This is very sad. In addition, it is very stupid. Compare this to what happened recently to a parolee, a 70-year-old retired Navy man, who had been convicted of touching his granddaughter inappropriately once when she was in the bathtub—incidentally, a typical type of sex offense that did not involve lurking or abduction, happened at home between two people who already knew each other and was unlikely to happen again.

After this grandfather had been out of prison nine months, a couple of carloads of officers showed up at his house one day. They didn't stop at the door, like in the Garrido case. They came right in, searched, and found several "contraband" items: three stuffed animals that they dug out of his wife's closet, calling them "toys that could be used to solicit children." Then the grandfather's parole officer put a no-bail parole hold on him and took him to prison, without permitting him to bring his medication, thus traumatizing his wife. He stayed incommunicado in prison for three weeks without his heart medication. He was finally given a hearing and, only because the hearing officer turned out to be a reasonable person, was released.

If carloads of officers did not waste their time—and taxpayer money—harassing low-risk people such as the man mentioned above, they would have resources to focus on truly dangerous people. Nobody can be 100 percent sure that if the officers checking Garrido had not been hampered by the weight of Jessica's law and other over-reaching laws, they would have taken the time to come inside Garrido's house and find Jaycee. But it is clear that if sex offender laws were narrowed down to something reasonable, officers could focus on dangerous criminals instead of filling the prisons with men whose wives own teddy bears. [3]

Those shadowy forces

Looking at the Garrido case and others, a writer in the Los Angeles Times in the summer of 2009 saw a "string of horrific, high-profile kidnappings, beatings and killings," (10) which always seems to bring forth a string of irresponsible, ineffective high-profile laws.

And indeed, the perceived crime wave did have some consequences. The Garrido case hit the news while Gov. Schwarzenegger was in the midst of dealing with the aforementioned court order to reduce the number of people in prison. This caused fear in many quarters that, in the wake of the "crime wave"—a "wave" all too similar to the one we have 3 In 1990, according to Jerome Miller, over one third of the inmates in California state prisons had been put there by their parole officers, often for technical violations such as forgetting a parole appointment. (After California State Assembly Bill 109 passed in 2011, the number of individuals in prison

---

[3] In 1990, according to Jerome Miller, over one third of the inmates in California state prisons had been put there by their parole officers, often for technical violations such as forgetting a parole appointment. (After California State Assembly Bill 109 passed in 2011, the number of individuals in prison for violation of parole diminished.)

for violation of parole diminished.) chronicled from the Summer of the Abducted White Girl—a flood of dangerous people would soon be set free, creating danger in the community. So, the Garrido case and the "crime wave" were probably what caused Governor Schwarzenegger, faced with a great deal of media-induced outrage, to delay in following the court order and to petition the Supreme Court to block the court's order.

But at least the latest "crime wave" didn't cause any proposals for new laws. One might have concluded that the abysmal state of the budget was too well known. Or was it just that the right ingredients—murder of an attractive white girl by a stranger, politician facing re-election, parents who could be brought on board, media willing to fan the flames of public fear—were not yet present?

However, those ingredients fell into place in another case that cropped up. Soon, those shadowy forces—the prison guards union, politicians?—that always seem to be waiting in the wings for the right moment, would pull out yet another proposed law aimed at draining taxpayers of money while keeping correctional personnel gainfully employed.

Things started to look up for these dark forces in early 2010, with the death of not just one attractive, white teenager, but two—Chelsea King and Amber Dubois, both from suburban San Diego. Seeming to justify the call for yet tougher laws, John Gardner, the man eventually convicted in these killings, had previously spent five years of a six-year sentence in prison after conviction for an earlier sex offense in the year 2000, when he was 21 years old, against a 13-year-old girl he knew from his neighborhood. The girl testified that Gardner hit her before she talked him out of raping her, after which he apologized.

After Gardner murdered Chelsea and Amber, there was the feeling that if he'd stayed in prison longer, Chelsea and Amber would still be alive. Moreover, Gardner was apparently a stranger to Chelsea and Amber (unlike the girl in his first crime), and had almost literally jumped out of the bushes in a park and along a road—exactly the type of crime that, although rare, causes the public's fears, understandingly, to go ballistic.

Slightly before Chelsea King disappeared, a state legislator had introduced Assembly Bill 1844, which was related to prison inmate labor. What happened next was all too similar to what happened with the Three Strikes law and Jessica's law.

Just after Chelsea's body was found in February, with lightning speed, AB 1844 was kidnapped. By April 13, it had become "Chelsea's law" and mutated into a monster mandating expensive measures such as life imprisonment without parole, lifetime parole or double parole for some crimes, parks off limits to sex offenders and yet more GPS monitoring. Of course, everyone was painfully aware of the fiscal collapse of the state, and one newspaper that spring said the annual cost of GPS was already at $15.3

million (11). But in the panicked rush to get Chelsea's law rolling, that important tidbit of news seemed to fall on deaf ears, even as other sound projects, such as a women's drug treatment facility named Freedom House, which had assisted women with substance abuse problems for 20 years, were denied funding.

The legislator who originally proposed AB 1844 was lost in the shuffle and to the fore came a young and promising military veteran and first term Assembly member, Nathan Fletcher, roped in by the forces that are always ready to seize on tragedies. Fletcher had no experience in criminal justice or sex crimes, but what he did have was an upcoming primary election on his plate. We know that nothing is as likely to ensure that a politician's name is mentioned over and over as a savior of young girls in peril as sponsorship of a designer law named after an attractive murdered girl.

The pact made with the forces probably went something like: you get re-elected, we get monster law. So Chelsea's law seemed to be on its way to sure passage, with objections by the American Civil Liberties Union and California Attorneys for Criminal Justice brushed aside by legislators with the scent of blood and victory in their nostrils.

With Fletcher's fortunes thus bolstered, other politicians sashayed in, with the news media as their eager partners. Former Governor Schwarzenegger gave Chelsea's law his imprimatur. And former San Diego County District Attorney Bonnie Dumanis exhumed some moldering arguments that should have remained in the tomb: "We all know that sex offenders don't get cured. There's no real treatment and anything that we can do that keeps those that do this locked up is, I think, what we need to do," she intoned in an April panel discussion sponsored by the San Diego Union Tribune newspaper. (12)

Former San Diego County Supervisor Dianne Jacob, after all those years still the queen of vitriol in the parallel universe, got into the act again voicing a death wish—"anyone who commits a violent or sexual crime against a child should either be executed or thrown in prison and not let out," she declared. (13)

The battle drums were beaten incessantly. This was particularly true in newspapers—a medium much beleaguered by loss of readership, loss of advertising revenue and bankruptcy due to the growth of the Internet and the economic crisis. And on radio—a ratings-driven medium which, due to its fleeting electronic nature is usually found at the top of the irresponsibility meter—coverage was intense and dramatic. Certainly, Chelsea's fate boosted readership and ratings from February clear through June 2010, as the case made headlines, often multiple headlines, daily, even many weeks after the man had been convicted, sentenced and sent off to prison.

And Assemblyman Fletcher likewise was able to leverage Chelsea King—via Chelsea's Light Foundation with its slick logo and photo of the red-haired teen—into a smashing victory in the June primary. Chelsea's law was passed well before the November general election, so, to keep the ball rolling, Fletcher stayed busy during the summer scouting other states that might be in need of a similar law, which by then was being called a "one-strike" law for sex offenders. (14) Thus buoyed by the swell of publicity generated by the murdered girl, Fletcher coasted on to victory in the November general election.

Of course, nobody is saying that murdered girls should not be mourned. They should, but appropriately—as real girls known and loved by real people, not as instant stars gruesomely exploited by politicians and the media. And although the girls' parents seemed eager to get behind this reactionary law that would fruitlessly increase penalties, they too are mere cogs in a great, cold publicity machine—the War on Crime machine—whose true ends have little to do with their children.

So when people ponder headline-grabbing cases and wonder why laws dealing with sex offenders didn't seem to prevent individuals with a long rap sheet from striking again, the answers are not intuitive or immediately obvious—they require clear thinking.

The lesson we can take from the Jaycee Dugard-Phillip Garrido backyard imprisonment case is that supervision for sex crimes might do some good if registration wasn't so broadly applied, making it impossible for officers to supervise truly dangerous people.

In the Chelsea King-Amber Dubois-John Gardner case, we do not know if tougher laws or stricter enforcement would have insured that Gardner would still have been in prison at the time of the girls' killings. What we do know is that he certainly did not get help while doing his time, nor did he have his issues addressed after his release. We may also surmise that, after his release from prison, the untouchable status given to all sex offenders due to harsh policies that are in place impeded him from becoming a functional member of the community and could have prodded him into more outlandish actions. Both cases show us that, unfortunately, there is no way to prevent all crime. But we can be more effective by using our resources for prevention rather than reacting after the fact. The solution is not to whip up another Frankenstein proposal with an astronomical price tag and slap the name of a murdered child on it—which is exactly what happened with Chelsea's law. Instead, we need focused, responsible policies with reasonable price tags.

24. PV dreams

April 2003 to January 2004

ELAINE HALLECK

Puerto Vallarta—what a place! Kari Fernandez remembered how long it had taken to get there, Dad complaining how much gas "the hog" was using, and herself sitting for days—days that became weeks—in a puddle of sweat, until she got the bright idea to put a towel on the seat.

But it was worth it when they emerged from the jungle arching over the narrow, curving highway, and got a look at the ocean and the steep green hills tumbling right down into it. And then eating ceviche—something like shrimp cocktail—at an outdoor place where you could almost see the ocean, and everybody so happy and friendly. Kari suspected people may not have been so friendly towards her and Dad if they knew.

Too bad they didn't stay very long in PV, as everyone called it—in English. Longer than the road trip from TJ…Tijuana…had taken. Long enough for Dad to get a job and an apartment, and buy the bug, or boche, as Mexicans called the little Volkswagens. It was another German car, although probably made in Mexico, and way better than the Mercedes on gas. Dad sold the Mercedes for parts because it had a problem with the license plates.

Dad eventually decided PV had a problem too. But at first, he thought it was okay, especially when the waiter at the ceviche restaurant told him about a job as a concierge, and he got it the next day.

The apartment they stayed in was outside the hotel zone, up under a golf course that overlooked the bay, Bahia de Banderas. But even though PV wasn't big, the apartment was really too far from the hotel to walk, especially since Dad worked long hours six days a week. He didn't want Kari to stay home all day alone, so she went with him and hung around during his workdays, first in the Mercedes, then using the computers in what they called a cyber cafe in the hotel, then sometimes exploring nearby streets.

"Be careful," Dad told her. "Be nice, but don't talk much to anyone, and don't go by the pool or restaurants where the guests are. But don't go far away. You're a good girl, and smart, so help me figure things out." Dad got the job because of his English, the language of most of the guests in PV. He wore a black suit with a black bow tie. Kari thought that suit was a big part of the reason he liked the job. He looked nice in it, although he had to change out of it before he left work. He'd only worn a regular tie a few times, when he went to court back in L.A.

Dad's job was at a big reception desk, and he spent a lot of time getting trained. It wasn't that easy, he said. After a few days, Kari found a shady, open-air taco restaurant with stools at a high counter and a few tables. It wasn't in a busy area, and they didn't seem to mind if she sat for a long time drinking an agua fresca, which literally means "fresh water" but is actually fruit and water put in a blender with sugar. Her favorite was "jamaica," made from red flowers. She knew how to pronounce it because of her Spanish class. At first Kari was afraid she might get sick from drinking it, but they showed her the huge bottles of purified water they used, and said it was even boiled. "Real sugar too," they said, although Kari didn't get that. Wasn't all sugar real?

Almost everyone around PV spoke English—sometimes not well, but well enough to deal with the so-called gringos pouring off the cruise ships looking for something to do. Kari wondered if she was a gringo. One day she bought a couple postcards and wrote to people back home. And she found a little bookstore called Gringo's with used English books and bought a young-adult novel called "Refugees," a local English newspaper and another in Spanish, thinking it would help her get fluent. She had managed to bring her University of Chicago Spanish-English dictionary from her Spanish class, and she always had it in her bag. It had already helped. With it she could look up words in the newspaper articles, although the one they used a lot—and the dictionary didn't really help with—was "se." It could be "sé," with an accent, or it could go before or after words, sometimes even attached to them. "Se" drove her crazy.

One reason Kari had chosen that taco restaurant the first day was that she noticed a girl about her age sitting at the counter with her nose buried in a book, partly out of sight behind the kitchen equipment. Kari didn't sit near her, but seeing someone like herself—with a dark complexion and obviously not a tourist because she was dressed so ordinarily, in a short-sleeved blouse, not a colorful halter top—gave Kari confidence that she could kill some time there without being taken for a…she didn't know what.

"Do you like that book?" the girl unexpectedly asked Kari as she passed on the way back from the bathroom. Kari saw that she was wearing flat sandals and a knee-length skirt with a pretty design on it. Her English seemed normal, but Kari had heard her speak what sounded like good Spanish to the restaurant people. The girl seemed to be prepared for a quick answer and to walk on past, but Kari forgot what Dad had said, and perked up in a friendly way.

"I just started, but it seems good so far—it's about three different kids and their families who had to run away from three different countries, all in boats. I just got it…" she pointed in the direction of the bookstore.

"At Gringo's!" the girl said, smiling. "My name is Marie."

Kari might have noticed that it wasn't Maria, but Marie, that the accent and appearance didn't quite seem American or Mexican, although basically Marie didn't stick out as unusual in PV, and that, like Kari, she was too dark to be the average tourist. Up close, Kari realized Marie was very pretty, but her clothes and manner downplayed her looks.

Kari held out the book so Marie could look at the cover, which depicted a boy looking out at a stormy sea from the deck of a boat. "I'm Kari."

"Enchantée! I read this! Then I resold it back to Gringo's," Marie said smiling, looking at the cover briefly and handing it back. "It's the story of my life."

What a coincidence, Kari thought. But she said "Really?" then realized that sounded dumb.

"Not exactly," Marie admitted. "But...mmm...a big story."

"You mean you're a refugee?"

"For a while I was. Now we're here. My father works at the Grand Fiesta Americana."

Kari was taken aback. "My father works at the Grand Fiesta too!" Then she paused and indicated the seat next to her, "Would you like to sit here?" Only then did she realize it was going to be hard to heed Dad's warning not to talk too much. She'd have to be careful. But it had been so long since she had a friend. Maybe since Ashley. What a disaster.

"Is your father a concierge?" she asked as soon as Marie sat down, sensing it was less dangerous if she kept control of things by asking questions.

"I think so," Marie nodded. "He does many things. He's an artist. That's how he brought us here. By drawing portraits on a cruise ship from Spain to Mexico. My mother and I worked in the laundry."

"Are you from Spain?"

"No. We're from Guinea. Well, my mother is Mexican. She was a missionary in Guinea. They had me before they left."

"A missionary. Wow! What kind?" The only missionaries Kari had heard of were Catholic priests, not women, and not single women. After she asked, Kari took advantage of Marie's turn to answer by sipping her agua fresca. It was hard work being in charge of a conversation—hard to find time to eat and drink.

"Jehovah's Witnesses."

Kari wasn't sure where Guinea was, but now suddenly guessed Africa. She wasn't sure about Jehovah's Witnesses either but didn't think it was polite to ask a lot of questions about somebody's religion. And a Mexican Jehovah's Witness missionary going to Spain with her African artist husband and ending up in PV was a lot to take in. But then, Kari's own story was pretty weird too. She suddenly wondered if she was a refugee herself. Gringo...refugee...all questions that couldn't be decided now. "Why did you decide to leave...Guinea?" After she asked, Kari realized that was pretty personal too. She had never been that talkative and now realized it wasn't that easy. But how could she ever have friends if she had to be so careful? On the other hand, she was starting to see that Marie was in a similar situation to her own, and she didn't seem that worried about opening up.

Marie rolled her eyes slightly. "We didn't exactly decide. Guinea is Islamic. My father converted to Jehovah's Witness. His family is…in the politics. Some of them didn't like Jehovah's Witnesses. So we had to leave."

Kari backed off that line of questions. "Your English is good. How did you learn?" she asked.

"In Guinea everybody speaks French. In a small country, in Africa, you have to speak foreign languages. Nobody outside Guinea speaks Mandinka or Susu or Pulaar. I had a good education, at my mother's school and at home. French, English, Spanish."

"Dios mio," Kari said, impressed. "I'm Mexican-American but I hardly speak Spanish. 'Dios mio' is about it." Something prodded her again, warning that any pauses in the conversation would naturally lead to questions from Marie that might be hard to answer. She looked at her Mexican newspaper sitting on the counter next to her book.

"What's this mean?" she said, pulling the newspaper near and pointing at a headline. "'Se busca responsable de hospicio.'" There was that stupid "se" again.

"They're looking for…someone who's…like, the director of a…" Marie pulled the paper closer, and her brown eyes scanned the story. "…a hospital or…no, an…orphanage."

"Orphanage?" Kari said, frowning slightly. "Why?"

"Voyons voir," said Marie, continuing to read. "The police think he…the police received complaints from boys about…I don't know this word…pederasta…Maybe it is…"

Kari got out her dictionary and looked. "It's not here," she reported. Marie tried a little device she had, a translator. "In English, 'pederast.' In French, 'pédéraste,'" she announced. Kari shook her head. That didn't help.

It didn't seem to help Marie either. "Disculpe…" she said to a lady behind the counter. "She's a Jehovah's Witness," Marie confided to Kari, as the woman moved nearer. Then, after a short conversation in Spanish, Marie turned to Kari. "Eh bien, a pederasta is a bad person—someone who abuses sexually to children," Marie explained. Now the woman was reading the article. She and Marie talked a little more and then the woman went back to her work.

"The pederast, Joseph Corrigan, he had an orphanage…for boys… here in PV, and…over the years some of the boys complained."

"San José!" the woman called out to Marie, along with more Spanish.

"The name of the orphanage," Marie told Kari. "Named after Saint Joseph, the father of Jesus. Now he disappeared."

"Saint Joseph?" Kari asked. She knew Marie meant the director but once more she didn't like where the conversation was going and sensed a joke would be good.

Marie shook her head no, and mumbled, "The director," but she was interrupted by the woman behind the counter calling out something else in Spanish, including "gringo."

"She says he was…gringo. Not Mexican," Marie told Kari. "My mother told me not to say that. You can tell by the name. She says the police do not pursue Mexicans. They receive help from the…gringo police." At this second "gringo," Marie raised her hands and shook her head helplessly.

So gringo was a bad word, Kari thought. Maybe it was a good thing, at least here in Mexico, if she wasn't one.

"Am I a gringo?" Kari asked.

"Gringa, with a," Marie corrected her, smiling. "What's your last name?" Kari doubted that she should tell her, but the name came out of her mouth anyway. "Fernandez." Somehow, Marie seemed trustworthy.

"I don't think you are a gringa. You don't look gringa."

Kari felt relief. Perhaps that was why she felt encouraged to ask a question. "So the police are after this guy?"

But Marie just looked at her, and repeated, "After this guy?"

"Yeah. Looking for the gringo."

"Ah. Yes. Looking for this guy. Yes, the newspaper writes they are after this guy."

"What if they get him?" Again, Marie looked at her blankly. "Find him," Kari explained. "What if they find him?"

"Prison?" Marie said.

"Are the police here…good?" Kari herself wasn't sure what she meant by this. "Do people…like them?"

"Do people like the police?" Marie repeated, then spoke to the woman behind the counter, who replied with a little laugh.

"I don't think so," Marie interpreted. "'Malditos,' she said. It's not a nice word. And now I remember…my father said everybody here hates the police. In Guinea too. They're worse than the criminals."

Kari took that in. But Marie wasn't finished.

"My father said that…many of the gringos who live here in PV, the majority of the gringos, he said, are…what is the word? Fuyant et éludant…" Kari had no idea what this meant, but she had a fleeting memory of Ronald Rose, who she'd read earlier that year had been captured by an American bounty hunter right here in PV. So she put two and two together and interpreted what, in French, somehow sounded both funny and elegant. "You mean they did something bad and they're…escaping from the gringo police?"

"Yes," Marie said.

Like Dad and me, Kari thought, as a wave of emotion hit her. She sensed that tonight, when she tried to tell Dad this, he and even she would find the whole conversation incredible. And she knew it couldn't continue like this—how could she hide from Marie the worry on her face?

But to her relief—at least for a moment—Marie launched into a story. "My mother is from Guadalajara. She has friends there…Jehovah's Witnesses."

Kari was beginning to think everybody here in Mexico was a Jehovah's Witness. Where were all the Catholics Tata had told her about?

"Their son, Diego, when he was younger, he was…mmm… secuestrado." Kari didn't have time to try her dictionary before Marie added, "'Kidnappé.'"

"Kidnapped!" Kari proclaimed.

"He was at a papelería with a friend from school. The friend's uncle said, 'Diego, want a ride home?' But they drove with Diego for three hours, here, to PV. They put him in a big, dark building with no floor and no windows and many other little boys.

"For days, they only gave them oranges to eat. Diego heard trains pass, far away, again and again. So he and other boys made a tunnel and escaped. Diego ran toward the sound of the train, ran and ran. Some of the little boys were too afraid, and they didn't escape."

Kari felt so sad when she heard about the little boys that her eyes teared up.

"Diego jumped on a train. He didn't know where it was going, but finally he recognized a road and he jumped off the train. He was in the Primavera forest. People in a car, they stopped, and they drove Diego to his home."

Kari breathed another question. "What did his parents do?"

"They were…misérables…désespérés…aliviados…but they couldn't call the police. They drove Diego back to PV to find the building, but they couldn't."

Horrible, Kari thought. But now, besides the story providing a distraction from her and Dad's predicament, she felt a little better thinking about someone else's problems—far worse than hers.

"Why did they kidnap him? What were they going to do with the boys?" But Marie shook her head and didn't say. Maybe she didn't know.

*

That night when Kari told Dad, he didn't seem to know either. She'd been bursting to tell him everything—and started in the car on the way back to the apartment after work. Marie escaping from Guinea and coming on a ship from Spain to Mexico, the Jehovah's Witnesses, Marie's father working at the Grand Fiesta Americana, the orphanage and the pederasta from the newspaper, everybody hating the police, all the gringo criminals living here in PV, and, finally, the kidnapping of Diego and the untrustworthiness of the police.

Dad didn't say much, except for little sounds of interest and surprise. "Dad, Marie did most of the talking. I didn't tell her very much about us. I did tell her our last name though."

"Oh, you did?" he replied. He didn't seem mad, but not happy either.

"Yeah, well, I asked her if we're gringos. So she asked my last name."

"Are we gringos?" Kari couldn't see Dad's face in the dark car very well, but he seemed to find his question funny.

"Marie said no. She said it depends on your name and how you look."

"There are a lot of guys like me in the hotel—American, but Hispanic."

"The guests?" Kari asked.

"No, no. Some of the guests are Mexicans...from Mexico...but mostly...gringos." This time he laughed for sure. "No, I'm talking about the guys who work there. And ladies too. They do everything...meet the guests who come in cars, work at the reception, give them ideas on things to do—wind surfing and stuff."

"Are they from California?"

"Yeah, California, Texas. One from Iowa, I think. They don't even really speak Spanish."

"Like us. What are they doing here?"

"I don't know. They have family with them. We don't talk that much except about work. Everybody's minding their own business. One guy from L.A. said something about getting away from gangs."

"Ee-yu," Kari moaned.

"Yeah, but to work at the hotel, you can't have tattoos, or weird haircuts or anything."

"Did you meet Marie's father?"

"I think so. There's only one black guy there and I guess he didn't seem American. He's kinda tall, but skinny."

"Is he nice?"

"Yeah, he's OK."

"Does he speak English?"

"Yeah, and Spanish."

"He speaks French too," Kari threw in.

"I didn't know he was from..."

"Guinea," Kari put in.

"Yeah, he's not American."

At the apartment, Kari showed Dad the book she'd bought. "It's really interesting. There's people all over the world who...had to leave home. Like Marie and her father and, well, a lot of them are like us, Dad. They were in trouble, or in jail. Sometimes there was like a war in their country, and it started with…with gangs."

But Dad was quiet, and pretty soon after they each ate a couple of tamales they had gotten at a stand in their neighborhood, he opened the sofa-bed and turned in. So Kari went in the bedroom. But she read more of "Refugees" before she went to sleep.

*

"His name is Laye," Dad told Kari. "His daughter told him she likes you."

Kari thought it was a funny name, pronounced "lie." And it surprised her to hear Marie liked her.

"She's nice," Kari said, thinking that maybe Marie liked her because of the book, "Refugees"—the story of her life, she'd said.

"She says you ask good questions," Dad said.

Kari just raised her eyebrows in surprise and started on her second tamale—chicken in green sauce tonight. It was great. But she didn't like the hot drink in a styrofoam cup—atole. She liked the cold, ruby-red jamaica way better. She even loved looking at it—like a liquid jewel.

"He gave me this." Dad reached for the map he'd asked Kari to bring home, along with her books and newspapers, and he started to open it on the small table. She saw it was a very large map in Spanish. "Jalisco," it said on the outside.

"Where's Jalisco?" Kari asked.

"It's here! It's the state we're in!"

"Oh, that's right," Kari replied, embarrassed that her navigational skills had evaporated so quickly now that they were here in PV. This map looked way more detailed than the ones they'd used driving here from Tijuana. "Why'd he give you a map?"

"I don't know. We talked today. He's the friendliest person there, maybe because of you and his daughter. He asked how long we're gonna stay."

"What'd you say?"

"I told him I don't know. It's true. But…it was a funny question—like he automatically didn't think we'd stay long. He said they might not. He told me not to tell anyone at the hotel. They might move to Guada… Guadalajara."

"It's where his wife is from. Did you meet her?"

"No. He said she works at a school. He said PV is mostly just a tourist place, but Guadalajara is a real city. He said there are no jobs here except in tourism. He said he can't even sell his sculptures here, because the tourists only want Mexican stuff, not African stuff.

"He's down on the USA," Dad went on. "The government. He said he had the money to fly from Guinea to Mexico, but all the flights went through New York, and the good ol' USA wouldn't let him in for a second, even just to change flights in the airport. And he said the USA cops are here in PV. They watch the airport to see who's coming in, and sometimes they get the Mexicans to deport people. It's something they call 'Guardian Angels.'"

Kari thought maybe "Guardian Devils" was more like it. She looked at Dad to see if he seemed worried.

"It's only at the airport. And it's for gringo types, not paisanos. That's the word Mexicans use for other Mexicans, especially ones who went to the USA and then came back—that's what Laye told me.

"He said I'm a paisano. It was like maybe he thought I'd be nervous, and he was trying to calm me down. Somewhere along the line, I told him about Tata's uncles and cousins who live in…Yahualica de Gonzalez Gallo." Both he and Kari could pronounce it now.

"I don't think Tata's really sure they're still there," Kari pointed out, then added slowly, "If I had a phone, I could call Trevor and ask." Kari had still never had a cell phone, and never really wanted one, but the idea of calling Trevor had just popped into her mind.

Dad didn't say anything but got the map all spread out until a lot of it was hanging off the table.

"Do you think it would work? To call Trevor?" Dad said.

"I think so. The lady at the Tacos del Mar restaurant has a cell phone, and she has kids in California. Maybe she's talking to them."

"But that'd be expensive, wouldn't it? Maybe you can find out more about it. You're a smart girl," Dad said as he pulled the far corner of the map up off the floor and examined it for a few long seconds. "There it is," he breathed.

Kari looked closer. Yahualica de Gonzalez Gallo. "Do you think they call it YDGG?"

*

"Hey! Paisano!" the man under the "Recepción" sign sang out as soon as Dad got "Buenas tardes" out of his mouth.

We don't have suitcases or anything, Kari thought. Our accents are a giveaway.

Dad put the kleenex to his nose—he had a nosebleed—and looked at the guy and then at Kari, so she said, "Nos gustaría una habitación. Cuanto cuesta?" She didn't know how great that sounded—she'd gotten it from her new translator, bought with Marie's help in Guadalajara, along with a cell phone, a little Nokia. Although Marie didn't have a cell phone herself, she sometimes used her father's. She had warned Kari the phone might not work that well in Yahualica de Gonzalez Gallo. And she was pretty sure it wouldn't work to call the USA.

"No speak English?" the man asked, looking friendly but a little pained.

"Well, yeah," Kari said. "We'd like a room, please."

"Sure thing!" the man said. "Matrimonial bed? Doscientos noventa y nueve. Two hundred ninety-nine, one night. Two hours, ciento noventa y nueve, one hundred ninety-nine."

Kari knew that prices in pesos always turned out to be way less than they seemed once you converted them to dollars. She figured that 299 would be maybe 15 dollars, and 199 about eight, and she told Dad that, even though he was paying everything in pesos, of course. In the back of her mind, she wondered why anybody would get a hotel room for two hours. Someone on break from work? But she hadn't seen many people around town so far.

Dad said, "Can we see the room?"

"Sure thing!" As they crossed the tiny lobby, he gestured at Dad's nose and said, "Many paisanos have this problem. Yahualica is…alto!" Alto meant high. Dad started with the nosebleeds in Guadalajara. Laye got them too. He said that Guadalajara is high…like a mile high…and he thought Yahualica was even higher, located in an area called "Los Altos de Jalisco"—the heights of Jalisco, or something like that.

They passed a girl about Kari's age, sitting on a small, leather sofa. She had her legs crossed, and was wearing shorts and high heels and maybe nylons, and looking at a cell phone on her knee.

"He my niece!" the man said. "No…nieta! Grandson! Anita! Hi!"

Anita said hi. Kari observed that Anita's cell phone was apparently working fine.

But the room on the second floor was tiny, with no windows, and only a double bed. Kari guessed that was what he meant by matrimonial.

"We need two beds. Dos camas. Cuanto cuesta?" Dad said, taking the kleenex away from his nose. Turning to Kari, he said, "Ask him if there's one with two rooms, with a bathroom in between."

Kari was pondering how to express this, when the man replied, "No family suite. Old construction." They didn't seem to have anything with two twin beds either, or two double beds. But the man led them to a bigger, corner room, with windows and a matrimonial bed, explaining: "We put more bed. Three hundred ninety nine."

After they put their stuff in the room, Kari asked Dad when the 399 beds were coming. Dad laughed and said he was starving. Kari had seen a restaurant nearby advertising "Tacos árabes" —Arabic tacos—and wanted to eat there. On the way down the stairs, Dad muttered, "He thought we were married?" and shook his head.

In the recepción, the man seemed to be waiting. "You guys hungry? We make carne asada. In dining room." They hesitated. The weather was pleasant, even though the streets here had barely a tree in sight except for the occasional, small lollipop tree, and Kari really wanted to try Arabic tacos.

"Carne asada!" the man coaxed. "Delicious! Come on! I show you jukebox."

"Dining room" was kind of a stretch, Kari thought, surveying what was basically a bar with a pretty, rusty-colored stone floor and two tables. The highlight seemed to be the digital jukebox.

"You select!" the man explained as he walked away. "Is free."

"I've never seen a digital jukebox before," Dad said. "Must be expensive. Pick out some music, princess." He probably said this to make Kari feel better about no tacos árabes.

"Beer?" the man called out to Dad, as the first song played. Three songs later, with half of Dad's beer gone, the girl appeared, serious-faced, and wearing a black apron that was the same length as her shorts. White running shoes had replaced the high heels.

"Dos platillos de carne asada?" she asked. Sí, they nodded.

"Excelente!" the man called out. "You gonna like. My partner start the fire."

Kari's "starving" father gave her a desperate look. "Is there any bread—pan—or...snacks?" he asked.

"Sure thing!" said the man, and soon plunked down a plate of chips—"Totopos!"—and a little bowl filled with orange liquid and a spoon—"The salsa of Porki! Factory in Yahualica! Chiles de arbol! Seven species!"

Kari had her translator out by the time the man disappeared through the door behind the bar. She looked for "species," as Dad downed an oil-saturated corn chip.

"'Species' is English, I think. Maybe...he meant..."

Dad started on another totopo, which he dipped in salsa this time. "Maybe 'especies'," Kari began, "which means spices..." But she stopped when she saw the expression on Dad's face.

"Oh no," he said. He braced his hands against the edge of the table, opened his mouth and, after a few long seconds of looking miserable, his eyes filled with tears.

The dining room was now empty except for the girl, back to her cell phone. Kari walked over to her. "Necesito leche. Pan. Mi padre..."

"Aaah. Much picante." The girl walked behind the bar. She was a little chubby, like Kari used to be, but that didn't seem to discourage her from wearing tight, shiny black shorts and those awful pantyhose. She got a shot glass, filled it with something, walked to the table and put it in front of Dad. "Tequila," she announced. "Sorry for you."

But Dad didn't drink the tequila, just shook his head no.

"No leche? No pan?" Kari asked.

The girl walked through the same door into which the man had disappeared, returned with a cup and a carton marked "LALA," and half-filled the cup with milk. Dad swished it around his mouth and swallowed. She brought him a napkin and he wiped his eyes and blew his nose. The napkin was bloody.

"Sorry for you," the girl repeated. "Salsa de Porki muy picante."

"Baño?" Dad said.

"Bathroom," the girl said, and pointed to a door with a washbasin outside.

"He's never liked hot stuff," Kari explained as Dad walked away. "Me neither. Do you? You like picante?"

"Me like picante?" Anita said, and nodded yes. "Sí. La salsa pica rica. We friends?" the girl said. "Your name?"

"Kari," Kari said. "You're Anita, right?

Now Dad was outside the bathroom, washing his hands and face.

"Sí, soy Anita. You job here?"

"Me? A job here?" Kari replied. Anita seemed to nod yes. "A job? Doing what? I'm 13."

"I have 15," Anita said. "Merry Christmas soon. Much paisanos."

But now Dad was getting near the table and Anita started to move off. "We friends," she said.

"Sure thing," Kari replied, not sure about anything.

*

"Dad, stop!" Kari twisted left and tried to get a better look at the small house with the rich red paint job. But now they were already past, driving a little too fast as they approached Yahualica's outskirts and the road got rougher. Kari wasn't sure she had really seen a sign on the red house saying, "Salon del Reino de los Testigos de Jehová." Kingdom Hall of Jehovah's Witnesses.

"Why? Was that Francisco's house?" Dad asked. "There's a car behind me. I can pull off up here…Oh no. Look. It's the Porki store."

A small building painted bright yellow and hot pink, with a pig cartoon on the garage door and a pig sculpture on the roof was next to the road where they pulled off.

The bug had taken the ridged dirt and stone roadside pretty well and, as the other car sped past, they sat for a bit as the cloud of beige dust cleared, but not before a lot came in through the car windows. Dad coughed. Kari handed him his bottle of Peñafiel water and he drank. At least he didn't have a nosebleed at the moment.

"Look, Dad, it's Porfi's, not Porki, but…I think they make salsa too." They were stopped behind a large truck and a man was bringing boxes on a dolly out of the building and loading them into the truck.

"Hot salsa, I bet," Dad said. "So why'd we stop, Kari? What'd you see? Francisco's house?"

Kari glanced at the map and the address she'd written on the edge while she was in Guadalajara, when she'd talked to Trevor and then Tata, using the special phone—called Magic Mack or something—in the office in the Jehovah's Witnesses hall. It had taken several calls to track down the name of Tata's uncle in Yahualica, and eventually even an address.

"Maybe," said Kari. "It's on this street somewhere. But no, I thought I saw…a Jehovah's Witness place. Marie said there's one in Yahualica."

Dad looked a little pained. "Aren't they kind of a cult?"

"A cult!" Kari repeated. "You mean Marie and her father and…?"

"Oh, forget it. Let's go back and look. What's Francisco's street number?" He pulled the car forward past the truck and stopped again. "Look," he said, pointing across the road and ahead. "Another church. Templo Buenos Cristianos." They both knew what that meant. Good Christians Church.

"A lot of churches here," Dad said, "for such a little place." On their way through the town today, they had passed several big, Catholic churches.

"And salsa too," Kari replied. "Anita is telling me salsa is what Yahualica is famous for."

"Anita? Oh yeah, Anita. Does she call you?"

"She sends text messages," Kari said. "She's the only one. Marie has my number, but she doesn't have a phone. I don't know anyone else."

"I'm not sure why we got the phone," Dad said as he started to inch the car forward to turn back to the red house. "Can't even call home on it. Kari, Anita is probably not such a great friend, okay? She reminds me of Ashley. I don't want to stay at that hotel anymore. It's not expensive, but…maybe Francisco can give us a tip."

"You mean, I shouldn't talk to Anita?"

"Well, be polite but…you know."

Yes, she knew. Polite but not friendly.

"How long you think we're gonna stay here, Dad?"

Kari had liked Guadalajara better. The weather was nice there, not muggy like PV, and there were trees—although not as many as in PV—with pretty flowers growing on them. Marie's family had found them a room above a little store that sold stuff like Coca-Cola and Sabritas potato chips. A huge, red Coca-Cola truck unloaded there almost every day. It was a lot smaller even than the apartment in PV, and the bathroom was downstairs behind the store. But everyone was really nice, and sometimes she, and even Dad, sat in on the discussions in the hall.

She loved the small books they had there—about the Bible and their Jehovah's Witnesses' ideas—and she especially loved the pictures in them. They must have had a great artist who made them, showing people of all races, and everyone looking happy. Sometimes they showed modern people, and some were of Bible days, which were even better—people in colorful, ancient clothes doing interesting things, like drowning outside Noah's Ark or going into a cave full of hungry lions.

Well, those people didn't look happy. But the queens and kings in beautiful clothes, and people like Moses holding the Ten Commandments from God—they looked happy. The people who got resurrected, and their relatives, they looked happy too.

The books were all in Spanish, of course. Kari didn't mind that—it was a chance to improve her Spanish, but Dad got bored. He had brought along his old gold-edged Bible all the way from Los Angeles, but it didn't help him much in the Spanish meetings, even when Marie's mom sat next to him and helped him find the parts they were discussing.

Dad hadn't answered Kari's question—he was concentrating on driving and looking for Francisco's address. So Kari started looking too. The houses in this area were scarce, and numbers on them even more scarce. They were almost back to the red house—maybe scarlet was a better word—when she noticed the number they were looking for on the stone entrance to a large house right before the scarlet house. This house stretched around the corner, was painted a beautiful, rich, shade of yellow-gold, and was very neat and clean. Suddenly she remembered Tio Francisco telling Marie, who'd helped Kari with the call, that his house was yellow.

"That's it!" Kari almost screamed. "That's Uncle Francisco's house."

*

Since the golden house was enclosed all along the two streets it faced by sturdy, iron railings about five feet high, broken only by two orange-ish stone columns marking an entranceway, Dad turned right on the side road and parked on the shoulder. All Dad was carrying was a bottle of water, and Kari her small pink pack from junior high, which she used now for carrying her old dictionary and new translator and cell phone.

Dad was wearing black pants and his nicest polo shirt, so Kari sensed the stakes were high. She may have wanted to return to Guadalajara and Marie and the nice people they'd met at their church, but Dad must have felt he didn't fit in there, maybe because of the super-religious little JW world they were in. With both PV and Guadalajara a disappointment for him, Yahualica probably seemed like the most promising option, maybe the only option.

Kari had called Francisco again yesterday and, although they had struggled to communicate, he sounded very warm, and she knew he was expecting them. Glancing up the road, she could still see a bit of the yellow and pink Porfi's factory and almost see the Buenos Cristianos temple in the distance.

She pressed a button on what looked like an intercom mounted on one stone column. Next to it, a niche in the stone with some capped wires sticking out contained two cigarette butts. In one nicely trimmed lollipop tree nearby, someone had wedged an empty can of Coca-Cola between two branches. Only part of one wall of the scarlet building, the one right next to Francisco's house, was visible, but Kari saw the paint was flaking into white in a few places.

The bright blue sky was half full of cotton-ball clouds and the temperature was pleasant, but the area was so exposed and dusty that Kari suddenly felt a sense of oppression. But then, when a fit, light-skinned, gray-haired, tall man—a lot taller than Dad or most other Mexicans—came bounding out of the house and toward them, smiling, Kari's feeling of desperation was replaced by something like awe.

"Buenas tardes!" he called out, while behind him, a smiling woman who looked more Mexican than Francisco—short and chubby and wearing an apron over her dress—waited in the doorway.

But were they really smiling or just squinting in the bright light? Kari decided they were genuine smiles after Francisco grabbed her lightly by both shoulders, bent down, looked her right in the eyes and said, "Hola, princesa!" with a twinkle in his own eyes. That was funny because Dad was the only one to call her Princess up until then.

Francisco was just as warm towards Dad, and Kari noticed he was kind of dressed up too. "Bienvenidos. Pasen. Pasen. Tienen hambre?"

Kari wasn't especially hungry, but she said, "Un poco! Gracias!" And that began a three- or four-hour get-together that wound up with Dad taking a nap in a bedroom off the living room. "Con confianza!" Francisco chuckled as he shepherded Dad into the room, urging him to get comfortable. "Shoes…bye-bye!" he chortled.

Somewhere along the line, Kari realized that Tio Francisco and Tia Sofia, seemed to be the living incarnation of "Mi casa es tu casa." They seemed to be more Mexican in that respect than any other Mexican Kari had ever met. Which was odd, when you thought about it, because they had lived for decades in Middletown, in the north of California, even north of Sacramento, a place Kari had never heard of and certainly never visited.

Yes, Francisco was Tata's uncle, and they both had their roots right here in Yahualica de Gonzalez Gallo, but it seemed that it was a huge family and that their paths had hardly crossed. Francisco and Sofia had nine children, they said, Francisco holding up nine fingers to prove his point. And he was older than Tata's mother, who had already died; Tata had said maybe around 80.

Kari didn't think he looked 80. From what she put together from his storytelling and Tia Sofia's additions—in much better English than Francisco could muster—he had begun going to California every year just after they got married here in Yahualica and started having kids.

"A truck on the streets with a loudspeaker," Sofia said. "'Come and work on farms in California!' Every year they took the men in buses. Returned before Christmas." After a while, Francisco could legally stay in California, and even bring his family.

They used to have a nice house in Middletown, Sofia said. Now about half their kids lived in California. One was a hydrological engineer; another managed a winery; a daughter worked at the Los Angeles airport. Of his kids that lived in Mexico, one was a doctor in Guadalajara, and a couple had stayed here in Yahualica.

And it was no coincidence that Francisco and Sofia had built this gorgeous house right next to the scarlet Salon del Reino de los Testigos de Jehová. Francisco had been one of the people—the only one, Sofia almost whispered to Dad and Kari—to found and construct the Kingdom Hall. Kari had many questions that she kept to herself. Why didn't he learn English better during all those years in the USA? Why did he leave California if everything was so nice there? Of course, she wouldn't have dared to ask that for fear it was too nosy, or that his reasons for leaving were similar to Dad's.

But her main reaction to Tio Francisco wasn't a question at all, but amazement that he had raised a family of nine so well by being a farm worker! In L.A., the "old-timers"—Hispanics like Kari and Dad who felt American through and through—looked down on the newbies, who were now mostly from Central America instead of Mexico. These were the people you saw hanging on street corners with signs saying they wanted a job or money, people who didn't speak much English and wore dirty clothes.

Yet Francisco's amazing accomplishments didn't stop at a big family full of engineers and doctors, a house in northern California, a scarlet church and a beautiful gold house in Yahualica. He had also built that other church they had glimpsed up the road—Templo Buenos Cristianos—though unfortunately it had closed. Neither Francisco nor Sofia said why, and Kari wasn't going to ask that either.

Kari was in awe for other reasons besides the success of her Mexican great-uncle. For one thing, here were the Jehovah's Witnesses popping up in her life again. She was starting to suspect she must be destined to be a JW prophet—if Jehovah's Witnesses even had prophets. Meeting Marie and Laye, and Dad working at the same hotel as Laye, going to the Guadalajara Salon del Reino with Marie's family, then coming to her grandmother's hometown and landing smack in the lap of JW again. Wasn't that just too many coincidences to not mean something important? Kari wasn't going to tell Dad her suspicion—it would sound too silly. What did a prophet even do? But the idea seemed okay to her—she liked the JW, their books with the beautiful pictures, their sincerity, their ideas about the Resurrection of ordinary people who loved God. The fact they didn't go in the army was kind of cool, and she didn't even mind that they didn't celebrate Christmas—only Easter. Besides, trying to celebrate Christmas this year in Yahualica might be pathetic.

However, Francisco told them a lot of people were coming for Christmas—people from California, relatives and friends. Maybe that was what Anita had meant: Merry Christmas soon. Much paisanos.

But when Kari mentioned Anita and the name of the hotel and Merry Christmas soon, Francisco's eyes didn't twinkle. And it wasn't long before he and Dad got talking, just the two of them. When she and Dad got back in the car later that afternoon, and he told her they were coming back here tomorrow—to live—she wasn't that surprised.

"For how long?" she asked, sensing her desire to return to Guadalajara floating up and away into the blue, blue sky.

"I don't know. But they have a lot of space. You'll have your own room. It's big enough for overnights. Maybe Marie can visit you. He wants us to go to the Jehovah's Witnesses meetings. You wouldn't mind that, would you?"

"No, I don't mind. Is Francisco the…elder?" Kari asked, dredging up the word from her memories of Marie's church in Guadalajara.

"Maybe," Dad answered. "But not right now. I guess they had a problem and…I don't know…Francisco backed off. He said we don't have to do anything, just attend the meetings."

"Is he going to be there?"

"I don't think so. He wants us to tell him what's happening."

"Are we, like, spies?"

Dad sighed. "I hope not. But anyway, he's not charging us rent. He said maybe later after I get a job. He thinks I can get one at Porki. Or maybe at his store. He's got a little naturista, he calls it, where he sells healthy stuff. Some of it comes from California. He showed me his office where he keeps it. The store's downtown. Near the hotel. But he says to stay away from Anita. He thinks you should start school in January. He doesn't think Anita goes to that school, or any school."

"Dad, Anita sent me some messages when we were at Francisco's. I told her about the Testigos de Jehová. You know what she calls them? Don't get mad. She called them Testículos de Jehová. I looked up testículos. It's almost like in English."

"Testículos," Dad repeated. He glanced at Kari and shook his head like he had about the matrimonial bed. "I told you," he said after a second. "Don't answer her. Kari, I'm going to take that phone away if you keep on with her. Tell her you can't answer anymore because I'm using your phone. Maybe I will be. Maybe I'll need it at my new job. Come on, we have better things to think about. We're going to be staying with Francisco and Sofia. Christmas is almost here."

"Whupass? What kind of name is that?" Dad asked.

He was putting a few small boxes into the boche to take downtown, if you could call it that, to Francisco's naturista store—small boxes of polen de abeja, which was bee pollen, dropper bottles with Spanish herb names on them, Shampoo Secreto de Las Yeguadas, cold-cream type jars that said PEYOTE in capital letters—stuff like that.

"Look, Dad. Laci Le Beau Super Dieter's Tea. In English."

"I was asking about Whupass."

"It's English," Kari said. "You know, like 'Kick your…'"

"I know it's English, and I know what it means, but whose you-know-what are they gonna whup? And what do they make…or do?"

"They make different stuff. T-shirts. Francisco gave me one. It's black and it just says 'Whupass' on it. I don't think Francisco gets it—the name."

"Aa-ah," Dad said in a guttural way that sounded like "yuk." "You're not gonna wear that, are you?"

"Well, no," Kari answered softly.

"Did you talk to them? Where are they from?"

"I didn't talk to them much, just saw them. Sofia says they're from L.A.—West Adams."

Another "Aa-ah" came from Dad, with a shake of his head—everybody knew West Adams was bad. "How long they been living at Buenos Cristianos?"

"I don't know. Sofia says nobody was using the building after the church…dried up. Sofia and Francisco were the only ones going. Not even Lola and Jack—they're the ones from West Adams."

They were driving now, and Dad didn't reply, so Kari added, hopefully, "They go to Guadalajara sometimes…on business." Kari was hesitant to come out and say that she'd like to go with them to see Marie, so instead she said, "They might have extra room in their car."

That seemed to get the point across, because Dad said, "We'll see," which didn't sound very hopeful. "Maybe they could bring Marie here for a visit," he added after a minute, so Kari perked up.

She and Dad had already been to a JW meeting at the scarlet hall—Dad not very enthusiastically—maybe the spy idea bothered him. But then he hadn't been enthusiastic about the meetings in Guadalajara either. I bet they remind him of that class where they called him a deviant, Kari thought. She remembered when she didn't even know what deviant meant. Kari wasn't aware of why she liked JW. If she had tried to put it into words, she might have said it was because they had a grip on things, on why you're alive and what happens after you die. Tata had a grip too, with her rosary and going to church, and it seemed pretty unshakeable, but JW was a lot more compelling. Everyone there was so sincere. And people who studied so much must know what they were talking about.

She also liked the fact they accepted Kari and Dad, despite Dad's problems. Of course, they didn't know about his problems, but Kari sensed they might not care.

Kari also figured that Dad wasn't enthusiastic about JW because in his mind, there was the suspicion that if the JW people in Guadalajara or Yahualica saw his name and photo on that California web page, and actually knew he was a sex offender, or a predator, or sick, as people sometimes said, they'd be just as horrified as their manager back in Green Manor. But luckily, in Yahualica people didn't use the internet as much as at home. Francisco had a computer in his office, but he didn't use it, as far as Kari could see. She didn't think Anita used the internet—just the phone. She didn't know about Lola and Jack. But Yahualica didn't seem like an internet kind of place. It hardly had any stores downtown.

Oh, if you could leave your past behind, and make a fresh start. That's what Kari had hoped for Dad when they left California. She hadn't really needed a fresh start herself, but she couldn't imagine herself without Dad. When they were on their way to PV in November, she had asked him if they could ever go back to California. He didn't answer right away.

When they'd left California a week or two earlier, the border crossing seemed the same—easy—as when the family had gone to Tijuana one Sunday a few years earlier.

That time they wanted to have carne asada and just to say they went. That was the time they bought that stupid, huge Mexican sombrero that Trevor had worn the time he took down the Megan's law sign on Dad at Green Manor. None of them—especially Tata—had liked Tijuana very much that Sunday afternoon and none of them ever really wanted to go back.

At the time, for people traveling south, the Mexicans usually didn't ask for any ID. Even going north, the only thing Americans had to show Immigration at the time was a California driver's license. Kari didn't think it had changed when they crossed the border in a hurry in November, and since they weren't planning on returning, they hadn't given a thought to passports—and didn't have one anyway.

That's what Dad mentioned in answer to her question at first.

"Maybe you could go back," he finally added. "But I don't think I can." Kari was sure that Dad missed Tata and Trevor a lot. When she'd called Trevor from Guadalajara for help locating Francisco, Dad had taken the phone every time to ask how they were and cried a little when he talked to them.

"No, no, you can't do that—it's too far and too dangerous," Kari heard Dad say to Tata, followed by "Maybe a week, two weeks…" Later he said that Tata had wanted to visit them in Yahualica for Christmas. But he needed to be settled down before anything like that happened.

*

Christmas came and went faster than Kari remembered it ever doing before. She and Dad had dinner outdoors on the patio late at night on Christmas Eve with Francisco, Sofia and a whole group of six people from Los Angeles who had arrived that afternoon in two pickups loaded with stuff. As it got later and later, they could hear and sometimes see fireworks being shot off by neighbors, but at Francisco's house they didn't have a Christmas tree, or lights, or gifts, or anything. The new people from California seemed totally okay with everything, so Kari imagined they were JW too. Lola and Jack were in Guadalajara, so three of the new people were staying at Buenos Cristianos, while the others stayed at Francisco's house.

They did play a game Francisco had cooked up, which had to do with stories from the Bible written on little pieces of paper, but they weren't just Christmas stories. Mostly the party was eating turkey and tamales and stuff, drinking cider and beer and tequila, and later having dessert. All done by the magic of Sofia. One of the things she made was a casserole with green beans, mixed with mushroom soup and with onion rings on top, that was exactly like what Tata used to make.

Kari helped a little, and also a boy named Diego, who was one of the ones staying at Buenos Cristianos with an older couple, the Sullivans, who were Americans—that is, gringos—except they spoke Spanish a little. Diego set up chairs and carried stuff from the kitchen. He was a little younger than Kari, but pretty strong. He was kind of tall and his hair was cut in a cool way, with short wisps on top dyed blond and sticking up, and he was wearing a choker necklace made of a single strand of small, white seashells. Kari didn't think she'd ever seen a guy wear a necklace before, but Diego didn't seem weird—in fact, he was nice—and he didn't have tattoos or anything.

There was no gift giving either, although Dad had privately given Kari a stuffed Mickey Mouse, about the same height as a Barbie doll but a lot chubbier. Kari had nothing against Mickey Mouse, but she wasn't really a fan of his either. She guessed that Dad must've been hard up to find places to shop in Yahualica.

She took Diego upstairs for a minute after dinner to show him Mickey Mouse. "He got me a telephone a couple weeks ago," Kari told him with a little laugh, as if to explain the insufficiency of Mickey Mouse, which Diego was turning over with a deadpan expression, as if he were looking for a battery or chip.

"Does it do anything?" he asked.

Back downstairs, Kari asked Dad if she could have the phone, which he'd been using for talking to Francisco back and forth about the naturista store. Diego had asked to see it, and before she knew it, he put his number in Kari's phone, and hers in his phone.

"But they don't work for calling across the border, do they?" Kari asked, as she glanced at the phone and noticed there was a text message from Anita.

"No, but my phone is Mexican, and it'll work while I'm here. And we come here a lot," Diego explained.

He said his family was building a house in Yahualica, and also a community center. Was the community center for Jehovah's Witnesses? Diego said he didn't know, but maybe. He said he might even go to high school here, so his Spanish would get better, although it was already tons better than Kari's. He was thinking he would eventually go to medical school somewhere in Mexico, maybe in Guadalajara, which has two medical schools.

"To be a doctor?" Kari asked.

"Yeah. My grandparents want me to. My grandmother embroiders pillowcases for me that say 'Doctor Diego.'"

"Oh, they're your grandparents!" Kari said. She couldn't even remember their names, but Diego said it was a long story, and he'd been born in Guadalajara, but years ago was adopted by these Americans—who he called his grandparents, although they weren't actually related to him by blood—and went to Los Angeles to live with them.

"Why'd you come here?" Diego asked. Oops, Kari thought, what should she say?

"Well, Uncle Francisco is my grandmother's uncle," she said. There was a silence and Kari realized Diego was waiting for more. "It's a long story too, like yours" she added. Diego nodded.

By the next day, Christmas, Kari had realized that Diego's story almost beat Marie's in terms of how complicated it was, although Diego's distances were not as big as Marie's, coming from Africa and all.

And then, as if thinking of Marie had created some magic, Lola and Jack returned from Guadalajara with Marie and her parents in the back seat. Dad had arranged it on the phone, as a secret surprise. It was only for a couple days. Marie would share Kari's room and Laye and his wife would stay in another one.

Kari was amazed at how the number of people in and around the golden house had exploded, just like Anita had predicted with her "Merry Christmas soon. Much paisanos." And Francisco and Sofia, far from being irritated, seemed to be loving all the guests. When everybody went to a meeting at the scarlet Hall the day after Christmas, Francisco went with them, and the small group of people whom Kari and Dad had been spying on before seemed totally okay with Francisco. He was even asked to give a half-hour talk.

But the most amazing thing of all was that after the meeting, Marie's mother walked up to Diego—who wasn't wearing his seashell necklace that day, Kari noticed—and said with a big smile, "Aren't you Diego?" Diego nodded yes and they talked in a friendly way for a few minutes. Kari and Marie were nearby and could hear the conversation, but Kari didn't think too much of it until, much later that day, after all Francisco's guests had finished eating comida on his patio, and Marie and Kari were getting ready for bed, Marie said, "Diego's the one I told you about. The secuestrado."

Oh wow, Kari thought. That Diego. And later she wondered why it was that everybody she was meeting here in Mexico seemed to have some dark cloud over their lives.

But at that moment, Kari only listened with awe, while Marie explained that her mother had told her that after Diego managed to get back to Guadalajara, everyone including Diego thought he might get kidnapped again. The boy who'd tricked him into getting in his uncle's car was still going to the same school where Diego was supposed to return. The police were no help, and in fact would probably have made things worse if they'd been contacted. So Diego's father asked the American man, Mr. Sullivan— now Diego's "grandfather"—who was his partner at the time in an electronics factory in Guadalajara that was going out of business, for a favor: could Diego go live with him and his wife in Los Angeles? And that's how they arranged the adoption. They thought it was the only legal way to get Diego out of Guadalajara. The parents and the rest of the family, traumatized almost as badly as Diego, soon moved to a different house on the west side of the city in a gated cuota and became JW.

By then Kari was in bed and, before turning off her phone, she remembered to read the message from Anita. "kari in naturista you can to sell me laci le beau super dieter tea?"

She powered off the phone and picked up the book Diego had given her, "The Giver." It was a Christmas present, Kari supposed, though not wrapped. Marie was laying on her side, reading something that looked like a JW book. Thank God for Diego's book, thought Kari, because "The Refugees" was long since finished, and there was sure no Gringo's bookstore here in Yahualica. It seemed like "The Giver" was going to be good, about kids living in a town in the future where everything seemed fine, except for little hints that something weird might be going on.

But Kari got sleepy almost immediately. Marie turned off her light and soon Kari did too. Contentedly, she put her head on the pillow, which seemed to softly welcome her.

"So is Diego related to me?" she murmured to Marie, who may have already been asleep. Kari didn't realize that she already knew the answer to the question, and it was "Definitely not."

25. The Road Less Traveled
2005 to 2021
ALEX LANDON

It was 2010 and Janice Bellucci had a good plumber.

"It's hard to find good plumbers," said the retired lawyer, who was living in Los Angeles.

The plumber, Frank Lindsay, had written a book. He didn't tell Bellucci what it was about, but the title, "We're All in This Together," piqued her interest.

"I got very upset when I read it," she recalled. But at that time, she still didn't guess that this story by a victim of the California sex-offender registry—sometimes called Megan's List—would redefine her life.

Before retirement she had worked in aerospace and government-contract law, and had been a "card-carrying feminist" with leadership positions in the National Organization for Women. But with the impact of her plumber's book, she would venture into a different area of civil rights—one that some consider opposed to women's rights—as well as into constitutional matters, and become a major contributor, perhaps the major contributor, certainly in California, to a sea change.

The worst thing that ever happened to her

Not surprisingly, as this sea change swept in, women have played a big role, both for the better and the worse. The large role of women in responding to sex crimes is not surprising considering that, as demonstrated in the #MeToo movement starting around 2017 (some of it centered on sexual harassment by powerful men in California's entertainment industry), women are very often the injured parties.

A lot of what came out of #MeToo was positive. Since abuse of women on the job is often hidden, allegations were made by groups of women supporting each other. And consequences outside the criminal justice system, such as firing the accused men, became an accessible solution. Firings took place at Fox News, where Bill O'Reilly was fired after pressure was put on sponsors. Sometimes courts were used, as with Harvey Weinstein when the abuse was clear—and the punishment was appropriate.

However, sometimes the consequences for the men were extreme. The childish behavior of Al Franken, for example, came to light when the notion of "zero tolerance" had taken hold, and he was pressured to resign from the U.S. Senate in 2017. I don't condone Franken's behavior—nor any of the offenses discussed in this book (with the possible exception of skinny dipping) — but the point is that discerning differences between offenses, and not lumping them all together, is crucial. It is a costly error to fail to distinguish between the Al Frankens and the Harvey Weinsteins, just as it is to fail to distinguish between the 16-year-old Romeos with their 13-year-old Juliets and the Jeffrey Epsteins.

Another cameo illustrating the growth of discernment versus knee-jerk thinking is illustrated by the radically different trajectories of two California girls who were both victims of shocking crimes.

Both Chelsea King and Jaycee Dugard were very young victims of men who had long rap sheets of sexual offenses. Both girls were pretty, both were white, and both their causes were taken up by their families and the media, putting them in the spotlight at around the same time, roughly 2010. But there the similarities end.

For one thing, Chelsea, tragically, was killed, while Jaycee was not. Chelsea's trauma was relatively violent and short, while Jaycee's trauma was long, beginning in 1991 and finally ending when she was rescued as an adult 18 long years later.

The aftermath of the two crimes were also drastically different. The legacy of the crime against Chelsea was taken up by her parents and a politician, Nathan Fletcher, who backed a publicity effort, an unnecessary designer law, a foundation and an annual run, all commemorating the worst thing that ever happened to Chelsea.

But the aftermath of the crime against Jaycee proceeded in an entirely different direction. Besides making a strong effort to maintain her privacy and that of her two children (fathered by her kidnapper, who later went to prison), Jaycee did two remarkable things that were very different from an annual run.

One was winning a $20 million court settlement from the state of California, due to the failure of officers to discover her in any of their visits to the home of her captor, who was on parole, during the years she was locked up in his backyard. This is an example of how laws born in hysteria and hate fail to accomplish anything except keeping law enforcement too busy. Jaycee's kidnapper obviously needed a lot more supervision from P.O.s than he got, and it is clear that if the officers had not been stretched so thin, they might have detected Jaycee, sealed off from the world a few feet from their noses.

Another of Jaycee's achievements after she was freed was to write a book. Other crime victims have written books and part of the reason Dugard did so must have been to earn money. She had been unable to attend school while in captivity, and would certainly have needed a means of support.

But Dugard's book stood out because, reportedly written in her own words, it had an admirable tone and content. According to a review in the

New York Times, rather than being "lurid" or "laced with self pity," as are many similar books, Dugard's "A Stolen Life" was "brave" and full of "dignified, hard-hitting understatement." What was missing from her book is also key: there were no calls for new, stricter laws, and very little bitterness. "Phillip [her captor] seemed like a nice guy when he wasn't using me for sex," she wrote. (1)

I'm not going to paint Jaycee Dugard as a crusader against designer laws, but her choices—the fact she didn't get roped in by tough-on-crime forces, or by police or political publicity machines, or by the tentacles of bitterness—do suggest an awareness that her road to healing after this crime was the one less traveled.

Could Jaycee Dugard be a harbinger of a new era, of the sea change in the last decade that I am tentatively describing? Is she evidence that California may reclaim its reputation as a state of clear thinkers? Is it possible that the fear and hatred surrounding sex crimes has dissipated? Dugard's unique achievements—plus, described just ahead, the emergence of non-coercive rehabilitative programs for convicted people, as well as that "card-carrying feminist" wielding her legal tools—all suggest a solid path through the quicksand of our present terrain.

No more victims

One new and much-needed project called Circles of Support and Accountability has become a far healthier alternative to what used to be practically the only choice for people convicted of sex offenses—police-affiliated psychotherapy. By 2019, COSA Circles had been established in Canada, the United States, Europe and the U.K. A Circle at an Anglican church in Canada, one of 300 in the country, even built housing for released people. In the United States, there are COSA projects in California, Colorado, Minnesota, North Carolina, Oregon and Vermont. Circles are groups of ordinary people in faith communities such as churches, who volunteer and get training in order to take a high-risk, released man under their wing. (High-risk is not at all the typical person convicted of a sex offense, but is the type that causes intense fear and media coverage when released into communities.)

Circles, which are not psychotherapy but have some of the same effects, meet with the man regularly to help him find a job, a place to live, or simply to offer him regular, friendly contact and advice, which is what most high-risk people released from prison completely lack—and exactly what makes them so risky, says COSA spokesperson and clinical psychologist Robin Wilson. Dr. Wilson has worked with thousands of high-risk people, who were released after doing time for sex offenses and benefited from what might be described as a rehabilitation project carried out by a caring community.

Wilson said his work with COSA has been his most rewarding professional experience, mostly because of the COSA's superior results. According to research, the project boasts 70 percent fewer re-offenses for high-risk men than any published treatment program. (Perhaps to highlight the difference between COSA and other approaches to sex offenders, Wilson mentions meeting the inventor of the penile plethysmograph, which is still often used on convicted people in police-affiliated "therapy").

Wilson emphasizes the obstacles to public safety that harsh laws (such as Megan's law and Jessica's law) paradoxically create:

"Where you have really, really stringent restrictions ...and make it difficult for people to develop any lifestyle stability, you increase the risk level simply by making it difficult for them to reintegrate. So even a person who's at the lower risk end, becomes somewhat more risky, because of the [stringent] policies we institute." (2)

So stringent restrictions, such as registration as it currently exists, according to Dr. Wilson, actually creates more victims. This happens because shunning ignores a crucial component of our criminal justice system—rehabilitation.

"We will find safety not by ostracizing the bad guys but by finding ways to bring them back," he emphasizes.

Wilson's critics bristle at his sympathetic attitude and call him a "thug hugger." But he explains that "No more victims" is the motto closest to his heart and that of hundreds of COSA volunteers. It means the Circle has failed.

"I was on fire"

It surprises some people to know that the way a convicted person rises above the temptation to reoffend can be pretty mundane, as Dr. Wilson explains it: after COSA has helped someone reconstruct his life—with a positive social circle, a decent job and the material "stuff" that comes with it—he now has so much to lose that reoffending becomes much less attractive. So even though the caring community that COSA Circles comprise do perform a sort of spiritual alchemy, Dr. Wilson emphasizes that a significant part of the transformation is achieved by making sure the released person has something—rather than nothing—to lose.

Starting from a radically different position—as a convicted person rather than as a psychologist who treats them—Alex Gittinger arrived at many of the same conclusions as Wilson—and, ultimately, at a similar professional position and level of discernment.

Gittinger was caught up in the parallel universe—"the twilight zone," as he calls it—for more than a decade after his conviction in Los Angeles in 2005.

He recounts his successful career in entertainment in Germany before Hollywood enticed him to relocate. But when he was convicted of sexual battery against a minor in 2005, his involvement in the entertainment world ended.

"It was a life changer," he reflected in 2020. He spent time in jail and in court-ordered therapy, which he now calls "useless," except for clarifying the difference between confrontational treatment and constructive rehabilitation.

After serving time, even with his conviction he could have returned to the entertainment world and worked behind the scenes, he explained. But then he began to suspect he had another calling. He got this inkling soon after he joined a 12-step group, Sex Addicts Anonymous, got a good sponsor and wrote his sexual history for him.

"My sponsor told me what I wrote showed no empathy for my victims — I didn't even see what I did as victimization." The sponsor emphasized that Gittinger needed better treatment than the court-ordered program he was in. But when Gittinger looked around, he found the price tag for such programs was tens of thousands of dollars.

"But you can't afford to offend again," the sponsor insisted. So Gittinger found a 42-day residential sex-addiction treatment program at Del Amo Hospital in Torrance, California. Its cost was a mere 50,000 dollars and his parole officer gave him the green light.

"It was the best 50,000 dollars I spent in my life. It changed me fundamentally. My P.O. at first had said she was going to try to put me back into jail, but after the treatment she said she was proud of me."

But it was a comment by his new wife that firmly planted the seed of a calling outside the entertainment industry.

"She overheard me talking on the phone to a sponsee in Sex Addicts Anonymous, and she said, 'Wow…you're so good at that. Why don't you make it a career?'" At the time, Gittinger did not even have a bachelor's degree — and he needed a master's to be certified as a therapist.

"But I was on fire. I started studying at Loyola Marymount in 2008." However, for a person convicted — especially of a sex offense — the process of education and certification was far from smooth. Gittinger was starting school at around the same time Janice Bellucci was reading her plumber's book. And the group she was about to found, which became the Alliance for Constitutional Sex Offense Laws (ACSOL), would turn out to be very helpful to Gittinger, since a lawyer in the group assisted him in winning a certificate of rehabilitation and getting off the sex offender registry, which helped with some of the obstacles to becoming a certified sex addiction therapist.

"That was a nail biter," says Gittinger, "because we had to petition the court and face any issues the district attorney had with it. But I was able to provide ample evidence of rehabilitation."

As he worked toward his new professional goals, Gittinger found that his unique experiences—both convicted for a sex offense and trained as a sex therapist—gave him special insight and promised to make him a leader in transforming court-ordered therapy into a process yielding excellent results.

"I can't make direct amends to my victims, so I help others not to offend," he said.

As Gittinger's education moved toward certification as a therapist, he volunteered as the leader of a 12-step-format "emotional support group" (under the umbrella of ACSOL, which had aided him in a harrowing, four-year legal battle to get a provisional license). Some participants in that group were still receiving old-school treatment, he explained.

"I encourage the people in the group who are on parole to tell their parole officers about it. Everyone has to be aware they are not violating parole restrictions and usually the P.O.s are okay with the support group. "It's not therapy," he underscores, "but it's had quite some therapeutic value. There's one tight-lipped homophobic guy, for example, who became good friends with a flamboyant gay guy. There's a woman who'd been on the registry for 30 years, meek and quiet…borderline suicidal. Through the group, she became a fierce advocate for people like us. When we got to Sacramento [to advocate for legislative change], she was leading the charge. The group has gotten people out of isolation."

Gittinger laments that "there are far too many treatment providers who are still doing primarily shaming and confronting, with the old-school emphasis on denial. Instead of saying, 'Oh, wow, you have a big blind spot. Let's look at your idea of boundaries,' they call people 'deviant' and put them into a state of toxic shame."

The confrontational groups are based on what is called the "containment model" and they use devices like polygraphs—lie detectors—not because they work, but as a fear tactic," Gittinger explained.

"Polygraphs are not even very accurate," he went on. "The P.O. might ask a subject 'Have you had any contact with minors?' and you say 'No, I didn't,' but you get so worked up, you might have a visceral reaction that causes you to fail the polygraph."

He is enthusiastic about therapists and projects, such as COSA, that stay away from the confrontational model, but says that such changes are "glacially slow."

"Just follow the money if you want to see why. I went to a conference put on by a federal government office called SMART [for Sex Offender Sentencing, Monitoring, Apprehending, Registering and Tracking], where there were 500 old-style professionals whose livelihood depends on the sex-offender registry. It was there it became clear to me that the registry is big business, not only for treatment providers, but for other professionals—specifically law enforcement."

The card-carrying feminist

Now we return to a force that helped Gittinger transform himself, and which is probably the clearest harbinger of a change for the better: the "card-carrying feminist" spurred by her "good plumber" to form an organization I have so far only touched upon. (Full disclosure: I have been a volunteer board member in this group since 2012.)

But in order to more fully account for Janice Bellucci and Alliance for Constitutional Sex Offense Laws, first a brief detour is in order—a look at another woman who was key in the mess that California's laws on sex offenses became, a politician of that old-school, fear-and-loathing mentality, who was thus an antagonist to Bellucci and the new era she hopefully represents.

It is unsettling to admit that the early death of this one person, Sharon Runner, from a rare disease in 2016, was an undeniable reason for the positive sea change in California. Runner was a religious and political conservative, who, in her long career as both a state assemblywoman and state senator, left a smear on California criminal justice that took years even to partially erase.

In 2006 Runner leveraged a designer law—Jessica's law or Proposition 83—as her vehicle for victory in an election. Jessica's Law, after it was approved by voters frightened by its full title, "The Sexual Predator Punishment and Control Act," ushered in a slew of severe punishments. One of the most notorious was to forbid people convicted of certain offenses to live closer than 2,000 feet to any school or park—for life. After Jessica's law was enacted, homelessness in California, already a major problem here, shot up.

Yet Jessica's law was apparently Sharon Runner's proudest achievement—she vigorously defended it until her death. For 10 long years, Runner continued to trumpet it, even as its provisions were being shot down by court after court and shown to be unworkable, expensive, without positive results and—after 14 court battles and a mountain of suffering and legal costs—partially unconstitutional.

And so we now pick up the story of ACSOL and Janice Bellucci, whose clear thinking, background as a lawyer, and indignation over injustice led her to take on the legacy of this dreadful politician.

"I hadn't known that Frank was on the registry," said Bellucci, after reading her plumber's book. "I couldn't believe any group of Americans could be treated like that. I decided I had to do something."

On the internet, Bellucci located a national group, RSOL, for Reform Sex Offender Laws.

"I contacted them and mentioned I'm a lawyer living in California. They immediately got back with me and asked me to become an affiliate in California, because there was such a large number of sex offenders here, but no organization." So, in September 2011, Bellucci started the California affiliate of RSOL. "I set it up as a non-profit with the IRS and created articles of incorporation. That was the easy part."

The first problem Bellucci ran into was one that would continue to plague the group. She and her plumber Frank Lindsay mailed out 500 letters asking Californians registered for sex offenses and their families, as well as professionals in law, psychology and the like, to attend a first meeting, planned for a Los Angeles church known for its commitment to civil rights. As it turned out, that inaugural meeting of California RSOL happened, and it had a respectable turnout, but not at the church.

"They cancelled a week after we announced, so we had to scramble to find another location. That's been an ongoing problem. Even law schools and organizations I belong to have refused to let us meet there, sometimes even though we were going to rent the space."

This was a clue that things were worse than Bellucci suspected. However, although these problems finding a meeting place surprised her—and continued—the meetings continued too, attracting from 12 to 82 people each time.

"It seems odd that fears in the community are so strong since one of our principal aims is to help convicted citizens comply with registration laws," she mused. (Her observations bolster studies demonstrating that, although registration with public notification began with the promise of calming parents who feared a killer might be living nearby, the laws have caused a rise in anxiety—and among a far larger group than only parents. (3))

Bellucci's early experiences also revealed how poorly the laws had been written. "Registered people need a lot of help with registration and residence, because the laws are unclear and can be enforced in confusing ways. One man was properly registered at his home and working 9-to-5 giving eldercare to a woman who knew about his background, but he was convicted for failing to register. They told him he was spending so much time at his job, that he should have registered at his employer's home too.

Another man had to register in four places," she said with exasperation. Some people in the group, she soon learned, had been locked up for years due to such confusion.

More shocks were coming Bellucci's way. "Then there are the suicides and murders of registered people. We had a suicide last month," she said in a 2019 interview. "An Orange County man killed himself just before sentencing because he couldn't face the prospect of registration." Bellucci said she has also tracked 17 vigilante killings of registered citizens that happened between December 2005, and December 2017. In fact, one of her group's accomplishments has been keeping track of suicides and vigilante killings, since nobody in the past had bothered. "There are generally no consequences for the killers. If he beats his chest like Tarzan, he might get prosecuted, but otherwise the police do nothing.

"An example is what happened to Frank. One morning a vigilante walked into his home and damaged some computers. When Frank discovered him, the intruder bruised him and threatened to kill him." Later that day, the same person held up a convenience store.

"One reason there have been so many vigilante murders of registered citizens is that they cannot own firearms and are sitting ducks," Bellucci explained. And advertising their home locations on official websites, and sometimes with official signs on their homes, gives the appearance that authorities are vouching that they are dangerous— a procedure so similar to putting up a wanted poster that it generally attracts fringe types. Bellucci notes that in Washington state, three registered people had been killed by a skinhead.

Low-hanging fruit

Injustices such as these tore at Bellucci and board members. Thus, some of the early moves of the group, which eventually migrated into the Alliance for Constitutional Sex Offense Laws (ACSOL), were taking on local laws around California that were patterned after Jessica's law—the "Sons of Jessica's Law."

"I get asked to hold meetings in out-of-the-way places around the state," Bellucci explained, "usually because there's some particularly troublesome law there." One that would be comical if it weren't for the people hurt was the Halloween-lawn-sign law. Bellucci called these laws the "low-hanging fruit"—laws so quirky she hoped they would not be that difficult to get rid of.

For example, in Simi Valley (a small city near Los Angeles), officials began requiring people convicted of sex offenses to put up a sign on their lawn around Halloween warning trick-or-treaters.

"In our cases against the Halloween sign laws, and there were three of them, communities even went to the extreme of specifying that on Halloween a [homeless or camping] registered person in a sleeping bag had to post the warning sign on their sleeping bag. Can you imagine any child walking up to a person in a sleeping bag to trick-or-treat?"

It is well established that people once convicted of sex offenses have low re-offense rates—much lower than for drug and property crimes, Bellucci reiterated—so it makes no sense to destabilize them, either through vigilante attacks or simply through provoking neighbors to show up on their front porch to "talk" to them.

So Bellucci and the group sued in federal court over the Halloween signs. And they won. "The judge agreed that these laws pose a danger to the registered person and their family."

Cheered by this success, the group also took aim at "presence restrictions," which forbid convicted people from being present at places such as parks and schools. ACSOL found that 79 California communities had enacted their own presence restrictions, inspired by Jessica's law. The group decided to focus on one of them—Lancaster (which also had a Halloween sign law).

"Lancaster had a law forbidding registered people not only from being near schools, but in swimming pools, bowling alleys, movie theaters and in most of the downtown area. They weren't allowed to go hiking either!" Bellucci said incredulously.

"We filed only 31 lawsuits against local governments. We did that on purpose. The result was we got rid of many presence restrictions throughout California, except for people on parole or probation." Besides taking aim at presence restrictions, Bellucci and the group began looking at laws on where registered people could live (called living or residence restrictions). Living restrictions in California had taken a great leap forward with Jessica's law in 2006, and this emboldened individual cities and counties to come up with their own rules. Bellucci initiated dozens of challenges to living restrictions around California, but found local politicians slow to respond. "They were afraid of getting voted out of office," she explained.

It was San Diego deputy public defender Laura Arnold who put the living restrictions of Jessica's law squarely in her sights, when she began her legal challenge, which eventually went to the California Supreme Court, against the over-broad enforcement of Jessica's law's residence rules on every registered citizen in the county who was also on parole, even if their offense had not been against a child and was decades old.

This was the situation with William Taylor, the man after whom Laura Arnold's challenge, the Taylor case, was named. Mr. Taylor was probably the most long-suffering plaintiff named in the case, although all the plaintiffs had stories that read like a Charles Dickens novel, with spiraling repercussions that had gotten them hopelessly entangled in the justice system, combined with other problems, such as illness and poverty. (4) William Taylor had committed a sex offense against an adult woman in Arizona, and by the time Jessica's law—supposedly aimed at protecting children—came into force about 20 years later, he was living in southern California. Mr. Taylor had been re-arrested and re-paroled three times in San Diego County, once for drugs and twice for parole violations, but never for another sex crime. All too typically, one of his violations had been a mistake in registering as a sex offender, which by California's over-broad registration law at that time, he would have to continue doing for the rest of his life. I would underscore that Mr. Taylor made this mistake because he was in intensive care in a hospital, suffering from at least seven, severe physical and emotional maladies.

Following his last release in 2008, after a prison term he should never have had to serve in the first place, Taylor had hoped to live in nearby Spring Valley at the home of relatives, one of whom was a health care professional. It seemed an ideal option, considering the welfare of both Mr. Taylor and the community, since living in a stable situation with family members goes a long way toward ensuring a parolee will not commit another offense.

But by 2008 the living restrictions of Jessica's law had been in place for two years, so Mr. Taylor's parole officer gave a thumb's-down to his Spring Valley plan. Later the same thing happened with a residential drug treatment center where Mr. Taylor could have gotten help with addiction. Both were too close to schools and parks where children would be—but remember that Mr. Taylor had never committed any crime against a child. At his wits' end, he slept for a time in an alley behind the parole office (at the suggestion of his parole officer) and in a boarding house three hours by bus from his parole officer and just as far from a clinic where he was getting medical care.

A boost to public safety

When Laura Arnold stepped in and chose Mr. Taylor and the other plaintiffs, it was not just because of the sadness of their situations. The most compelling reason for Arnold's case was the self-defeating nature of Jessica's law's living restrictions. Even the California Department of Corrections and Rehabilitation, responsible for carrying out Jessica's law, supported the outcome in Taylor when they stated: "The dramatic increase in homelessness has a profound impact on public safety" and "the residency restriction[s] [have] significant and serious consequences that were not foreseen when it was enacted." (4)

After all, when Jessica's law had appeared before voters as a proposition, its stated purpose was to "help Californians better protect themselves." Instead, by forcing people like Mr. Taylor and other low-level offenders into homelessness, where they overtaxed parole officers trying to supervise them, Jessica's law was clearly making things more dangerous for the average Californian.

On March 2, 2015, the California Supreme Court, including four women justices, agreed in a unanimous decision—something of a rarity— and struck down Jessica's law's living restrictions, since they put the public at greater risk than before.

By the time of the decision, nine long years had passed since Jessica's law was enacted, huge amounts of taxpayer money had been spent trying to enforce its many provisions—and Sharon Runner had died.

It is hard to think of a stronger rebuke to Sharon Runner's law than a unanimous state Supreme Court decision that included four women justices. But in testimony to the persistence of hatred, her husband George Runner bad-mouthed the Taylor decision as a win for "sex offenders and molesters," (5) never acknowledging the court's main point: that Jessica's law was a failure that had actually increased the danger to the people of California, who now, with the ruling, would no longer be as endangered by the widespread homelessness the law caused, and could instead rejoice that supervising the dangerous few had become easier.

After all, the court clearly ruled that living restrictions could still be applied to someone on parole when a parole officer thinks it necessary in a particular case. The problem was that California's Jessica's law, named after a little girl sexually assaulted and horribly murdered in Florida, had been designed much too broadly, and applied to all sorts of people, such as Mr. Taylor, long finished with parole for a crime against an adult. So when the court pruned the law back, it actually brought it closer to the original spirit of designer laws mentioned in this book, since it is normally people still on parole for crimes against young people who understandably cause public fear and anger to surge if they go on to commit a similar crime.

A formidable policy

In 2015, observing the positive outcome of the Taylor case, Janice Bellucci and other ACSOL members allowed themselves to feel hopeful about a complementary attack they were building, this one against an older and more formidable policy: the lifetime registration mandated in California. This reform took years of work by ACSOL and fortunately was done in collaboration with such heavyweight forces as the California Police Chiefs Association and former Los Angeles County District Attorney Jackie Lacey—law enforcement people who well knew what an impossible task they faced trying to monitor so many low-level convicted people for their entire lives.

The big moment arrived in October 2017, when former Governor Jerry Brown signed a measure converting the old one-size-fits-all list into a "Tiered Registry." And starting in the summer of 2021, the reform began to free approximately 80 percent of the 100,000-plus people on the state registry from the burden of registering with police for their entire lives. Janice Bellucci was elated by what ACSOL had gained after starting from one person's outrage at her plumber's predicament: "The new tiered registry law is where I see the most progress in our years of work," she said with guarded satisfaction.

Like the justices in the Taylor case, the author of the tiered-registry reform, Sen. Scott Wiener of San Francisco was quick to emphasize the main point—the boost to public safety: "Our law enforcement agencies will be able to better protect people from violent sex offenders rather than wasting resources tracking low-level offenders." (6)

The old law had made California one of just a few states requiring lifetime registration, sometimes even for a conviction of indecent exposure—yes, for peeing on a tree. Instead, the reform classified people into different levels or "tiers," depending on the crime. Some—convicted for crimes the legislature considered the least severe—are put into Tier One and can ask to be removed from the list after 10 years. Tier One is for crimes such as misdemeanor sexual battery and indecent exposure— behavior that nobody condones (with the possible exception of peeing on a tree), but that should not provoke intelligent citizens to shoot themselves in the foot by transforming low-risk convicted people, estimated at two-thirds of the total, into outcasts. (6)

The next largest group, Tier Two (roughly one-quarter of the total), consists of people convicted for offenses such as lewd acts with a minor under 14. Being in this group means a person must remain on the registry for 20 years. In the opinion of many in ACSOL, this is too long in most cases, but the legislature decided it was appropriate.

Tier Three, the smallest group, was originally estimated at less than 10 percent of the total and requires lifetime registration. Rape, sex crimes against children 10 and younger, repeated sex crimes and the sex trafficking of young people put people in this most punitive group. (The modest size of Tier Three was later bloated by a single politician's move to include possession of child pornography, as we will see ahead.)

A wild ride

But the road to a better world is bumpy, and bombs dropped by two California state legislators, Melissa Melendez and Lorena Gonzalez, threatened to swell Tier Three to a much larger size. The potholes—one better described as a crater—originated from these two women of opposing political parties, who had both linked themselves with the #MeToo movement. (7, 8)

Melendez took ACSOL on a wild ride as it progressed through the legislature, attacking the Tiered Registry by introducing a bill to move a big group—people convicted of child molestation—into the strictest tier, requiring them to register for their entire lives instead of 20 years.

During my career, I've represented many people on molestation charges. Usually it's a one-time thing, and there was something else going on—the person was drunk or high—and later they are horrified by what they did. Since the re-offense rate for this type of crime is extraordinarily low and avoiding re-offending is the stated purpose of the registry, even

20 years of registration does not usually make sense, much less lifetim
registration. Nevertheless, in April 2019, Melendez tried to resuscitate th
unproveable assertion that needs a stake through its heart.

"The average child molester," harms at least 200 children before he i
caught, she claimed at a hearing of the Assembly's Public Safety Committee. Was she channeling a ghost from a couple of decades earlier—former
San Diego County Supervisor Dianne Jacob claiming that "an average sex
offender, in their lifetime, commits 360 sex offenses"? The tribe of "alternative facts" proponents who emerged on the national scene a few years
later had nothing on these politicians.

Next, Melendez called her one "expert" witness, who gave equally flab-
bergasting testimony, claiming there is no treatment available for anyone
diagnosed as a pedophile! (9)

But this time, "alternative facts" lacking an evidentiary basis did not
go unchallenged. Like knights on white horses, Janice Bellucci, over 75
ACSOL members, and a representative of the California Sex Offender
Management Board showed up at the committee hearing and, at the end
of the day, Melendez and her expert were voted down 4 to 3. And so,
the thousands who would have been moved in the Tiered Registry from
20 years to lifetime registration—up to 40,000 people, Bellucci said—
breathed another brief sigh of relief.

But Lorena Gonzalez was able to conjure up the ghosts of fearmon-
gers past more easily than Melendez. Gonzalez took aim at the Tiered
Registry in 2017 and 2018, as it was making its way through the Legislature and its Public Safety Committee. She got her hands on the bill,
insisting on moving mere possession or viewing of child pornography
(not its making or selling) into Tier Three, the strictest tier, requiring
lifetime registration. Gonzalez's move defied both logic and the vision of
the prosecutors and police who had been in on designing the reform. Tier
Three is the level for people who have committed the most severe crimes
and are likely to be a public danger if they reoffend. But pornography
possession or viewing is a non-contact crime and there is little chance it
will be repeated, especially after conviction. So it was absurd to bloat Tier
Three by including possession.

To rationalize her move, Gonzalez claimed she was motivated by
motherly fear that a child of hers could be molested. (10) One might be
tempted to advise her to get a grip, but was she really so overwhelmed by
emotion, or was she crazy like a fox? Early in 2017, Gonzalez had married
Nathan Fletcher—the very Nathan Fletcher who had skated to election
victory in 2010 on Chelsea King's murder and Chelsea's Law infamy. Is it
a stretch to imagine Fletcher pointing out to his new wife the benefits that
posing as an enemy of child rapists can yield for the ambitious politician?
And, even more chilling, is it far-fetched to suppose that the couple were

trying to fill the shoes of the Runners, since Sharon Runner had died just the year before Gonzalez dropped her bomb on the Tiered Registry? Indeed, soon after hobbling the Tiered Registry law, Gonzalez announced plans to make a run for California Secretary of State.

There is one more reason to discredit the surge of motherly concern Gonzalez claimed to feel. An emerging "crime" in the United States is teenagers who "sext" other teens racy photos of themselves or others and are brought up on child pornography charges. In 2018, for example, the American Civil Liberties Union brought to light the case of a 14-year-old Minnesota girl facing the sex-offender registry for sending a boy she liked an explicit photo of herself. Nonsensically, she was considered both victim and perpetrator. (11)

Yet a survey of 18-year-olds had found that 30 percent had sent nude pictures during high school. What if all these kids were to end up on the sex-crime registry? What if a child of Lorena Gonzalez should be convicted of possessing or viewing child pornography due to "sexting" and put in Tier 3 for life, as her mangling of the Tiered Registry dictated? Would she then come to her senses as to whether including possession of child porn in Tier 3 was about protecting children or in reality just another hateful, neo-Puritan punishment?

Sadly, Gonzalez did succeed in ruining that part of the Tiered Registry law. However, around the same time, in December 2019, the California Supreme Court made a very positive decision that negated Gonzalez's claim that super-strict laws on viewing child porn images are justified by the goal of protecting real children.

Completely theoretical harm

Here's what happened. The usual way people try to justify over-the-top child porn laws is that if nobody bought and looked at porn, nobody would make and sell it—just as when you drink a beer, you support the alcohol industry. But would it be logical to claim that everyone who has an alcoholic drink is responsible for everyone killed by a drunken driver? Obviously not.

The state Supreme Court used this more valid logic when they ended a rule that psychotherapists had to report a patient's viewing of child porn to authorities. The case was Mathews vs. Becerra, named for Don Mathews, a California therapist who treats patients for problems such as compulsive behavior. Mathews argued that his obligation to report patients to police if they admitted to looking at child pornography made it impossible to treat people who came to him for help with pornography compulsions, since successful therapy is based on opening up about the inner workings of your mind. (12)

Legal scholars supported Mathews by pointing out that the notion that possessing child porn harms real children is completely theoretical. And a majority of the judges agreed, deciding that it was up to the state to prove that the reporting requirement for therapists truly protects children. (Ironically, it is the state that sometimes harms real young people when it informs them, usually years after the fact, that they were once unwitting "stars" of child porn. This information can be very upsetting for youngsters who didn't know about their victimization until prosecutors told them. Dramatic examples of girls being traumatized for exactly this reason were presented in a 2019 New York Times series. But in an illogical twist, the gist of the article was the girls' understandable horror at learning the crime was recorded on the internet forever—the article didn't touch on the fact that law enforcement in reality accelerated their trauma by informing them of the porn. (13))

The Mathews vs. Becerra decision did not address whether possessing child pornography should be seen as a serious crime, only whether therapists have to turn in patients in this one situation when they know a patient looks at child pornography. But it was still a substantial victory for rationality in a situation that often gets a knee-jerk reaction. However, unencumbered by common sense, Gonzalez plowed ahead in 2018, getting the California legislature to pass other senseless laws on sex crimes. Perhaps legislators were hesitant to seem insensitive to the issues raised by #MeToo, but thankfully former California Governor Jerry Brown stepped in and restrained Gonzalez by vetoing eight of her bills. (14)

Janice Bellucci and ACSOL have found at least three more purely malicious measures in California in recent years: after completing sentences and parole or probation, people convicted of sex-related felonies are the only type of felons who may not serve on juries; they are also prohibited from being poll workers for elections; and they may not apply for compensation from the state Victims Compensation Fund.

Such absurd measures, based on fanciful notions of the harm that might follow from a convicted person's participation in civic life, make it clear that rage against people who once committed a sex offense persists alongside smoldering racism, sexism and other irrational prejudices—and that the rage probably comes from the same dark place in the human psyche. This is the reason that, instead of simply calling bad laws on sex offenses "designer laws," reflecting their use of attractive victims relentlessly advertised in a perverse branding process, I have come to believe that "hate laws" is an equally accurate term.

And so, the Tiered Registry crept toward and then reached its implementation date in 2021, as registrants began engaging public defenders and private attorneys to help them petition courts to be removed from the registry. And Janice Bellucci kept her fingers crossed. "I warn people in ACSOL that if another high-profile crime happens— another Megan Kanka [whose 1994 murder by a neighbor previously convicted of sex crimes spurred Megan's laws]—it could cause a big setback for the Tiered Registry," she said.

Clearly, progress has been made, but there are miles to go before we sleep—and there are people energized to go the distance.

26. The Tower of Hope

June 2017 to April 2018

ELAINE HALLECK

Not all heads turned as 27-year-old Kari Fernandez, with a bounce in her step and wearing a grey fleece jacket, black tights and running shoes, covered the distance between her parked white, 12-seater Mercedes van and the umbrella-covered tables and chairs where a scattering of people were eating or waiting.

But one head that did turn was that of Kevin Sullivan, another driver in Kari's company. Kevin was always glad to see Kari and he thought he probably would have been her boyfriend if he was 10 years older, and she wasn't married to his brother—or his "almost-brother," as he usually called Diego.

Kevin was sitting in Otay Mesa, California, outside the sleek complex at the U.S. end of the two-way, air-conditioned pedestrian footbridge connecting the Tijuana airport to the United States. The two-year-old building housed U.S. Customs and Immigration and a few car rental and food businesses. The complex sometimes seemed like the only sign of life in the otherwise rather desolate area. You had to get on a freeway and travel six miles east to get to the much busier San Ysidro border crossing— all clang and clamor of trolleys and buses, with roads and traffic packed together so tightly there was barely room for the shopping outlets, McDonald's, crosswalks, and more of the same everywhere you looked.

Then a few more miles northeast and you'd be almost in downtown San Diego and the bay with its fleets of parked Navy ships. Kevin, Kari— sometimes with her baby—and another driver separately buzzed back and forth several times every day on freeways between Otay Mesa, San Ysidro and downtown San Diego.

Now, in a bit of down time here at Otay, Kevin could sit in the shade of an umbrella, sip a Starbuck's and catch up on phone chats. Behind his back and to the south, actually only a few feet away, were the TJ airport and some inklings of that beleaguered city's pell-mell character.

In front of him, to the north in the misty distance, were sedate, almost magical, mountains that he liked to look at. The mountains were tantalizing as they loomed beyond CBX's new parking lots and the nearby, somber-hued office parks that never showed any sign of life, despite their nice landscaping.

As Kari approached, Kevin didn't exactly have to tear himself away from the mostly nonsense on his phone. Maybe it was that bounce in her Converses, or her quiet friendly ways. It wasn't that she was so sexy—her long hair was tied back, and she wore just a little make-up and looked like she was ready for a run on that surprisingly cool, but sunny June afternoon of 2017. But those clothes would do the job when she was loading and unloading luggage at the back of the van.

Kari didn't sit down, just greeted Kevin and asked if he could take the regular run. "Dad texted me this morning about a special job. I brought some American politicians from the airport to downtown TJ, not far from the Zona Norte. Now I've gotta pick them up and get them back."

Since they weren't supposed to read texts while driving, Kevin figured he must have missed that one. He raised his eyebrows in surprise.

It wasn't that he was going to refuse to drive the regular run—after all, Kari was more or less his boss. But the company, Kari-U, didn't usually go to the notorious Zona Norte, even though these days there wasn't nearly the same level of vice as years ago, when the place was a magnet for thousands of bored Navy guys on shore leave, who would head to the Zona Norte for excitement—in the form of drinking, marijuana and sex. Kevin couldn't imagine why American politicians would want to go there and then to the TJ airport.

When Kevin asked Kari this, she explained that she was only picking up the politicians near the Zona, not in the Zona. It was some sort of organization for American soldiers, believe it or not. And she'd picked them up at the San Diego airport, not TJ, and that's where she was taking them this evening. She'd be back here at Otay with them in an hour, crossing the border in the lane for vehicles with Sentri passes of course, before heading off to the San Diego airport, less than a half hour away if traffic was good.

"How many are there?" Kevin asked.

"I got four of them at the airport this morning. One's a lady. One more met us at our destination—a guy from the American consulate, I think. The lady's from Texas. She sat up front with me—I don't have Dani and her car seat today. The lady was nice. She told me they're from the Hispanic Caucus. That little storefront where I dropped them off, in TJ, actually had an American flag hanging out front."

"You said it's for American soldiers?" Kevin asked incredulously.

Kari shook her head yes. "I don't get it either. The sign in the window said 'Deported Veterans' but the guys I saw there all looked Hispanic, and they were wearing U.S. military uniforms, with medals and everything. But I have to go—I'm late because I got the van washed. Their flight back to Washington is at 7 and they're probably already wrapping up their speeches and stuff."

As Kevin watched the van and Kari pull away, he mulled over the deported veterans business. He didn't think they could deport American citizens, and didn't you have to be a citizen to get in the military?

But no, he suddenly remembered a high school friend of Diego's in L.A. What was his name? Jack. Yes, Jack Esparta. Kevin had called him Jack Sprat, and he was a little fat, just like in the poem. After high school, Jack was thinking about going in the Army and he tried to talk Diego into it too, telling him it was a path to citizenship. Jack didn't realize Diego was JW and didn't do army. And anyway, Diego's citizenship had long been squared away, since he was legally adopted.

Kevin only saw Jack once or twice after he finished with the Army—or was it the Marines?—but through Jack and other friends, he learned that, even though Jack lost weight to get in, he didn't gain his citizenship through his military service after all. Jack actually thought citizenship would be automatic and never followed up on it. On top of that, when he later applied for a passport using his birth certificate from a midwife in Texas, they thought it was forged, threw Jack into an immigration detention center, and tried to deport him, until he got a lawyer, who somehow fixed it.

So much for citizenship for Hispanics, even those who served in the Army. That was probably why Kari's grandmother, Tata, who didn't know where she was born but jumped through hoops to get her U.S. passport so she could visit Kari and her father in Yahualica, was always so nervous at the border when she came back into San Diego. Later, after Kari and her dad's move to TJ, Tata got a Sentri fast pass for herself and her car, and was less jumpy about crossing back into San Diego. But the fear was still there.

Of course, Kari's dad never even tried to get back in. Kevin knew some of his story and Kari said her father had thought for a second about paying a ton of money to get smuggled in with a new identity and no passport, but at that point, with no job or house waiting for him—and not much money for paying a coyote either—it didn't make any sense to go back.

Kari, soon after moving to TJ, had started getting her passport squared away, with the help of an American lady who had a business there. After all, Kari had left California in 2003 with nothing except her clothes and her Spanish-English dictionary. Tata and Trevor had eventually brought across her hospital birth certificate and other documents she needed.

So now Kari was good as gold, and she never even seemed nervous crossing the border, which she did a lot. But she and Diego—along with Kari's father—had a pretty house in a decent, gated fraccionamiento in Tijuana that would have cost them three times as much north of the border.

Now that Kari's father had stopped working at Hyundai, he put in as many hours as possible at JW's Tower of Hope, a substance-addiction program that most ironically had the same name—in English yet—as the old abusive one in L.A., which he'd been forced to attend all those years ago. He also helped Kari with the baby. While still in Yahualica, he had become a Mexican citizen under the name of Juan—Juan Fernandez.

He only changed his first name, maybe figuring that with two common names, he could more easily get lost in the crowd.

Now he kept quiet, lived clean and probably passed for Mexican, as long as he didn't talk too much. He had a girlfriend, Rosy, who lived nearby, in Rosarito beach. Rosy in Rosarito, everyone called her. She was one of the many Hispanic-Americans who'd moved south to TJ to be with some family member who got deported, in Rosy's case, her mother. That family was among the lucky ones who managed to exit America involuntarily but in some kind of style, or who at least didn't end up like those sad deportees who had nothing but the clothes on their back and lived in the canal near the Zona Norte, where people injected drugs.

The Americans had started getting tough about deportations, passports and everything else—when was it?—2005? 2007? 2009? Kevin only remembered that it was about the time Kari and her dad moved north to Tijuana, which was ironic when you thought about it. But they only moved to be closer to Tata and Trevor, and because JW had addiction programs where Juan could work, and because Juan also thought a job at Hyundai sounded good. They didn't move to TJ with the idea of trying to go back to California. Anyway, around that time was when you suddenly started needing more documents when you wanted to get back in the States after traveling to Mexico for even a few hours.

But at that point, hardly any gringos were coming to Tijuana for fun. The rip-roaring party scene in the Zona Norte, or Sin City as some Americans called it, had dried up when the U.S. military suddenly made TJ off-limits for soldiers and sailors—under pain of court-martial. The anti-drug war started by Calderon, the Mexican president, and urged on by President Bush, had wreaked havoc in TJ, and still was. Kevin remembered that murders of cartel members and police officers had increased so much—over 800 one year, including spectacles like bodies hanging from bridges—that the American military brass figured all the drunk, pot-smoking, sex-hungry young soldiers were bound to get into big trouble in TJ. Besides, with a big ol' drug war going on, it didn't make any sense for the U.S. military to allow thousands and thousands of sailors to go to Tijuana and buy pot and meth and you name it.

But even back then, all that narco drama didn't have much effect on Diego, Kari, her father, or anyone Kevin knew. Kevin's parents, the Sullivans, still lived in L.A. and had helped Diego and Kari buy the house in TJ, which was in a nice but not luxurious area not too far from Rosarito beach. And that's where Kari, Diego and Kari's dad stayed most of the time. They hardly ever did things like go out to restaurants and movies and never to bars or rock concerts. They just went back and forth to work or, in Diego's case, to medical school, and that was it. After all, JWs could hardly be called big partyers. Kevin's parents had told him a long time ago that if you don't want trouble, don't look for it, and that meant staying away from bars and party scenes.

Kevin had been lost in thought, but now he was done with his java chip frappuccino and could see a couple people with luggage hanging around near the Kari-U pickup area. It was getting close to 4, but he still had some time, so he went inside the complex to talk again with the cute barista, Marisol, and get another frappuccino for the road.

Less than an hour later, while waiting at a light to get on the 905 with his load of passengers and luggage, Kevin heard a ping from a text Kari had sent Juan, and he quickly read it: Dad, I found out something cool at the vets office from the founder Omar. Can't wait to tell you.

*

Juan Fernandez quickly grabbed two of the three chihuahuas playing in his patio and put them in their cages, then scooped up Rikki, his favorite, and headed for the front door. All five of his dogs, even Rikki, put up a ruckus of barking—or squeaking, as Rosy called it—in response to the doorbell.

Juan knew it was only Omar, bringing over a newly deported veteran with an addiction problem. But the dogs didn't know that, and barked as if there were an invasion. Chihuahuas could be nervous and even aggressive, but Juan refused to have their vocal cords operated on, like some breeders did. Together with the parakeets he bred in the same patio, they caused quite a racket. But Juan didn't mind—it wasn't nearly as loud as the noise in the factory where he used to work, and the parakeets, if not the chihuahuas, sounded a lot more pleasant.

Juan expected the new deportee to look and act rattled, but he was surprised that Omar looked a bit sourpuss too; Juan thought he'd be walking on clouds today. They all shook hands quickly. No carrying on in the Mexican manner; they were Americans, after all. Then Omar asked for a glass of water. In the kitchen, while the new guy looked at the animals in the patio, Omar shook his head, sighed, rolled his eyes, and confessed he wasn't feeling well.

"It's a circus, man. CNN has been calling non-stop, plus Jorge Ramirez, and my daughter Jennifer from L.A. I can't get any sleep. My blood pressure is up, my diabetes is acting up. This is what I've wanted for years. But now that it's here…holy crap."

Juan had long been a little worried about Omar's weight and his eating habits, and now he didn't know what to say. "Well, Kari's taking you across tomorrow," he responded. It was all he could think of, and Kari's presence was always calm and cheerful—as if she had a magic wand. Tata called her Santa Kari—Saint Kari.

"Yeah, Kari's great. Anyhow, Immigration Services is taking care of everything. It's never been done before. A bunch of people will be at the ceremony in San Diego: some politicians—including one guy who made a name on your anti-sex-offender laws—and Jennifer. It's like getting married times 100."

"Hang in there," Juan said, and clapped Omar on the shoulder. He still remembered when his lawyer had done that decades ago after a tough day in court, and it made a difference.

Omar's distress was perplexing to Juan, who deep down was jealous that Omar was being repatriated, and also realized that he was going to miss him. There were definite boundaries to their friendship. Omar had told Juan when they first met last year that he felt for Juan, but couldn't afford to let him spend time at the deported veterans office. For one thing, Juan wasn't a veteran. For another, there was too much chance of law enforcement types showing up, between the lawyers who helped out sometimes and everything else.

Not that Juan really wanted to hang around the veterans office—he was happy at home—a hell of a lot happier than working at Hyundai. He'd decided to visit Omar's office—after a lot of hesitation—because Kari told him that she learned from Omar that a new law—a Tiered Registry law— was about to be passed in California and it would drastically improve things for people on Megan's List for a sex crime. After the law was passed, most guys would be on track to get off the registry eventually, whereas before they had to be on it all their lives, as Juan knew all too well.

Besides that, Kari said there were people at the office, a couple of them even living there, who were in different stages of getting a pardon from Governor Brown for the crimes that got them deported. Kari heard the word "pardon" and got excited, not remembering how different her father was from those deported veterans. He had committed a crime, yes, but it wasn't any old crime; it was the kind they want to put your eyes out for. And he fled California; he wasn't kicked out. So, he wouldn't be eligible for a pardon, like Omar, or a certificate of rehabilitation, which some guys used to get off Megan's List. Also, he was a citizen, although Kari doubted that he'd be any more able to prove it than the deported guys.

Despite the limitations of the friendship between Omar and Juan, what Omar could do for Juan—or, better said, what Juan could do for Omar— was to get deported veterans who had addictions into the 12-step-style program that Juan led at the Tower of Hope.

Now, Juan and Omar walked out into the patio, where the new deportee was eating an orange Juan had given him, and looking at a JW pamphlet on addiction, in English. It was a bilingual program, since most of the participants were at least a little bilingual.

"You know that Juan here is the pastor at Tower of Hope," Omar said. "You two will head over there in a while. It's a good program and it's free. We're still gonna need to help you find a place to stay, but you're in good hands with Juan today. You went through treatment yourself, Juan, right?"

"Sure did," Juan replied. "But, well, maybe the word 'treatment' is a little strong." He wanted to say maybe the word "pastor" was a little strong too, but he didn't.

"It's more like a daisy chain of guys—and gals—helping each other. We ask that participants come every day—three hours. Pretty soon you'll get a sponsor. And you might meet someone who can help with finding a place and a job."

"Is there a rule I have to stop drinking before I can start?" the guy asked. Juan and Omar both laughed. "If there was a rule like that, nobody would start,"

Juan said. "But obviously we don't encourage drinking. Jehovah's Witnesses don't go in for it. Anyway, do you have money for that?" The guy sheepishly shook his head no.

Just like Omar had his limitations with Juan, Juan had his limitations with the guys in the addiction groups. He never let them stay at his house and they normally didn't even see it—Omar had brought the new guy this time because he wanted to say goodbye to Juan.

There were also limitations on what Juan revealed about himself when he led meetings. He didn't talk about his background or even where he was born. Of course, he talked about his past with alcohol, but he never referred to the huge problem alcohol caused him with the law. He was friendly, but he really didn't make friends because he didn't want to be asked the kind of questions about his past that had been his terror ever since coming to Mexico.

Juan mostly talked about how God—and prayer, he believed—had lifted his compulsions from his shoulders. Well, Santa Kari and San Francisco had helped too. These days he felt completely okay with alcohol—he didn't abstain, but he didn't buy beer and seldom drank. A lot of that was due to JW influence.

Actually, drinking alcohol stopped abruptly that day in 2003 when Kari and Juan—he was called Danny, at the time—had crossed the border and headed south. With all the responsibilities of the car, driving and taking care of Kari in a country where he really didn't speak the language, he hardly ever even thought about having a beer. Now he thought that alcoholism had more to do with his environment back in L.A.—with trying to relax, with watching TV and hanging with certain friends.

But when his environment changed—drastically—his desire for beer evaporated. It hadn't been difficult at all to stop drinking. In fact, he hadn't really even noticed that he'd stopped until he began meeting with that JW study group in Yahualica, and it branched off into a group about addiction.

The leadership was sending study materials about addiction and addiction groups, and encouraging people to get training.

Juan didn't know exactly why he went into the addiction group—maybe it was because Tio Francisco, who ended up being his sponsor, suggested it. Or maybe he just wanted to talk about something besides the Bible, although even people in the small Bible group in Yahualica sometimes talked about personal things. The nice thing was that, in both the Bible and addiction group, you didn't have to talk—not like that so-called therapy group back in L.A. led by the psychologist who, if you didn't talk, would write down that you weren't participating and tell your P.O. It was a memory that gave Juan the creeps, and sometimes even used to make him feel like throwing up. Yes, he was jealous about Omar getting repatriated, but when he thought about it harder, not that jealous. What kind of a country would treat people like he'd been treated?

Of course, Mexico's system was probably a mess too, and politically they generally seemed to want to copy whatever America did, with the idea of not being seen as a "poor" country. However, Omar had told him about an American guy who was in a TJ prison, and got help from the U.S. Consulate to transfer to a Florida prison to serve out his time, according to an international agreement. Later Omar called the guy in Florida and he said he wished he'd stayed in TJ. Although he'd been "scared shitless" when he started his prison time in Mexico, it had turned out to be much easier than in Florida.

It was in the Yahualica addiction group that Juan had first talked about Ashley. Other people had talked about their screw-ups, and Francisco had mentioned legal problems he had in the States, with taxes or something. Maybe they were even the reason he moved back to Mexico.

But the first time Juan told Francisco about his neighbor's daughter Ashley, they weren't actually in a meeting—they were working at the store. Juan said that if he hadn't been drinking, the mess with the girl would never have happened. Drinking wasn't the only reason, but it was the biggest one. Later he told Kari the same thing. She didn't seem surprised, even though he had never actually admitted to her that he messed with Ashley. He also told Kari he was sorry he disrupted her life. Kari didn't say much to that either—just shook her head a bit, said thank you, and that he didn't have to be sorry.

Juan told Francisco that he hoped he hadn't hurt Ashley. She seemed like she was on a road, with her parents and their ways, to a life that wasn't so great, but what he did to her certainly didn't help. Sometimes even now he thought about her—she would be the same age as Kari and he wondered if she was married with kids too. He hoped the experience hadn't messed her up, but sometimes suspected that if it had, it would be more due to the reaction of the rest of the world than to him messing with her.

Often Juan wondered if he was the best person to lead an addiction group, since his problem with beer hadn't been nearly as bad as what he heard a million times a day at the Tower of Hope, about alcohol and other drugs.

Well, the legal problem Juan had caused himself because of what he did to Ashley—now that was bad. These days, he couldn't believe he'd done something that stupid and ridiculous. He'd been so buzzed he wasn't even sure he remembered it. By now, what he'd heard, read, and said after the fact had all blended together with his few drunken memories. The one certain thing was that he didn't ever want to repeat being addicted. That was what motivated him to work with the addicts and drunks. He knew the program could help them and he was happier leading it than at any other time in his life, except when the kids were very young and Patty was still on board, as he still fondly recalled.

27. There's a lot of that going on!

1994 to 2021

ALEX LANDON

Has there been a sea change in America regarding sex crimes and their "solution" by designer laws—laws named after attractive victims and relentlessly advertised by public figures promoting their personal brand? Although pessimists may believe that the web of designer laws (or hate laws as I now call them) is beyond redemption, I argue that California has been seeing a positive sea change—in the form of enlightened court decisions, refreshing approaches to therapy and registration, and the emergence of the Alliance for Constitutional Sex Offense Laws led by a courageous woman. All these positive elements have worked in synchrony to forge slow change in the nation's most populous state.

Still, a wider snapshot of America's sex offender laws in the last decade shows a mixed picture—at times improving, but at times revealing the persistence of an outlandish juxtaposition of zero benefits to the public with severe repercussions to about a million convicted citizens. This persistence—sometimes coupled with a refusal to look at the evidence— was what led me to add "hate laws" to my term "designer laws."

In the "plus" column nationally are people I've been hard on in the past, but who now are critical of the current constellation of "Megan's Laws"—in the plural—all based on the impact of the murder of Megan Kanka in 1994. One such group is the Association for the Treatment of Sexual Abusers (ATSA), which, in earlier times, advocated a hardline treatment approach that could not be dignified as "therapy." However, ATSA has recently done some important reforming work by listing in their 2020 report 12 recent court decisions unfavorable to Megan's Laws. Three decisions mentioned violations of free speech (meaning registered people shouldn't be compelled to publicize damaging information about themselves), six decisions called registration a violation of ex post facto (meaning punishment imposed for actions that happened before Megan's Law was passed), two found registration is cruel and unusual punishment, and five found that the laws are a violation of equal protection and due process (meaning registered people are not individually assessed). What's more, a 2021 decision by the South Carolina Supreme Court likewise ruled there are equal protection and due process problems with Megan's Laws. (1) (2)

If that wasn't enough of a turnabout, ATSA listed 12 academic studies done between 2007 and 2019, some on Megan's Law's home turf of New Jersey, demonstrating that registration and community notification laws have not achieved their stated purpose: a reduction in sexual re-offending by convicted people.

Also in the plus column nationally is the work of another courageous woman. Patty Wetterling is the mother of an abducted boy and she used to be a prominent advocate for Megan's Laws (including one named after her son). But in a recent report by Human Rights Watch, she changed her opinion, asserting that registration should only be used to help police locate convicted people in the event of a new crime and not for community notification, which was begun with the first Megan's Law in 1994. (3)

This is what many who have critically appraised Megan's Laws now advocate, including the American Law Institute, called the most prestigious non-governmental law reform organization in the United States, in their seismic 2021 draft report recommending changes to the U.S. Penal Code. (4) In addition, the California Sex Offender Management Board, a prestigious state advisory group, chimed in with their 2016 educational booklet, "What you may not know about California's Sex Offender Registry," warning that "research shows registration systems do not reduce recidivism or prevent new sex crimes."

Even Maureen Kanka, mother of the murdered Megan and for decades a driving force behind Megan's Laws, spoke out in 2009 against charging a 14-year-old New Jersey girl with disseminating pornography for posting nude photos of herself, an offense that would lead to the girl's registration as a sex offender. (5) Although Maureen Kanka saw past her pain in this instance, she has still not expressed the change of heart that Patty Wetterling has. Perhaps Kanka's husband's run for public office—and the political benefits that accrue from his name recognition as Megan's father—is the reason she has to date remained a strong booster of Megan's Laws, apparently not realizing, or not caring, how rare the egregious crime suffered by her daughter was, and what damage it does to base sweeping laws on worst cases.

However, the sensible statements by ATSA, Patty Wetterling and ALI, and even that one remark by Maureen Kanka must be appreciated as bits of progress. Just like the changes in California, these marvels at the national level do suggest that much-needed reform is percolating.

Birth of a monster

Still, other developments have been ominous—and all of them are related to a dreadful new law, passed in 2016, International Megan's Law .

IML, like many hate laws targeting people convicted of sex crimes, was a convulsion in the very foundations of law, extending into uncharted international terrain where registration has severe consequences unlike anything seen before. But even more importantly, IML offers no chance of getting closer to that goal we all share: preventing sex crimes against women and children.

IML was authored by Congressman Chris Smith of New Jersey, home of the original 1994 Megan's law. After decades of experience with Megan's Laws (in the plural) at the state and federal level, as well as the 12 unfavorable studies showing they yield no benefits, the news that Megan's Laws are a flop didn't faze Smith. (The studies didn't faze Megan Kanka's mom either, who dismissed them with the illogical claim that "We never said [the law] was going to stop them from reoffending." (6)) Perhaps, letting the winds of hate fill his sails, Smith simply didn't care whether Megan's Laws worked. After all, the anti-sex-crime branding he invested in, using Megan's murder as a steppingstone, helped make him the longest- serving congressman in New Jersey history.

As IML got under way, it floated on a raft of novel propaganda—new and misleading language that, as George Orwell famously sketched in his novel "1984," is key in greasing authoritarianism's wheels. The novel phrases coined to support the novel repressions of IML—starting around 2000, according to law professor Dina Francesca Haynes, with "human trafficking," "sex trafficking" and "child sex trafficking" and escalating to "modern day slavery" (7)—dovetail with a tradition of older disturbing and misused terminology on sex crimes: "convicted predator," "convicted pedophile" and the like.

Other turnabouts we see in the brave new world of IML and its sister hate laws have been in who is promoting them. I don't mean individual people, although of course that is happening too, but a juggernaut formed of specific demographic and professional groups. The new groups include chic and charismatic entertainers, NGOs, women, evangelistic religious groups, businesses that contract with federal authorities, and African Americans, who have been prominent in a worrisome shift in Congressional power dynamics.

IML was born in February 2016, when it was signed by former President Obama. It mandates blacklisting and unprecedented travel restrictions for almost a million Americans who are registered on the "Megan's List" database due to conviction for a "sex crime." IML is tied by its name to New Jersey's "Megan's Law," signed a mere month after the murder of Megan Kanka in 1994, and to the federal "Megan's Law" of 1996, signed by Bill Clinton. These early laws added wide public notification about where convicted people were living to their inclusion in an older database used only by police, which had already existed in some states, such as California. It is worth noting that in many jurisdictions, "sex crimes" can include streaking, urinating in public and consensual sex between teens, as well as sexual "thought crimes," such as viewing child porn, or texting racy content to a teenager—or even to someone merely thought to be a teenager, but who, in reality was an officer. Amazingly, people convicted of these last two crimes—looking at sexy images of underage teens, and sending such images or raunchy text—are frequently teens themselves, caught in the internet-age crime of "sexting," a form of high-tech flirting (or sometimes high-tech revenge).

A principal provision of Rep. Chris Smith's IML is that registered citizens, including teens, are required to get passport stamps announcing their past conviction. Passport marks that generate restrictions have not been seen before, outside of Nazi Germany and the former Soviet Union, which used them to prevent Jewish people from emigrating. The mark is part of a process that triggers notification of a destination country where the person plans to travel and/or his expulsion from foreign airports—sometimes not until he arrives, suitcase in hand.

Sounds harsh, complicated, and constitutionally suspect, doesn't it? It is all three. And IML thus results in erroneous, arbitrary, unjust, and malicious enforcement on the U.S. side—and the foreign side too, considering the huge variety of foreign cultures and justice systems that the law impacts. Basically, foreign authorities can do whatever they want with the notification the U.S. government sends them about convicted citizens, and although the language of international aviation is English, staff in foreign airports may not even understand the notification. According to analysts who have studied or experienced IML, the notification is interpreted by foreign authorities as "There's a warrant for your arrest and you're on the run." The fallout could even include execution, which is the law in some countries as punishment for sex crimes, and I doubt that U.S. embassies would defend registered citizens traveling abroad from execution, since the U.S. State Department is part of the machinery depicting them as dangerous.

One pertinent example (documented in the unsuccessful 2016 challenge to IML in the U.S. District Court for the Northern District of California) is the California man who couldn't visit his dying father in Iran, since Iran is one of the countries that use the death penalty against sex offenders and might have executed him due to his passport mark. Then there was the California lawyer who was once registered but had, with much difficulty, earned a certificate of rehabilitation and was no longer on Megan's List but was nevertheless kicked out of the Philippines, since the IML bureaucracy had failed to take his certificate into account. Another registered American had been regularly visiting his 81-year-old mother, who lived alone in Mexico, where he was usually admitted—but was unexpectedly deported during one trip. Another couldn't marry a sweetheart in Mexico; another was barred from returning to his wife and kids in the Philippines after visiting his parents in New York.

These are stories that the average person will never hear, simply because registered citizens are often too afflicted by shame to complain loudly. But those same registered citizens are all too full of accounts about their surprise deportations and surprise arrests—not for new sex offenses but for incorrectly handling planned travel. This should banish from readers' minds any thought that IML simply results in a million Americans missing out on a frolic at one of the world's great beaches—or, as frequently stated by IML boosters, missing out on a vacation for "sex tourism."

Harmless, titillating entertainment?

One scholar has written of Megan's Laws in general as the "result of the publicity that some of history's most heinous sex offenders have received." (8) And, indeed, we can identify a handful of worst-case crimes as sparks, or perhaps better said, pretexts, behind IML. However, as we will see, there is no evidence that the crimes sparking IML are rampant—although the publicity around them certainly is.

Such publicity causes ordinary people, saturated in internet, radio, TV and print accounts of the worst horrors, to begin to believe "There's a lot of that going on!" and it has become "a crisis that has reached previously unimagined proportions" in the words of a U.S. State Department report on "Trafficking in Persons." (9) Sadly, these alarming statements do not turn out to be mere harmless, titillating entertainment—they go on to spark sweeping political and legal "solutions" that promise to rein things in.

Several heinous characters clearly emerge as engines that drove IML during the years it was in the works. The notorious Jack Sporich is one, with his unsavory crimes that titillate the imagination and his timeline of infamy that tracks IML's rise. Sporich is a well-off, California aerospace engineer released from prison in 2004 after serving time for molesting boys on camping trips. He was rearrested five years later in Cambodia, where he was said to troll the streets on a motorcycle dropping money to attract boys. 2009, the year Sporich was rearrested, was just a year after Rep. Smith began pushing IML in the U.S. Congress.

Besides Sporich, the depredations of the beyond-notorious financier Jeffrey Epstein also dovetail IML's timeline. Epstein's first conviction for procuring a child for prostitution came in the same year, 2008, when Rep. Smith started his campaign, and Epstein's last arrest on charges of sex trafficking minors was in 2020, four years after Smith got IML passed.

Also propelling IML was an Islamic paramilitary group in Nigeria, Boko Haram, who loomed large in infamy during the years IML was in the works. The brutal group was said to deal in "child sex trafficking," "sexual slavery" and "modern day slavery"—new terms they helped embed into the American lexicon—due to their 2014 kidnapping of 276 teenage girls from a village school and their threat to sell the girls as wives. Coming just two years before Rep. Smith finally got IML passed, the kidnapping incident and slavery terminology made a perfect storm to propel the law, especially since they tapped into the frustration felt by women and African Americans that was about to surface.

Rep. Smith's attempts to get IML passed spanned almost a decade, and besides surfing the waves generated by Sporich, Epstein and Boko Haram, Smith conjured up the ghost of that much older, worst-case crime by bringing Megan Kanka's parents to a press conference on IML two decades after the murder of their daughter. This was a publicity move pure and simple, since the content of International Megan's Law has little to do with Megan's Law except for the name and the fact that both relate to sex offenses. [4]

Sporich, Epstein, Boko Haram and Megan Kanka's killer too. In this maelstrom of sensationalism, it is sensible to ask if IML could in reality have prevented any of these worst-case crimes that so boosted the law's passage.

Of the criminals mentioned, Sporich is the one whose deeds in Cambodia seem, almost rationally, as if they might have been prevented by the notification of foreign governments mandated by IML. Yet he was brought down—seven years before IML came online—by a panoply of pre- existing forces: the U.S. Justice Department's "Operation Twisted Traveler," U.S. Immigration and Customs Enforcement ("ICE"), the International Criminal Police Organization ("Interpol") and an aid-to-children agency. ICE even stationed agents in Cambodia working on Sporich's case. It is fair to say, then, that even though popular disgust over Sporich's case surely drove IML's passage, this law, like other hate laws, was unnecessary and redundant in stopping Sporich.

A detour here illustrates one principle trampled in de-fanging Sporich. His investigation, arrest, deportation and trial in Los Angeles—for acts in the sovereign country of Cambodia, which has and enforces its own laws against child molestation (though not harshly enough for American tastes), were due to the U.S. Protect Act of 2003 (Chapter 21), which facilitated U.S. hegemony over foreign countries.

Cambodian officials apparently agreed to this violation of national sovereignty. However, perhaps the agreement was not so freely reached, considering a recent history of strong-arming—the U.S. bombing of Cambodia from 1965 to 1975, including indiscriminate "carpet bombing" that killed untold thousands of civilians (as revealed in atrocity

---

[4] IML doesn't mandate public notification, which had been the crux of Megan's Law of 1994, but the notification of foreign police.

investigations). (10) (11) How would Americans react if police agents of a country that once bombed us—say, Saudi Arabia, of which 15 of the September 11 terrorists were citizens—set up shop in New York to root out journalists they believe are heinous?

Indeed, such incursions against citizens on foreign soil generate the same head-scratching as many hate laws. It's like America telling an American she must observe the U.S. speed limit of 70 mph on a German autobahn (which has no speed limit) in order to protect German citizens, and even stationing U.S. police in Germany to arrest American speeders and drag them back to American soil.

Returning to whether IML could have prevented the crimes sparking it, what about Epstein—couldn't he have been thwarted by IML? Again no, because, although Epstein was registered after 2008 as a sex offender on "Megan's List" and certainly sailed on international trade winds, IML and the foreign-government notification it mandates were completely irrelevant to him, since the U.S. Virgin Islands are not a foreign country. Although I am focusing on International Megan's Law here, it is also worth asking if the mothership—the original Megan's law of 1994— measures up as a law that could conceivably have prevented the worst-case crime that ignited it.

It is difficult to argue with Megan's parents, who said that if they had known that a man twice convicted of sex crimes against little girls was living almost across the street, Megan would still be alive. Yes, "community notification" on released prisoners—the core of Megan's Law—seems in this case to be a rational reaction to the circumstances of the horrible murder of Megan.

But an extra measure of clear thinking and patience is necessary here, in order to avoid the bruising pitfalls following the emotional reactions that bring designer and hate laws in their wake. And our first instance of clear thinking is the sociological, meta-analysis of Megan's Laws mentioned earlier, which revealed that designer laws are uniformly named after photogenic white victims and spearheaded by articulate parents in the grip of self-dealing politicians. This analysis is but one powerful antidote to falling under the spell of Megan's Laws. There are more.

"Inspiration and beauty irreversibly transform the soul"

Another good remedy for the seductive but superficial logic that claims Megan's Law could have prevented Megan's murder is scholarly analysis of whether community notification and public listing of sex offenders have achieved their articulated goal—the reduction of sex crimes. Before discussing such analyses, we must point out that causation—not to mention prevention—is the classic, hair-tearing concept in philosophy, logic and science. There are weighty logical and logistical problems in proving that anything causes or prevents anything, even with simpler questions, such as if broccoli prevents cancer.

Nevertheless, as mentioned at the start of this chapter, good scholarly studies have been done in the three decades since New Jersey passed the first, groundbreaking community notification law, Megan's Law, and other jurisdictions followed suit. So, let's take a very brief overview of these studies, keeping in mind the many social forces in play and the date—1994—that the first Megan's Law took effect in New Jersey.

In the words of one of the most respected researchers on rates of child sexual abuse, sociologist David Finkelhor of the University of New Hampshire, "the pattern for really close to 30 years has been one of decline." Finkelhor points out that between 1992 and 2018—over 25 years—the overall rate of child sexual abuse dropped an astounding 62 percent.[5] However, since New Jersey's Megan's Law took force in 1994, and the decrease started two years before, in 1992, the claim by Megan's Law boosters that the decrease proves Megan's Law is "working" is suspect.

In fact, as Finkelhor states, there is still no strong consensus about the reasons for the long, steady decrease, and scholars generally link it to many practices. (12) (13)

Yes, some of these practices could be harsher laws, such as Megan's Laws, and even a rising, general awareness of sexual abuse from tell-all TV shows such as "The Oprah Winfrey Show" and the highly voyeuristic blockbuster film about sexual psychopathology, "Silence of the Lambs"— both major American cultural phenomena of the 1990s, when the decrease began. It is plausible to suppose that such cultural forces—news programs, television and movies—made the average child molester—an inebriated relative or friend molesting a young teen in the home—realize that he or she had better watch their step.

But caution is in order before reaching this conclusion, because Finkelhor and other scholars mention many other plausible reasons for the reduction. These are "charges reduced from sex to nonsex crimes"—since reasonable prosecutors began hesitating, with lower-level crimes, to trigger the devastation that community notification causes convicted people (14). Reductions have also been linked to "civilly committing those sex offenders found to present the highest risk to the community," (15) a practice begun in earnest in New Jersey four years after Megan's Law came online. Yet another cause of the reduction could be convicted people's

---

[5] A six-percent upward blip between 2017 and 2018 was attributed to increased reporting spurred by the MeToo movement and such scandals as Harvey Weinstein.

participation in rehabilitative psychological treatment, some of it better than earlier forms. (16)

This mention of rehabilitating criminals instead of punishing them brings us to another key in analyzing whether Megan's murder could have been thwarted by community notification. It is important to realize thatMegan's killer apparently received no good services during the time he spent in prison for his sex crimes before killing Megan. Records showthat he was normally incarcerated, not civilly committed, and, although he did participate in psychological treatment, a counselor said that he slept a lot and she believed he remained unreformed. Records also show that, although Megan's killer had a horrific childhood (17), starting with fetal alcohol syndrome, which left him mentally impaired, he was not under any type of parole supervision at the time of the murder, since he completed his entire sentence before killing Megan. He even shared his house with another man convicted of a sex offense. Such fatal oversights make it understandable that Megan's parents were appalled when they learned of them after she was murdered.

However, at least in California, these lapses would be very unlikely at this writing. A person such as Megan's killer, intellectually challenged and with two prior sex crimes against children, could well be civilly committedand if released, would be under 24-hour supervision.[6]

But Megan's killer had first been imprisoned in an era when the enlightened, community-based Circles of Support and Accountability, COSA, was still a wild idea in some doctoral thesis, and non-coercive sex-addiction treatment was likewise undeveloped. COSA's founder Dr. Robin Wilson, who focuses on high-risk people such as Megan's killer, said recently that old-school sex therapists call him an "offender defender" and denigrate the services he pioneered. Indeed, such critics pan all the good services that are nowadays sometimes available to those who committed a sex crime, such as non-coercive rehabilitative programs, and emotional support and advocacy groups. Yet in the contemporary world, especially post-George-Floyd, many voices are calling for alternatives to policing that offer services—sometimes surprising services—instead of punishment. To "defund the police," and instead offer services, is what many of us involved in defending accused people have long advocated. In Chapter 1 of this book, written over a decade ago, I criticized California prison guards earning 35 percent more than schoolteachers, while having less preparation.

---

[6] Likewise, California's new Tiered Registry law means that authorities now have moretime for supervising dangerous people instead of skinny dippers, as the law's sponsor Sen. Scott Wiener emphasized.

Of course, guards are generally thought to rely less on education than brawn and bravado — unless they work with Norwegian rapists and killers in the highest-security Norwegian prisons, where guards explained in a film documentary that their goal is to "to help [prisoners] back to society." As one put it, "the main idea is…we're just supposed to take away their freedom. That's the only punishment we're giving them." Because the goal is "rehabilitation, not revenge," Norwegian prisons have nice libraries, and offer classes and art and recording studios for inmates. (18)

A recording studio in a prison may be a shocker for some, but the real shocker is the degree to which musical education has been used worldwide to help people overcome overwhelming problems. Jose Antonio Abreu created a network of free, youth orchestras in Venezuela, which lifted many young people out of slums and into top orchestras, including his best-known protege, Gustavo Dudamel, director of the Los Angeles Philharmonic.

"Maestro Abreu taught us that art is a universal right and that inspiration and beauty irreversibly transform the soul," Dudamel said when Abreu died in 2018. (19) It is safe to say that very few U.S. inmates, in the 1990s or now, have been exposed to any inspiration and beauty while in prison. But if arts education like that in Norway and Venezuela were given to convicted Americans, we could see how much farther those services go than the polygraph and the penile plethysmograph in lifting people out of terrible circumstances.

The happiness of IML?

Now that the notion has been demolished that Megan's Laws have any benefit for ordinary women and children, a question stares us in the face: "How did this happen?" The short answer: it happened due to violations of principles, not only principles that have been written down in the U.S. Constitution, but older principles that were articulated by people who were pillars of modern thinking on law, as well as ancient principles written on stone and in our hearts, such as telling the truth.

It is crucial to look at these violations of principle, since the original "community notification" law, Megan's Law of 1994, has become a prototype bringing in its wake the newer hate laws we are analyzing here: IML, the Frederick Douglass Law, and so on, and their tsunami of federal bureaucracy and private contractors. [7]

---

[7] A partial listing of the bureaucracy includes the U.S. Attorney General, State Department, Department of Homeland Security, Department of Justice, Angel Watch Center, FBI and U.S. Marshals Service.

Huge bureaucracy sparks huge consequences, and, indeed, a 2019 New Jersey lawsuit points out that being registered triggers more than 600 federal, state, and local consequences and a "minefield of collateral effects" for the person. (20) The scholar Catherine L. Carpenter was on the same wavelength as this "minefield" study when she wrote in the Buffalo Law Review that sex-offender laws are part of an American "legislative epidemic" that threatens to deteriorate into "systemic failure." (21)

Rep. Smith tried to obscure the oobleck-like rain of IML when he said the passport mark is only for people whose crimes were against children and "when their state decides to remove their name from the state registry, the passport identifier will no longer be required," suggesting that IML only applies to people convicted of crimes against young people. (22) But Smith, as it turns out, is guilty of deception, since one of IML's enforcers, the U.S. Marshals Service, warns that "IML has notable provisions that may impact all registered sex offenders who intend to travel outside of the United States" (23). Besides that, a California attorney specializing in helping registered citizens avoid running afoul of the many restrictions of Megan's Laws says that IML "impacts more than current registrants. It also covers those who have suffered a conviction involving a minor who have been relieved of the requirement to register.

"And there's a new law every five minutes," the attorney observed. "What's that about?"

What it's about is the same kind of institutionalized fear and hatred seen in the myriad Jim Crow laws that were enacted in all but 10 U.S. states over a period of 90 years, severely impacting another disfavored group of citizens—former slaves. Strictly speaking, there may be nothing unconstitutional about the sheer quantity of laws restricting former slaves or former sex offenders. But obviously, since courts have frequently called the constitutionality of Megan's Laws (and Jim Crow laws) into question, shouldn't a responsible legislator vet the laws she or he writes in order to avoid wreaking constitutional and social havoc?

When Rep. Smith authored IML, he apparently had to take a stab at ensuring its constitutionality. And what he came up with was the ludicrous claim on the official record that "Congress has the power to enact this legislation pursuant to…Article I, Section 8, Clause 3 of the United States Constitution, as sex offenders are traveling in foreign commerce." (24)

Puh-leeze, Rep. Smith. Yes, that clause does give Congress the power "to regulate commerce with foreign nations," but it doesn't take a constitutional scholar to see that someone who wants to visit a dying father in Iran or marry a sweetheart in Mexico isn't "traveling in foreign commerce." Convicted citizens, like anyone else, have myriad reasons for traveling. But Smith didn't check with the million or so Americans convicted of sex crimes, including streaking and "thought crimes" such as viewing pornography, and when he claims they all travel in search of illicit "commercial" sex ("sex tourism") it is ludicrous to say the least—a lie dressed up in constitutional clothing.

And since we have spoken of the legislative epidemic, we should look at Rep. Smith's official biography, which boasts that he ranks "second among all 435 Members of the House over the last two decades in the number of laws authored."(25)[8] Some of Smith's laws advanced apparently worthy causes such as services for veterans, torture victims and autistic people, and, hopefully, brought benefits to those people. But the six related to sex offenses merely advance a sham benefit, "protecting children," which we know is not verified.

In the case of Smith's IML, the goal and supposed benefit that he articulated, believe it or not, is protecting foreign children. Studies will never be done on this benefit, since "before" and "after" statistics on sex crimes rarely exist in the world's expanse of cultures and languages, and, if they did, scholarly access to them would be complicated, making any benefits from IML unverifiable. The bottom line: it is very doubtful that American children have been protected by Megan's Laws, we'll never know if foreign children will be protected by IML, and, even if this benefit were verifiable, there is no reason to expect better with IML than we have seen from Megan's Laws.

So, since this "benefit" cannot be established, ordinary Americans are left holding the bag, with only the restrictions on registered citizens, and the price tag, to show for Megan's Laws. (The costs for Smith's six sex-offense laws, as estimated by the Congressional Budget Office and a scholar, was nearly 1.5 billion dollars at the time of the analysis. (24) (26)) When I count the ways that IML is a cataclysm shaking the pillars of law—its violations of national sovereignty and the Constitution, its basis in untruth, its Jim-Crow-like restrictions on a disfavored group, and so on—the absence of any benefits is high on my list.

It may surprise many to know that the necessity that a law demonstrate benefits, as well as the nature of those benefits, figure as foundational legal principles in the West. The influential, 18th-century British philosopher Jeremy Bentham was always quick to point out that, because laws necessarily restrict freedom, they are in themselves "evil." Sometimes I want to shout this from the rooftop of our Capitol. Evidencing a sympathy for lawbreakers that is way out of fashion today

---

[8] Smith is not the only representative sponsoring a profusion of legislative actions—another one boasted an astounding total of 9,674, according to an official congressional tally, and a five-minute search revealed that none passed.

but was paramount to the founders of our legal system, Bentham called the "evil" of restricting a lawbreaker "unhappiness" and wrote that if this unhappiness is greater than the benefits or "happiness" to ordinary people, then the law lacks "utility," the capacity to bring the "greatest happiness to the greatest number of people." In Bentham's eyes, a bad law reflects governmental "misrule" and is evil, while a good law—a law that works—balances lawbreakers' "unhappiness" with the average Jane or Joe's "happiness." Rep. Smith must have been aware that Megan's Laws upset this balance. After all, he specializes in sex-offense laws. Surely he was up-to-date on the 12 critical studies, the 13 unfavorable court decisions, and the important 2007 critiques by Human Rights Watch and the victim mother Patty Wetterling, most of which came about before IML was passed in 2016. But instead of giving credence to this genuine evidence against Megan's Laws and, by inference, his newest baby, IML, Rep. Smith pulled out the big guns of deception and emotion to sell IML.

For example, let's look at one of his pro-IML articles, "International Megan's Law working to protect children," which bristles with emotional deception. (27) Smith began the article with a nod to "protecting children," which, leaving aside that the children are foreign, should be the benefit of IML. But this alleged "happiness"—full of more holes than Swiss cheese, as Smith must have known—was quickly pushed aside and replaced by vitriol toward registered Americans. Smith hammered away at them with salacious language: they are "pedophiles," he wrote six times in the rather short article, "predators" (seven times), and "convicted child sex predators," "convicted predators" or "convicted pedophiles" (four times). The glaring problem with Rep. Smith saying "pedophiles" and "convicted pedophiles" is that pedophilia is a very specific and rare medical diagnosis spelled out in the American Psychiatric Association's manual of mental disorders, and very few offenders, even those convicted of offenses against minors, are truly pedophiles. And in any case, since pedophilia is a medical condition, not a crime, it is impossible to be convicted of it.

What's more, a "predator" is an animal, and although some people use it and other colorful words (such as "dog" or "worm") to describe humans, nobody can be a "convicted predator" (or convicted dog or convicted worm). However, "convicted predator" conjures up a lot more loathing than "convicted American"—and more support for "evil" laws (using Bentham's terminology).

Yes, "predator" was a favorite in Rep. Smith's lexicon. But what about the young Maine resident, William Elliott, convicted at age 20 for having sex with his girlfriend shortly before her 16th birthday? Was he a "convicted predator" as Rep. Smith would have it? (Elliott, sadly, was murdered in 2007, at the age of 24, by a Canadian vigilante who found his address on a public sex-offender registry. (28)) What about the 14-year- old Minnesota girl facing the sex-offender registry for sending a boy she liked an explicit photo of herself? (29) A "predator" too? What about the Naked Bike Ride participants, the streakers, the skinny-dippers, the people who peed on trees? All predators?

And what about my client convicted of inappropriately touching his young granddaughter in the bathtub? Since a predator in the animal kingdom hunts its prey, or sneaks up on it, this term has some similarity to a stranger attacking out of the shadows—perhaps Jack the Ripper—but not to this grandfather. He can't be classified as a pedophile either, since that medical term means a person with a longstanding attraction for prepubescent children, not my client, for whom it was a one-time thing that was bolstered by drinking and later horrified him.

So, first Smith waves the bloody shirts of "predator" and "pedophile," getting readers sufficiently worked up to overlook IML's lack of any true benefits (and the fact that its alleged beneficiaries are foreigners). Next, he slaps on some numbers—3,500 "predators" fingered by IML administrators and 2,000 actually denied permission to enter foreign countries—thus adding a numerical sheen suggesting evidence that the law is "working."

But wait. Restricting the travel of convicted citizens is not a benefit at all, in Jeremy Bentham's classic sense of "happiness" for ordinary people. Instead, travel restrictions impose "unhappiness" on lawbreakers, which is supposed to be outweighed by the children being protected. But—excuse me, Jeremy Bentham, if I'm repeating myself—there is no evidence that children in foreign countries are protected by IML, and there never will be. So Smith's attempt at alchemy—transforming the lead of "unhappiness" into the gold of "happiness"—is simply a lie, a grand foray into the parallel universe where fiction is fact.

Some IML proponents have tried to conjure up benefits for foreigners that give an appearance of legitimacy. Perhaps a young Thai sex worker, who may (or may not) be happy if IML prevents her from getting American clients in the gorgeous beach city of Pattaya. Maybe a Korean woman promised a job as a cleaner in a U.S. home, flown to Tijuana and smuggled into San Diego and happy because IML somehow thwarted her smugglers' plans to get her to work in a massage parlor. Perhaps a Nigerian teenager, happy she was not kidnapped by Boko Haram militants (aided by a mythical troupe of American sex tourists) because IML somehow deterred them. Some of these benefits are doubtful, some ludicrous. Some may be noble. But all are anecdotal, all slippery as a wet bar of soap since they involve clandestine activities. And all are anomalies, since the supposed beneficiaries are foreign people living in foreign countries.

In fact, I would argue that these alleged "benefits" for foreigners are mere window dressing for IML, which, although sparked by disgusting crimes, quickly evolved into a hate law pure and simple, motivated not by any concern for foreign victims, but by disgust for the tiny number of worst-case criminals.

Jeremy Bentham, looking down on this mess nearly two centuries after his death, would not be pleased.

28. A tiger in TJ

September 18, 2019, to January 20, 2020

ELAINE HALLECK

"Hijole!" Marie Camara burst out. Her eyes were on the sky to the right, in the direction of all the noise. Since Pera Fernandez was driving the always wicked U.S. 15, she couldn't really take her eyes off the road. But she did wonder fleetingly which language this mild-mannered, multilingual African-Mexican-American girl was using—this tall, lovely girl who was married to her grandson and had spent her teenage and young adult years deep in the heart of Mexico. But there wasn't much doubt that "Hijole!" meant something like "Dios mio!" and knowing Marie, Pera was sure it wasn't anything rude.

But the point was, what was making all that noise? Must be that clot of oddly shaped black things she'd glimpsed percolating in the sky over the Miramar Marine Air Station, like a bunch of Trevor's old Transformer toys come to life.

Then something clicked in Pera's mind. "It's Trump!" she cried, suddenly remembering that she'd heard he was due in San Diego today to visit his wall. Making a big fuss with all the helicopters, or whatever they were, was so totally Trump. Pera began to wish she'd left home in the San Diego suburb of Vista earlier, in case this fanfare was going to close the border and make it hard to visit her Hijo—she just couldn't get used to calling him Juan—and little Dani.

Pera well remembered the mess last November, the day she visited them and got stuck in traffic for hours trying to cross back into San Diego when they closed the San Ysidro port of entry for hours. The caravans had just arrived from Honduras and supposedly threatened to rush the gates. Pera and Marie, who was with her that day too, had been trapped in the Sentri lane for hours trying to reenter San Diego. She'd turned the engine off—some people even ran out of gas, causing worse traffic jams. How she wished she'd gone a little farther east and crossed at Otay Mesa, where Kari came and went in her van on the California side, and where she didn't think the caravans had caused any closure.

While sitting in her car for hours, Pera thought she had seen some of the migrants. She couldn't be sure, but their clothes were different from Tijuanenses—most wore backpacks and had plaid blankets that somebody had probably given them along the way. They were being sheltered at different places in Tijuana, including the JW church where her Hijo worked.

Yes, there were lots of shelters, but there were many angry Tijuanenses too, waving Mexican flags, telling the migrants to go away, and saying they were a disease like gonorrhea. On TV, Pera had even seen Mayor Gastelum calling the migrants bums and wearing a "Make Tijuana Great Again" hat, a copy of Trump's ridiculous hat. Some demonstrators even attacked a group of migrants who were camping at the beach not far from her Hijo's house.

Pera thought that was a shame. But what she couldn't understand was why the caravans were coming in the first place. Didn't they know how hard it was to get into the USA? Hadn't they heard Trump loosing his evil mouth on them and sending soldiers to flex their muscles at the border? All that was in no way welcoming, yet still they came, aiming to be admitted as asylum seekers, Pera heard.

Marie had explained that things were very bad for people in Honduras, Guatemala and El Salvador—the countries where the caravans were coming from and the ones where America had carried on wars over the years, usually with the idea of fighting some Communist group. Marie had attended a conference at Tower of Hope where American Quakers, JWs, and other anti-war people came to explain why the "Northern Triangle" had been completely destabilized by guns the Americans had given them during those wars. Years—even decades—later, the arms were still there, but no courts or other institutions. So when disputes came up, people settled things with those guns.

Pera knew Marie fled Africa as a girl and had some "hellacious" experiences, as Trevor put it, in the process. That explained why she was so interested in refugees.

Further shedding light on the mystery of why the caravans were coming, Trevor had come home one day and said that a guy he worked with at the San Diego airport said his brother, a Mexican federale cop, told him the caravans were organized and paid for by Trump's people. Yes, Trump people were paying for buses for the Hondureños and posting in their Facebook groups that it was a good time to go north. That meant Trump was actually encouraging the caravans at the same time he was saying how terrible they were! That news seemed to throw Trevor for a loop, since he loved Trump and didn't love the caravans.

Oh, Trevor. He'd never really gotten over the mess with Danny, and getting in trouble himself as a juvenile. No, he didn't have a record, gracias a Dios, but Pera thought it was mostly his girlfriends and, later, Marie who pulled him back from the edge. He didn't have a religion either, despite her and Kari's and Diego's and Marie's influence.

But he didn't drink much and Pera was almost sure he didn't use drugs—TSA kept its employees on a pretty short leash. And he'd suddenly taken to Taekwondo, through the same buddy whose brother was a federale. It fit with his security job, although Pera didn't imagine TSA employees had much opportunity for those high kicks. And then, through the same friend, he started Qigong—no kicking and more breathing and emphasis on balance and energy. Pera had some hopes for Trevor and Qigong. It was much better than some crazy religion, or believing the earth was flat or the government was behind earthquakes.

After Trevor got the news about what the federale said about Trump's people facilitating the caravans, he quieted down about Trump. Pera said rosary after rosary that he was getting over his idolization. Anyway, all he'd ever articulated to explain it was, "A lot of people are getting a raw deal and Trump understands that."

Pera couldn't argue with that, at least the first part. Her Hijo had gotten a raw deal. And Trevor too, for throwing a nut at a school bus! But as for Trump understanding people's pain, she thought it was really a matter of him taking advantage of it. She couldn't articulate why she disliked Trump so much, nor why he scared her, nor why she didn't want to hate him as much as some people did.

Pera came back to the here and now when Marie, after spending long minutes with her nose buried in her phone, emerged with a nugget: "Trump's on his way to the airport! He's going to start a motorcade there and visit the wall near Otay Mesa."

"Is Trevor gonna see Trump?"

"He didn't say…" But Marie kept fiddling, and soon announced, "They're pausing almost everything at the airport now, so he might. Trevor's a federal employee, so…"

*

Pera was so American that she hadn't really known what pozole was before she started coming to the Tower of Hope once a week. And here she was tending a big pot of the pork and corn stew, while Marie chopped cabbage and onions to sprinkle, along with oregano and lime juice, on top. In an hour or so, at the comida hour, which to Pera's thinking was much too early, a few hungry people, including some refugees who'd been in last November's caravans, which had by now dissipated, would sit down to dig into the pozole, using plastic spoons and plastic bowls, while sitting at plastic tables near the kitchen. Maybe a deported veteran, from Juan's meeting in another part of the building, would join them. They were refugees too, Marie had said, but coming from the other direction.

Luckily, Trump's motorcade hadn't had any effect at all this morning on the several lanes of traffic entering Mexico at the San Ysidro border station. And when he and his entourage did get to the border later this afternoon, they'd hopefully be far enough away not to affect Pera and Marie's 45-minute drive north to Vista. They'd moved there 10 years ago, to be closer to "Juan," Kari and Diego in Tijuana.

It was Marie who was really keen on helping displaced people at Tower of Hope, from the moment she found out the place was part of the network of shelters in Tijuana.

Sometimes she wondered how Marie and Trevor could be happily married considering their divergent attitudes on refugees, which was a hot topic these days, especially in San Diego. Trevor's "go-back-home" attitude toward Hispanics sneaking across the border was not unusual among Mexican Americans, many of whom once had to pay a lawyer a lot of money in order to enter legally, or more or less legally.

Ironically, that group of "more or less" legals included Marie. When she was 19 and got engaged to Trevor, she got a visa to visit the USA, but had to pretend she wasn't visiting for the purpose of getting married, even though she did get married during her "visit." People in Marie's shoes were trying to avoid applying for a daunting, multi-page "fiancée visa." Trevor had heard of one that was 400 pages! Pera thought the iconic Statue of Liberty holding out a beacon didn't have much to do with the reality of immigration these days, if it ever did.

Trevor came out of his experience of that white lie, like many Mexican Americans, still firm in his opposition to illegal border crossers, while Marie remained unwavering in her sympathy for migrants.

And it wasn't like Marie didn't have anything better to do than make lunch for refugees in a shelter. She had become an accomplished artist, although her strong point wasn't sculpture like her father, but drawing and painting. She was taking a drawing class now and always carried a drawing pad, and today after dinner, she'd be sketching people in the dining room, or whatever she turned up—an orange on a plate, an empty table, a window, even her own feet. Unlike most students in her community college art program, Marie was interested in hands-on art, not computer art, which she joked was like "drawing with your left foot."

Pera thought Marie would be teaching the classes pretty soon. She'd done tons of drawings of baby Dani, usually while the baby was sleeping, and of anyone around her who would sit quietly. She drew Juan's chihuahuas too, but just like with Dani, the trick with animals was getting them to stay still. Marie had showed Pera Rembrandt's sketch of two women teaching a child to walk.

"This would be difficult," she explained, "but look how well he captured their gestures."

Sure enough, a bit later, while people were eating pozole, there was Marie, sitting in the dining room sketching a baby sleeping on a blanket on the floor near his parents, two other kids, a big black sports bag and a window.

Marie had taken a liking to this family on their earlier visits at the shelter, and had listened eagerly and sympathetically to their story. With great animation, the father, Alberto, told her in good English how he'd been deported back to El Salvador from the United States, then worked in a call center doing tech support in San Salvador, where he could put his English to good use. But then he began to be extorted by gangs due to his relatively high wages, and so finally returned to the U.S.-Mexico border with a caravan. Alberto expected the family to be accepted for asylum any day, but said he wouldn't be able to enter with them, since he'd been deported. This struck Marie and Pera as odd, but they hadn't asked Alberto what he planned to do after he was separated from his family. He said maybe he'd leave Tijuana and go east to Matamoros, which was possibly even more of a vice capital than Tijuana, so Marie wondered if he was planning to cross illegally.

Today Alberto was excited, telling Marie that an American immigration official at the pedestrian crossing, where they only accepted 30 asylum applications a day, had called out 1847, the number before his family's, at the end of the morning. So he knew his family's number, 1848, would be called first thing tomorrow.

Marie was sitting on a chair with the sketchbook on her lap, still drawing the sleeping baby, as she talked to Alberto. Pera was nearby, picking up plastic dishes as people finished eating, when she heard Marie say, "Alberto, your duffel bag is moving."

Alberto came over, lowered his body and began unzipping the bag. As Pera craned her neck, she saw Alberto move a pink blanket inside the bag and reveal, first, a fluffy, silver-dollar-sized, white-and-rust-colored paw with two thin, black stripes. He pushed aside more of the blanket, and there was the rust-and-black-striped head of the largest kitten Pera had ever seen. It appeared to be sleeping, but with one eye open.

Still carrying the dishes, Pera came closer, and whispered "Oh my God." Marie had stopped drawing and seemed frozen as she gaped at the fluffy head and ears. The two children had rushed over to the bag, with expressions of wonder on their faces, as if Alberto were opening a bag of magic tricks or Christmas presents.

"Maybe the tranquilizer is…" Alberto began, but then hesitated. Pera finished his sentence. "Wearing off?"

*

"He said he called her a fat bitch before he drove away. He thinks that's why they came after him," Juan said. He was cleaning the chihuahuas' cages, while Trevor knelt on the floor playing with Stripe.

Pera knew her Hijo wouldn't normally talk like that in front of her, but she was on the other side of the patio, standing on a chair taking down Christmas lights. It was high time—January 20—way past Three Kings

Day. The television was on in the kitchen, where Kari was making something for Dani, and a momentary lull in its noise had made it easier for Pera to overhear Juan and Trevor.

"That's messed up," Trevor growled, the edge in his voice contrasting with the way he rubbed Stripe's tummy and playfully stuck his knuckle between the cub's jaws, daring him to bite.

Oh, little Stripe. Pera recalled driving back to Vista from the Tower of Hope that day that Trump visited the wall—was it just four months ago? Marie had breathlessly read out a message from Hijo saying he'd found a black bag in the bathroom and a "baby animal" inside. Pera sensed right away that the cub was going to be huge for them, and not just when it became an adult.

Later, they'd surmised that Alberto had realized that his family's unexpected acceptance as asylum seekers in the USA meant that the cub, which he'd been given a few days earlier on the spur of the moment by a guy who was walking an adult tiger down a TJ street, was going to complicate his life too much. Alberto was told he could sell Stripe for a lot of money in San Diego. But he hadn't thought it through, and when his wife and kids' asylum number came up, and he contemplated going solo to Matamoros, a tiger cub in a sports bag didn't fit in with his new plans. It was amazing how Trevor had taken to the little guy, and to driving over the border to her Hijo's house almost every day to take care of him. Stripe had injected new meaning into Trevor's life when he came crashing into their world like a meteor from outer space. To Pera, the day of Stripe's arrival seemed a fateful day—almost as tumultuous as the one in 2000 when the "justice" system had come crashing into her Hijo's world.

With Stripe, Trevor's idolization of Trump had evaporated. That first night when Hijo, who adored animals too, took Stripe home, and immediately started feeding him with one of Dani's baby bottles, he texted Trevor asking him to find out how to make formula for a tiger cub. Trevor did so in a flash and was there the next day with the ingredients, Trump's visit all forgotten. Then he bought Stripe a bigger cage than Hijo's chihuahua cages, and even put in a small, shallow, concrete swimming pool and sturdy, sliding glass and screen doors to separate the pool, with its little grass and dirt area, from the covered patio, where the cages were.

Now Trevor and Juan continued talking and Pera couldn't help but listen. She thought Trevor was getting that edge in his voice like he used to get when talking about Trump.

"It's nuts they arrest people for stuff like that. And then deport them too?" Trevor shook his head from side to side and seemed to be at a loss to express his indignation, just like Pera felt when she talked about Trump.

"He said he was buzzed when it happened," Hijo answered. "He said he got the munchies and went to McDonald's drive-thru in just his boxers. Now he says it was stupid. The girl at the window said something about his clothes, and he flipped out at her. But he says he didn't take his weenie out of his shorts. She said he did. He got six months in the county jail. It's considered a sex crime. Then they deported him. After he was in the Marines and everything. But he isn't a citizen. Now he's crying. He has a house in Vista, and a business, and kids.

"In Vista?" Trevor repeated.

Pera heard Kari call out from the kitchen. "Tata, the CDC confirmed the first case of Covid-19 in Portland, Oregon. Somebody who just got back from Wuhan, in China."

Pera didn't think Hijo and Trevor had heard, or if they had, their own conversation was more engrossing to them. But Marie had heard. Pera glimpsed her walk into the kitchen from the front room. Dani squealed when she saw Marie, like she always did.

"Is it in Mexico yet?" Pera called back.

"Who knows?" Marie answered. "But it will be."

"I think he's gonna try and cross back," Juan went on. "He's got money. He can pay. I told him maybe he should try what Omar did—get a pardon. But he'd need a lot of help. There's a lawyer who comes to the Deported Veterans office and helps people—he was in the military too. But it'd take a long time to get a certificate of rehabilitation and a pardon. He'd have to get counseling too. I don't know if he wants to wait, and live, well, a tougher life over here, until he gets on his feet. He doesn't speak much Spanish. But at least his kids will bring him money."

"What about that new law? The one that gets people off that police list for sex crimes."

Pera thought she could feel a change in her Hijo's voice, or maybe it was just a decrease in volume. "Oh yeah, Megan's List. I think he'd have to wait 10 years, with his offense. Penal Code 314. And get a lawyer for that too. Anyway, he just got out of jail. He's not thinking about that. He may not even realize it yet."

"Didn't you tell him?"

"No, no. I don't talk about myself. All I did is suggest he talk to the lawyer that comes to Deported Vets."

"How long would you have to wait to get off the list?" Trevor asked. "With my offense, I think 20 years, which isn't that much longer now—I finished my sentence in 2003. Bu-ut, the tiered registry doesn't do me any good. I ran while I was on probation. That'd be another offense, unless my P.O. was asleep and never noticed. I'm sure there's a warrant for my arrest and I'd get caught right at the border."

"After all this time?" Trevor asked.

"I don't have a passport anyway. Nah, it's hopeless. I'll stay here in TJ forever. It's OK. I like it. Better now that I'm not at Hyundai."

Pera remembered how good her Hijo's job at Hyundai sounded at first—good enough to tempt him and Kari to move from Yahualica to TJ and be closer to her and Trevor—and Diego, who had proposed to Kari and was headed for medical school in TJ.

Pera had once worked for Hyundai in Long Beach, making 12 or 13 dollars an hour, which was good at the time. But when Juan was at Hyundai in Tijuana, much later, they only paid him two or three dollars an hour. The work wasn't that different from what he'd done in the U.S. back when he was Danny, but as Juan he was a lot older, and the long hours got to him. By then, Kari was working at a call center in TJ, was doing OK, and was about to get married, and get the house near Rosarito Beach, courtesy of Diego's parents, who wanted to situate Diego for med school. So Juan's "retirement" from Hyundai and his switch to full-time counselor at Tower of Hope seemed natural.

Diego was an agreeable guy and now was very busy with his medical residency, so he hadn't had much to say about Stripe in September, except "He can't be here for long." Pera and everyone else totally agreed, so Diego never got any argument on that. Now that Stripe was four months older and about the size of a bulldog, although still using a bottle, what to do with him was almost the only topic of conversation among everyone living in the house—Hijo, Kari, and Diego—and everyone who visited regularly—Trevor, Marie, Pera and Rosy.

Funny, almost everybody in the family had a soft spot in their heart for refugees—and Stripe was a big-time refugee—except for Trevor, who had almost zero sympathy for them. Yet Trevor was the one who went to bat for Stripe in the biggest way. Trevor talked about almost nothing except how to engineer a soft landing for that furry refugee. He'd even started saying he might go to veterinary school.

"They get new animals all the time at the zoo," Pera now heard him telling Juan. "I see them at the airport. And they ship animals to other zoos too. Maybe once a month or so. You know, it's like the best zoo in the world."

This was Trevor's tack about trying to get the San Diego Zoo to take Stripe. Trevor had managed to make the acquaintance of a guy who worked there. The guy wasn't encouraging, talking about permits and shots, but Trevor had this idea that if he just got Stripe across the border, he could drop him off in his covered cage near some back entrance to the zoo and make a run for it. It would be like abandoning a baby on the steps of an orphanage. The only problem would be that Trevor wouldn't get to see much of Stripe again—unless he visited the zoo or got a job there, which had probably spurred his fantasy about veterinary school, Pera thought.

Kari and her big brother had almost gotten into an argument over Trevor's idea that she could transport Stripe across the border as covered luggage in her Kari-U van.

"They never check you," he said.

"That's because they know me. And trust me. I'm not going to blow that."

"OK, I'll be the driver."

"You're not on the Sentri permit."

"Yes I am. Remember? You put me and Diego on it."

"No, Trevor. It's too dangerous. And it's my van."

Then Trevor had said he'd take Stripe through in his own car. Juan said he wouldn't permit it. Besides, Juan said, they had drug-sniffing dogs at San Ysidro and Otay. Wouldn't a trained dog smell a tiger? Trevor said he'd wax his car with pork fat, to confuse the dogs. Juan just looked at him, then shook his head and said maybe he'd better try a dry run first, with a pork-fat wax job and no Stripe.

Rosy had pointed out that Tijuana had a zoo. And Marie said there was a beautiful zoo in Guadalajara, where her parents lived. She and Diego could drive down there with Stripe, although it was a long drive—and how would they deal with exercising Stripe? And did anyone know if the Guadalajara Zoo would accept him?

So Trevor and Diego, whose Spanish was better than anybody else's, drove over to the TJ Zoo a couple weeks ago. They didn't take Stripe, just photos of him on Trevor's phone. They returned discouraged, saying there was a chance the zoo would take Stripe—they already had some Bengal tigers—but first they'd have to improve their enclosure area, which included a pool and individual cages. That would take time and, Diego even surmised, a donation. He wondered if his parents would cover that. But the people at the zoo didn't know how much time, and Stripe was growing. He was still using a baby bottle, but he was getting teeth.

"What about some rich person?" Juan asked.

"Actually, the guy at the zoo suggested a narco," Diego replied. "He said there are big, enclosed ranchos around Tijuana, and all kinds of stuff goes on there. Some have animals. All kinds. He asked me if I heard about Pablo Escobar's hippos in Colombia.'"

Juan blanched at that. "I don't want dealings with narcos. And who's gonna take Stripe to the rancho? Are we gonna rent a car to do it, so they don't trace us? They're as bad as the Border Patrol. No…how about a rich person in California?"

Trevor laughed—with a distinctly un-merry tone. "Yeah, people there do keep all kinds of animals illegally. You know it's even illegal to have a freakin' gerbil in California? It's a misdemeanor but you can get fined $1,000 and six months in jail."

"Ay! Just like Steve, the deported veteran in my group," Juan put in. "Indecent exposure is a misdemeanor too, with a thousand-dollar fine and a year in jail. And later your life ruined by Megan's List."

Pera had finished taking down the Christmas lights, and now she was packing them in a box. Trevor had moved outdoors and was playing in the pool with Stripe. Pera still didn't like his tone of voice when he called out, "Next they'll be putting you on Megan's List for having a gerbil."

The sliding glass and screen doors were open and by that time almost everybody—Marie, Kari and baby Dani, Diego, Juan and Rosy, were in or near the covered patio.

"I'm thinking maybe Steve, the deported vet, would take Stripe to Vista," Juan said to Trevor. "If he runs. But...I don't know..."

"Yeah, why would he do that?" Trevor called out in response to Juan's hesitation. "Stripe would just slow him down. And in a sports bag, or what? He'd have to be tranquilized big time. It's not good for him."

"Maybe we could pay Steve," Juan said. "But on the other hand, he doesn't need money."

"The guy at the San Diego Zoo said sometimes, even at that zoo, they have to euthanize animals," Trevor threw in.

"Listen, listen..." Marie said. Everyone got quiet and looked at her expectantly, since she usually didn't say much. "All the options are risky. There is going to be danger for someone, including Stripe. But he is growing. The Chinese flu is coming, and it will make the border worse. We have to do something very soon."

Nobody spoke immediately.

Then Trevor said, "I got a new idea." He looked directly at Diego. "Kevin is only 17. If he got caught smuggling Stripe, he'd get in trouble, but he wouldn't be prosecuted as an adult. Kevin has an honest face—teachers always love him. He's on the Sentri permit and he could drive Stripe through in Kari's van. Or in my car, or we could rent a car. Anyway, y'know, if the Americans confiscate Stripe, it might actually be better. They'll at least put him in the care of someone who knows what they're doing, not some narco, and hopefully they won't euthanize him. If Kevin makes it, I'll be waiting for him at Otay and take it from there."

Diego sighed and looked at the ceiling. "Well, crap. Maybe. My father would kill me. I wouldn't tell him beforehand, but at least he could bail out Kevin if it came to that. And Kevin's pretty brave. He'd probably do it—if Kari asked him..."

He smiled at Kari, who raised her eyebrows, let out a little sigh, and tilted her head, but didn't say anything.

29. Trick or trafficking?

19th century to 2021

ALEX LANDON

"This is actually really, really messed up," begins comic actress Amy Schumer, trying to convince the Instagram audience not to click off the short, sophisticated 2018 video made with fellow comic Seth Meyers. Her light hair is pulled back severely, and her serious face looms out of blackness. "Today you can go online and buy a child for sex. It's as easy as ordering a pizza," she says confidently. (1)

Echoing her, a cast of youngish, racially diverse faces surge one by one from the darkness. The tempo and repetition give the PSA a musical, rap-ish feel. "Thousands of children are raped every day…It's all just a click away…They call it human trafficking…Every hour…on the hour…24/7…24/7…24/7…It happens in every town, in every city across America…And the websites where they're advertised, they make millions and millions of dollars every year…This is a crisis," the faces intone.

Older faces, again racially diverse, react: "It's inconceivable to me…I was not aware…I'm totally shocked and flabbergasted."

"It is slavery," a middle-aged black woman insists, in a fillip that has become a classic in the halls of opposition to "human trafficking." Although the tide of opinion, certainly in this video, may seem overwhelming, contrast its rhythmic, sweeping statements with those of George Washington University sociologist Ronald Weitzer, a recognized expert on the sex industry with many books and articles on the topic to his name. In "New Directions in Research on Human Trafficking," he writes:

"No evidence or verifiable sources have been supplied to support these claims [of widespread "human sex trafficking"] and, in fact, they are impossible to substantiate given the clandestine nature of…human trafficking," Weitzer states. "One conclusion is inescapable: The claim that human trafficking victimizes a massive number of people is unsubstantiated…The glaring evidentiary problems are so severe that even rough estimates of the worldwide magnitude of this hidden enterprise are destined to be fatally flawed." (2)

Even common sense would cast doubt on the comedians' vaguely quantitative "thousands of children raped every day" and websites making "millions and millions"—the same common sense that a 17-year-old budding actor showed while exiting a Burbank, California, studio on a sunny afternoon after participating from the audience in a live taping of a major network's long-running and particularly mendacious "advice" talk show.

"How can they say that stuff?" his mother wondered, mulling over the fabrications she had just witnessed—as ridiculous as the afternoon "wrestling" TV shows of her childhood.

"Mom, there are no consequences!" the teen informed her.

"No consequences" may be accurate in the sense of no threat of lawsuits holding media personalities or their guests accountable for spinning their unverifiable tales. (The very existence of Schumer and friends' video is particularly fragile due to the nature of Instagram, which someday soon will make the video as hard to verify as the existence of 1950s TV wrestler Whipper Billy Watson.) But the lack of negative "consequences" does not mean no consequences at all. The annals of infotainment history, from Instagram videos to mainstream TV talk shows, are full of positive consequences for the net worth of those making titillating claims. When Oprah urges a young woman to give details of her claimed sodomization by her father (assuring her that it is "not to pry in your business but to educate parents." (3)), we can be sure nobody will step forward to ask for evidence. And so Oprah's worth—estimated at $3 billion—only rises, and presidents and princes are willing to take a ride through her parallel universe. (4)

Wait a moment please

It is galling for anyone who believes, as I do, that human trafficking is most likely a serious problem, to see wild claims with little basis in evidence rule the day. It's not a matter of one star airing alarming material that arouses indignation today but is forgotten tomorrow. No, the purpose of Schumer's video was to close a "stupid loophole," she said, in a law known as Section 230—called "one of the most important pieces of internet legislation ever created," (5) but criticized by her for making child sexual abuse like "ordering a pizza." (Section 230 is criticized by others for facilitating a massive flow of disinformation and giving Big Tech immunity from any bad results of what it publicizes, but this was not the basis of Schumer's video, which was itself part of the massive flow of disinformation.)

The aftermath of this video was that the U.S. Congress and former President Donald Trump enacted the new policy she urged, making online platforms such as Craigslist responsible for policing ads and thus drying up personal's sections that have sexually enticing ads, among other ads for people seeking romance. But then angry voices lambasted closing the "stupid loophole" as an example of censorship and clipping sex workers' wings. In fact, social worker Marisa B. Ugarte, who directs a San Diegoanti-trafficking assistance group for which I volunteered, told me the new law would only drive the sex

300

trade underground and make it harder for her to assist victims. Yet it seems doubtful that a star would ever regret an indignant video on human trafficking—clickbait far more potent than most topics.

The video on "child sex trafficking" and Section 230 was just one room—a small closet, in fact—in a huge and teetering edifice devoted to fighting "human trafficking" and associated evils, such as "modern day slavery." At this writing, many people are familiar with these terms, but I sometimes put them in quotation marks because they were all but unknown in 2000, the year the first U.S. Trafficking Victims Protection Act was passed. 2000 was also almost the same year the State Department began producing its annual and now-controversial Trafficking in Persons (TIP) report, which as the acronym implies, "names and shames" countries that the department rates as having bad human rights and trafficking practices.

In fact, since 2000, efforts against "human trafficking" have grown so much that by now nearly everyone has heard of it, and it has morphed into the scarier "child sex trafficking" and "modern day slavery," and a great family of laws, all accompanied by a dazzling phalanx of indignant actors and singers, such as Schumer.

But alongside this imposing edifice, a small cohort of respected academics, such as sociologist Weitzer, has also emerged, saying "Wait a moment please." Another one of them, law professor Dina Francesca Haynes, focuses just on the singers and actors in her sobering 2013 report "The Celebritization of Human Trafficking." (6)

The title nearly says it all, yet it is in Hayes and Weitzer's details that we get the naked picture of the extent of the stars' activities in such bodies as the U.S. Congress, the United Nations and the World Economic Forum at Davos, and the effect of this parade of "experts" on public policy and perception.

Pop singer Madonna, for example, and her foundation Raising Malawi targeting sex trafficking in Africa, promoted Gucci's new Fifth Avenue store on the lawn of the UN Secretariat in New York during Fashion Week. Actress Demi Moore and her foundation introduced a Tiffany's line of diamond pendants with a handcuffs theme that was supposed to signify "bonds of love and the plight of human trafficking victims trapped in slavery." Actress Jada Pinkett-Smith said she first learned about human trafficking from her preteen daughter in 2012, and then, mere months later, accepted an invitation to speak as an "expert" before the U.S. Senate Foreign Relations Committee. She launched her campaign against sex trafficking with a music video, "Don't Sell Bodies," in which she sings in the nude from a mattress in a stone cell with shadows of bars falling across her flawless skin.

Such voyeurism-tinged efforts raise the celebrities' public profile at minimum, and sometimes their net worth too, as there can be millions of dollars in grants at play and the stars are not obligated to disclose important financial information.

Similarly, Ricky Martin was transformed from a Latin pop singer into an expert, and testified before the U.S. Congress, giving terrifying statistics: "Each year 2 million people are victims of human trafficking. Of those, 1 million children are forced into the sex trade," he assured lawmakers. But Professor Haynes debunked these claims as decisively as sociologist Weitzer decimates those of the F.B.I. and U.S. State Department, writing that Martin's (conveniently round) figures "do not correspond to any verified data, nor did Martin cite any source to support his figures."

From merry old England comes a chilling tale illustrating just how statistics such as Martin's come to run wild in an infotainment world in which there are "no consequences."

In a 2009 article in The Guardian, "Prostitution and trafficking—the anatomy of a moral panic," investigative journalist Nick Davies, recipient of British Press Awards as Reporter and Journalist of the Year, traces the genesis of the panic about human trafficking to "the mid 1990s, when the collapse of economies in the old Warsaw Pact countries saw the working flats of London flooded with young women from eastern Europe. Soon, there were rumours and media reports that attached a new word to these women. They had been 'trafficked.'" (7)

Like Weitzer and Haynes, Davies also uncovered a nonchalant attitude on the part of authorities toward evidence on human trafficking. He traced the beginning of statistics gone wild to a 1998 study by two cautious U.K. researchers. Their numbers on trafficking were quickly "stripped of caution, stretched to their most alarming possible meaning and tossed into the public domain," then "picked up by the media who have stretched them even further in stories which have then been treated as reliable sources by politicians, who in turn provided quotes for more misleading stories."

Thus, the researchers' initial figure of 71 women "trafficked" (willingly or unwillingly) in 1998 quickly mushroomed to 142 based on considerations the researchers themselves called "speculative." This figure was then crunched up to the maximum end of the "speculative" range—to 1,420— by adding in such "trafficking" as mail-order brides. With the aid of a British evangelical group called Chaste (Churches Alert to Sex Trafficking Across Europe), that began hammering in the new terminology of "sexual enslavement" and "sex slavery," such fluid statistics came to appear more solid.

By 2003, bringing in more "highly speculative" assumptions, the figure was further crunched up to 3,812, then rounded off to 4,000 in 2006. But 2007 saw a statistical explosion—to "25,000 sex slaves"—thanks to two public officials who claimed they were using "Home Office estimates," although this Home Office source was never found. The juicy 25,000 figure was picked up and repeated by the media. Then one of the same public officials lowered the figure to 18,000, based on a 2008 report by a constable heading up a national police operation. But later the constable said his figure was incorrect, and was actually the total number of prostitutes in Britain. His associate even added that he "may have meant to say 1,800 and just got his figures mixed up."

From 71 "trafficked women" to 25,000 "sex slaves" is a tremendous jump. But given the absence of consequences—there are no peer reviewers at the level of constables and politicians, and sex traffickers were unlikely to sue a newspaper or anyone else for defamation—the damage was done. Everyone but the most careful researchers was left with the impression that "There's a lot of that going on!"

Brain dead

The ignominious International Megan's Law of 2016 has major sections on sex trafficking, and so occupies several floors in the slapdash tower erected to combat this evil. IML had many nay-sayers during its nearly decade-long trail through the halls of the U.S. Congress, while its dogged sponsor, New Jersey's Chris Smith, resuscitated and re-resuscitated it, even producing the aging parents of Megan Kanka to capitalize on the publicity around the original Megan's Law of 1994, which is related to IML in name only, not in design or intent.

Despite the healthy suspicion toward the dreadful IML, it was finally passed and then signed by former President Barack Obama in February 2016, near the end of his two terms. But Obama had never been considered a tough-on-crime president. In fact, he had reduced the federal prison population, granted clemency much more often than other recent presidents, and spearheaded an initiative to undo punitive sentences (8), surely realizing that they disproportionately affect his fellow African Americans. In fact, Obama had been part and parcel of a small but cohesive core of black public officials who had long worked to slow down the seemingly inexorable march of tough-on-crime laws.

IML's passage was puzzling for these reasons and several more. Another head-scratcher was the fact that IML had been recognized as a turkey when Rep. Smith first introduced it, since lawmakers had apparently seen the studies showing the original Megan's Law hadn't reduced sex crimes against American kids and wondered why IML should work to protect foreign ones. How was it then, that this proposed law that was repeatedly rejected by Congress, was finally passed unanimously—unanimously—in 2016? No hip or glamorous celebrities had been seen specifically promoting IML (other than that juggernaut of stars lining up with jewelry sales, nude videos and inane statistics on "sexual slavery" and human trafficking in general).

303

Another oddity was that Obama, who had broken records for personal popularity with his Nobel Peace Prize and his reign at the head of Gallup Poll's most admired people, nevertheless signed this turkey of a law.

One of the sad facts explaining these mysteries was that by 2016, late in Obama's presidency, he had been hobbled by the implacable enmity of the Tea Party, a faction that was partly, maybe principally, driven by racial resentments. So Obama ended his terms hard pressed to get anything approved. Thus, the Tea party and Obama's desire not to be remembered as a loser probably explain what he was doing signing the bipartisan IML and helping transform it from a turkey into an eagle.

Another piece of the puzzle emerges in a strange photo in a New Jersey newspaper that same February. It ran above a headline "Obama signs International Megan's Law." The photo showed Obama and four professionals—three African Americans and an Asian—smiling for the camera in a homey setting called Integrity House, a facility in Newark for helping convicted drug and alcohol addicts. (9)

Usually when presidents sign laws, they are photographed in the White House, pen in hand, surrounded by the law's supporters. So why was Obama shown at Integrity House? What was Integrity House? Who were the four professionals? None of this was evident, and in fact a little digging revealed more anomalies. First, the photo had in fact been taken three months before IML's signing. Second, Integrity House was an addiction rehab center, and the multi-ethnic group was its staff. What did an old photo related to drug offenders have to do with a law targeting sex offenders?

The answer, my friend, is blowing in the wind—unless you look at the symbolism of the photo.

To see this symbolism clearly, we must take a moment to dig into the particulars of IML's passage in 2016—and into the pre-Obama past, for example the mostly black vote against President Bush's 2003 Protect Act by 16 African American legislators (who had unfortunately been drowned out by the swell of 400 tough-on-crime lawmakers voting in favor of the Protect Act; see Chapter 21).

Although the voice vote in 2016 on IML was recorded as unanimous, including of course all African Americans, there was one black voice raised in dissent. It was Virginia Rep. Bobby Scott, the lone remnant of the bloc that had stood with incarcerated and convicted people in 2003. By 2016 five Black Caucus members from 2003 had died and seven had stepped down, leaving only four blacks remaining, including Rep. Scott, from this original bloc recognizing the unjust impact of tough-on-crime laws on African Americans.

But Rep. Scott's renegade doubts in 2016 about IML seemed to be a slap in the face to President Obama's leadership, as Scott valiantly pointed out some obvious but overlooked problems. For one thing, the passport mark that IML would require for Megan's List registrants was redundant, Rep. Scott asserted, since registrants' travel was already being reported to foreign countries. Secondly, IML ignored the huge variation in risk of reoffending, Rep. Scott said, pointing out the many "Romeo and Juliet" registrants. And for his third reason, Rep. Scott asked why IML singled out just one type of criminal for its unprecedented travel restrictions and scarlet-letter passports; why did it treat sex offenders even more harshly than murderers and terrorists? (10)

But the tsunami of approval by both black and white lawmakers roiled right over Rep. Scott. And nobody even seemed to notice that healthy black resistance to the tough-on-crime movement had suddenly broken down, and that the breakdown could be at least partially explained by Obama's sway as an apparent supporter of IML. To black representatives, it must have seemed ridiculous to suppose that this respected African American leader who had shown an awareness of the struggles faced by blacks would sign a law that would generate a bureaucracy harming civil and constitutional rights.

And for anyone who may have questioned this reversal by black lawmakers, there was that photo of the happy, mostly black group in the newspaper story on IML. That the photo was window dressing having nothing to do with IML seemed a detail lost in the daily press of life.

The purveyors of political publicity must think the public is brain dead. But I believe they're wrong and, moreover, that such deceptive publicity and bad laws cause mistrust in authority to surge. My hope that the public's anger can be constructively channeled is in large measure the reason for this book.

"We'd better keep watching to stay on top of it"

One last story of a publicity machine gone awry will not leave anyone more confident that truth is being served in matters of human trafficking or that effective antidotes to it will ever arrive.

We can begin this final story in February 2017 with another photograph and headline—after all, they are the only parts of print media reports that most people read, and likewise all that people generally take away from a TV report or YouTube video. The photo showed an attractive, uniformed, black flight attendant smiling for the camera as she leaned against a seat inside an empty airplane. This same photo cropped up in a publicity blizzard over a few days that February, appearing in many news outlets, such as NBC, Business Insider, USA Today, the BBC, Fox News and others. It is thought to have first appeared on the NBC webpage, where it ran below a headline, "'Frederick Douglass Bill Introduced in

Congress to Curb Human Trafficking" (11). Lower in the NBC story, an enormous head shot of Frederick Douglass fixes a regal gaze upon you, his silver-streaked mane of hair helping create a monumental effect.

Douglass was the 19th-century slave turned eloquent anti-slavery orator, a newspaper publisher and an advisor to Abraham Lincoln.[9] And the flight attendant was Alaska Airlines employee Shelia Fedrick.[10] The reports said Fedrick had "rescued girl from human trafficking" or "saved a teenage girl from human trafficking after seeing a secret note." Exciting stuff. But the reality of the Frederick Douglass Law, most of whose provisions deal with administrative and educational matters, was less exciting. And the part most relevant to the story about Shelia Fedrick's "heroism" was the chunk of the law's $430 million that would go towards training for airline employees to spot potential trafficking victims.

The February date of this media blitz was very near 2017's Super Bowl, played in Houston's NRG Stadium February 5. The lead-up to the game had been electrified by Texas Sen. John Cornyn's assertion that the Super Bowl has "one of the highest levels of human sex trafficking activity of any event in the country," a claim disputed by Politifact and several researchers, and called by Snopes a "myth." But—key to our story—the myth had spurred a large anti-trafficking training course given in Houston by a flight attendants organization, Airline Ambassadors International, a week before the big game.

In fact, the law featured in the story with the rescuing airline attendant—its full name is the Frederick Douglass Trafficking Victims Prevention and Protection Reauthorization Act of 2018—would mandate such training courses and thus make more contracts available. The untiring Rep. Chris Smith, whom we have seen frequently in these pages, was about to introduce the law in Congress just a few weeks after the 2017 Houston Super Bowl. Airline Ambassadors International then, was clearly feathering its own nest by running this well-timed campaign claiming that flight attendant Shelia Fedrick had foiled a sex trafficker.

But nest-feathering, like the handcuff-themed jewelry, nude music videos, and specious statistics, would be overlooked, as was any question about who had strategically showered news outlets with those press releases about the heroic flight attendant. The resulting flood of media stories were strikingly similar, down to identical government figures alleging that U.S. Immigration and Customs Enforcement had arrested 2,000 human

---

[9] Frederick Douglass is the historical figure who, just days before this media blitz, had been the subject of Trump's gaffe seeming to refer to him in the present tense.

[10] Fedrick's first and last names were spelled in various ways by the various news outlets, leading to the first doubts about the care taken in preparing the story.

traffickers and identified 400 victims in 2016. Who could blame Super Bowl fans, dazzled by so many reports on "teenage girl saved from human trafficking" whizzing by on their screens, if they exclaimed, "My God, there's a lot of that going on! We'd better keep watching to stay on top of it."

But the biggest problem with the story, according to the fact-checking groups such as Snopes, is that "it may not be true." For one thing, most media outlets downplayed or completely left out the fact that the incident on Alaska Airlines had in reality happened six years before the 2017 Super Bowl! (This means that the Shelia Fedrick photo was far more out of sync with the story on the Frederick Douglass Law than was the misleading, 3-month-old photo at Integrity House "illustrating" Obama's signing of IML.)

There were other problems too: nobody, such as the airlines or the police, who supposedly arrested the trafficker when he landed at the San Francisco airport, would confirm the incident. In addition, Fedrick and the girl she supposedly rescued could not be found. Etcetera. Snopes rated the story as "Unproven" (12) and Politifact said it was "Mostly False," acknowledging that something similar may have happened, although not as dramatic as in the articles and video.

Knowing the juggernaut that International Megan's Law became, you probably have little doubt about the ultimate success of Rep. Smith's Frederick Douglass Law—if success is measured by acclaim, funding, and unanimous votes in Congress. Who could resist a bill named after the imposing Douglass, said to be the best orator of his day? Certainly not the African American legislators who cosponsored the Frederick Douglass Law—especially in the Trump era when black rights were under fire, when white supremacist groups were on the march in places such as Charlottesville, Virginia, and when men such as George Floyd were being murdered by police. Under such circumstances, not standing with Frederick Douglass seemed out of the question, even if the bill and its call to end "modern day slavery" were mostly gimmicks to enrich contractors and swell government bureaucracy.[11]

If the mysterious story of the Alaska Airlines attendant saving a girl from human trafficking leaves you wondering "Where's the beef " of trafficking in the "bun" of publicity, you will not be reassured by knowing that Snopes reported that eight years after the incident, Airline Ambassadors International was "still promoting the story as proof that flight attendants can and do stop human trafficking"—and to help justify the

---

[11] The law did have one good section providing assistance to people identified as trafficking victims.

taxpayer money spent on their growing international training program. And AAI continues to churn out similar publicity. A 2010 story in American Way in-flight magazine, headlined "Human Cost of Trafficking," is long on drama and short on corroborating detail. (13) Its photos show a cute Cambodian toddler being hugged by retired flight attendant Deborah Quigley, but there is no mention at all in the body of the story about the trafficking that the headline screams. Even the article's allegation that the girl was neglected are thin—one photo shows her with alarming red marks on her face and hands, which turn out to be from a red marker she was playing with. Despite this lack of evidence, Quigley, whom the article said had traveled to Cambodia "to deal a blow to the international human-trafficking racket that sells 2 million women and children into slavery each year," nevertheless "scooped the child in her arms and took her to the nearby New Hope clinic, run by Australian Kerry Hunter."

"Kerry is Somnang's foster mother now." the article concluded, causing one to wonder if this could have been a case of kidnapping by overbearing foreigners.

NBC ran another glowing story stating that Airline Ambassador's Sandra Fiorini, urging that the training given by her group be made mandatory, testified in Congress about the "trafficking" she had witnessed during her airline career. However, the only example mentioned was her suspicion that she had seen "girls" flying from Moscow to the United States, who appeared to be hoping for modeling or acting careers, and who might be "trafficked." (14)

Some would call a savvy, established group manipulating publicity to secure lucrative government contracts a self-dealing elite.

With equally scarce detail, press releases from government agencies claim to be making strides in fighting trafficking. (15) Agencies almost too numerous to mention have been involved in the many recent laws passed against trafficking (the U.S. Attorney's Office, U.S. Marshals Service, Internal Revenue Service, Drug Enforcement Agency, California Highway Patrol, District Attorney's Offices and many others). But it is the FBI that seems most adept at publicity, probably due to its long history in the infotainment industry. Its public affairs release in January 2021, claiming agents had just rescued 33 missing children from "modern day slavery" in the "Lost Angels" operation during "Trafficking Awareness Month" was probably related to the public education mandated by all these laws. But this FBI claim of a big bust was again completely lacking in corroborating details that would enable verification. The article is further thrown into doubt by elastic definitions of "human trafficking," which can include labor trafficking, human smuggling, and the movement of willing, adult sex professionals (according to researchers Weitzer, Haynes and Davies). Thus, the main utility of the FBI report

308

was to shore up the job security of staff—and "Lost Angels" remains in the parallel universe of questionable accuracy.

"Missing White Girl Syndrome"

Let me again point out that I believe human trafficking is a problem. The legal work I did for a San Diego outreach organization called Bilateral Safety Corridor Coalition, run by an energetic social worker named Marisa B. Ugarte, involved the case of a young Korean who contacted her. The woman had left Korea due to an agent's promise of a job as a house cleaner in the United States. Instead, she was taken to Tijuana, Mexico, just across the border from San Diego, where her identity and passport were laundered so she could "legally" enter the United States, where she was put to work in a massage parlor. Once she contacted Ugarte, she was helped to a shelter and eventually received monetary assistance from the federal government. (This is the service-oriented provision of anti-trafficking law I believe is helpful, while willy-nilly restrictions and enforcement accomplish little except shoring up the job security of people working in the government bureaucracy.)

Some might consider the huge edifice of restrictions constructed by bad laws on trafficking a case of harmless overkill—so what if we go overboard in fighting this dreadful evil? But hyper-vigilance does harm. Just ask Brian and Renee Smith, who were traveling with their adopted Asian teenager on Southwest Airlines and were pulled aside and questioned by officers after their arrival at the Phoenix airport because of the suspicions of a flight attendant. The Smiths even said they thought they were racially profiled because their daughter is Asian and they are not. (16)

In addition, there is the high cost of this huge edifice, which prevents us from doing so many things that need doing: drug treatment, education, and retooling for protection of the environment, just to name a few. Analysts have said that the United States has become like a dinosaur: big body and small brain. Our system to fight human trafficking is part of this enormous, dumb dinosaur.

To those who insist that human trafficking is such an entrenched problem that it is insoluble, I point to the recommendations of sociologist Weitzer, who, besides studying human trafficking, specializes in the similar, seemingly intractable phenomenon of prostitution as well. He notes that several countries, including New Zealand, have developed well-functioning systems for legalizing and controlling the sex trade. (17) In fact, reforming policies on prostitution could be a good place for the United States to begin to control trafficking, since so much trafficking is apparently related to the sex trade.

I began this chapter with an example of a video in which a symbol of racial justice—an African American calling child sex trafficking an example of "slavery"—was employed as an attempt to legitimize a bad law. I followed with two more similar symbols—African American flight attendants and drug counselors used deceptively in publicity for bad laws. And while this publicity was probably not motivated by outright racism on the part of the speakers, it still amounts to harmful deception. It's as if the speakers are saying, "I want racial justice, most people want racial justice, so I'm invoking a symbol of racial justice to make this law I'm supporting look good."

Race is not always used to prop up the bad laws that I call designer laws and hate laws. California's Sharon Runner, to my knowledge, never used a symbol of racial justice to try to make Jessica's law look good. Instead, she relied on people's natural disgust over a gruesome crime, as well as the face of a very cute child, in her quest to gain fame for herself and her law, which was a reprehensible non-solution to Jessica Lunsford's murder.

However, I argue that this natural disgust is in certain cases magnified by an unconscious racial fear among America's powerful classes. It is a fugitive fear that is mostly visible by way of circumstantial evidence—especially the fact that no designer or hate law has ever utilized a non-white victim. The annals of law enforcement are full of white victims who garnered high levels of publicity, had laws named after them (Megan's law, Chelsea's law, Danielle's law, Jessica's law, on and on), and were part of social paroxysms such as the one in 2002 that I call the Summer of the Abducted White Girl (Chapter 3). But never, to my knowledge, have these high-profile campaigns centered on a brown or black victim. The only time African Americans appear in publicity for designer and hate laws is when they are being used in publicity as a shield to deflect suspicions that the law has racist features.

I am far from the only one who has observed this. "Missing White Woman Syndrome" has its own page on Wikipedia now. Analysts, of whom journalist Gwen Ifill is the best known, have noted that victims of color may go missing or be murdered near the same time and place as white victims, but they do not receive much attention—and they certainly don't get laws named after them. Ifill pointed out the media's hunger for stories about white "damsels in distress," to the exclusion of all others. Recently, an initiative called BlackAndMissing Inc. was started in order to correct this imbalance. Another writer, Karen Attiah, lamented that this was necessary, but noted how powerful "Missing White Girl Syndrome" was, using the 2021 murder of the blonde Gabby Petito as an example of this type of media frenzy. (18) Attiah named four black, brown, native American and LGBTQ victims whose cases had languished unsolved, while media and police attention (including the publicity-savvy

310

FBI) flourished around Petito's case. Another analysis from the University of Wyoming found 710 all but unknown cases of Native Americans who disappeared over 10 years in the state, while the remains of Gabby Petito were quickly located there.

"There is no doubt that the Petito family is going through unimaginable shock and pain over her killing," Attiah wrote. "Her case deserves attention and justice. But all of the missing deserve this."

A fear that never departed

The reason for the persistence of racially skewed interest in disappearances of white females is that the fear invoked by their cases is not simply fear for someone's safety. No, fear in America reaches the point at which it moves mountains when it belongs to people of the most powerful classes—and when at its root lies a deeper, historical fear on the part of slaveholders that they might suffer mayhem at the hands of angry, marauding slaves.

In 1967, the Virginia-born author William Styron researched an account about the 1831 insurrection that the slave Nat Turner led in that state's rural Tidewater area, one of only three violent revolts that happened during the 250 years of what Styron described as "American Negro slavery...the worst the world has ever known...so despotic and emasculating as to render organized revolt next to impossible." (19) (At this writing, this despotic form of slavery was legal in America for 90 more years than it has been illegal.) About 60 white people were murdered by Turner's rampaging band, including many females and at least one baby—although the rebels did not indulge in rape. Later, an estimated 200 African Americans were tortured and killed by vigilante groups who overran Tidewater seeking vengeance, and 17 band members including the leader Nat Turner were quickly executed.

More relevant to my argument about the roots of designer and hate laws was the intense general reaction to Nat Turner's rebellion that radiated far and wide of Virginia. "A shock wave of anguish and terror ran through the entire South," Styron wrote, "a fear that never departed."

Nowadays, we may like to think that the place from which the fear never departed was only the South, not the United States as a whole. But all 13 original colonies except Vermont had slavery at some point, 15 of 23 states had slavery in 1820, and after the Civil War southerners migrated in great numbers to other parts of the country. "Census takers at the end of the century [in 1900] counted over one million southern-born whites living outside their birth region," writes historian Gregory James. (20)

Thus, I argue that a sort of zombie fear—alive but not conscious—is at the bottom of the otherwise inexplicable and steady surge of designer and hate laws throughout the United States.

This zombie fear could explain why, in black Judge Ketanji Brown Jackson's 2022 confirmation hearings for the U.S. Supreme Court, white U.S. senators attacked her as "soft on crime" for her sensible statements on harsh sentencing for the possession (not creation) of child porn—as if Brown Jackson were a reincarnation of Nat Turner and set to run amok endangering innocent white people. The fear William Styron laid out was likewise perceived by Michael Moore in "Bowling for Columbine," when he explained widespread gun-carrying and mass shootings as results of some white people's fears rooted in the history of U.S. slavery. (21)

This argument has become well enough known—through the work of black journalists such as Ifill—that those who push bad, tough-on-crime policies have started to react defensively.

And so, the National Center for Missing and Exploited Children plunks down a black child model on the cover of its annual report; a campaign against human trafficking is renovated as a campaign against "modern slavery;" black professionals greeting a black president are utilized in publicity for laws that will fall heavily on black men; and black historical icon Frederick Douglass is used to promote such bad laws.

But still, no black victims have been used as symbols promoting designer and hate measures—only white victims, usually exceptionally pretty girls and young women, often blonde. One of the latest is Dru Sjodin, a white teenager so lovely she was selected as homecoming queen at her Minnesota high school. After she was murdered by a registered sex offender in 2003 near her university in North Dakota, the name of the National Sex Offender Public Registry was changed to the Dru Sjodin National Sex Offender Public Website (22), and her photo graces the site. But ironically, the page doesn't mention that Dru's murder is a good example of why sex-offender registries don't work—her killer was registered for a previous sex crime, yet registration obviously didn't stop him.

But we have seen that reaction to sex offenses is rarely rational, so Dru Sjodin's selection to grace this website is no exception.

Is the ploy mentioned earlier—using the former slave Frederick Douglass's name and photo to promote a law offering pork-barrel contracts to flight attendants—any worse than the ploy of using Dru Sjodin's name and photo to promote policies that didn't help her? Is taking advantage of Frederick Douglass any worse than using the red-haired Chelsea King's beautiful photo and memory to promote an unnecessary, redundant law named after her? Is it worse than using the adorable face of murdered Florida resident Jessica Lunsford in her fuzzy pink hat to cement the election of Sharon Runner with a dreadful, unconstitutional California law wreaking punishments on Romeo-and-Juliet couples and people who urinate on trees?

No, using Frederick Douglass deceptively is not any worse than the other ploys used to build up the whole sorry mountain of ill-conceived and hateful policies that severely harm a million convicted Americans while not impeding sex crimes. But it is still disappointing to see the current lack of discernment by a group of elected officials who used to be more sensitive. Although I am glad to see more photos of African Americans in the media, this is no substitute for all of us seeing real people of other backgrounds in our everyday life—living, working, studying, worshipping, talking and playing together. I hope progress is being made in these areas but, meanwhile, illogic and race-based deception will be no cure for the genuine cases of human trafficking.

Conclusion—The hopeful and the dismal

"Read it and weep" was the way one sympathetic reader summarized the first edition of "A Parallel Universe" in 2011. We trust that not all our readers actually wept, but we do believe that nobody can turn the final page of either the first or second edition of this book with less sympathy for convicted people and less frustration over the American criminal justice system than they felt on page one. Nevertheless, a big part of what prompted this second edition is that there has been improvement in the decade since the first edition. As yet, none of these improvements are cause for jumping up and clicking our heels; there is still a cloud over people convicted of sexual offenses that is much darker than the one over other convicted. people.

Three excellent cameos of the fluid situation in 2022—all mixtures of the hopeful and the dismal—are seen in the confirmation hearings of Ketanji Brown Jackson for the U.S. Supreme Court; in the wavering progress of the American Legal Institute's new draft guidelines for reforming registration laws for convicted people; and in the abundant debunking of the false statistics on sex-offense recidivism, which warped the earthshaking 2003 U.S. Supreme Court decision on Alaska's "Megan's list."

The first cameo: a black female judge exuding credibility is called on the carpet by senators considered possible presidential candidates, who grill her about her "soft" sentences for possession of child pornography. Meanwhile Wesley Hawkins, a young man whom Judge Jackson sentenced to three months in prison (instead of the eight years under the federal guidelines), saying she didn't want him to be "introduced to incorrigible influences such that you are lost to society forever," says that now, about a decade after his sentencing, he hopes that when people look at him, "they can see he was just a young man, that he's grown and learned from his actions." (1)

What a juxtaposition of grandstanding politicians with common sense. And perhaps there was even a silver lining behind the dark cloud of scathing accusations from the politicians — the opportunity for Judge Jackson and Wesley Hawkins to calmly articulate their points of view as the nation watched.

In another collision of contrasts, many of us reformers were elated in 2022 when the American Law Institute drafted its Model Penal Code, which would mostly do away with public sex-offense registries (allowing access only to police) and would restrict the type of offenses that can get someone on the registry (eliminating skinny dippers and teenagers who "sext" other teens, you can be sure). But our optimism at ALI's actions was given a chilly shower when opposition arose to the ALI draft proposal from the U.S. Justice Department and 37 state attorneys general. We recognized that these opponents were mostly fighting for their job security. But it was still sad to see the welcome mat for the Model Penal Code yanked away almost as soon as it was put out, and frustrating to know that the Code, which if approved would carry weight as the recommendation of some fine legal minds, faced an uncertain future.

The last cameo illustrating mixed hope and frustration after decades of advocating for reform is not just one or two discrete events in a short time period. No, the slow crumbling of the statistics that drove the momentous 2003 U.S. Supreme Court decision in Smith v. Doe, which let Alaska's online "Megan's list" stand (described in Chapter 13 of this book), took place over about 20 years. But this crumbling gradually turned into a landslide of dissent against a ruling that had kindled hate among some Americans and meant life or death for too many registered citizens. (One was William Elliott, described in our Chapter 27—murdered by a young man who in 2007, four years after Smith v. Doe sent "Megan's list" ballistic, traveled 560 miles to shoot Elliott after finding his name in an online public registry due to conviction for sex with his girlfriend when she was almost 16 and Elliott was 19.)

A 2017 article by David Feige in the New York Times was just one in this steady flow of reports eating away at the claims about recidivism that had been key in the decision. Feige pointed out how baseless were former U.S. Solicitor General Theodore Olson's statistics that led former Justice Anthony Kennedy to call the re-offense rate for sex offenses "frightening and high." Kennedy's phrase has actually been so derided over the years, that those who studied the matter said if he had checked the rate, he would have had to describe it as "among the lowest rates of same-crime recidivism of any category of offender." (2)

Feige's article was far from the only one lambasting Justice Kennedy's "frightening and high" phrase. But unfortunately, the abundance of debunking couldn't undo the murders, attacks and suicides provoked by letting Alaska's "Megan's list" stand. Nor could it undo the measures in other states that had been unleashed by Olson and Kennedy's "frightening" statistics, or the harm done 13 years later by International Megan's Law of 2016, whose author so blithely used similar scare tactics to frighten the U.S. Congress into unanimously passing it (Chapter 27). Nor could all the debunking come close to reversing the deeply punitive nature of many other official American responses to sex crimes that had surged since the false statistics were given credibility by Justice Kennedy. For example, in the parallel universe that has emerged after the decision, there is no question of offering services rather than punishment, rehabilitation rather than revenge.

In fact, as Feige pointed out, the bad statistics became a self-fulfilling prophecy. They have helped fuel punitive measures all over America: making lawbreakers pay real money for being in prison, for penile plethysmograph tests, for Abel and polygraph tests, for "therapy," for appointments with their probation and parole officers—and if they don't pay, are late for appointments or don't register correctly, they go to prison. As Feige wrote, "a study by the California Department of Corrections concluded that 91 percent of sex offenders returned to California prisons were returned for these technical violations, while only 1.8 percent were returned as a result of having committed a new sex crime." In short, statistics that drove a momentous court decision have been questioned over and over, but the harm the decision caused not only still stands but has been magnified.

In 2017, when Feige wrote his article debunking the sex-offense statistics, he expressed hope that the U.S. Supreme Court would take another look at the situation. However, as in other years since 2003, the court declined to review both cases he mentioned.

But as 2023 and the 20th anniversary approaches of the Supreme Court's momentous 2003 decision approach, another look at registration by the high court is on the minds of about a million registered Americans and the people who care about them and about justice. ACSOL founder Janice Bellucci and leaders of similar groups note that 2023 will be imbued with gravity and hope, and stress how imperative it is that concerned people speak up.

Speaking up—particularly to defend people who are sometimes considered the lowest of the low—brings to mind the words of Martin Niemoller, a German clergyman who was imprisoned in a Nazi concentration camp and, in 1946, made a speech about the failure of ordinary Germans to resist the Nazis.

"They came first for the Communists," he said, "and I didn't speak up because I wasn't a Communist. Then they came for the Jews, and I didn't speak up because I wasn't a Jew. Then they came for the trade unionists, and I didn't speak up because I wasn't a trade unionist. Then they came for me and by that time no one was left to speak up."

Notes

Chapter 1. Golden State or Police State?

1. "Prevalence of Imprisonment in the U.S. Population, 1974-2001," http://bjs. ojp.usdoj.gov/index.cfm?ty=pbdetail&iid=503.

2. Joe Domanick, senior fellow in criminal justice at the USC Annenberg Institute for Justice and Journalism, "Prison Fix: Call in the Feds," Los Angeles Times, Opinion: Op-Ed, August 6, 2006.

Chapter 3. The Baby Kissers

1. Office of the Attorney General, Calif. Dept. of Justice, "California Sex Offender Information," www.caag.state.ca.us/megan/pdf/ca_sexoff.pdf Accessed July 2002.

2. Center for Sex Offender Management, U.S. Department of Justice, "Myths and Facts about Sex Offenders," August 2000, http//www.csom.org/pubs/ mythsfacts.html, Accessed June 2002.

3. Eric Lotke, "Politics and Irrelevance: Community Notification Statutes," http://www.igc.org/ncia/cns.html, Accessed July 2002.

4. Bill Lockyer, California Attorney General, "Report to the California Legislature, July 2002, California Sex Offender Information, Megan's Law," ca_sexoff_0702.pdf, Accessed January 2, 2003. (December 31, 2001: Totalregistrants: 93,139; Serious: 75,188; Other: 16,236; High-risk: 1,715).

5. www.kfmb.com/crime_fighters/details.php?storyID=8127, Accessed June 18, 2002.

6. Books supporting the idea that mass hysteria and over-zealous prosecution caused this wave of allegations of child sexual abuse and Satanism in preschools include: Paul and Shirley Eberle, The Politics of Child Abuse, Lyle Stuart, 1986; and Michael R .Snedeker, Debbie Nathan, Satan's silence: ritual abuse and the making of a modern American witch hunt, New York: Basic Books, 1995; among books challenging the hysteria hypothesis is Alex Constantine, Virtual Government – CIA Mind Control Operations in America, Feral House, 1997.

7. Kyle Zirpolo, as told to Debbie Nathan, "McMartin Pre-Schooler: 'I Lied'," October 30, 2005.

Chapter 7. Blue is Green

1. Phone conversation with D. F. Tweedie, December 7, 2002.

2. Eric Lotke, "Issues and Answers: Sex Offenders: Does Treatment Work?" http://www.igc.org/ncianet/sexo.html. Accessed July 2002.

Chapter 9. Inquisition

1. McKune, Warden v. Lile, 536 U.S. 24 (2002).

2. Tanya Caldwell, "U.S. Appeals Court Rejects Arousal Test for Sex Offender," Los Angeles Times, June 21, 2006.

Chapter 11. Spy vs. Spy

1. Phone conversation with D. F. Tweedie, December 2002.

2. "The CIA's MKULTRA Program Explored the Use of LSD and Hypnosis in Covert Operations: The Mind Control Connection" http://www.parascope.com/articles/0397/kubark03.htm. Accessed July 10, 2002.

3. Phone conversation with Mindy Mechanic, October 2002.

Chapter 13. A Parallel Universe

1. Center for Sex Offender Management, "Myths and Facts about Sex Offenders," U.S. Department of Justice, August 2000. http//www.csom.org/pubs/mythsfacts.html Accessed June 22, 2002.

2. "Report to the Legislature on the California Sex Offender Information and Megan's Law," caag.state.ca.us/megan/pdf/july2001.pdf, pg. 6. From http://caag.state.ca.us/megan/publications.htm. Accessed July 14, 2002.

3. Smith v. Doe, 538 U.S. 84 (2003).

4. Godfrey v. Doe - Amicus Curiae (Merits). On Writ of Certiorari from the United States Court of Appeals for the Ninth Circuit, in the Supreme Court of the United States. 2001 term. https://www.justice.gov/osg/brief/godfrey-v-doe-amicus-curiae-merits

5. Richard B. Schmitt, "Crime Victims Speak Up," Los Angeles Times, March10, 2003.

6. Eric Lotke, "Issues and Answers: Sex Offenders: Does Treatment Work?" www.igc.org/ncianet/sexo.html. July 2002.

7. Connecticut Department of Safety v. John Doe – Amicus (Petition). On Petition for a Writ of Certiorari to the United States Court of Appeals for the Second Circuit, Brief for the United States as Amicus Curiae Supporting Petitioners. No. 01-1231 in the Supreme Court of the United States. 2001 Term. https://www.justice.gov/osg/brief/connecticut-department-public-safety-v-john-doe-amicus-petition

8. Center for Sex Offender Management, August 2000.

9. Camille Paglia, interviewed by Celia Farber, Spin, September and October 1991.

10. Smith v. Doe, 538 U.S. 84, 103 (2003)

11. Center for Sex Offender Management, August 2000.

---

12. Marc Klaas, "Reexamining Sex Offender Notification," Klaas Action Review (newsletter), Winter 2003. http://www.klaaskids.org.

13. Office of the Attorney General, "California Sex Offender Information," California Department of Justice Web site. www.caag.state.ca.us/megan/pdf/ca_sexoff.pdf.

14. Office of the Attorney General, "Report to the California Legislature," Calif. Dept. of Justice Web site. July 2002. ca_sexoff_0702.pdf.

15. Phone Interview with Howard Barbaree, May 26, 2002.

16. Bureau of Justice Statistics, "Recidivism of Prisoners Released in 1994," www.ojp.usdoj.gov/bjs/

17. Connecticut Department of Safety v. John Doe – Amicus (Petition). On Petition for a Writ of Certiorari to the United States Court of Appeals for the Second Circuit, Brief for the United States as Amicus Curiae Supporting Petitioners. No. 01-1231 in the Supreme Court of the United States. 2001 Term. https://www.justice.gov/osg/brief/connecticut-department-public-safety-v- john-doe-amicus-petition

18. Kathlyn Gaubatz, Crime in the public mind, Ann Arbor: University of Michigan Press, 1995; in William Lyons; Stuart Scheingold, "The Politics of Crime and Punishment," National Institute of Justice/NCJRS, 2000.

Chapter 15. War on Crime

1. James Vorenberg, "The War on Crime: The First Five Years," The Atlantic Monthly, May 1972

2. Los Angeles Times, "Let Judges Be Judges," August 18, 2003.

3. Vorenberg, May 1972.

4. Leonard Gilroy, "Taking on California's Mighty Public Engineers, Prison Guards Unions," Reason Foundation, August 13, 2009. http://reason.org/blog/show/taking-on-californias-mighty-p

5. Ibid.

6. Joe Domanick, senior fellow in criminal justice at the USC Annenberg Institute for Justice and Journalism, "Prison Fix: Call in the Feds," Los Angeles Times, Opinion: Op-Ed, August 6, 2006.

7. Ibid.

8. Gilroy, August 13, 2009.

9. Marc Klaas, "Reexamining Sex Offender Notification," Klaas Action Review (newsletter), Winter 2003. http://www.klaaskids.org.

10. Associated Press, "High-profile attorney retained by parents of Danielle van Dam," North County Times, November 20, 2002. Kimberly Epler, "Danielle van Dam's mother to push for new law," North County Times, January 4, 2003. Kimberly Epler, "Van Dams sue daughter's convicted murderer," North County

Times, January 3, 2003. Kimberly Epler, "Mother pushes for 'Danielle's Law,'" North County Times, January 17, 2003. Tony Perry, "Westerfield Sentenced to Death," Los Angeles Times, January 4, 2003.

11. Ibid.

12. Radley Balko, "Targeting the Social Drinker is Just MADD," Los Angeles Times, Dec. 9, 2002.

13. National Center for Missing and Exploited Children, 2008 Annual Report, http://www.missingkids.com/missingkids/servlet/ResourceServlet?LanguageC ountry=en_US&PageId=3679, NC171.pdf. Accessed Dec. 24, 2009.

14. Associated Press, "Security Agency Targets Molesters," Los Angeles Times, July 10, 2003.

15. Mary McNamara, "O to a higher power," Los Angeles Times, December 11, 2005.

16. "Man pleads not guilty to rape charges," North County Times, December 3, 2002. Ilana Mignon, "Sexual Offender Strikes Out," The Coast News, December 5-11, 2002.

17. Stephanie Simon, "Ex-Cons Exiled to Outskirts," Los Angeles Times, December 5, 2002.

18. Linda Grant, "My cousin, Eva Braun," The Guardian, April 27, 2002.

Chapter 17. Sounds Good

1. Charles Piller and Lee Romney, "Jessica's Law may not be hospitalizing more post-prison sex offenders," Los Angeles Times, August 11, 2008.

2. US v. Juvenile Male, 581 F.3d 977 (9th Cir. Sept. 10, 2009).

3. Smith v. Doe, 538 U.S. 84 (2003).

4. The Associated Press, "Supreme Court Bars Death Penalty for Juvenile Killers," New York Times, March 1, 2005.

5. http://www.meganslaw.ca.gov/pdf/LegislativeReportMegansLaw2008.pdf.

6. Piller and Romney, August 11, 2008.

7. Jocelyn Y. Stewart and Claudia Zequeira, "Troubles Beyond a Girl's 11 Years," Los Angeles Times, August 3, 2005.

8. Nancy Vogel and Gregg Jones, "Davis Demands Megan's Law Be Extended," Los Angeles Times, September 18, 2003.

Chapter 19. Sting of the Thought Police

1. Ron Garmon, "Mutaytor won't die," Los Angeles Times, February 9, 2007.

2. Greg Moran, "War hero sentenced to prison for child-porn possession," San Diego Union-Tribune, May 4, 2009.

3. Richard Abshire, Marissa Alanis, Jennifer Emily, "Sex sting leads to suicide for former Kaufman D.A.," The Dallas Morning News, November 6, 2006.

4. P.J. Huffstutter, "U.S. Indicts Porn Sellers, Vowing Extensive Attack," Los Angeles Times, August 8, 2003.

5. Kamenko Pajic, Justice Department covers partially nude statues, January 29, 2002, http://www.usatoday.com/news/nation/2002/01/29/statues.htm

6. Henry Chu, "Britain to start full-body scans at Heathrow," Los Angeles Times, January 5, 2010.

Chapter 21. Crusade

1. Laurie Kellman, "Elizabeth's dad urges Amber bill passage," The San Diego Union Tribune, March 14, 2003.

2. Ibid.

3. U.S. Department of Justice, "Fact Sheet, Protect Act," April 30, 2003, http://www.justice.gov/opa/pr/2003/April/03_ag_266.htm. Accessed Jan. 2, 2010.

4. "Straitjackets for Judges," New York Times, April 14, 2003.

Chapter 23. But Grandma, You Have Such Big Teeth!

1. Joe Domanick, senior fellow in criminal justice at the USC Annenberg Institute for Justice and Journalism, "Prison Fix: Call in the Feds," Los Angeles Times, Opinion: Op-Ed, August 6, 2006.

2. Stephanie Simon, "Ex-Cons Exiled to Outskirts," Los Angeles Times, Dec. 5, 2002.

3. Peter Y. Hong, "On his block, a molester," Los Angeles Times, Dec. 5, 2006.

4. Ibid.

5. Piller and Romney, August 11, 2008.

6. Denise Zapata and Kevin Crowe, "Jessica's Law too vague to enforce?" Watchdog Institute, November 29, 2009.

7. Piller and Romney, August 11, 2008.

8. Charles Piller and Lee Romney, "State pays millions for contract psychologists to keep up with Jessica's Law," Los Angeles Times, August 10, 2008.

9. Elaine Halleck, Calculations from California Auditor General Report, "figures 09 CA budget, sexoff."

10. Sandy Banks, "Can the wrongs in California's criminal justice system be righted?" Los Angeles Times, September 4, 2009.

11. Sarah Gordon, "GPS monitoring of sex offenders is useful, but limited, experts say," North County Times, March 20, 2010.

12. San Diego Union-Tribune, "Law enforcement solutions: A panel discussion," April 25, 2010.

13. Michael Stetz, "Outrage is justified, rush for laws isn't," San Diego Union-Tribune, March 10, 2010.

14. Julie Pendray, "Chelsea's Law parents spread idea for 'one-strike' sex law," The Washington Times, September 27, 2010.

Chapter 25. The Road Less Traveled

1. Janet Maslin, "A Captivity No Novelist Could Invent," New York Times, July 17, 2011.

2. Circles of Support and Accountability training session given by Robin Wilson, ABPP, and National Reentry Resource Center, https://nationalreentryresourcecenter.org/circles-of-support-and-accountability#:~:text=Robin%20J.,convicted%20of%20a%20sexual%20offense, Accessed Sept. 20, 2020.

3. Danielle Viera, "Try as They Might, Just Can't Get it Right: Shortcomings of the International Megan's Law of 2010," in 25 Emory International Law Review 1517 (2011), https://scholarlycommons.law.emory.edu/eilr/vol25/iss3/14, Accessed Oct. 5, 2021.

4. In re Taylor, 60 C4th 1019

5. Lesley Warren, "Calif. Supreme Court Ruling Reveals Unintended Consequences of Jessica's Law," The Imprint Youth and Family News, Apr. 28, 2015, https://imprintnews.org/journalism-for-social-change/calif-supreme-court-ruling-reveals-unintended-consequences-of-jessicas-law/10856, Accessed Oct. 5, 2021.

6. Melody Gutierrez, "New California law allows sex offenders to be removed from registry," SF Gate, Oct. 6, 2017, https://www.sfgate.com/politics/article/California-law-sex-offenders-Jerry- Brown-12259564.php, Accessed Oct. 5, 2021.

7. George Skelton, "California's Capitol always has been a sexual playground with bullies from both parties. Now, empowered women could change things," Los Angeles Times, Oct. 30, 2017.

8. Abby Hamblin, Luis Gomez, "Q&A: Assemblywoman Lorena Gonzalez on California's Democrats, running for secretary of state," San Diego Union Tribune, Mar. 19, 2019.

9. "Public Safety Committees stop AB 884, pass SB 145," ACSOL website, April 9, 2019, https://all4consolaws.org/2019/04/public-safety-committee-stops-assembly-bill-884/comment-page-2/, Accessed Oct. 6, 2021.

10. Florida Action Committee, "CA: Gov. Brown supports bill sent to him that would end lifetime listing of many sex offenders on public registry," Sept. 18, 2017, https://floridaactioncommittee.org/ca-gov-brown-supports-bill-sent-end-lifetime-listing-many-sex-offenders-public-registry/, Accessed Oct. 7, 2021.

11. Teresa Nelson, "Minnesota prosecutor charges sexting teenage girl with child pornography," American Civil Liberties website, Jan. 5, 2018, https://www.aclu.

org/blog/juvenile-justice/minnesota-prosecutor-charges- sexting-teenage-girl-child-pornography, Accessed Oct. 7, 2021.

12. Mathews v. Becerra (12-26-2019) 8 C5th 756

13. Michael H. Keller, Gabriel J.X. Dance, "Child Abusers Run Rampant as Tech Companies Look the Other Way," New York Times, Nov. 9, 2019.

14. Florida Action Committee, "CA: Governor Vetoes Eight Sex Offender Bills," Oct 26, 2018, https://floridaactioncommittee.org/ca-governor-vetoes-eight-sex-offender-bills/, Accessed Oct. 7, 2021.

Chapter 27. There's a lot of that going on!

1. Katherine Gotch, Andy Harris, Kimberly Kras, Chris Lobanov-Rostovsky Ann Snyder, Tom Tobin, Seth Wescott, "Registration and Community Notification of Adults Convicted of a Sexual Crime: Recommendations for Evidence-Based Reform, 2020," Association for the Treatment of SexualAbusers report, https://www.atsa.com/policy-papers/adultsorn, Accessed Oct. 8, 2021.

2. Joseph Cranney, Gregory Lee, "Lifetime placement on sex-offender list unconstitutional, SC Supreme Court Rules," June 9, 2021, The Post and Courier.

3. "No Easy Answers—Sex Offender Laws in the US," Human Rights Watch report, September 2007, https://www.hrw.org/reports/2007/us0907/us0907webwcover.pdf, Accessed July 1, 2021.

4. "Model Penal Code: Sexual Assault and Related Offenses, Tentative Draft No. 5," May 4, 2021, The American Law Institute.

5. "Megan's Law Mom Criticizes 'Sexting' Charges," NPR, Mar. 26, 2009, http://www.npr.org/templates/story/story.php ?storyId=102399198, Accessed Oct. 8, 2021.

6. Susan K. Livio, "Report finds Megan's Law fails to reduce sex crimes, deter repeat offenders in N.J," NJ.com, February 7, 2009, https://www.nj.com/news/2009/02/study_finds_megans_law_fails_t_1.html, Accessed Oct. 8, 2021.

7. Dina Francesca Haynes, "The Celebritization of Human Trafficking," The Annals of the American Academy of Political and Social Sciences, Vol. 653, p. 25-30, May 2014. .

8. Danielle Viera, "Try as They Might, Just Can't Get It Right: Shortcomings of the International Megan's Law of 2010," 25 Emory International Law Review. 1517 (2011).

9. "2020 Trafficking in Persons Report," U.S. State Department, https://www.state.gov/reports/2020-trafficking-in-persons-report/, Accessed Oct. 8, 2021.

10. "Mass Atrocity Endings," Tufts University, https://sites.tufts.edu/atrocityendings/2015/08/07/cambodia-u-s-bombing- civil-war-khmer-rouge/, Accessed Sept. 1, 2021.

11. Ben Kiernan and Taylor Owen, "Bombs Over Cambodia," Genocide Studies Program, Yale University, https://gsp.yale.edu/sites/default/files/walrus_cambodiabombing_oct06.pdf, Accessed Sept. 1, 2021.

12. Alyssa Dandrea, "New data shows reports of child sexual abuse increasing nationally and in New Hampshire," Concord Monitor, Mar. 6, 2020.

13. David Finkelhor and Lisa M. Jones, "Explanations for the Decline in Child Sexual Abuse Cases," U.S. Department of Justice, Juvenile Justice Bulletin, Jan. 2004.

14. Letourneau, E., Levenson, J., "Evaluating the Effectiveness of Sex Offender Registration and Notification Policies for Reducing Sexual Violence against Women," September 2013. https://www.ojp.gov/pdffiles1/nij/grants/231989 pdf

15. Zgoba, Kristen, et al. "Megan's Law: Assessing the Practical and Monetary Efficacy," December 2008, https://www.ojp.gov/pdffiles1/nij/grants/225370.pdf, Accessed May 15, 2021.

16. Mercado, C., Jeglic, E., "Sex Offender Management, Treatment, and Civil Commitment: An Evidence Based Analysis Aimed at Reducing Sexual Violence," September 2013. https://www.ojp.gov/pdffiles1/nij/grants/243551.pdf, Accessed May 15, 2021.

17. Dale Russakoff, "Defense Describes Tortured Childhood of Megan's Killer," Washington Post, June 10, 1997.

18. "Where to Invade Next," 2015 movie, Michael Moore.

19. Sonaiya Kelley, "Jose Abreu, Founder of Venezuela's El Sistema youth orchestra, dies at 78," Los Angeles Times, March 25, 2018.

20. Joe Atmonavage, "He was labeled a sex offender as a teen. Now he is challenging the law that made him register as one." NJ, Sept. 19, 2019, https://www.nj.com/news/2019/09/he-was-labeled-a-sex-offender-as-a-teen- now-he-is-challenging-the-law-that-made-him-register-as-one.html. Accessed Oct. 13, 2021.

21. Catherine L. Carpenter, "Legislative Epidemics: A Cautionary Tale of Criminal Laws that Have Swept the Country," Buffalo Law Review, Jan. 2010.

22. Chris Smith, "SMITH: International Megan's Law working to protect children," App.com, Dec. 5, 2017, https://www.app.com/story/opinion/columnists/2017/12/05/international- megans-law-chris-smith/108327518/, Accessed Sept. 19, 2021.

23. "International Megan's Law—FAQ Sheet." U.S. Marshals Service. https://www.usmarshals.gov/megans-law-faqs.html. Accessed July 19, 2021.

24. "Legislation Sponsored or Cosponsored by Christopher H. Smith." Congress.gov. Accessed July 18, 2021. https://www.congress.gov/member/christopher- smith/S000522?q=%7b%22congress%22%3a%22all%22%2c%22sponsorship %22%3a%22sponsored%22%2c%22bill-stus%22%3a%22law%22%7d

25. U.S. Congressman Chris Smith. Biography. https://chrissmith.house.gov/biography/

---

26. "Sex Offender Registration and Notification Laws at Home and Abroad: Is an International Megan's Law Good Policy?" Christopher King, City University of New York Law Review, Winter 2011, Volume 15, Issue 1.

27. Chris Smith, "SMITH: International Megan's Law working to protect children," Dec. 5, 2017, https://www.app.com/story/opinion/columnists/2017/12/05/international- megans-law-chris-smith/108327518/, Accessed June 7, 2021.

28. Charles Montaldo, The History of Megan's Law. ThoughtCo, November 6, 2019. https://www.thoughtco.com/history-of-megans-law-973197#:~:text=Paul%20Kramer%2C%20a%20Republican%20Party,kidnappe d%2C%20raped%2C%20and%20murdered, Accessed Oct. 15, 2021.

29. Teresa Nelson, "Minnesota prosecutor charges sexting teenage girl with child pornography," American Civil Liberties website, Jan. 5, 2018, https://www.aclu.org/blog/juvenile-justice/minnesota-prosecutor-charges- sexting-teenage-girl-child-pornography, Accessed Oct. 7, 2021.

Chapter 29. Trick or Trafficking?

1. Untitled video, kristinanniebell Instagram site, https://www.instagram.com/p/Bd3WH3Plabu/, Accessed Sept. 4, 2021.

2. Ronald Weitzer, "New Directions in Research on Human Trafficking," The Annals of the American Academy of Political and Social Science, March 2014.

3. Vicki Abt, "How TV Talkshows Deconstruct Society," Penn State News, Mar. 1, 1996, https://news.psu.edu/story/141522/1996/03/01/research/how-tv-talkshows-deconstruct-society, Accessed Sept. 12, 2021.

4. Rachel Cavanaugh, "Best and worst talk shows in TV history," Stacker, May 22, 2021, https://stacker.com/stories/1978/best-and-worst-talk-shows-tv-history, Accessed Sept. 4, 2021.

5.Aja Romano, "A new law intended to curb sex trafficking threatens the future of the internet as we know it," Vox, July 2, 2018. https://www.vox.com/culture/2018/4/13/17172762/fosta-sesta-backpage- 230-internet-freedom, Accessed Sept. 4, 2021.

6. Dina Francesca Haynes, "The Celebritization of Human Trafficking," The Annals of the American Academy of Political and Social Sciences, Vol. 653, p. 25-30, May 2014. https://papers.ssrn.com/sol3/papers.cfm?abstract_id=2250705, Accessed Oct. 8, 2021.

7. Davies, Nick, "Prostitution and trafficking – the anatomy of a moral panic," The Guardian, Oct. 20, 2009.

8. Lopez, German, "One way Obama has quietly worked to reverse 'tough on crime' policies," Vox, Dec. 10, 2016, https://www.vox.com/policy-and-politics/2016/12/10/13901888/obama-clemency-mass-incarceration, Accessed Sept. 24, 2021.

9. Jonathan D. Salant, "Obama signs International Megan's Law," Feb. 9, 2016, nj.com newspaper, https://www.nj.com/politics/2016/02/obama_signs_international_megans_la w.html, Accessed Dec. 13, 2020.

10. "International Megan's Law to prevent demand for child sex trafficking," webpage of Congressman Bobby Scott, Feb. 1, 2016. https://bobbyscott.house.gov/media-center/floor-statements/international- megans-law-to-prevent-demand-for-child-sex-trafficking, Accessed Sept. 25, 2021.

11. Kalhan Rosenblatt and Chandelis R. Duster, "'Frederick Douglass' Bill Introduced in Congress to Curb Human Trafficking," NBC News, April 27, 2017, https://www.nbcnews.com/news/nbcblk/frederick-douglass-bill-introduced-congress-curb-human-trafficking-n752096, Accessed Sept. 25, 2021.

12. David Mikkelson, "Did Flight Attendant Shelia Fedrick Save a Girl from Human Trafficking?" Snopes, Feb. 7, 2019, https://www.snopes.com/fact-check/shelia-fedrick-human-traffickers/, Accessed Aug. 10, 2021.

13. Adam Pitluk, "Human Cost of Trafficking," American Way, Sept. 15, 2010, https://airlineamb.org/wp-content/uploads/2019/01/American-Way-9-15-10-copy.pdf, Accessed Sept. 28, 2021.

14. Kalhan Rosenblatt, "Flight Attendants Train to Spot Human Trafficking," NBC News, Feb. 4, 2017, https://www.nbcnews.com/storyline/airplane- mode/flight-attendants-train-spot-human-trafficking-n716181, Accessed Sept. 5, 2021.

15. Laura Eimiller, "Multi-Day Joint Agency Operation 'Lost Angels' Leads to the Recovery of 33 Missing Children During Trafficking Awareness Month," FBI Los Angeles, Jan. 22, 2021, https://www.fbi.gov/contact-us/field- offices/losangeles/news/press-releases/multi-day-joint-agency-operation-lost- angels-leads-to-the-recovery-of-33-missing-children-during-trafficking- awareness-month, Accessed Sept. 16, 2021.

16. Christine Negroni, "Dad Questioned After Southwest Flight Attendant Suspects Human Trafficking," Forbes Debunks, Dec 22, 2017, https://www.forbes.com/sites/christinenegroni/2017/12/22/dad-questioned- southwest-flight-attendant-suspects-human-trafficking/?sh=42189c6023ae, Accessed Sept. 26, 2021.

17. Ronald Weitzer, 2012, "Legalizing Prostitution: From Illicit Vice to Lawful Business," New York: New York University Press.

18. Karen Attiah, "Gabby Petito deserves justice, but 'missing White girl syndrome' hurts us all," The Washington Post, Sept. 29, 2010.

19. William Styron, "This Quiet Dust and Other Writings," Vintage International, Vintage Books, Random House International, New York, 1993.

20. Gregory James, "The Southern Diaspora (Black, White, and Latinx)," The Great

Index

CPSIA information can be obtained
at www.ICGtesting.com
Printed in the USA
LVHW041642030723
751453LV00005B/29